Women of the
American South

Women of the American South

A Multicultural Reader

EDITED BY

Christie Anne Farnham

New York University Press

NEW YORK AND LONDON

NEW YORK UNIVERSITY PRESS
New York and London

Copyright © 1997 by New York University

Chapter 1 © 1996 by THE JOURNAL OF WOMEN'S HISTORY.
Reprinted with permission from the Summer 1996 issue of THE
JOURNAL OF WOMEN'S HISTORY.
Chapter 17 © 1997 by Jane Sherron De Hart

Library of Congress Cataloging-in-Publication Data
Women of the American South : a multicultural reader / edited by
Christie Anne Farnham.
p.   cm.
Includes index.
ISBN 0-8147-2654-2 (alk. paper). — ISBN 0-8147-2655-0 (pbk. :
alk. paper)
1. Women—Southern States—History.   2. Minority women—Southern
States—History.   3. Afro-American women—Southern States—History.
I. Farnham, Christie.
HQ1438.S63W67   1997
305.4'0975—dc21   97-33778
                          CIP

New York University Press books are printed on acid-free paper,
and their binding materials are chosen for strength and durability.

Manufactured in the United States of America

10 9 8 7 6 5 4 3 2 1

To my children
Dulany Lucetta Pope
Delanie Penrose Pope
Whitney Bancroft Pope
and
Norwood Braxton Pope

Contents

Preface

This collection owes its existence to Niko Pfund, one of the first to take cognizance of the sudden surge of interest in southern women. Although Anne Firor Scott initiated contemporary interest in the subject as early as 1970 with the publication of *The Southern Lady: From Pedestal to Politics, 1830–1930*, the initial emphasis of women's history on paradigms based on the Northeast, together with the concurrent focus inspired by black nationalists on the history of African American men, absorbed southern research agendas to such a degree that a full flowering of southern women's history was delayed. Although some important studies appeared during the seventies, like that of Lois Green Carr and Lorena S. Walsh on early female settlers in the Chesapeake, it was not until the eighties that the number of such studies increased significantly. Authors of these works and their colleagues in women's history, by necessity largely self-taught, have now trained a new generation of historians of southern women whose research, along with the continued productivity of their predecessors, has produced this surge of studies in the nineties.

Today's scholarship seeks to uncover a more inclusive history by examining southern women in all of their rich diversity and moving beyond a biracial focus on the region's past. Such diversity counters popular notions of a monolithic South in which the prototypical southern woman is a white "lady." All other women in the region too often are seen merely as members of some residual categories of difference, not part of the main story. However, southerner is not a regional identity that belongs only to whites, for example, nor is southern history limited to the story of how whites maintained dominance over multicultural challengers. Instead, the essays in this volume are sensitive to the perspectives of various groups, recognizing that to be a southern woman has meant different things to different women through the years.

This collection is an effort to be both a comprehensive general history of southern women and an in-depth exploration of some of the major differences among them. An editor's note introducing each essay sets forth the national and regional contexts of southern women's history and charts the chronology of major events and changes in their lives. As a consequence of space limitations and the availability of previously unpublished research projects (Scott's contribution is the only previously published work, and it had not yet appeared when these manuscripts were selected), not all multicultural categories are addressed in the essays. However, the editor's notes are a means of partially compensating for such omissions.

As with any anthology of such geographic and historical scope, the dilemma of how to organize the essays posed a problem. I have adopted a loosely chronological structure, one that allows interaction among these many women—and groups of women—to emerge organically, with earlier essays providing a foundation, implicit and explicit, for later chapters.

The collection demonstrates that a dominant standard, like the southern lady, is socially constructed. Consequently, other southern women are not portrayed here as marginal to some larger story, for southern women's history is the history of all the women of the South.

This anthology would not have been possible without the willingness of almost fifty scholars to submit their work for consideration and dozens more who offered to do so. I am most grateful to them and to Iowa State University for released time to pursue this project, as well as to colleagues too numerous to mention for their helpful suggestions. Lastly, I want to thank my spouse, Whitney Pope, for the sacrifices and deprivations that his longtime commitment to my scholarly endeavors have entailed, and without which such projects would not have come to fruition.

Chapter One

Writing the History of Southern Women

Anne Firor Scott

EDITOR'S NOTE: *History as a profession with recognized evidentiary standards based on research in primary documents developed only toward the end of the nineteenth century. The conventional view held that history was about change; therefore, it was thought that men made history, women being confined to an unchanging round of domestic activities. Even when a rare book focused on women, like Julia Cherry Spruill's* Women's Life and Work in the Southern Colonies *(1938), it gathered dust on library shelves.*

That all changed with the advent of the Civil Rights Movement and feminism. An increasing number of women had moved into graduate training in the fifties, taking advantage of opportunities for women in higher education in the post–World War II era. Consequently they were well positioned to write women's history when their engagement in civil rights and feminism opened their eyes to the omission of over half of the world's population from the pages of history. The result was what often has been described as an "explosion" of studies in women's history.

Yet southern women, with the exception of elite white women and female slaves, received less attention. Historians of the South were drawn by their engagement in civil rights struggles and concern with black nationalism to focus on African American men, and historians of women were involved in developing interpretations drawn largely from the experiences of northeastern middle-class white women. By the mid-eighties, however, this was beginning to change. Inspired by a rapidly developing scholarship on black women, scholars writing

This essay is adapted from a much longer one called "Unfinished Business" published in the *Journal of Women's History* 8 (summer 1996): 111–21 and used here by permission.

on southern women began expanding their concerns to a wider range of subjects.

One reason was that increasing numbers of women being trained as historians were members or descendants of these excluded groups. If we are to a large degree creatures of our cultures, the admission to the profession of persons from a wide range of backgrounds — the democratization of history — guarantees that limited views of any one group will be challenged by the work of another. This is not to say that each group is seeking to dominate the historical record with its own political identity and agenda or that one interpretation of history is as good as any other. Rather, historians put forward for consideration interpretations, driven in part by their own experiences and perspectives but based on documentation, which the entire profession then judges by its evidentiary standards.

In addition, each generation asks new questions drawn from its own experiences in a changing world, enlarging our understanding of the complex nature of historical truth. The complete truth may never be attained, but the democratization of the profession and its commitment to evidentiary standards bring that goal close to realization. The following essay by Anne Firor Scott, a founder of southern women's history, combines the story of her own background and contemporary influences with the larger narrative of attempts to preserve southern women's history and establish it as a legitimate subfield within the discipline.

• • •

I suppose the writing of southern women's history may be said to have begun in 1861, when a woman writing under the name Mary Forrest (her real name was Julia Deane Freeman) published *Women of the South Distinguished in Literature*, a collection of carefully researched biographies of writers. In the last half of the nineteenth century the southern writers who might be said to have dealt with the history of women were those who wrote memoirs and novels; no male historian, academic or amateur, paid any attention to women. In the Reconstruction years the Daughters of the Confederacy collected and preserved documents; in 1920 the organization published a fascinating volume called *Representative Women of the South*, which, after a flowery introduction, turned out to be a rather thorough documentation of women's public activities. When U. B. Phillips came to write his history of slavery in the 1920s, he paid some attention to white women.[1]

The first effort to produce a scholarly monograph came in the late 1920s, when, for reasons now lost to sight, a young woman studying at the University of Wisconsin decided to write her dissertation on the subject of antebellum southern women. Virginia Gearhart had been an honors student at Goucher, a school notable for faculty women with a strong community orientation. Gearhart, a Marylander, thought of herself as a southerner, and her pioneering research is punctuated now and then with familiar southern mythology.[2] Still, in view of the total absence of any secondary literature in her chosen field, she made a brave beginning. In the 1930s came the work of two first-rate scholars, Julia Cherry Spruill and Guion Griffis Johnson, and two others whose work was impressive, Marjorie Mendenhall and Eleanor Boatwright. Though all five of these women wrote important scholarly articles or books, none of them, as far as I can tell, had the slightest impact on those who controlled the teaching and writing of southern history. Not only was their excellent scholarship ignored, but not one was able to find an academic post worthy of her talents. Each worked out such accommodations as she could. Boatwright and Mendenhall were cut off in their prime, one by suicide, the other by a medical error. Of the three who lived a normal life span, one spent her life as a manuscript librarian, one as an organizer of women's associations (while she wrote history on the side), and one as a Christian Science reader. Their work was excellent, but it was in an area not yet recognized by the gatekeepers as a legitimate field of study.[3]

Fortunately the printed word does not perish as readily as the people who write, and much of this work was destined to reappear when there were people ready to listen. This time began to come in the 1960s.[4]

By then the context in which southern history was being written was changing rapidly. The Second World War had brought numbers of southern women into the labor force, the armed services, and other places. If they went home immediately after the war, they did not necessarily stay there long. More and more young women were going to college. Organizations like the League of Women Voters were growing rapidly, and by the early 1950s league members were joining southern white church women in actively preparing for school integration. Before long southern women were publicly taking sides in the debate about school integration.

It was my good fortune to come upon evidence for the post–Civil War emergence of southern women as a political force just in time to benefit from this changing contemporary context. I was asked to present a paper called "The 'New Woman' in the New South" to the 1961 meeting of the Southern Historical Association. It was the first dealing with the history of southern women to appear on the program of that august body, and probably the second on the subject ever presented to a learned society in this country. (In 1951 Elizabeth Taylor had given a paper on the Texas suffrage movement to the Mississippi Valley Historical Society.) The paper was warmly received by a generous audience (mostly male), so generous, indeed, that I was emboldened to submit it to the *South Atlantic Quarterly*, where, after what I later learned had been a spirited debate, it was accepted and published.

Nine years later *The Southern Lady*, the book foreshadowed by that paper, came out—only a step ahead, as it turned out, of what became an avalanche of work on the subject.[5] This acceleration of interest reflected the continuing change in the context: by 1970 young southern women had been exhilarated and energized by the Civil Rights Movement. The gentle breeze that preceded the hurricane of feminism had begun to blow.[6] Numbers of women began to enter history graduate programs, boldly proposing to study the history of their own sex.

So it came to be that the subject that had merited three citations in the index of a 1965 work on southern historiography by Arthur S. Link and Rembert W. Patrick filled more than fifty pages in its successor in 1987.[7] I wonder whether any new field in the discipline has ever grown so rapidly. Like our predecessors, the twentieth-century historians of women have been profoundly concerned with social and political issues and with our own status. For this reason more than in most other subfields of American history, our books, even at their most scholarly, speak to women who are not historians.[8]

We may have reached a point at which the study of women's history has become self-propelling, less dependent, perhaps, on a favorable context, for though feminism itself is under attack and often declared to be dead—a rumor that is vastly exaggerated—feminist scholars continue to produce books, articles, and monographs and organize panels with unabated enthusiasm.

The field continues to grow both in substance—new questions are constantly being raised, new groups and individuals being studied—and in theoretical sophistication. Some current developments in the field include the strong emphasis on theory, a good deal of crossover from literary criticism, the extraordinary burgeoning of black women's history, and the ever increasing interest in lower-class women, farmers' wives, and the like. What elements in the present context encourage these particular developments. To examine that issue would require another essay as long as this one.[9]

For the moment, perhaps, it is enough to say that over its long history—since Judith Sergeant Murray began to draft her essays in 1776—women's history has developed in close relationship with women's activism and has itself affected that activism, providing the basis for many efforts to broaden women's world. Also, from the beginning it has run on its own track, ignored by the so-called mainstream (mostly male) historians. The first characteristic continues to this day and perhaps accounts in part for the extraordinary amount of work accomplished since 1960. The second is, I believe, beginning to change. Perhaps the day is not far distant when every scholar working in a relevant field will pay close attention to women's records as well as men's.

History is always unfinished. It is necessary to remember that what we are doing today will be seen as equally unfinished fifty years from now. Historians writing over the years have done the best they knew how (and we should not for a moment suggest that they were any less intelligent or perceptive than we are). We write by our lights, as they did by theirs. As Charles Darwin once remarked to his friend and codiscoverer of natural selection, Alfred Russell Wallace, "the firmest conviction of the truth of a doctrine by its author seems, alas, not to be the slightest guarantee of its truth." Many of the formulations that seem to us so exactly to tell the truth about the past will probably be discarded by the next generation of scholars on the basis of new evidence, new insights, new theories.

More and more we are recognizing how important it is to understand the background and experience from which any historian views her or his chosen subject. Perhaps my own case is instructive. Faced with the challenge of writing an afterword for the twenty-fifth anniversary edition of *The Southern Lady,* I began to reflect on the context of my life and what it had to do with my work. The first thing I realized was that the context was not confined to the actual years since I was born, but in many ways began long before.

Growing up in the 1920s, I was surrounded by white southern women, some of whom considered themselves ladies. As children must, I absorbed offhand, giveaway comments of grown-ups. Once I spoke of a black woman I admired as a lady; I was reproved. Long after her death I discovered that my grandmother, whose picture appears on the cover of the new edition, fitted almost exactly the description I had worked out from the records of many of her contemporaries: a description of well-to-do, highly respectable southern girls who yearned for education, made do with what they could persuade their parents to provide, and created careers in church work and voluntary associations. My grandmother was a Virginian named Byrd Lee Hill. Her father and her planter grandfather had been Confederate officers. Her mother, already an orphan when the Civil War began, had found herself almost destitute when one brother wound up in a Yankee prison and the other in the army. She had applied for a job in the Confederate treasury. Whether she got the job is not clear, but she had married John Booten Hill while the war went on. Byrd Lee, the only daughter, was born in 1869 and grew up with a high measure of intellectual ambition. She yearned to go to college, but had to settle for a teacher's college. She had married young, had five children, was a pillar of her church and an active member of the Browning club, helped some black clubwomen set up a day care center, and—after suffrage—traveled through Georgia organizing branches of the newly created League of Women Voters.

She didn't like to keep house, my mother said, but loved to read and write. Her patriarchal father-in-law ordered her not to sign articles she wrote for the local paper. Yet she had enough independence to stay with her own church instead of joining her husband's. She died when I was five, but the stories I heard about her captured my imagination.

As I grew up, there were others who shaped my understanding of southern women: the hardworking farm wives who were everywhere in Georgia before the Second World War, four of my college teachers, a black woman who came to nurse my little brothers and then went to college. She came home to become a schoolteacher.

Much of this effort to unravel my own past as it fits into the larger past is described in the afterword to the new edition. Even there I'm sure I have only begun to address what an all-seeing eye could discern. How, I wondered, as I tried to decipher my own development and relate it to all that came later, does anyone dare to try to reconstruct the past?

But we do and we will continue to, but clearly it must be with a certain tentativeness, a decent humility. There is, as I said, a very large amount of work in progress dealing with southern women. Many surprises are in store, much discussion and argument will ensue. Above all it is clear that the history of southern women is only beginning to be written.

NOTES

1. Mary Forrest, *Women of the South Distinguished in Literature* (New York: Derby and Jackson, 1860); Mrs. Bryan Wells Collier, *Biographies of Representative Women of the South*, 6 vols. (n.p., n.d.). Memoirs, particularly those focused on the Civil War,

abounded in the years after the war. Novelists whose work is enlightening include Sarah Barnwell Elliott, George Washington Cable, Grace King, Charles Chesnutt (for black women), and later Ellen Glasgow.

2. Virginia Gearhart, "The Southern Woman, 1840–1860" (Ph.D. diss., University of Wisconsin, 1927).

3. For an extended analysis of the lives and work of these women, see Anne Firor Scott, ed., *Unheard Voices: The First Historians of Southern Women* (Charlottesville: University Press of Virginia, 1993). See also Jacqueline Goggin, "Arthur M. Schlesinger and the Feminization of American History" (paper presented to the History of Education Society, October 1992).

4. Now, in the 1990s, Julia Spruill's *Women's Life and Work in the Southern Colonies* has been reissued by W. W. Norton (which brought out the first reprint in 1972), Eleanor Boatwright's Duke University thesis of 1940 has been published by Ralph Carlson, and the University of North Carolina Press hopes to reissue Guion Johnson's *Antebellum North Carolina*. Excerpts from the works of all five women appear in Scott, *Unheard Voices*.

5. Anne Firor Scott, *The Southern Lady: From Pedestal to Politics, 1830–1930* (Chicago: University of Chicago Press, 1970).

6. See Sara Evans, *Personal Politics: The Roots of Women's Liberation in the Civil Rights Movement and the New Left* (New York: Knopf, 1979).

7. See Jacquelyn Hall and Anne F. Scott, "Women in the South," in John Boles and Evelyn Nolen, eds., *Interpreting Southern History: Historiographical Essays in Honor of Sanford W. Higginbotham* (Baton Rouge: Louisiana State University Press, 1987), 454–509. The earlier volume was Rembert W. Patrick and Arthur S. Link, eds., *Writing Southern History: Essays in Historiography in Honor of Fletcher M. Green* (Baton Rouge: Louisiana State University Press, 1965).

8. Evidence comes from the triennial sessions of the Berkshire Conference of Women Historians, which attracts women from many disciplines and a good number who are not academic at all.

9. In the decade since Boles and Nolen went to press, many monographs, collections of essays, biographies, and special issues of journals have added to the mountain of material on southern women's history. Many more studies are in progress, so the future looks to be as exciting as the present. The Association of Southern Women Historians is growing and becoming more active every year. Its triennial conference has become a major historical event. A bibliographical essay taking up where Hall and Scott left off in the mid-1980s would be exceedingly useful.

Chapter Two

From Corn Mothers to Cotton Spinners

Continuity in Choctaw Women's Economic Life, A.D. 950–1830

James Taylor Carson

EDITOR'S NOTE: *Histories of the South often begin with the first permanent English settlement at Jamestown in 1607 or perhaps with the earlier unsuccessful attempt in 1587 at Roanoke Island, where the first English women were present. But the South, which stretches from just above the Chesapeake Bay in the north to Florida in the south and as far west as central Texas, was home to women as early as twelve to fifteen thousand years ago. To be true to the historical record, southern women's history must begin with these descendants of Asians who in many migrations, beginning perhaps as much as 30,000 to 45,000 years ago,* crossed the land bridge connecting Siberia with Alaska that was exposed when the formation of glaciers lowered sea levels.*

Little is known about these early peoples who settled in what is presently the United States, but Paleo-Indian culture developed after about 11,500 B.C.E., based on the use of stone spearheads and the hunting of large animals like mammoths. The extinction of these mammals by 7000 B.C.E. together with climatic changes brought forth the Archaic tradition (ca 8000 B.C.E.), which survived in isolated areas until the arrival of the Europeans. In the South, Indian communities hunted small game in the forests, which covered the region, and gathered seeds, nuts, and roots. They also burned areas to produce more harvestable food and attract grazing animals.

About nine thousand years ago, present-day Mexico was home to developing horticultural societies, based on the cultivation of wild grasses. Over the course of three thousand years, corn, beans, and squash were bred into high-yielding crops that spread from Mesoamerica to the Anasazi of the Southwest and eventually formed the basis of the Woodland tradition that emerged in the South about

1000 B.C.E., *appearing first along the Mississippi and Ohio river valleys with the cultivation of squash and bottle gourd. The semipermanent villages that the resulting harvests made possible encouraged the elaboration of cultural practices and trade across the entire continent.*

The most advanced Indian civilization in North America, the Mississippian, arose between 700 and 900 C.E. on the floodplains between present-day Vicksburg and St. Louis. The domestication of corn, beans, and other plants from Mesoamerica became the basis of Mississippian culture. Indeed, corn continues to be the South's most important cereal crop today. Beans supplement corn by resupplying nitrogen to the land, thereby preventing soil exhaustion, and by providing niacin, which cannot be digested from corn, preventing pellagra. With this abundant and nutritious food source, the population increased dramatically, which necessitated the development of more complex political organizations. For example, in 1540 de Soto was impressed with the wealth of Queen Cofitachequi, who headed a confederacy of peoples in South Carolina. A settlement at the confluence of the Missouri and Mississippi had a population of forty thousand by 1200 C.E., making it larger than any American city at the time of the Revolution. The lower Mississippi region, with its flat-topped earthen pyramids like the one at Emerald, Mississippi, covering seven acres, demonstrated its debt to Mexican civilization.

Although other cultures existed when Europeans arrived — the Powhatan confederacy was composed of Algonquians from Canada, for example — by the time of Columbus most southeastern Indians lived in semipermanent villages, women did most of the agricultural labor, and men hunted with bows and arrows. The Mississippian tradition of matrilineal families and ceremonies for the Corn Mother goddess were widespread. Clearly, conceptions of appropriate gender roles conflicted with those of Europeans, remaining a continuing source of tension, which is explored in detail as it affected the Choctaws.

· · ·

Mrs. Gaines, the wife of an American trader who worked among the Choctaw Indians of Mississippi, looked out the window of her cabin to check on the Choctaws she had hired to weed her garden, and what she saw disturbed her. While the mothers and daughters stooped between the rows of corn, beans, and potatoes, and scratched the earth with their hoes, their sons and brothers ran about laughing and playing, chasing squirrels, birds, and rabbits with their blowguns. She approached the women and explained to them the error of their ways. Men, the trader's wife insisted, were supposed to work in the fields while their women tended the home and hearth. Angered by Mrs. Gaines's lecture, one of the workers replied,

"Would you have me make a woman of my son? He is to be a man and a warrior & he is not going to work like a woman!"[1]

The confrontation in Mrs. Gaines's garden mirrored the broader experience of Native Americans in the post-Columbian world. Besieged by Europeans and Americans who held entirely different cultural beliefs as well as tremendous economic, military, and political clout, Native Americans continually had to refute, refuse, or adapt to the blandishments of missionaries, politicians, traders, and settlers. What had been a way of life in the prehistoric Southeast became after contact and colonization a culture in contention with what the invaders held up as "civilization." To survive in what one historian has called the "Indians' New World," Choctaws drew on the power of their belief system to shape its contours and define their place within it. For Choctaw women the process of adaptation centered on preserving the traditional rights and prerogatives associated with their horticultural labors, the work that the women in Mrs. Gaines's garden refused to share with their sons and brothers.[2]

The number of times Choctaw women appear in the historical sources before their removal from Mississippi in 1830 can be counted on one hand. Women's imprint on the archaeology of the American Southeast is even fainter. Students of Native American history compensate for such problems by resorting to theory to help explain the evidence and to fill in the gaps in the historical and archaeological records. By bringing together anthropological theories about kinship, economic production, gender relations, and even language, ethnohistorians can construct an interpretation of cultural change and persistence over time based on fragmentary evidence.

One theory of great use in understanding Native American women and the changes and persistences related to their economic life is the idea of the moral economy, a system of beliefs and values that structured how, for example, the prehistoric Choctaws viewed labor, production, and exchange. When, after contact with Europeans and Africans, Choctaw women decided to adapt Old World introductions by planting their first cotton seeds, applying their feet to the treadles of spinning wheels, or herding their first cattle, they made *moral* decisions based on what the received values of their culture deemed right or wrong.[3] By using innovations that were consonant with their moral economy, Choctaw women conserved their culture and maintained their identity as women, an identity that dated to the original settlement of North America.

Archaeologists have theorized that the first hunting and gathering societies that crossed the Asian land bridge into North America divided their labor according to gender. Groups of men hunted big game animals like woolly mammoths and ancient bison, while the women scoured the forests and grasslands for edible plants, roots, berries, and nuts. The division became an important part of many Native American belief systems in which men enjoyed a special relationship with the animal world and women shared the same with the plant world.

Horticulture, the cultivation of plants, did not begin until between 3400 and 2300 B.C., when Native peoples of Mesoamerica domesticated corn. By 900 B.C. the crop had become a staple of their societies, and it diffused northward into North America, reaching the Mississippi Valley in the middle of the tenth century A.D.[4] According to Choctaw oral tradition, corn came to them from a crow that had flown up from the south and dropped a grain at the feet of a little girl. "What is this?" the girl asked. "Corn," replied her mother.[5]

Corn revolutionized life for the prehistoric ancestors of the Choctaws. Thanks to the new plant, female farmers in the lowlands of the American South provided a far more reliable and bounteous supply of food than the men who hunted, and the population increased accordingly. With greater numbers of people came the need for greater stores of food and increasingly more complex political and social structures to coordinate the cultivation, harvest, and storage of corn. These developments culminated in a cultural era known as the Mississippian phase. The Mississippians' legacy is today most visible in the mound centers scattered throughout the Southeast and in the rich store of artifacts that they left behind.[6]

Among the beautifully crafted copper ornaments, shell gorgets, and catlinite pipes that the Mississippians produced are several figurines that depict the central relationship of Mississippian women to horticulture. One figurine excavated from a site near Cahokia, Illinois, depicts a kneeling woman, surrounded by a snake, a symbol of fertility, in which she has sunk the blade of her digging stick. Another artifact associated with the Spiro site in southeastern Oklahoma portrays a woman preparing to pound corn in a mortar. Similar artifacts characterize men as hunters and warriors.[7]

How scholars have viewed the relationship between female farmers and male hunters has changed considerably over the last three decades. Anthropologists once used the phrase "stratification" to describe the division of labor by gender and the greater prestige that was usually attached to male work and the lack of prestige that was attached to female work. The women's rights movement of the early 1970s influenced this interpretation, causing a later generation of historians and anthropologists to react against the imposition of contemporary understandings and interpretations on past gender relations.[8]

In the case of the Mississippians, the term "stratification" rings hollow because there is no evidence to suggest that women's work as farmers was held in lower esteem than men's work as hunters and warriors, or vice versa. For these reasons, scholars now use the term "complementarity" to describe gender relations among most Native Americans. Activities like hunting and fighting, for example, carried men far and wide. Women, however, lived their lives in the fields and households that made up the many towns and chiefdoms of the Mississippian countryside. Together, both sexes provided for the sustenance of their societies.[9]

How men and women in complementary societies like the Mississippian partitioned economic and political power and influence is the most pressing question confronting students of Native American women today. Because of their association with warfare, men controlled diplomatic relations with other tribes and dominated political offices. Vested with the official power to make decisions on behalf of the communities they represented, men held what scholars have defined as "authority." Lacking access to formal expressions of power, women possessed "influence," the power that came with ownership of houses, domestic property, and farmland. Moreover, Mississippians were matrilineal, that is, they traced kinship and descent through the female line, so that when male chiefs died they were succeeded by their sisters' sons. Women thus used their power to influence homelife, town affairs, and political succession, but they still lacked the formal and publicly organized institutions that legitimized the men's authority.[10]

The division between female farming and male hunting embodied the broader patterns of Mississippian cosmology. Mississippians conceived of the world in sets of opposites. The sun, fire, and eagles, symbols of order, were offset by the moon, water, and serpents, symbols of disorder. Similarly, men, who were associated with the symbols of order, were counterbalanced by women, who were associated with the symbols of disorder. To ensure divine favor, Mississippians had to prevent the mixing of opposites. Otherwise, their society would become polluted and their lives would be in jeopardy.[11]

Mississippians and their Choctaw descendants regarded blood as a particularly dangerous pollutant, because it contained the unpredictable and dangerous power of life. To avoid polluting themselves and their world with blood, they followed numerous taboos regarding blood, all of which reinforced gender differences. Men, for example, isolated themselves in sweathouses to purify themselves in preparation for war, and afterwards, they returned to the ceremonial buildings to cleanse themselves of the blood they had spilled so that they could reenter society without polluting it. Likewise, women isolated themselves during their menstrual periods in huts built specifically for the purpose. What went on in the menstrual huts is unknown, but, as ethnohistorian Patricia Galloway has theorized, they were meeting points for large numbers of women who undoubtedly performed special rituals much as the men did.[12] Men avoided contact with such women at all costs because, as one French traveler noted, "the men think that if they approach a menstruating woman they will become ill and will have bad luck in battle."[13]

Each year, when the first corn crop ripened, the Mississippians of the American South gathered at Green Corn Ceremonies to absolve themselves of pollution and restore the equilibrium of their world.[14] The ceremony was, in the words of one Choctaw, "a sacred religious duty [that] was held in honor of, and to conciliate and secure a continuation of favors from the great sun."[15] Indeed, the prosperity of the agricultural economy was linked inextricably with the sacred ideology on which the Mississippian belief system rested. Male and female, moon and sun, water and fire, and farming and hunting counterbalanced one another in a dualistic cosmology that explained and ordered the Mississippian world. For the corn to grow and for the society to prosper, men and women had to remain separate but complementary.[16]

Contact with Europeans and Africans brought an end to the Mississippian phase in the Southeast. Recent scholarship in demography and archaeology has revealed that populations collapsed in the region because of the spread by the new arrivals of epidemic diseases to which Indians lacked immunity and the warfare and slave raiding that usually accompanied European imperialism. The demographic collapse that followed the early exploration and colonization of the Southeast, however, did not wholly obliterate the Mississippian cultures that had inhabited the region. Rather, contact led to "deculturation." In all respects, from personal adornment to settlement patterns, the polished culture of the prehistoric Mississippians dulled to a dim reflection of its original brilliance.[17]

Many deculturated peoples were no longer viable economic, social, and political entities, and throughout the region remnant groups amalgamated into multiethnic confederations. Sometime in the sixteenth century, remnants of three Mississippian groups fled into what is today east-central Mississippi, where they formed the society and culture that became the Choctaws. Face-to-face contact between Choctaws and Europeans, however, did not occur until 1699, when Pierre Le Moyne, Sieur d'Iberville, sailed up the mouth of the Mississippi River and encountered the three "villages," or ethnic divisions, of the Choctaws.[18]

Early reports of European contact with Choctaws confirm the persistence of the Mississippian gendered division of labor. As early as 1702, one French observer noted that after the men had cleared the fields, Choctaw women planted corn in river bottomlands. Others reported that they raised two corn crops, the first in family gardens and the second in communal fields. By one historian's estimate, women harvested two-thirds of the Choctaw diet from their fields. Farming was so important that one English traveler called the Choctaws of the eighteenth century a "nation of farmers."[19]

In addition to farming, the deerskin trade was an important part of the Choctaw economy in the eighteenth century. As the hunters of their society, Choctaw men began spending more and more time, energy, and resources providing French and English traders with deer and other animal skins. What role Choctaw women played in the trade is unclear, but, like the women of the culturally similar Creek Indians of present-day Georgia and Alabama, they probably devoted more time to processing skins and less time to traditional activities like making clothing, earthenware vessels, and other household items. For this reason, students of Native American history have viewed the deerskin trade as a pivotal process in the economic subordination of women. For example, women in hunting and gathering tribes like the Montagnais-Naskapi and Micmac in northeastern Canada and the Sioux of the American Great Plains devoted so much time to the processing of animal skins that they became dependent on the copper kettles, sewing thread, metal tools, and foodstuffs offered by European traders. These women soon had no alternative but to spend every waking hour processing deerskins, beaver pelts, and buffalo hides in order to obtain the necessities of life.[20]

While women in hunting and gathering societies changed from producers to processors and consumers, women among horticultural and matrilineal peoples like the Choctaws retained their principal roles as producers. Moreover, although the women spent less time performing traditional tasks, they did not abandon them. A recent archaeological investigation of several Choctaw towns has shown that while European trade goods became increasingly important to Choctaws over the course of the eighteenth century, the frequency and number of pottery sherds present in the sites suggest that women refused to substitute copper kettles and glass bottles for cooking and storage vessels of their own manufacture. Unwilling to forsake their important roles as potters and handicrafters, Choctaw women were able to keep the entanglements of the deerskin trade at arm's length.[21]

Other economic opportunities for women existed outside the deerskin trade. European colonists and their African slaves had introduced new plants and even livestock to the Choctaws, and these new goods, in addition to old staples like corn and beans, enabled Choctaw women to meet the growing demands of colonial towns like Mobile, Biloxi, and New Orleans for food. Many of the new crops were raised exclusively for trade to colonists. One visitor to the Choctaws in the mid-1770s reported that "they have carried the spirit of husbandry so far as to cultivate leeks, garlic, cabbage and some other garden plants, of which they make no use, in order to make profit of them to the traders."[22] To obtain valued goods like paints, beads, and sewing items, women exploited their roles as farmers to tap into the burgeoning "frontier exchange economy" that increasingly linked the Indians, slaves, and settlers of the Lower Mississippi Valley in a subsistence-level trade in foodstuffs, household items, and labor.[23]

By the early nineteenth century the frontier exchange economy began to evolve into a market economy as cash replaced reciprocal trade as the medium of exchange. At the sprawling town market in New Orleans, Choctaw women sold vegetables, cane baskets, mats, sifters, and moccasins that they made in their small camps on the outskirts of town. In addition to the produce of their gardens and the work of their hands, mothers and daughters gathered and sold scarce firewood in Mobile and other towns.[24] Among rural farmsteads, Choctaw women offered "cooking vessels, pitchers, and trinkets" to their American counterparts, and hired themselves out to women like Mrs. Gaines who needed laborers to help keep up their farms.[25] Whether in the marketplace, the urban camps, or the countryside, Choctaw women seemed to be employed constantly in producing goods for sale or working to earn money. More important, each of these activities fit within the accepted parameters of female economic life.

Not all opportunities, however, lay in the bustling ports and sleepy hamlets of the Lower Mississippi Valley. Within the boundaries of their nation, Choctaw women did a considerable business selling to travelers on the Natchez Trace, a public road authorized in the 1801 Treaty of Fort Adams to be constructed between Nashville and New Orleans via the Choctaw nation. The treaty provided for taverns and ferries to be opened along the road. Most of the business of feeding and sheltering travelers fell to Choctaw entrepreneurs like David Folsom and Greenwood LeFlore, who ran taverns, and to women who peddled their goods along the roadside.[26]

Travelers on the trace were not of one mind when it came to their Choctaw hosts. Martha Philips Martin remembered, "When ever we stopt [sic], they treated us with great kindness, if you showed you had confidence in them." Others complained frequently about the prices Choctaws charged and the avidity with which they pursued their business. On his way to New Orleans, John H. B. Latrobe remarked that "Hospitality exists everywhere, where food cannot be bought and sold. [But] A good market in the neighborhood always puts an end to it." "[A]lmost every Indian we passed," remarked the Reverend Jacob Young in 1807, "had something to sell, especially corn at two dollars per bushel, corn blades at a bit, pumkins [sic] for a quarter, and hickory-nuts, walnuts, [and] hazel-nuts for a bit."[27] The successful businesswomen used their earnings to purchase cloth, sewing items, and agricultural implements at the trading post Mrs. Gaines's husband ran.[28] Nineteenth-century travelers soon came to expect women running up beside their horses and wagons, offering their produce, and crying out, "Bit. Bit."[29]

In addition to the pumpkins, nuts, and corn ears that they offered to travelers, Choctaw women began trading and selling milk and beef. Men and women owned their stock separately and impressed on their nephews, nieces, and children at an early age the value and importance of stock raising. Generally speaking, infant sons and daughters received from their mothers and uncles a cow and calf, a sow and piglet, and a mare and colt. As the child grew older, his or her herd would multiply and provide the owner with a sound source of income and subsistence in adulthood.[30]

Together, such small beginnings produced an enormous economic resource. By 1828 the national herd numbered over forty-three thousand head, a ratio of 2.07 cattle per capita, which compares favorably to the 1840 ratio for the state of Mississippi of 1.8 per capita. The average price of a cow in 1828 was between $8 and $10, so the Choctaw herd had a maximum market value of over $300,000 on the hoof.[31] "These people," one observer remarked, "have stocks of horses, cattle, hogs, etc. some of them have *large* stocks, and appear to live plentifully."[32]

That women owned cattle suggests a fundamental contradiction of their moral economy, because animals traditionally had been associated with men. But to Choctaw women, cattle were not animals—they were plants. One Choctaw term for cattle—*alhpoa*—means literally "fruit trees such as are cultivated" and suggests a uniquely feminine construction of the value and utility of livestock.[33] The fruit trees that proliferated among Choctaw towns offered an analogy to cattle for several reasons. Women tended both to extract valuable food, whether it be plums, peaches, or milk. The association of women with the great power of fertility also may have created a special relationship between women and cattle; the annual reproduction of cattle made them particularly valuable. Above all, orchards were a part of the domestic landscape, and other cattle-related terms derived from *alhpoa* suggest that this held true for cattle as well. For example, *alhpoa aiimpa* meant pasture, and *alhpoa imilhpak* meant fodder. Both terms imply the careful tending that characterized women's horticulture as opposed to the neglect that characterized the free-range herding practiced by the men.[34]

The linguistic construction of mobile cattle as stationary fruit trees may have enabled Choctaw women to adapt to changes in settlement patterns that occurred in the late eighteenth century. At that time, Choctaw families began moving out of their towns and settling on isolated farmsteads, and women had to abandon the orchards that had been an integral part of their landholdings and subsistence cycle. But since cattle were "fruit trees," women could, in a cognitive sense, take their orchards/cattle with them into the previously unsettled borderlands that had been reserved previously for male hunting and fighting. Women were thus able to maintain what had been an integral part of stable village life in a new and forbidding environment.[35]

By designating cattle as fruit trees, Choctaw women maintained a continuity with the past in the face of a changing present. In so doing, they also improved their prospects in the American market economy. How often they sold or traded cattle is unclear, but in at least one instance a young woman used her cow to pay for her education. In July 1820 a thirteen-year-old girl tried to enter the Elliot missionary school, located in present-day west-central Mississippi. The missionaries, however, denied her request for admission because the school was already overcrowded. Reluctant to crush the girl's hopes of going to the school, her friends told her that she needed nice clothes to be accepted to the mission school. Encouraged by this news, the girl determined to sell her cow for cash to buy some new clothes. Touched by her resolve, the missionaries agreed to take the girl in, and her uncle offered to pay any expenses to cover the cost of her schooling.[36]

What the missionaries mistook for youthful precocity, and what some might mistake for an everyday occurrence in the Old Southwest, in fact, revealed two things—an accommodation between the Mississippian moral economy of the Choctaw Indians and the market sensibilities of nineteenth-century Americans, and how the cultural construct of language mediated relations between the two. The girl's conception of the cow as a good that could be sold for cash suggests the prevalence of a distinctly market-oriented mindset. But because she could conceive of the cow as a plant, she did not have to transgress her moral economy to raise and dispose of the animal. Unlike bourgeois Anglo-American women, who were increasingly being confined to "separate spheres," or other Native American women in hunting and gathering societies, who were finding themselves trapped in the vicissitudes of the skin trade, Choctaw women could draw on their own culture to sanction an innovative economic activity like stock raising and carve out a small place in the emerging American economic order.

The Choctaw language enabled women to participate in the cattle economy without compromising their relationship to farming and to plants. At the same time, women's supervision of the plant world made them agents of change in Choctaw horticulture, for it was women who adopted cotton cultivation from the Americans who lived in their midst. In 1800 Samuel Mitchell, the first federal Choctaw agent, disbursed cotton seed to his Choctaw neighbors and showed them how to plant it. Women took to the new crop quickly, and the fluffy white bolls spread from small patches at traders' homes and appeared alongside the corn, pumpkins, and squashes in their gardens.[37]

At home, Choctaw women spun and wove thread into homespun cloth for their families, and soon they began to produce surpluses. In 1817 missionary Elias Cornelius reported that federally supported mechanics in the Nation had manufactured two thousand spinning wheels and several hundred looms for Choctaw use. "They raise cotton & manufacture it into cloth for their ordinary use," he reported. Some years later, another observer remarked that Choctaw women had spun and woven over ten thousand yards of cotton cloth in one year. One federal official admitted, "I have myself bought many yards of cloth from full blooded Indians of their own make." Women ventured into the towns and farmsteads of the countryside to sell their cloth, but according to one citizen of Mississippi, they were "cheated out of the proceeds" of their labors.[38]

By joining the slave labor forces to pick cotton on plantations in Mississippi and Alabama, Choctaw women supplemented their earnings from selling cotton cloth, fruits, vegetables, and handicrafts. Early settlers of the region attempted to hire Choctaw men for the work, but their unwillingness to engage in such labor put an end to the experiment. Women, however, did work as itinerant farm laborers. After gathering their own crops of corn and cotton, Choctaw women, frequently accompanied by men, camped on the outskirts of plantations to look for employment opportunities. While the men hunted, the women joined the slaves to pick the planters' cotton before it rotted on the stalk. Women received blankets, cloth, handkerchiefs, other manufactured items, or cash wages for their work.[39]

Choctaw women's acceptance of cotton and cattle as commodities and spinning, weaving, stock raising, and wage labor as acceptable activities suggests a convergence between their own culture and that of Anglo-America. But beneath such surface appearances ran deep Mississippian metaphors. Clothing styles, in particular, embodied the juxtaposition of American styles and Mississippian meanings. Choctaw women in the early nineteenth century substituted cloth that they had purchased or manufactured for animal skins in the fabrication of garments. Their scarlet skirts reached beneath their knees, and bright calico shirts and shiny silver jewelry completed their outfits. But their hair told a sacred story obscured by the flash and color of their attire, for in the part of their black hair they traced a line of vermilion to represent the path of the sun that had always given life to the green fields of corn and now nourished the long rows of cotton.[40]

Farmland had remained an important part of Choctaw women's economic life and identity throughout the first century of contact, but events beyond their control threatened to dispossess them of this most important possession. On September 15, 1830, a federal commission made up of John Eaton and John Coffee arrived in the Choctaw Nation to negotiate on behalf of President Andrew Jackson the cession of their land and their removal from Mississippi to a reserve in what became "Indian Territory" in present-day Oklahoma. The commissioners found lodging near the council ground, which lay on a wooded patch of land between the two forks of Dancing Rabbit Creek, and on the morning of September 22, they met with the Choctaw chiefs and councilmen. Coffee and Eaton took their seats on a log that was oriented with the path of the sun. Before them sat the Choctaw men in a broad semicircle that stretched southward under the shade of several oak, pine, and mulberry trees. The documents left behind by the treaty commission do not mention any women at the proceedings, but a Choctaw account stated that in the middle of the semicircle of chiefs and councilmen sat seven women.[41]

Each councilman stood before Coffee and Eaton and offered his thoughts on removal, but only one, Killihota, advocated it. He urged that "the Choctaws ought to sell everything they owned, land, cattle, horses, and hogs, and all in a body emigrate west." Land, however, lay outside his and the other men's authority, and the women made this clear. "Killihota," snapped one of the seven women, "I could cut you open with this knife. You have two hearts." "You may hang me," replied the councilman, "and cut my bosom open and you will see that I have only one heart and [it is] for my people." Though he survived the confrontation, Killihota's entreaties fell on deaf ears, and each subsequent speaker backed the women and denounced removal. The Choctaw women had transformed their influence into authority, and, for the time being, succeeded in defending their land.[42]

The women's opposition to removal ended these discussions, and some days later most of the Choctaws left for home, secure in the knowledge that they had thwarted the federal commissioners. Meanwhile, several chiefs remained at the treaty ground, determined to reach a final agreement with Eaton and Coffee because they, like Killihota, believed the Choctaws could no longer live in an America that was growing increasingly hostile toward its Indian peoples. The resulting treaty stipulated that the Choctaws would remove over a three year period and that each man would receive an allotment of land, which he could sell for profit or remain upon after the removal. Reflective of the biases of the Anglo-American commissioners, the women received nothing. For them, the treaty was a disaster. Over the next few years, nearly fifteen thousand of the twenty-one thousand Choctaws packed up their belongings, bade farewell to their homes and fields, and struck out for an uncertain future in Indian Territory.

By casting economic innovations like cotton and cattle into traditionally accepted categories of belief and modes of production, Choctaw women changed with the world around them without losing their place in it. However, regardless of the power of their culture and the convictions of their beliefs, they could not resist the expansion of the United States. But contact was as much a phenomenon of interaction between individuals as it was between political sovereignties. So long as the conflicts and accommodations encountered in the "Indians' New World" remained on the level of the individual, Choctaw women defended successfully what was theirs. No, they had told Mrs. Gaines, their sons would not work like women. More important, the mothers and daughters refused to surrender the rights and responsibilities that had defined them and empowered them as women ever since the crow dropped the first corn seed at the feet of a little Choctaw girl.

NOTES

1. "Papers of George S. Gaines, Copied from the Original Now on File in the Mississippi State Department of Archives and History in a Collection of Letters Once Owned by J. F. H. Claiborne," 1, Indian Archives, Oklahoma State Historical Society, Norman, Okla.

2. James Merrell, *The Indians' New World: Catawbas and Their Neighbors from European Contact through the Era of Removal* (Chapel Hill: University of North Carolina Press, 1989).

3. For the original example of economic choices based on cultural views of morality, see E. P. Thompson, "The Moral Economy of the English Crowd in the Eighteenth Century," in *Customs in Common: Studies in Traditional Popular Culture* (New York: New Press, 1993), 185–258.

4. R. Douglas Hurt, *Indian Agriculture in America: Prehistory to the Present* (Lawrence: University of Kansas Press, 1987), 6–11.

5. Folder 42, microfilm reel 2, Henry S. Halbert Papers, Mississippi Department of Archives and History, Jackson, Miss.

6. For a discussion of the Mississippians, see Charles Hudson, *The Southeastern Indians* (Knoxville: University of Tennessee Press, 1976); Chester B. DePratter, *Late Prehistoric and Early Historic Chiefdoms in the Southeastern United States* (New York: Garland, 1991); John H. Blitz, *Ancient Chiefdoms of the Tombigbee* (Tuscaloosa: Uni-

versity of Alabama Press, 1993); and Charles Hudson and Carmen Chaves Tesser, eds., *The Forgotten Centuries: Indians and Europeans in the American South, 1521–1704* (Athens: University of Georgia Press, 1994).

7. Thomas E. Emerson, "Water, Serpents, and the Underworld: An Exploration into Cahokian Symbolism," in *The Southeastern Ceremonial Complex: Artifacts and Analysis, the Cottonlandia Conference,* ed. Patricia K. Galloway (Lincoln: University of Nebraska Press, 1984), 50–55.

8. Michelle Zimbalist Rosaldo, "Women, Culture, and Society: A Theoretical Overview," in *Women, Culture, and Society,* ed. Michelle Zimbalist Rosaldo and Louise Lamphere (Stanford: Stanford University Press, 1974), 17–42 represents the early understanding of Native American women. See Jane Fishburne Collier and Sylvia Junko Yamagisako, "Toward a Unified Analysis of Gender and Kinship," in *Gender and Kinship: Essays toward a Unified Analysis,* ed. Jane Fishburne Collier and Sylvia Junko Yamagisako (Stanford: Stanford University Press, 1987), 14–52 for a revisionist interpretation.

9. Diane Rothenberg, "The Mothers of the Nation: Seneca Resistance to Quaker Intervention," in *Women and Colonization: Anthropological Perspectives,* ed. Mona Etienne and Eleanor Laycock (New York: Praeger, 1980), 68; and Joy Bilharz, "First among Equals? The Changing Status of Seneca Women," in *Women and Power in Native North America,* ed. Laura F. Klein and Lillian A. Ackerman (Norman: University of Oklahoma Press, 1995), 103.

10. Daniel Maltz and JoAllyn Archambault, "Gender and Power in Native North America," in *Women and Power,* ed. Klein and Ackerman, 234.

11. Hudson, *Southeastern Indians,* chaps. 2, 3; and Mary Douglas, *Purity and Danger: An Analysis of Concepts of Pollution and Taboo* (Harmondworth, U.K.: Penguin, 1970), 13–14.

12. James Adair, *Adair's History of the American Indians,* ed. Samuel Cole Williams (1930; reprint, Nashville: National Society of the Colonial Dames of America, in Tennessee, 1953), 130, 185; John R. Swanton, "An Early Account of the Choctaw Indians," *Memoirs of the American Anthropological Association,* vol. 5, no. 2 (Lancaster, Penn.: American Anthropological Association, 1918), 59–60; and Patricia K. Galloway, "Where Have All the Menstrual Huts Gone? The Invisibility of Menstrual Seclusion in the Late Prehistoric Southeast" (paper presented at the Southeastern Archaeological Conference, 1991).

13. Jean-Bernard Bossu, *Travels in the Interior of North America, 1751–1762,* trans. and ed. Seymour Feiler (Norman: University of Oklahoma Press, 1962), 171.

14. John A. Walthall, *Prehistoric Indians of the Southeast: Archaeology of Alabama and the Middle South* (Tuscaloosa: University of Alabama Press, 1980), 194.

15. Gideon Lincecum, "History of the Chahta Nation," 250, Gideon Lincecum Papers, Center for American History, University of Texas at Austin, microfilm.

16. Lincecum, "History," 251; and Alfred Wright, "Choctaws: Religious Opinions, Traditions, Etc.," *Missionary Herald* 24 (June 1828): 179–80.

17. Henry Dobyns, *Their Number Become Thinned: Native American Population Dynamics in Eastern North America* (Knoxville: University of Tennessee Press, 1983); Ann F. Ramenofsky, *Vectors of Death: The Archaeology of European Contact* (Albuquerque: University of New Mexico Press, 1987); and Marvin T. Smith, *Archaeology of Aboriginal Culture Change in the Interior Southeast: Depopulation during the Early Historic Period* (Gainesville: University Press of Florida, 1987).

18. Patricia K. Galloway, "Confederacy as a Solution to Chiefdom Dissolution," in *Forgotten Centuries*, ed. Hudson and Tesser, 393–420.

19. Patricia K. Galloway, "Henri de Tonti du Village des Chacta, 1702: Beginnings of the French Alliance," in *La Salle and His Legacy: Frenchmen and Indians in the Lower Mississippi Valley,* ed. Patricia K. Galloway (Jackson: University Press of Mississippi, 1982), 167; Swanton, "An Early Account," 59; Richard White, *The Roots of Dependency: Subsistence, Environment, and Social Change among the Choctaws, Pawnees, and Navajos* (Lincoln: University of Nebraska Press, 1983), 26; Hudson, *Southeastern Indians,* 259, 266–67; and Bernard Romans, *A Concise Natural History of East and West Florida; a Facsimile Reproduction of the 1775 Ed.* (Gainesville: University of Florida Press, 1962), 71.

20. Kathryn E. Holland Braund, "Guardians of Tradition and Handmaidens to Change: Women's Roles in Creek Economic and Social Life during the Eighteenth Century," *American Indian Quarterly* 14 (summer 1990): 239–58; Mary C. Wright, "Economic Development and Native American Women in the Early Nineteenth Century," *American Quarterly* 33 (1981): 525–36; Carol Devens, "Separate Confrontations: Gender as a Factor in Indian Adaptation to European Colonization in New France," *American Quarterly* 38 (1986): 461–80; and Alan Klein, "The Political Economy of Gender: A 19th Century Plains Indian Case Study," in *The Hidden Half: Studies of Plains Indian Women,* ed. Patricia Albers and Beatrice Medicine (Washington, D.C.: University Press of America, 1983), 143–74.

21. Rothenberg, "Mothers of the Nation," 82; Nancy Shoemaker, "The Rise or Fall of Iroquois Women," *Journal of Women's History* 2 (winter 1991): 39–57; Karen Anderson, "Commodity Exchange and Subordination: Montagnais-Naskapi and Huron Women, 1600–1650," *Signs* 11 (autumn 1985): 48–2; and Timothy Paul Mooney, "Many Choctaw Standing: An Archaeological Study of Culture Change in the Early Historic Period" (master's thesis, University of North Carolina at Chapel Hill, 1994).

22. Romans, *Concise Natural History,* 84.

23. Eron Opha Rowland, ed., "Peter Chester, Third Governor of the Province of West Florida under British Dominion, 1770–1781," *Publications of the Mississippi Historical Society, Centenary Series,* 5 (1925): 83–84; and Daniel H. Usner, Jr., *Indians, Settlers, and Slaves in a Frontier Exchange Economy: The Lower Mississippi Valley before 1763* (Chapel Hill: University of North Carolina Press, 1992), 211.

24. Benjamin Henry Boneval Latrobe, *Impressions Respecting New Orleans: Diary and Sketches, 1818–1820,* ed. Samuel Wilson, Jr. (New York: Columbia University

Press, 1951), 21–22, 76; Fortescue Cuming, *Sketches of a Tour to the Western Country* (Pittsburgh: Palmer, Spear and Eichbaum, 1810), 335–36; Berquin-Duvallon, *Travels in Louisiana and the Floridas, in the Year 1802, Giving a Correct Picture of Those Countries, Tr. from the French, with Notes, &c. by John Davis* (New York: I. Riley, 1806), 96; Paul Wilhelm, Duke of Württemberg, *Travels in North America, 1822–1824*, trans. W. Robert Nitske, ed. Savoie Lottinville (Norman: University of Oklahoma Press, 1973), 33; Gideon Lincecum, "Life of Apushimataha," *Publications of the Mississippi Historical Society* 9 (1906): 480.

25. "A Partial Biography of the James Ware Davis Family," 3–4, William Penn Davis Papers, Special Collections, William R. Perkins Library, Duke University, Durham, N.C.

26. Treaty of Fort Adams, December 12, 1801, United States, Records of the Bureau of Indian Affairs, National Archives Record Group 75, Documents Relating to the Negotiation of Ratified and Unratified Treaties with Various Indian Tribes, 1801–1869, microfilm series T494, reel 1.

27. Harriet Owsley, ed., "Travels through the Indian Country in the Early 1800s: Memoirs of Martha Philips Martin," *Tennessee Historical Quarterly* 21 (March 1962): 75; Latrobe, *Impressions*, 80; and Jacob Young, *Autobiography of a Pioneer* (Cincinnati: L. Swormstedt and A. Poe, 1857), 213–14.

28. Choctaw Trading House Daybooks, United States, Records of the Bureau of Indian Affairs, National Archives Record Group 75, Records of the Choctaw Trading House, 1803–1824, microfilm series T500.

29. Young, *Autobiography of a Pioneer*, 213–14.

30. *Missionary Herald* 17 (April 1821): 110.

31. Calculating livestock statistics for Americans, much less Choctaws, prior to the 1840 federal census is extremely difficult. However, figures do exist that give some indication of how large the Choctaw herd was. The American Board missionaries took a census of the people and the animals in the eastern division of the Choctaw Nation in 1828. Using these figures, I reconstructed a ration of people to cattle for the district and applied this figure to the total Choctaw population of twenty-one thousand. *Missionary Herald* 17 (April 1821): 110; 25 (May 1829): 153; 25 (February 1829): 61, 153; "Report on Indian Tribes," Senate Document 27, *Public Documents, Printed by Order of the Senate of the United States*, 2d sess., 20th Cong., 1828–29 (Washington, D.C.: Gales and Seaton, 1829), 6; and Lewis Cecil Gray, *History of Agriculture in the Southeastern United States to 1860*, 2 vols. (Washington, D.C.: Carnegie Institution of Washington, 1933), 2:812, 1042.

32. *Niles' Weekly Register* 38 (July 5, 1830): 345. Emphasis in original.

33. Cyrus Byington, *A Dictionary of the Choctaw Language*, ed. John R. Swanton and Henry S. Halbert, Bureau of American Ethnology Bulletin 46 (Washington, D.C.: U.S. Government Printing Office, 1915), 77.

34. Ibid., 77; Mary Haas, "Men's and Women's Speech in Koasati," in *Language in Culture and Society*, ed. Dell Hymes (New York: Harper and Row, 1964), 228–33;

Amelia Rector Bell, "Separate People: Speaking of Creek Men and Women," *American Anthropologist* 92 (June 1992): 332–45; Antoine Simon Le Page du Pratz, *The History of Louisiana Translated from the French of M. Le Page du Pratz,* ed. Joseph Tregle, Jr. (Baton Rouge: Louisiana State University Press, 1975), 234; Lauren C. Post, "The Domestic Animals and Plants of French Louisiana as Mentioned in the Literature with References to Sources, Varieties, and Uses," *Louisiana Historical Quarterly* 16 (October 1933): 560; and U. P. Hedrick, *The Peaches of New York* (Albany, N.Y.: J. B. Lynn, 1917), 44–45.

35. White, *Roots of Dependency,* 103–5, 130–37; *Missionary Herald* 25 (November 1829): 350.

36. *Panoplist and Missionary Herald* 16 (July 1820): 320.

37. John Forbes to Juan Ventura Morales, February 11, 1802, *Papers of Panton, Leslie and Co.* (Woodbridge, Conn.: Research Publications, 1986), microfilm, reel 14; James Wilkinson, Benjamin Hawkins, and Andrew Pickens to Henry Dearborn, December 18, 1802, United States, Records of the Bureau of Indian Affairs, National Archives Record Group 75, Office of the Secretary of War—Letters Received, 1824–1881, microfilm series M271, reel 1; and Samuel Mitchell to David Henley, January 17, 1800, David Henley Papers, Special Collections, William R. Perkins Library, Duke University, Durham, N.C.

38. Elias Cornelius, December 2, 1817, Indian Missionary Journals, part 1, Elias Cornelius Papers, Special Collections, William R. Perkins Library, Duke University; Jedidiah Morse, *A Report to the Secretary of War of the United States* (New Haven: Howe and Spalding, 1822), 182; *Niles' Weekly Register* 38 (July 3, 1830): 345; and L. R. Bakewell to James Barbour, September 2, 1825, United States, Records of the Office of Indian Affairs, National Archives Record Group 75, Correspondence of the Office of Indian Affairs and Related Records—Letters Received, 1800–1823, microfilm series M234, Choctaw Agency, reel 169.

39. Francis DuBose Richardson Memoirs, 27, 33, microfilm 3010, Manuscript Division, Wilson Library, Southern Historical Collection, University of North Carolina at Chapel Hill; George S. Gaines, "Gaines' Reminiscences," *Alabama Historical Quarterly* 26 (fall and winter 1964): 184; Horace Smith Fulkerson, *Random Recollections of Early Days in Mississippi* (Vicksburg: Vicksburg Printing and Publishing, 1885), 12; Mary J. Welsh, "Recollections of Pioneer Life in Mississippi," *Publications of the Mississippi Historical Society* 4 (1906): 350; H. G. Hawkins, "History of Port Gibson," *Publications of the Mississippi Historical Society,* 10 (1909): 283.

40. "Papers of George S. Gaines," 10; F. B. Young, "Notices of the Chactaw or Choktah Tribe," *Edinburgh Journal of Natural and Geographical Science* 2 (1830): 14; and Willard H. Rollings, *The Osage: An Ethnohistorical Study of Hegemony on the Prairie-Plains* (Columbia: University of Missouri Press, 1992), 18.

41. Henry S. Halbert, "Story of the Treaty of Dancing Rabbit Creek," *Publications of the Mississippi Historical Society* 6 (1902): 374–77.

42. Ibid., 384–91.

Chapter Three

A Struggle for Survival
Non-Elite White Women in Lowcountry Georgia, 1790–1830

Timothy J. Lockley

EDITOR'S NOTE: *Western Europe was a relatively unimportant collection of poor agricultural societies on the edge of the Eurasian landmass when Portuguese maritime advances encouraged ocean exploration in the 1420s. By 1492 Columbus had landed in the Bahamas, establishing the first permanent link between the two hemispheres, and soon initiated the transatlantic trade in African slaves. By 1535 the Spanish had conquered the wealthiest and most populous New World societies (Aztec, Incan, and Mayan peoples), bringing so much gold and silver to Europe that it doubled the money supply and led to massive inflation. This sixteenth-century "Price Revolution" was exacerbated by a rapid increase in population due to declining death rates as epidemics receded. The Dutch, English, and French were the primary beneficiaries of these changes, which led them to enter the competition for North America.*

Because of their isolation, Native American populations lacked the immunities to diseases like smallpox, measles, and influenza that the Old World had built up over the centuries. The resulting depopulation hastened European dominance. There were probably two million Indians in the South in 1500, but that number had been halved by the time Jamestown was settled in 1607, and by 1790 had fallen to 3 percent of pre-Columbian figures.

Spaniards like Juan Ponce de Leon and Hernando de Soto explored Florida and other parts of the Lower South. By 1590 a chain of military and Franciscan outposts stretched from present-day South Carolina to Florida, and St. Augustine (1565) became the first permanent European settlement on the North American mainland. The French focused their efforts on fur trading in present-day Canada, but the desire for a warm-water outlet led them to establish Gulf Coast colonies, the most important being New Orleans (1718). Ursuline nuns arrived in 1727 and founded what may have been the first school for Euroamerican girls. As the novel, opera, and ballet Manon Lescaut *illustrates, some French women from the streets and prisons also immigrated, as did "casket girls," rural women who brought their dowries with them. The French and Indian War (1763) brought the British removal of six thousand French families from present-day Nova Scotia to southern Louisiana, where they maintain their Cajun culture even today. Changing hands many times, Louisiana and Florida eventually became part of the United States in 1803 and 1819, respectively. Yet the influence of Latin culture remains larger than is usually recognized.*

Most Latin immigrants were male, a demographic pattern that produced racially mixed populations in Latin America and concubinage in New Orleans and other Deep South cities. White males formed relationships with slaves or free blacks, occasionally as an alternative to marriage. During the antebellum period New Orleans was a center of the "fancy-girl" trade in light-skinned women, who brought $5,000 when prime fieldhands sold for $1,600. Plaçage developed among free blacks, whereby light, well-educated, chaste women were introduced to white males at the city's quadroon balls. Ensuing relationships resulted in contracts with "protectors," stipulating support for the women and future children. From such interracial unions developed a caste of creoles of color, proud of their French cultural heritage.

French planters fleeing the uprising in Saint Domingue in the 1790s brought their slaves with them. Caribbean slaves had retained more of their African culture than those in British North America, because of the constant infusion of new slaves from Africa and because they vastly outnumbered whites. They were able to retain many African practices in New Orleans's Congo Square, where they were permitted to dance, make music, and trade. Women traded in the marketplace, as they did in Africa. African religious practices involving such things as signs and amulets were widespread in Louisiana. Marie Laveau, a free woman of color, and her daughter became powerful practitioners of Voodoo, an expression of African religious beliefs influenced by Catholicism.

If the Deep South was more Latin than is often realized, the Upper South was less English. Roanoke, birthplace of Virginia Dare (1587), the first English child born in the New World, was unsuccessful. Jamestown, founded in 1607, soon imported English women, mostly as indentured servants, but in 1619 the first Africans arrived, adding to the cultural mix. The Shenandoah Valley became a road down which families of Scots-Irish and Germans from Pennsylvania entered the southern backcountry. French Huguenots settled in Charleston and Jews established themselves in coastal cities. Swiss, Welsh, Irish, and Highland Scots also contributed to this pluralistic society.

Georgia, founded in 1732 as a refuge for the worthy English poor, was no different. With the influx of Welsh, Swiss, Scots, Irish, German, and Jewish immigrants, it soon became part of the rice-indigo society of the Carolina low-country. Perhaps as much as 80 percent of white women immigrants arrived as indentured servants. Not all were able to rise, however; and poor women re-mained ubiquitous throughout the South — even in Georgia.

· · ·

This essay offers a brief look at the lives of non-elite white women in and around Savannah in the early national period. The Georgia lowcountry, like the rest of the nineteenth-century South, was a highly stratified soci-ety dominated by white males. Most social historians have concentrated on the well-documented lives of the most prominent white men, and even those scholars who have explored the lives of white women focus almost exclusively on the wives of the elite.[1] Any historian studying white women of the early South is hampered by evidential problems. The poor-est white women were usually illiterate and left few of the direct historical records, such as letters and diaries, that could prove useful. Even official records that regularly encompass non-elite men are silent on non-elite women. Legal transactions, for example, were normally carried out by men (husbands, brothers, and fathers). By using Chatham County court documents, city council minutes from Savannah, and records of lowcoun-try churches and benevolent societies, this essay seeks to correct some of these omissions in current historiography. This study will delineate what may well have been the typical experience of non-elite white women in Savannah: lives of poverty, reliance on charity, and a constant and often futile struggle to make ends meet. Studying the everyday experiences of poor white women, their attitudes, hopes, and fears may give us some insight into the interaction among race, class, and gender in a slave society.

The southern myth of female gentility, especially pertinent in lowcoun-try cities like Savannah and Charleston, has tended to obscure the fact that many white women lived in poverty.[2] However, contemporary elites were cognizant of white destitution; by the early national period a com-plete network of benevolence had been formed in the lowcountry. The willingness of wealthy individuals to participate in charitable provision stemmed from a popular perception that benevolence had a beneficial impact on society generally. By alleviating the suffering of the poor, the elite hoped to inculcate in them "the habits of industry & virtue, and furnish the means of useful and respectable employment."[3] Girls were acknowledged to be especially vulnerable to economic pressures, and in this highly patriarchal society the sight of destitute young white girls aimlessly wandering the streets of Savannah was very moving.[4] Contemporary gender conventions presumed that "a boy can make his way through this cold world well enough; but the situation of a young orphan girl is one which has the strongest demand upon the best sympathies that belong to our nature."[5] Girls were denied the chance of learning the variety of trades to which boys were apprenticed, and their resultant inability to earn their keep through casual work meant that they often became a burden to their parents. Catherine Williams, for example, was turned out of her mother's home because "she was fatherless and her mother was not permitted by her present husband to give her the shelter of her roof."[6] Catherine's evident inability to contribute to the family income no doubt influenced her stepfather's decision. Consequently, a number of benevolent institutions in the Georgia lowcountry were established specifically to assist young girls, the first being the Savannah Female Asylum, founded in December 1801 by "a number of ladies." This gendering of benevolence, organized by elite women for poor women, clearly "called [them] into a full spectrum of public roles" and gave them a new influence in society, caring for "female orphan and other equally distressed female children."[7]

While giving poor white girls a decent start in life was the principal reason for establishing female asylums, the subtext of benevolence was social control. The misbehavior and lack of discipline of older girls on one occasion forced the board to issue the matron "a whip with directions to use it."[8] In an attempt to instill the habits of industry, the boards of female asylums bound out girls to learn viable occupations. Applications from women involved in a trade were particularly welcome, though offers like Mrs. Irvine's to the Beaufort Female Benevolent Society to train two girls in the millinery trade for two years were all too rare. To some extent, these working women were motivated by the chance to employ cheap labor; in Mrs. Irvine's case the benevolent society agreed to pay for bedding and clothing, while Mrs. Irvine provided the girls' food.[9] Yet above all, work of this kind was intended to be character building; thus, misuse of the girls by employers was not permitted. In Savannah, Mary Ann Flynn was quickly removed from Mrs. Monrow's service as the board had "every reason to think that she is kept for the sole purpose of attending on her [own] child."[10] The binding-out system allowed poor girls to encounter and learn from older white women who themselves may have lived meager existences, forming gender networks that crossed generational lines.

The social control exerted by charitable women on children also extended to their parents. All charitable institutions to some extent subscribed to the idea that parents who surrendered their children to the care of others were not fit to receive them back unless a substantial change in circumstances had occurred. Indeed, one of the stipulations of the Beaufort Female Benevolent Society to parents and guardians was that girls were "exclusively given up . . . to the control and directions of the society."[11] Even mothers who were permitted to take their children back sometimes had to sign "a bond authorizing the directresses to take the child back if they hear anything prejudicial to the future welfare of the child."[12] By restricting the rights of poor women over their own children, elite women exerted a class-based control that denied poor women the rights and responsibilities of motherhood.

The specific purpose of female asylums was to care for destitute white girls. Those parents who were not destitute, and therefore unable to enroll their daughters in the asylums, but who nevertheless lacked the means to educate their children could apply to the variety of lowcountry free schools and academies. The education of poor children formed an important part of the work of every charitable institution, for ignorance, it was believed, "leads to idleness, idleness to vice, and vice abandons to ruin."[13] Education therefore, while being intended to enlighten, primarily aimed to shape the behavior of the non-elite, who otherwise would "advance in vice." In Savannah the main provision of education fell to the Savannah Free School Society, which by 1820 taught more than two hundred children, slightly less than half of whom were female.[14] All applications to take a child resulted in an inquiry "into his or her circumstances, . . . that none be admitted who are not really indigent."[15]

A comparison of the membership lists of these societies and the federal census provides an estimate of the number of children in Savannah receiving some kind of charitable assistance. The pervasiveness of charity in the lives of the city's poorest inhabitants is clearly demonstrated by the fact that around 1820 nearly a third of the entire resident female population of Savannah under the age of twenty-one was in receipt of charity from either the Female Asylum or the Savannah Free School. The gendered nature of this benevolence is self-evident: only about a fifth of boys received charity in the same period.[16] This would seem to suggest that a significant portion of the non-elite whites resident in Savannah lacked sufficient resources to care for their children as they might have wished.

By providing for indigent whites, the elite reduced social disaffection while adopting the mantle of Christian charity. In the early nineteenth century more than five hundred individuals—about a quarter of the adult white population of Savannah—subscribed to either the Female Asylum, the Union Society, or the Free School.[17] As part of their attempts to control the lives of poor women, the elite fostered a close relationship between charity and religion. On Sundays the charitable institutions sent orphan girls to church in order "to impress [on] their minds . . . the great importance of a modest and virtuous behavior." Efforts were made not to prefer one denomination over another. Girls at the Female Asylum, for example, were taken to Sunday morning worship at the Independent Presbyterian Church, followed by an afternoon service at the First Baptist Church.[18] Children attending the Free School, in addition to hearing twice daily readings from Scripture, were expected to attend the church "as may be designated by their parents or guardians."[19] Religious observance was therefore intended not only to inform but to control the behavior of the poor by instilling in them the virtues and social ethic believed by the elite to best ensure social stability. By adopting and utilizing evangelical religion in this manner, the elite had found a useful tool in their attempts to control the lives of the poor through benevolence.

Those poor girls who survived to adulthood (and many did not) found their economic choices limited. Although occupational information about white women is difficult to locate, third party diaries, travelers' accounts, and newspapers show that poor white women concentrated in certain trades, especially cloth making, food preparation and marketing, housekeeping, and retailing. Other poor white women found work as domestics to the elite residents of Savannah, and newspaper advertisements show that versatility was the key to successful employment. However, many African American women, free as well as slave, also worked as domestics in Savannah.[20] Consequently, poor white women often struggled to find work in this area. House servants often worked long hours, and it was no doubt easier for owners to use older female slaves who were no longer productive in the fields than pay white women. This is not to say that white women who managed to obtain employment as domestics necessarily labored under better working conditions than African American women. In 1796, Nancy Burton obtained an order from the council to prohibit John Fitzpatrick from being violent toward her sister, Sarah. The council later gave Sarah Burton the option of renouncing her domestic indentures to Fitzpatrick in favor of her sister's care.[21] Clearly, working white women held no special status in the labor market of Savannah by virtue of their color.

The marginal social position of non-elite white women is reflected by the fact that they regularly worked alongside African American women. Emily Burke even saw "white women and black women" near Savannah working in fields together "without distinction." John Melish, visiting one lowcountry farm in 1806, noticed "a black girl carding cotton, and a daughter of the landlord spinning . . . they were quite busy and appeared to be industrious and happy." The new cotton mills established in the nineteenth century also offered employment to women of both races. One visitor observed "the white girls working in the same room and at the same loom with the black girls . . . without apparent repugnance or objection."[22] Cloth making had been part of the traditional female role in both England and Africa; it is therefore unsurprising that these roles should be re-created in the New World. What is significant is that white women were prepared to undertake this work with African American women on apparently similar terms of employment, enabling some women to form biracial gender networks that crossed and, therefore, weakened racial distinctions.

The most public sphere of economic interaction between women of different races and classes was the Savannah city market. Most market trading was undertaken by bondswomen, just as it was throughout the Caribbean islands and in West Africa.[23] Their dominance in the city market is shown by the numbers of licensed slave vendors. In 1801, Savannah City Council granted thirty trading licenses to slaves, twenty-five of whom were female. Free black women were also involved in trading goods. Ten free black women listed their occupation in 1817 as "huckstering"—selling goods on the streets, in direct competition to the licensed slave vendors.[24] White and black women, either daughters, wives, or domestics, were also the principal shoppers. This daily ritual of economic interaction brought white women into regular contact with Afro-American women on nondependency grounds. Race had little significance in these economic transactions.

Black and white women also interacted in Savannah's brothels, which were frequented by Afro-American and white men alike. These women could expect little leniency from civic authorities if prosecuted. Indeed, some scholars have argued that white women were effectively deprived of their racial identity and the protection it afforded after they engaged in interracial sexual activity. An overwhelming proportion of the prosecutions for "disorderly conduct" involved women, and while sex between white men and black women was frequently overlooked by the legal authorities, miscegenation involving white women was taken extremely seriously.[25] In both 1808 and 1809 the Chatham County grand jury cited "houses of ill fame," which "are suffered to be kept in the very center of the city" and where "the sacred ties of marriage are forgotten, and the foundation of diseases laid."[26] Street prostitution was also apparent in Savannah. In 1814 a warrant was issued for an unnamed white woman "who is in the habit of passing through town at all times, and holding improper conversations with persons of color."[27] Poor women had, of course, been traditionally associated with prostitution, and there is no reason to believe that Savannah was any different; however, in the South, the denial of racial identity that miscegenation entailed for white women generated significant social repercussions. Nevertheless, prostitution remained for some a necessary way of earning a living, despite the fact that it was the ultimate gendered rejection of the elite social ethic. The fact that this would bring poor white women into contact with both male and female Afro-Americans was evidently insufficient reason for them to abandon this line of work.[28]

Although the marginal socioeconomic situation of poor white women is clear, it formed but one part of lives that also encompassed the familial and the spiritual. Many non-elite women sought a husband to obtain a measure of economic security, love, and happiness; but marriages also entailed the subordination of wives to their husbands.[29] Of course many non-elite white women lived contented married lives: in a series of letters from her husband, William Garland, we learn that while Harriet Garland lived a materially impoverished existence, she took comfort from the love and support of her husband. William was an itinerant mechanic working mainly in the Savannah River area and was thus frequently absent from their home in Beaufort. In times of good employment Garland encouraged his wife to look out for the next wage packet he had sent to her, while regretting that his work took him away from home. In leaner times he was forced to warn her to be "as careful of your money as you can."[30] While lack of evidence makes it impossible to estimate just how many lowcountry marriages were unhappy, divorce petitions highlight some of the worst cases of abuse of poor wives by their husbands. Unlike residents of neighboring South Carolina, where divorce was prohibited, Georgians were able to petition county courts to obtain divorces.[31] One such petition to Chatham County Inferior Court is that of Mary Ryan.

According to surviving records, Mary Wood and William L. Ryan married in February 1817. Ryan was a merchant rich enough to own one slave, and even Mary acknowledged that in the early years their marriage had enjoyed "domestic peace and quiet." Around 1820 Ryan's business faltered, he no longer owned a slave, and the value of his property had fallen from $1,500 to $100. By 1821 he owned no property at all. Ryan began to drink heavily, though whether this was a cause of or a response to his economic problems is not known. But as a consequence, his wife stated, he for "three years beat, calumniated & in other ways ill-treated your petitioner, driving her from her home, compelling her to seek her personal safety by flying to her friends, leaving her at divers times unprotected & houseless, an object of the bounty and tenderness of an aged & infirm mother."[32]

Mary Ryan based her petition for divorce not only on the violence she had suffered but also—and probably more telling in terms of how gender relations were perceived in lowcountry society—on the marital failings of her husband. According to Mary, she "performed all those domestick duties which religion and the regulations of society require." In other words, William could not claim that he had beaten his wife to correct her failings. By throwing her out, he had forced her "to rely solely on her daily manual labor for support of herself and infant child," instead of fulfilling the traditional role of breadwinner. In a final damning appendage to her petition, Mary Ryan desired to be rescued from William's "unmanly, ungenerous and barbarous conduct." This manner of illuminating William's failings as a man was the clinching argument in her petition. Despite the fact that his lawyers pleaded innocence on his behalf, William was unable to convince the jury that he had dutifully fulfilled his matrimonial obligations. The jury heard testimony from three witnesses, all women, one of whom was Mary's mother, Catherine Wood. Their testimony has, unfortunately, not survived, but it is likely that these women were those friends Mary referred to as offering her refuge from her husband. Their testimony evidently gave weight to Mary's version of events, as the jury found "sufficient proofs" to grant the divorce petition.[33]

Mary Ryan was not the only non-elite white woman to obtain redress against her husband through the courts. Shortly after the Revolution, Mary Wade was granted full rights "to deal and transact all lawfull business in your name independent of any interference or control of your said husband [Hezekiah Wade]." Hezekiah had been a tavern keeper, but was evidently unemployed by the time of this petition. Mary Wade testified that he had become an alcoholic and incapable of providing for the family, even resorting to pawning those articles "furnished by charitable people." The court therefore ordered that Mary Wade be given the rights usually reserved to men, to trade and make contracts in her own name "for the purposes of acquiring an honest and competent support." While empowering Mary Wade was significant, considering her gender, it should be noted that the principal reason for the actions of the court was to protect those with whom she formed contracts. Mary Wade was what was termed a "femme covert." In other words, she did not have a separate legal identity from her husband, and contracts signed by her would have had no legal validity. By this ruling, the court gave her the same legal rights held by men. Other femmes coverts obtained redress against abusive husbands by seeking a guardian to handle their affairs. When Ann Chauvin was ejected by her husband, William, she succeeded in persuading the Superior Court to appoint David Gugel as her guardian to obtain "her just rights." [34]

Many white women found that an appeal to their local church brought a swift and public condemnation of mistreatment by husbands. In 1770 the Congregational church at Midway suspended three men who failed to treat their wives in what was perceived as the appropriate manner. [35] While these cases were comparatively rare in the discipline meetings of evangelical churches, when they did arise the public humiliation of the man in question was complete. In 1829 Little Ogechee Baptist Church went so far as to excommunicate Lucas Bob for leaving his wife and "taking up with another woman." [36] His actions were not tolerated by a community that expected husbands to live up to their familial responsibilities.

The interest of churches in the domestic arrangements of their members, of course, applied to women as well. Those living in adultery violated the ethic of female "passionlessness" promoted by churches and consequently could expect censure through either suspension or excommunication. Both Morning Shepherd and Mrs. Jenkinson were expelled from their religious communities for improper physical relations. [37] It is important to note, however, that while adultery would probably result in excommunication, separation from a violent husband would not necessarily involve long-term consequences. When the First Baptist Church in Savannah considered the case of Hannah Jordan, who had applied for a letter of dismissal to the Nevill's Creek church, they had to contend with the objections of several members who claimed that she had left her husband improperly. Hannah responded that her husband had thrown her out, forbidding her to live in town, and setting her at liberty to remarry. She was quick to point out that she had no intention of remarrying but that her husband intended to do so within two weeks. She also placed her faith in the church to effect a reconciliation, in which case she would stay. Evidently the church agonized over the proper course of action. Probably, the male members felt that she should not have left her husband, but so eloquently did she portray herself as the injured party that the church "unanimously agreed to dismiss her as an orderly member."[38]

Even though one of the major appeals of Baptist and Methodist churches to poorer white people was a theology that promised equality before God, they were not immune from contemporary perceptions about race and gender relations. In 1807 the Savannah River Baptist Association wrote a circular letter to its member churches concerning domestic relations. While it emphasized that husbands had a duty to care for and love their wives, it also stressed above all that women had a duty "to be obedient."[39] Such submission to the authority of husbands would "promote greater union, which will produce greater happiness." Similar sentiments motivated the exhortation to family worship by the Sunbury Baptist Association in 1823. This letter stated that not only was family worship the Christian duty of every white male to organize, but that it would also demonstrate that he was "the priest of his own little commonwealth." These public displays of Christian devotion would "enable him successfully to rule his own household."[40]

The shoring up of established gender structures that the associations were advocating also applied to race and familial responsibility. On the one hand, white males were held as the supreme temporal authority over their wives, their children, and their slaves. On the other hand, white women were meant to live up to the ideal of the hardworking Christian woman.[41] It is therefore unsurprising that the dominance of white men was reflected in the daily workings of evangelical churches. Discipline councils were organized and presided over by white men, despite the fact that the majority of members were female. On several occasions no busi-

ness was transacted at the meetings of the First Baptist Church in Savannah, since no male members were present.[42] Churches therefore provided
opportunities for women to develop female networks, but the structural
dominance of men generally prevented the development of an alternative
feminine social ethic.

Widowed and single women, without the economic support of males,
were often seen as fit objects for charity. The purpose of Widow's Society
in Savannah, founded in 1822, was expressly to "supply the wants of
destitute infirm widows and single women, of good characters" outside
an institution. Not that the Widow's Society worked on the same scale as
some of the other benevolent institutions in Savannah. In 1828 less than
$200 was expended on the support of only twelve women.[43] In 1816,
another exclusively female charity named the Savannah Dorcas Society
assisted about a hundred people in the city with "clothing and nourish-
ment."[44] Both of these societies ensured that they were assisting the
respectable poor: those who were elderly, infirm, or sick but who remained pious and humble. Charity, in these cases, was meant to tide a
family "in a distressed situation" over difficult times, rather than have
them become destitute.[45] In this sense we have come full circle: many of
the young girls helped by the Female Asylum or the Free School returned
to a dependence on charity in widowhood, never achieving the economic
independence they sought.

The typical experiences of non-elite women in Savannah can be encapsulated in a single biography. Diana Kirkland was born in Savannah in
1813 to James and Priscilla Kirkland, both of whom had migrated to
Georgia from the North.[46] While little is known of their life in Savannah,
evidently the family's economic situation was precarious: less than a year
after the death of her father, seven-year-old Diana was placed in the
Female Asylum by her mother, who had already lost one child in infancy.
Diana's mother married the innkeeper Isaiah Atkinson shortly afterwards,
leaving Diana in the Female Asylum until Atkinson himself died in 1823.[47]
Two years later Priscilla was again poised to marry; she petitioned the
Female Asylum for her daughter's return but was refused, "the ladies
knowing her character to be very bad." Despite this rebuff, Diana's
mother secretly took her from the asylum, and the ladies had to initiate
legal proceedings to get her back.[48] Returned by the civic authorities,
Diana spent the next two years chafing at the authority of the matron and
the board. She finally managed to escape the asylum in 1828, aged fifteen,
and moved in with her mother, who had been widowed for the third time.

In their search for economic survival, Diana and her mother, together with at least two other women, opened a brothel under the guise of a sailor's boardinghouse, choosing to live as "abandoned women" rather than rely on elite benevolence. Not that either had long to enjoy any security they gained from prostitution: Diana Kirkland died at age seventeen in 1830, and was survived by her forty-nine-year-old mother by only eighteen months.[49] The lives these women lived of poverty, social ostracism, prostitution, frequent marriage and remarriage, and a constant struggle for survival would have been familiar to many non-elite white women in Savannah.

This essay has illuminated some of the methods used by poor white women to alleviate their social condition: appeals to third parties, casual employment, acceptance of charity, and the formation of cross-class or biracial gender networks. Peculiarly isolated in the social fabric because of their gender, race, and class, non-elite white women in the Georgia lowcountry found that the avenues that facilitated economic self-sufficiency were extremely limited. Many died as they had lived, in poverty.

NOTES

1. For notable exceptions, see Victoria E. Bynum, *Unruly Women: The Politics of Social and Sexual Control* (Chapel Hill: University of North Carolina Press, 1992); D. Harland Hagler, "The Ideal Woman in the Antebellum South: Lady or Farmwife?" *Journal of Southern History* 46 (1980): 405–18; Eleanor M. Boatwright, "The Political and Civil Status of Women in Georgia, 1783–1860," *Georgia Historical Quarterly* 25 (1941): 301–24.

2. Hagler, "Ideal Woman," 405–18.

3. Oration of Rev. Willard Preston dated 23 April 1833, *Minutes of the Union Society: Being an Abstract of Existing Records from 1750 to 1858* (Savannah: J. M. Cooper, 1860), 120.

4. John B. Boles, "Henry Holcombe: A Southern Baptist Reformer in the Age of Jefferson," *Georgia Historical Quarterly* 54 (1970): 387–88 and *Georgia Analytical Repository* 1, 2 (July–August 1802): 68–74.

5. *Daily Georgian*, 22 April 1828.

6. Records of the Beaufort Female Benevolent Society (BFBS), minutes, 26 May 1836, South Caroliniana Library, University of South Carolina, Columbia, SC.

7. *Columbian Museum and Savannah Advertiser*, 22 December 1801; Henry Holcombe, *The First Fruits in a Series of Letters* (Philadelphia: n.p., 1812), 78–79; Gail S.

Murray, "Charity within the Bounds of Race and Class: Female Benevolence in the Old South," *South Carolina Historical Magazine* 96 (1995): 58; Savannah Home for Girls Records (SHGR), minutes of the board, 1810–1843, box 1, vol. 1, Rules of the Society, no. 1, Georgia Historical Society (GHS), Savannah. I would like to thank Parent and Child Development Services in Savannah for granting permission to utilize these records.

8. SHGR, minutes, 9 June 1827, 6 March 1828. See also 13 August 1823.

9. BFBS, minutes, 23 July 1820, 22 August 1820. For examples of girls bound out to do domestic work, see 8 August 1823, 30 March 1827.

10. SHGR, minutes, 24 April 1818.

11. Constitution of the BFBS, 1814, Article 9.

12. SHGR, minutes, 14 November 1822, 1 June 1826.

13. Oration of Rev. Willard Preston, 129.

14. Account of the Origin and Progress of the Savannah Free School Society, (SFSS) (New York: Day and Turner, 1819), 3; SFSS minutes, 5 January 1820, 3 March 1817, GHS. In 1820, 228 children attended the poor school, 129 boys and 99 girls.

15. SFSS minutes, 9 December 1816.

16. I obtained these estimates by comparing the number of children helped in this period with the 1820 census. It is impossible to ascertain exactly the number of children under twenty-one in Savannah, because census enumerators grouped young people aged sixteen to twenty-six. For the figures used here, I divided this age group by half and added it to figures for the under-sixteen group to obtain an overall estimate of the number of children under twenty-one. In 1820 it was estimated that 881 white girls in Savannah were under twenty-one. If 285 were receiving charity (186 from the Female Asylum and 99 at the Free School), they represented 32.3 percent of the total. A total of 126 boys were educated at the Free School, and a further 53 by the Union Society. In 1820, 839 males under twenty-one resided in Savannah; the proportion receiving charity was 21.6 percent.

17. The Female Asylum had 190 subscribers in 1820. SHGR, membership list, 1820. The Free School enumerated 259 subscribers. SFSS, minute book, 1820. The Union Society had 137 subscribers on 1 April 1822. *Minutes of the Union Society*, 100–101. Of the subscribers to the Free School, 57 were also subscribers to the Female Asylum. Of the subscribers to the Union Society, 80 were also members of either the Female Asylum or the Free School. Therefore 554 individuals were members of at least one society. In 1820 the federal census counted 2,092 adults over twenty-one in Savannah. Therefore, 26.4 percent of individuals were making charitable contributions.

18. SHGR, Rules of the Society, no. 5, minutes, 7 May 1811.

19. SFSS, Rules, 27–30.

20. Julia Cherry Spruill, *Women's Life and Work in the Southern Colonies* (Chapel Hill: University of North Carolina Press, 1938), 276–78. See advertisements for a "housekeeper, can work well at needle, and is a clear starcher," "a good cook,

washer and ironer," and "a good pastry cook, also a washerwoman and a chamber-maid," in *Columbian Museum and Savannah Advertiser,* 26 July 1796; and *Daily Georgian,* 27 November 1828, 12 March 1829. Of 116 free black women assigned an occupation in 1828, all but 19 recorded domestic/cook, seamstress, or washer-woman as their job. *Daily Georgian,* 10 March 1828. See also Betty Wood, *Women's Work, Men's Work: The Informal Slave Economies of Lowcountry Georgia, 1750–1830* (Athens: University of Georgia Press, 1995), 117.

21. *Georgia Gazette,* 21 March 1796, 26 March 1796.

22. Emily Burke, *Pleasure and Pain: Reminiscences of Georgia in the 1840s* (Savan-nah: Beehive Press, 1978), 77; Narrative of John Melish, in *The Rambler in Georgia,* ed. Mills Lane (Savannah: Beehive Press, 1973), 20; Richard W. Griffen, "Poor White Laborers in Southern Cotton Factories, 1789–1865," *South Carolina Historical Magazine* 61 (1960): 32.

23. Wood, *Women's Work,* 80–100.

24. Savannah City Council minutes, 26 January 1801, 9 February 1801; Register of Free People of Color, 1817, GHS.

25. Diane Miller Sommerville, "The Rape Myth in the Old South Reconsid-ered," *Journal of Southern History* 61 (1995): 495–98, 513–14; Catherine Clinton, "'Southern Dishonor': Flesh, Blood, Race and Bondage," in *In Joy and Sorrow: Women, Family and Marriage in the Victorian South,* ed. Carol Bleser (New York: Oxford University Press, 1991), 52–68; Bynum, *Unruly Women,* 41–47, 93–110. Women made up five of six defendants charged with "keeping a riotous and disorderly house" in Savannah. City Council minutes, 3 March 1805 (Priscilla Bilow); 21 September 1807 (Elizabeth Williams); 12 December 1807, 22 January 1810 (Black Hannah); 15 March 1811 (Rebecca Rust and John Fleetwood). See also Wood, *Women's Work,* 118.

26. Chatham County, Superior Court minutes, vol. 8, 1808–1812, January term 1808 and January term 1809; see also vol. 1, 1782–1789, October term 1787; vol. 2, 1790–1793, July term 1790; vol. 9, 1812–1818, January term 1814, Georgia Depart-ment of Archives and History, Atlanta.

27. City Council minutes, 13 May 1814.

28. Randall M. Miller, "The Enemy Within: Some Effects of Foreign Immigrants on Antebellum Southern Cities," *Southern Studies* 24, (1985): 43–53.

29. Stephanie McCurry, *Masters of Small Worlds: Yeoman Households, Gender Rela-tions and the Political Culture of the Antebellum South Carolina Lowcountry* (New York: Oxford University Press, 1995), 15–17; Bynum, *Unruly Women,* 2, 59–60.

30. William Harris Garland Papers, folder 4, letters dated 6 December 1835, 22 April 1840; folder 5, letters dated 23 March 1841, 4 May 1841, 9 June 1841; folder 6, letters dated 11 October 1841, 11 November 1841; folder 7, letter dated 18 March 1842, Southern Historical Collection, Wilson Library, University of North Carolina at Chapel Hill.

31. Divorces were still rare, however; between 1798 and 1835 only 291 were granted by the legislature. Constitution of the State of Georgia, passed 30 May 1798; *An Act to Carry into Effect the Ninth Section of the Third Article of the Constitution,* passed 1 December 1802; Oliver H. Prince, ed., *A Digest of the Laws of the State of Georgia* (Athens: Oliver H. Prince, 1837), 910, 187–88. Statistic from 187 n.

32. *Marriages in Chatham County, Georgia* (Savannah: Georgia Historical Society, 1993), 176. Deed dated 2 February 1817. Savannah Tax Digest, 1819, GDAH. Petition of Mary Ryan, Keith Read Collection, box 4, folder 51, Chatham County Court Records, Hargrett Rare Book and Manuscript Library, University of Georgia, Athens. Ryan owned a shop of some sort, and was fined ten dollars in 1818 for keeping it open after official hours, presumably to trade with slaves visiting Savannah. City Council minutes, 4 May 1818. Savannah Tax Digests, 1820 and 1821, GDAH.

33. Petition of Mary Ryan, Chatham County, Superior Court minutes, book 11, 1822–1826, January term 1824. Mary's mother was born in South Carolina in 1759 and died aged sixty-six on 14 July 1825. *Register of Deaths in Savannah, Georgia* (Savannah: Georgia Historical Society, 1989), 4:172.

34. Chatham County, Superior Court minutes, book 1, 1782–1789, October term 1785. See also book 7, 1804–1808, January term 1805. In 1809 Ann Chauvin was still filing a tax return separately from her husband. Savannah Tax Digest, 1809.

35. Minutes of the Congregational Church at Midway, vol. 1, dated 26 August 1770, GHS. Joseph Baker was suspended for "gitting in liquor and abusing his wife. John Goulding for suspicion of keeping his own wench and living in adultery with another man's wife, Adley Maxwell for unlawfully keeping his own wench in adultery."

36. Minutes of Little Ogechee Baptist Church, October 1829, Special Collections Department, Mercer University, Macon, GA.

37. Case of Morning Shepherd, Little Ogechee Baptist Church, 1 June 1797; case of Mrs. Jenkinson, First Baptist Church, Savannah, 1 May 1829, Mercer University; Nancy F. Cott, "Passionlessness: An Interpretation of Victorian Sexual Ideology, 1790–1850," *Signs* 4 (1978): 219–36.

38. First Baptist Church, Savannah, minutes, 12 October 1810, 21 December 1810, 11 January 1811, Mercer University.

39. Savannah River Baptist Association minutes, circular letter, November 1807, Mercer University.

40. Sunbury Baptist Association minutes, circular letter, 1823, Mercer University.

41. Hagler, "Ideal Woman," 412.

42. All lowcountry evangelical churches had a female majority among white members ranging from 60 percent to 80 percent. See, for example, First Baptist Church, Savannah, 71.3 percent; Darien Presbyterian Church, 59 percent; Indepen-

dent Presbyterian Church, 82.8 percent. GHS, Mercer University; McCurry, *Masters of Small Worlds*, 178–95; First Baptist Church, Savannah, minutes, 14 August 1813, 21 August 1813; 6 January 1815, 13 January 1815, Mercer University.

43. *Daily Georgian*, 28 January 1823, 5 January 1828.

44. *Savannah Gazette*, 25 January 1817.

45. BFBS, minutes, 25 March 1817.

46. James was born in Massachusetts, Priscilla in North Carolina.

47. SHGR, members list, 1 June 1820; *Register of Deaths*, 4:13, 38, 153. Atkinson was propertyless in 1821, and described as an innkeeper in 1823. Savannah Tax Digest, 1821.

48. SHGR, minutes, 7 April, 6 May 1825.

49. SHGR, minutes, 9 July 1827, 6 March 1828, 2 October 1828; *Marriages of Chatham County*, 147; Savannah Tax Digests, 1826, 1831, 1832. In 1830 two women aged twenty-five to thirty, as well as a male infant, lived with Priscilla Johnson. Federal Manuscript Census, Chatham County, 1830; *Register of Deaths*, 4:240, 257.

Chapter Four

Cherokee Women and Cultural Change

Alice Taylor-Colbert

EDITOR'S NOTE: *By the 1750s there were several distinctive subregions in the South. Maryland, tidewater Virginia, and the Albemarle area of North Carolina were tied together by tobacco cultivation; rice and indigo production united lowcountry South Carolina and Georgia. These areas featured large-scale production of staple crops for international markets, unlike the backcountry, which stretched west to the mountains, where small farms and subsistence agriculture led to mixed economies. The Latin South represented a light military occupation by France and Spain of land along the Gulf from Florida to Texas. The remaining area was Indian country. Whites pushed into Kentucky and Tennessee in the 1770s, bringing tobacco culture with them. South to the Gulf was inhabited by Creeks, Choctaws, and Cherokees, and Seminoles lived in Florida.*

By 1750 the British had developed water- and steam-driven machines to power textile looms and hammers for forging iron, thereby becoming the first country to undergo the Industrial Revolution. They were able to produce more goods at lower prices, raising living standards in what is known as the "consumer revolution." The desire for comfortable cotton clothing caused the demand for raw cotton to outstrip the world supply, leading to large profits for producers. A major impediment to large-scale cultivation of cotton in the South, however, was the difficulty of removing its seeds, but the invention of the cotton gin in 1793 solved this problem. Now Euroamericans coveted the fertile lands of the Native Americans and used fraud and force to expel them. In addition by 1800 technological breakthroughs in the processing of cane juice opened south Louisiana to sugar plantations.

The demand for cotton and sugar ensured that slavery took on new life in the South at a time when it was declining elsewhere. Slavery was declared illegal in 1772 in England. The British abolished the slave trade in 1807 and ended the institution in their Caribbean possessions in 1833. Saint Domingue (Haiti), in

43

the first of the independence struggles that freed most of Latin America's slaves by 1855, abolished slavery in 1803. However, slavery remained in Cuba and Brazil until 1886 and 1888, respectively. The Chesapeake, where slavery had been declining as a consequence of falling tobacco prices and soil exhaustion, now became a point of origin for a domestic slave trade to Alabama, Mississippi, and Louisiana. Many planters from this region and from the Carolina and Georgia lowcountry took their slaves with them to open new plantations in the Deep South.

Unlike African American slaves, Native Americans had no function in white society. Only their lands were coveted. Thus whites rationalized that Native Americans, as products of an "inferior" civilization, should be removed or exterminated to make way for a "superior" Anglo-American society.

. . .

In an 1826 essay, John Ridge extolled the progress toward "civilization" of his people, the Cherokees of the southeastern United States. One illustration of that progress was the change in the status of women. He explained that even in poor families, women rarely labored in the fields. "Duties assigned them by nature as Mothers and Wives are well attended to . . . and cheerfully do they prepare our meals, & for the family they sew, they spin and weave and are in fact a valuable portion of our citizens." Those more fortunate women, like his mother, Susanna Wickett Ridge, had frame or brick homes with superior furnishings and slaves to wait on them.

Such descriptions of Cherokee life were hailed in the American press as indicative of the remarkable achievement of an exceptional Indian people. John Ridge himself was a product of the new age. His parents had provided him with an excellent American education, through which he had attained leadership positions in both the Creek and Cherokee Nations. He was very proud of this, and in his essay he intended to give appropriate credit to his people. According to Ridge, the women had been responsible for most of the acculturation process. They had been the ones to adapt to white, Anglo-American society most readily.[1]

To understand how extensive these cultural changes were for women and what role women played in effecting those changes, one must examine the traditional role of Cherokee women. That is not a simple task. Some information about early Cherokee society comes from archaeologists who unearth artifacts like pottery, beads, and utensils. When anthropologists and historians combine this archaeological evidence with the few written accounts by early European travelers from the sixteenth to eighteenth centuries and with the oral history of the Cherokees themselves, one can begin to catch small glimpses of the women's lives, values, and contributions to their society.

The traditional Cherokee kinship system consisted of seven clans—blue or panther, long hair, bird, paint, wild potato or bear, deer, and wolf. When a woman bore a child, that baby became a member of the mother's clan. Although a father usually assisted in his child's upbringing, the clan members, not the father, were considered the child's blood relatives. In other words, Cherokee society was matrilineal. The clan could be considered an extended family. Male children were taught how to become men by their uncles and maternal grandfather, while females learned from their mother, aunts, and grandmother. For love and protection and to preserve the unity and longevity of the clan, one lived near one's close relatives, that is, one's mother's people. Either as a result of this kinship system and matrilocal residency or because of the value Cherokees placed on womanhood, Cherokee women controlled, or owned, the houses.[2] This is one of the most important examples of a woman's power in traditional Cherokee culture. That power gave her a measure of control over her own destiny, something European women of the time dared not dream.

As a Cherokee girl grew into a woman, the females in her clan taught her everything she needed to know to survive. They supervised her closely and encouraged her involvement in all aspects of the life of their town or village. When she matured, the young woman gained complete independence and responsibility for her own actions. She was free to decide with whom and when to mate. Although her family or clan might try to sway her opinions regarding the young men she encountered, the decision belonged to her. The only stipulation was that the man could not be a member of her own clan; in other words, he could not be a blood relative.[3]

In some rare instances, more than one Cherokee woman chose the same spouse. Polygamy appears to have occurred most often in times of war when men were scarce or when a powerful leader was so revered that children by him were highly desirable. The few recorded instances indicate that sisters might choose the same man, thus simplifying concerns about female property ownership and maintaining close kinship ties. In other cases a man might marry his brother's widow in order to protect her. Regardless of the situation, each Cherokee had the power to decide whom to wed.[4]

When the typical Cherokee couple chose to live together, they entered a partnership as equals. Theirs was not a marriage in the European style. (Indeed, no word for husband existed in the Cherokee language. The Cherokee word translates into "the man I live with.") Although the couple usually made their decision public with a simple ceremony, it did not entail a lifetime commitment. The words "until death do us part" were never spoken. The ceremony probably consisted of a town feast with much singing and dancing, followed by the exchange of items that suggested the roles each person would have in the partnership. In one recorded ceremony, the man brought meat, perhaps a leg of venison, and a blanket, and the woman brought corn and a blanket. After the festivities, the two exchanged the corn and meat and put the two blankets together. A pronouncement may have been added that "the blankets are joined." The couple then went home, a residence with or near the woman's mother and her clan. In contrast to European customs, the woman did not leave her kin to follow her mate; he was obliged to follow her.[5]

If choosing a partner in Cherokee society was a simple matter, divorce was just as easy. A couple's respect for each other's wishes meant that when one partner chose to end the relationship, the other accepted that decision. The man could simply walk away or not return from a hunting trip or war party. The woman could tell her mate to leave or put his personal belongings outside the door. He would then be obliged to return to his own clan. The woman's family, especially her brothers and uncles, would assure her welfare and that of her children. Therefore, unlike her European counterparts, a Cherokee woman did not have the issue of dependency to tie her to an unhappy relationship.[6]

This equalitarian relationship was represented in the nuptials by the gifts of meat and corn. Although the gifts were different, signifying gender-specific roles, both items were essential for survival. Men were hunters (thus the meat providers), fishermen, builders, and politicians. Women were child care providers; makers of clothing, pottery, and baskets; housekeepers; and farmers. Although the men cleared the fields and probably helped in planting, the women hoed, harvested, preserved, and prepared the fruits, vegetables, and grains that sustained the families. The women labored together to produce their crops, but they established divisions in the fields and each reaped the bounty from her own specific portion. Like the animal skins of the men, the women's agricultural products were theirs to control. They could use them, share them with those in need, or barter or sell them. In other words, the women were income producers, which made them even more valuable partners.[7]

Another example of gender equality in Cherokee culture is that both genders viewed sexual activity as a normal, important part of life and displayed no inhibitions regarding its practice. Some early travelers like James Adair wrote that even adultery, by either party, was not punishable by Cherokee law. In European cultures and most Native American ones, the woman was always punished for adultery and sometimes so was the man. However, social ostracism and public ridicule were apparently sufficient to limit adultery in Cherokee society. Premarital sex was common, but in marriage, both persons were expected to remain faithful, a requirement that the ease of divorce made feasible.[8]

One might expect that the Cherokees' obvious enjoyment of sex and lack of harsh restraints would have occasioned a burgeoning population. On the contrary, Cherokee women exercised control in this area of their lives as well, using various methods to limit births to only two or three. Monthly separation and cleansing rituals by the women as well as purification rituals performed by both men and women required abstinence; breastfeeding for two years depressed fertility; and men were away for months, sometimes years, on hunting trips or war parties. Cherokee women also used abortion and practiced infanticide of deformed infants.[9] Thus, for Cherokee women, controlling their lives was an integral part of what it meant to be female.

The coming of the Europeans, especially after Hernando de Soto's exploration in 1540, changed life for the Cherokees. At first, trading was the focus of exchange between the cultures. Since Cherokee men did most of the traveling, they did most of the shopping. They traded furs and skins, especially buffalo and deer, for guns, knives, swords, and tools. When the women realized that cooking utensils, metal needles for sewing, fine cloth that felt good close to the skin, and other valuable items were available, they began to grow more crops that could be used for barter. The colonists, mostly English by the mid-1600s, may not have realized that they were really trading with the women, with Cherokee men acting as middlemen. All they knew was that the Cherokee men were buying lots of things for the women. Sometimes this led them to the conclusion that the Cherokee men were henpecked.[10]

Other cultural differences led to misunderstandings between the two groups. Cherokee men ridiculed male colonists who labored in the fields.

Even Cherokee women wondered about such men. They seemed effeminate; cultivation was, after all, women's work. In contrast, the colonists viewed the Cherokee men as lazy good-for-nothings who made their women do all the work. When the Cherokees tried to explain their matrilineal social system, their clans, and even their town government, which allowed the participation of elder or honored women in council meetings as representatives of their clans, colonists called the Cherokee system "a petticoat government." Since European women, with the exception of royalty, did not participate in government, colonial leaders refused to acknowledge the leadership roles of Cherokee females. At a Charles Town council meeting, the noted Cherokee leader, Little Carpenter or Attakullakulla, asked the colonial governor why no women were allowed. He remarked, "White Men as well as the Red were born of Women." He left his white male audience speechless. For Little Carpenter, women's importance, even in government negotiations, was assumed. Anglo-Americans, on the other hand, could not appreciate the Cherokee government, which allowed the voices of all the people to be heard.[11]

Nor could they fathom Cherokee consensual politics. If a group or clan disagreed with a proposed action—going to war, trading with a certain tribe, ceding land—that action was not taken. Harmony was the key to Cherokee society—in government, in the fields, in the home, and on the hunting trip. The Cherokees thought about other members of their community and clan every time a decision was made. Isolation and its partner, individualism, were unheard of, either in living patterns or in decision making. So the colonists were right in their perception that the women were important, even in government. Unfortunately, they attributed that trait of Cherokee society to a primitive, heathen nature.[12]

Some of the colonists decided that what the Cherokees needed to correct their strange social system was education in the civilized ways of Europe. Perhaps the Cherokee men could be convinced that raising livestock was not a feminine activity. Since expanding colonization and land cession treaties were depleting the hunting grounds, livestock could supplement the meat supply. Nevertheless, Cherokee men could not reconcile themselves to tending the docile cows, "white men's buffalo." They continued to measure their manhood by their bounty in hunting and their victories in war and politics. On the other hand, Cherokee women recognized the value of livestock. When the men came home empty-handed from a hunting trip, meat could still be on the table. For a widow or divorced woman this food source could mean not having to depend on male relatives with families of their own. It could mean not only self-sufficiency but profit. Thus Cherokee women began to raise pigs, cows, and sheep, as well as crops.[13]

By the 1790s, the U.S. government began a concerted effort to "civilize" the southeastern Indians by supplying new farm tools and equipment, spinning wheels, looms, and the like, so that the Native Americans could redefine their occupational and cultural roles. Not surprisingly, the women were the ones who responded. They did not stay inside the home as Anglo-American women did, but they did add spinning, weaving, and cloth making to the list of their responsibilities. The Cherokee men refused to help with crops or livestock for years, and some never changed, viewing this as a threat to their manhood. Others eventually adapted, as game became more scarce, their women needed more help, and the profits to be gained became more apparent. One of the most influential leaders to respond to the government's new "civilization" program was a Cherokee named The Ridge.[14]

The Ridge had grown up as a traditional Cherokee warrior in the period after the American Revolution. His exploits are well documented; however, he grew tired of fighting and discouraged by the ever increasing numbers of whites moving into his area, so he repeatedly helped his mother and family move farther and farther west and south. The Ridge married Susanna Wickett in the early 1790s. Although they probably wed in a traditional ceremony, their lives were significantly different from that of their ancestors. Their families had long before adopted many European ways, including apparel and building styles. So instead of joining their blankets and going to Susanna's wattle and daub house (a structure made of hardened clay and sticks on a wooden frame), The Ridge took his bride to a log cabin he had built for her in Pine Log (northwest Georgia). Susanna moved away from her clan and its support to a home she did not own.

Although Susanna would have performed most of the same domestic tasks as her ancestors, The Ridge probably assisted in the labor-intensive chores. He found his calling, though, in political and military duties for the tribe. In the War of 1812 he earned the rank of major for his service under Andrew Jackson, adopting the title as part of his name. As a result of payment for such services and, no doubt, the thriftiness and work of Susanna, Major Ridge eventually acquired the means to adopt the southern whites' solution to the need for field labor: African slaves.[15]

Slavery had been a Cherokee institution for centuries, but it was different from the chattel system Europeans instituted with African slavery. Like other Native Americans, Cherokees took war captives who might be executed later, adopted into the tribe, or used as forced laborers. The decision regarding the fate of such prisoners usually rested with the elder female member of the clan to whom the prisoners were brought. Apparently, such women exercised great authority in their communities and could help their clans prosper through such arrangements. Indian slaves captured in war were not necessarily slaves for life, nor were their children automatically enslaved.[16]

In the early 1800s, Cherokees like the Ridges, most of whom had some white blood or heritage, realized the economic potential of slavery. The slaves could do the hardest manual labor and free both Cherokee men and women for other tasks. Susanna could spend more of her time making fine garments of imported silk, supervising the cooking and preparation of the fruits of their orchard and the vegetables of their gardens, and entertaining the numerous visitors to her new plantation home (now Chieftains Museum in Rome, Georgia).[17]

In the second and third decades of the nineteenth century, the new lifestyle afforded by slavery and entrepreneurship (operating a ferry across the Oostanaula River and owning with a white partner the only store in the area) allowed the Ridges to give their children a formal education. Although separation was emotionally painful for Susanna, she insisted that not only her son John, who limped because of a scrofulous hip, but also Nancy and Sarah be sent to school. Only Walter remained at home, because he did not have the necessary mental ability.

The Ridge children attended the Moravian mission school at Spring Place, many miles away, where they learned reading, writing, and arithmetic as well as European-defined gender tasks, like sewing and carpentry. In addition, religious instruction led to their conversion to Christianity. As a result of her contact with the Moravian missionaries who taught her children, Susanna also became a Christian. When John wrote in 1826 that "the influence of Religion on the life of the Indians is powerful & lasting," he was in part reflecting the experience of his own family.[18]

Susanna Ridge represents a profound change in Cherokee culture. Over her lifetime (late 1770s–1849), the definition of what it meant to be a woman in Cherokee society changed. Like white women of the period, Cherokee women were supposed to be devoted—not to clan or relatives—but to husbands and children. They were supposed to toil inside, not outside, their homes. Only the poorer, "backward" Cherokee women worked in the fields, for, as Theda Perdue demonstrates, to be considered civilized, Cherokee women of the nineteenth century had to adopt the Anglo-American "cult of true womanhood" of domesticity, submissiveness, piety, and selfless concern for family. By 1826, Elias Boudinot, a Ridge cousin, could write, "Polygamy is abolished. Female chastity and honor are protected by law." Infanticide had also been outlawed. As Susanna Ridge exemplifies, in many ways Cherokee women became like their white sisters. Susanna devoted most of her time to indoor activities; she enjoyed entertaining in a style befitting a plantation mistress; she became a Christian; she remained faithful to Major Ridge all her life; she kept a watchful eye over her daughters' choices of husbands; and she raised two children despite their deformities.[19]

Unlike Nancy Ward, a "War Woman" (a participant in battle and military negotiations) and respected Cherokee diplomat who died in 1822, Susanna could only offer her opinions to her husband, because the Cherokees slowly adopted the American legal and political system that excluded women. President Thomas Jefferson advised them to create patrilineal inheritance laws and to abolish the rights of women and clans. The Cherokee male leadership considered these ideas and began to develop paternalistic policies, but the Cherokees did not deny a woman's right to her property before marriage and to custody of her children. If Major Ridge had died, Susanna, unlike white women, would have kept the plantation and her children. Yet eventually even these property rights were restricted to only those Cherokee women who had been legally married by a minister or justice of the peace. Property cases concerning traditional Cherokee marriages (common law marriages) failed in the Cherokee-American court system.[20]

Ironically, Cherokee women had been responsible for much of the acculturation that deprived them of their traditional power. The changes in lifestyle were those that women desired. As the Cherokee leadership gradually excluded women and adopted the whites' patriarchal system, Cherokee women seemed not to object. Perhaps they believed that was the price to be paid for enjoying the benefits of reduced labor. While we know that women did not hold positions of political power after Nancy Ward, we know they continued to have a powerful voice in family governance and business. Susanna Ridge made the decisions about where and when her children went away to school, and she sent her daughters as well as her son—something most white women of the period never considered. Susanna continued to handle business affairs when her husband was away, and she apparently supervised crop production and preservation.[21]

Despite the successful acculturation of the Cherokees and the profound respect they received from many American leaders, or perhaps because of the economic prosperity that seemed to follow their move toward "civilization," whites, especially Georgians, began to lash out against the Cherokees in the late 1820s in an attempt to force their removal. Susanna supported her husband and son, even when they came to the conclusion that moving to Indian Territory west of the Mississippi River was the best alternative. When Major Ridge and John, along with a minority faction, signed the Treaty of New Echota in 1835, they legally and ethically committed treason by selling the Cherokee homeland. While Principal Chief John Ross and the official Cherokee government tried to fight the implementation of the fraudulent treaty, the Ridges faced animosity and threats of violence from those Cherokees who wanted revenge. As a dutiful wife and mother, Susanna packed their belongings and moved west with her husband and slaves to start life again in present-day Oklahoma.

Despite Ross's efforts to defeat the treaty in the U.S. Senate and before the Supreme Court, in 1838 federal troops arrived to force the Cherokees to move. After thousands died on the journey west, Susanna's husband and son were assassinated for their part in the "Trail of Tears." An aged Susanna watched as her son was dragged outside his house and stabbed repeatedly with a knife the same morning in June 1839 when her husband was shot to death in an ambush. When her white daughter-in-law fled in terror, Susanna faced the anger in the faces of her enemies and remained at her home until she could settle the estate and receive the money from the sale of the family store and lands.[22] Although deprived of most of the traditional powers of Cherokee womanhood, Susanna Ridge retained the determination and power of will that characterized her ancestors.

NOTES

1. William C. Sturtevant, ed., "John Ridge on Cherokee Civilization in 1826," *Journal of Cherokee Studies* 6, no. 2 (fall 1981): 79–82; Thurman Wilkins, *Cherokee Tragedy: The Ridge Family and the Decimation of a People*, 2d ed., rev. (Norman: University of Oklahoma Press, 1988), 164–67, 182–85, 216; Patrick H. Garrow, "An Archaeological Survey of Portions of the Chieftains Museum Property, Rome, Georgia," 17 February 1988, 14–15, Chieftains Museum, Rome, GA.

2. J. P. Evans, "Sketches of Cherokee Characteristics," *Journal of Cherokee Studies* 4, no. 1 (winter 1979): 10; John Phillip Reid, *A Law of Blood: The Primitive Law of the Cherokee Nation* (New York: New York University Press, 1970), 68, 120, 140; William G. McLoughlin, *Cherokee Renascence in the New Republic* (Princeton: Princeton University Press, 1992), 5–6; Theda Perdue, "Southern Indians and the Cult of True Womanhood," in *Half Sisters of History*, ed. Catherine Clinton (Durham: Duke University Press, 1994), 37; Thomas E. Mails, *The Cherokee People: The Story of the Cherokees from Earliest Origins to Contemporary Times* (Tulsa: Council Oak Books, 1992), ix–xiv.

3. Charles Hudson, *The Southeastern Indians* (Knoxville: University of Tennessee Press, 1976), 324; Rennard Strickland, *Fire and the Spirits: Cherokee Law from Clan to Court* (Norman: University of Oklahoma Press, 1975), 29–30; Mails, *Cherokee People*, 72; McLoughlin, *Cherokee Renascence*, 11.

4. McLoughlin, *Cherokee Renascence*, 13; Hudson, *Southeastern Indians*, 196–202; Perdue, "Southern Indians," 45; Reid, *Law of Blood*, 118–19, 300; James Mooney, *Myths of the Cherokee and Sacred Formulas of the Cherokees* (1900 and 1888; reprint, Nashville: Charles and Randy Elder, 1982), 162–64, 364–65.

5. William Bartram, *Travels through North and South Carolina, Georgia, East and West Florida* (1791; reprint, New York: Penguin, 1988), 354–55, 402–3; Mails, *Cherokee People*, 73, 75; McLoughlin, *Cherokee Renascence*, 13; Perdue, "Southern Indians," 38–39; Wilkins, *Cherokee Tragedy*, 31; Reid, *Law of Blood*, 68, 113–15, 120–21, 301. Reid adds that the Eastern Band still had no word for husband in the 1930s.

6. McLoughlin, *Cherokee Renascence*, 13; Perdue, "Southern Indians," 39; Reid, *Law of Blood*, 114, 117, 299.

7. Mooney, *Myths of the Cherokee*, 355; John Howard Payne Manuscripts, vol. 4, book 1, 61–62, Edward E. Ayer Collection, Newberry Library, Chicago, typescript in the Museum of the Cherokee Indian, Cherokee, NC; Bartram, *Travels*, 284, 399–401; Hudson, *Southeastern Indians*, 264–69; Mails, *Cherokee People*, 85; Perdue, "Southern Indians," 38; Reid, *Law of Blood*, 67, 125, 129, 138–39.

8. James Adair, *The History of the American Indians*, ed. Samuel Cole Williams (New York: Promontory Press, 1930), 152–53; William C. Sturtevant, ed., "Louis-Philippe on Cherokee Architecture and Clothing in 1797," *Journal of Cherokee Studies* 3, no. 4 (fall 1978): 199; Bartram, *Travels*, 183, 355–56, 403; McLoughlin, *Cherokee Renascence*, 13; Perdue, "Southern Indians," 39; Reid, *Law of Blood*, 69–70, 115; Strickland, *Fire and the Spirits*, 23, 31–39.

9. Pat Alderman, *Nancy Ward: Cherokee Chieftainess* (Johnson City, TN: Overmountain Press, 1978), 7; George Catlin, *North American Indians* (New York: Penguin, 1989), 462; Adair, *History of the American Indians*, 129–31; McLoughlin, *Cherokee Renascence*, 10, 333; Payne MSS, vol. 4, book 1, 48.

10. R. S. Cotterill, *The Southern Indians: The Story of the Civilized Tribes before Removal* (Norman: University of Oklahoma Press, 1989), 16–17; William L. McDowell, Jr., ed., *Colonial Records of South Carolina: Documents Relating to Indian Affairs,*

1754–1765 (Columbia: University of South Carolina Press, 1970), 566–69; Gary C. Goodwin, *Cherokees in Transition* (Chicago: Department of Geography, University of Chicago, 1977), 96; McLoughlin, *Cherokee Renascence*, 5–6.

11. Minutes, 9 February 1757, South Carolina Council Journal, in Reid, *Law of Blood*, 68–69; Adair, *History of the American Indians*, 152–53; McLoughlin, *Cherokee Renascence*, 65; Perdue, "Southern Indians," 40. For more information on Attakullakulla, see James C. Kelly, "Notable Persons in Cherokee History: Attakullakulla," *Journal of Cherokee Studies* 3, no. 1 (winter 1978): 2–34.

12. V. Richard Persico, Jr., "Early Nineteenth Century Cherokee Political Organization," in *The Cherokee Indian Nation: A Troubled History*, ed. Duane H. King (Knoxville: University of Tennessee Press, 1979), 92–109; McLoughlin, *Cherokee Renascence*, 326–27.

13. Charles J. Keppler, comp. and ed., *Indian Treaties, 1778–1883*, vol. 2 (Washington, D.C.: Government Printing Office, 1904; reprint, New York: Interland, 1973); McLoughlin, *Cherokee Renascence*, 62–65; Perdue, "Southern Indians," 42; Reid, *Law of Blood*, 68, 135.

14. C. L. Grant, ed., *Letters, Journals and Writings of Benjamin Hawkins*, vol. 1, *1796–1801* (Savannah: Beehive Press, 1980), 21–22; Theda Perdue, "Letters from Brainerd," *Journal of Cherokee Studies* 4, no. 1 (winter 1979): 7; Keppler, *Indian Treaties*, 31; McLoughlin, *Cherokee Renascence*, 62–63, 94, 330; Perdue, "Southern Indians," 41–42; Sturtevant, "Louis-Philippe," 201; Wilkins, *Cherokee Tragedy*, 32–33.

15. Wilkins, *Cherokee Tragedy*, 13–26, 31, 68, 73, 85; list of persons who enrolled for emigration after the treaty of 1835, 27 January 1837, Museum of the Cherokee Indian, Cherokee, NC. The document lists Major Ridge and his five slaves.

16. Louis De Vorsey, Jr., ed., *De Brahm's Report of the General Survey in the Southern District of North America* (Columbia: University of South Carolina Press, 1971), 109; Theda Perdue, "Cherokee Planters: The Development of Plantation Slavery before Removal," in *The Cherokee Indian Nation*, ed. King, 110–15; Adair, *History of the American Indians*, 418; McLoughlin, *Cherokee Renascence*, 67, 338; Reid, *Law of Blood*, 130, 190–91, 312. For more information on slavery, see Theda Perdue, *Slavery and the Evolution of Cherokee Society, 1540–1866* (Knoxville: University of Tennessee Press, 1979).

17. Gary E. Moulton, ed., *The Papers of Chief John Ross*, vol. 1, 1807–1839 (Norman: University of Oklahoma Press, 1985), 236; Don L. Shadburn, *Cherokee Planters in Georgia, 1832–1838* (Roswell, GA: W. H. Wolfe Associates, 1990), 128–29; McLoughlin, *Cherokee Renascence*, 338; Perdue, "Cherokee Planters," 123–25; Strickland, *Fire and the Spirits*, 79–83; Wilkins, *Cherokee Tragedy*, 4, 160, 186–89, 277–78.

18. Moravian Mission Diary, Spring Place, 1810, typescript in Rome/Floyd County Library, 84, 87, 125; Wilkins, *Cherokee Tragedy*, 33–35, 99–103, 111–14, 117, 119.

19. McLoughlin, *Cherokee Renascence*, 330–34; Perdue, "Southern Indians," 37;

Elias Boudinot, "An Address to the Whites," in *Cherokee Editor: The Writings of Elias Boudinot,* ed. Theda Perdue (Knoxville: University of Tennessee Press, 1983), 75.

20. Fred Gearing, "Priests and Warriors: Social Structures for Cherokee Politics in the 18th Century," *American Anthropologist* 64, no. 5, part 2 (October 1962): 26; idem, "Thomas Jefferson's Advice to the Cherokees," *Journal of Cherokee Studies* 4, no. 2 (spring 1979): 64–66; William P. Palmer, ed., *Calendar of Virginia State Papers and Other Manuscripts, 1652–1781* (Richmond: R. F. Walker, Superintendent of Public Printing, 1875), 435–36, copy in the Museum of the Cherokee Indian, Cherokee, NC; Alderman, *Nancy Ward*; McLoughlin, *Cherokee Renascence,* 140–41, 225, 294–95, 330–32; Perdue, "Southern Indians," 50; Reid, *Law of Blood,* 137, 140, 187, 305; Strickland, *Fire and the Spirits,* 58, 100, 211; John Ridge to Albert Gallatin, 27 February 1826, in *The Cherokee: A Brief History with Documents,* ed. Theda Perdue and Michael Green (Boston: Bedford Books of St. Martin's Press, 1995), 37–38.

21. George M. Battey, *History of Rome and Floyd County* (Atlanta: Webb and Vary, 1922; reprint, Atlanta: Cherokee Publishing Co., 1994), 212; Wilkins, *Cherokee Tragedy,* 99–100, 119, 294.

22. Dr. Elizur Butler to Rev. S. Whittelsey, Tahlequah, 3 October 1839, Museum of the Cherokee Indian, Cherokee, NC; Kenneth Penn Davis, "Chaos in the Indian Country: The Cherokee Nation, 1828–35," in *The Cherokee Indian Nation,* ed. King, 129–47; Wilson Lumpkin, *The Removal of the Cherokee Indians from Georgia* (New York: Dodd, Mead, 1907), 42–48; James W. Parins, *John Rollin Ridge: His Life and Works* (Lincoln: University of Nebraska Press, 1991), 28–31; Payne MSS, vol. 6, chap. 1, "National Characteristics of the Cherokees," 40; Grace Steele Woodward, *The Cherokees* (Norman: University of Oklahoma Press, 1963), 192–226; Moulton, *Papers of Chief John Ross,* 378, 385; Wilkins, *Cherokee Tragedy,* 241, 257–65, 301–7, 311, 315, 335–36, 341. For more information on this period of Cherokee history, see Gary E. Moulton, *John Ross: Cherokee Chief* (Athens: University of Georgia Press, 1978); Russell Thornton, "The Demography of the Trail of Tears Period: A New Estimate of Cherokee Population Losses," in *Cherokee Removal: Before and After,* ed. William L. Anderson (Athens: University of Georgia Press, 1991), 75–95; and the special issue "The Trail of Tears: Primary Documents of the Cherokee Removal," *Journal of Cherokee Studies* 4, no. 3 (summer 1978).

Chapter Five

The Politics of Pedagogy and Judaism in the Early Republican South

The Case of Rachel and Eliza Mordecai

Jean E. Friedman

EDITOR'S NOTE: *Cherokee women were not alone in their quest for a type of assimilation in which traditional identity could also be maintained and fostered. White women, because of their religious, ethnic, and socioeconomic differences, faced contemporary constructions of the ideal woman that both changed them and were changed by them. Society's concept of the ideal woman reflected the values and traditions of the dominant segment of society. As philanthropy for Georgia's "worthy poor" demonstrates, women as well as men of the middle and upper classes used the ideal as a standard by which women were judged. However, the ideal was not expected from other races, because they were considered too primitive to produce real women. The ideal afforded certain privileges and protections that were incompatible with taking the land of Native Americans and exploiting the labor of African American slaves in the fields.*

The subordination of white women to white men during the colonial period rested on European beliefs in a natural hierarchy between genders that was less evident in Native American and West African societies, especially those structured as matrilineages. Subordination was maintained by the exclusion of women from access to public life and economic independence, which made their absence from positions of power and authority appear both natural and God given. The hierarchical organization of European societies placed the husband at the head of the family, and everyone, including his wife, owed him obedience. The ideal good wife was characterized by modesty, industriousness, frugality, faithfulness, submissiveness, and deference toward men.

The American Revolution, with its republican ideology and Enlightenment ideas of contract, consent, and rationality, began to influence this concept of familial authority, which previously had rested on a perceived link between father, king, and God. Women came to be seen as rational individuals who transmitted society's values through their maternal role as the first teachers of the young. A new ideal of Republican Motherhood proved useful to those who argued for the education of girls beyond simple literacy and numeracy. Because education was thought to be primarily for the purpose of building character, educators argued that women, as teachers of rising generations of citizens on whose virtue the success of the Republican experiment rested, needed to be educated themselves in order to fulfill this task.

By the antebellum period the feminine ideal would be further transformed into the "cult of true womanhood." Developing first in the North, where the Industrial Revolution took men out of the home, where most families traditionally had worked together as farmers or artisans, the new ideals of femininity and masculinity emphasized "separate spheres" of activity and authority. Whereas man's sphere was the world, woman's sphere was the home. Her moral sensibility was deemed superior to man's, because she was thought to be inherently more pious, as a consequence of her dependent position in society and vulnerability to death in childbirth. But her authority came only from her powers of persuasion, for like her colonial predecessors, she was also submissive and obedient. Although men might stray, ladies were by definition virgins at marriage and faithful within it. Although the South remained an agricultural region, the ideology of separate spheres took strong hold there, because it functioned to explain a society built on slavery. The similarities between lords and planters and serfs and slaves glamorized the exploitation of African American labor by glorifying chivalry and romanticizing the ideal of the lady.

The privileges and protection afforded those who exhibited the characteristics of the reigning ideal of femininity, together with the denigration and vulnerability of those who could not or would not, made that ideal a powerful inducement for assimilation into the mainstream culture. Education became a prime method for inculcating the approved values. This strategy was not always successful, however, as the Cherokee seminary modeled on Mount Holyoke demonstrated: the socialization of girls into this ideal could not outweigh the greed for Indian land and the underlying motivation for excluding Native Americans from equal status.

Although never quite 1 percent of the southern population, Jews were more successful in laying claim to parts of the dominant gender ideology, because they were categorized as white. While they remained a group apart, maintaining their religious traditions, their wealth and business expertise provided some entry into southern society. Jewish identity had been sustained despite a history of persecu-

tion. Jews had been expelled from England in 1290 and France in 1306. They migrated to Germany, and in the next century many were driven on to Poland. The Spanish expelled both Moors and Jews in the same year that Columbus landed in the New World. Jews who found their way to British North America lived largely in coastal cities, engaging in commercial activities. They formed a particularly influential group in Charleston, where they had been encouraged to settle during the postrevolutionary depression to help lowland planters by providing needed capital. Their commitment to education also increased their ability to combine aspects of assimilation with the retention of their traditional identity.

• • •

"I thought you were conceited yourself." This sullen remark by ten-year-old Eliza Mordecai to her sister-mentor, Rachel, on August 19, 1819,[1] indicates more than petulance upon rebuke for a proud, wrongheaded intellectual challenge. Definition of self in the Early Republic carried with it ethnic and religious tensions that complicated a preadolescent's path to maturity. Role expectations for elite white women, "Republican Mother-hood,"[2] allowed little space for the dissident voice, the religio-ethnic self. The emergence of a female self was played out on a battleground of pedagogical relationships, and any categorization of diverse Republican women is difficult. Ethnic and religious women's adaptation, resistance, amplification, and rejection of Enlightenment notions of "Republican Motherhood" demonstrate the intense negotiation and compromise that shaped Republican women. The pedagogical experiment of Rachel Mordecai, an Orthodox Jew of German descent who taught her stepsister Eliza according to Enlightenment pedagogy, transformed secular female ideology into Enlightenment Jewish practice. Her experiment reveals the struggle to create a moral and religious self in the Early Republic.

The pedagogy of "Republican Motherhood" delineated certain teaching principles—the nurturance of independent male citizens, not dependent subjects, and the education of virtuous and knowledgeable children. The model mother exemplified the virtue and wisdom needed to stabilize the Republic and taught Enlightenment rational values by the dialogic method. A benevolent but cautious patriarchy encouraged the educative precepts of "Republican Motherhood." Although Enlightenment pedagogy necessitated the virtuous character of the parent-teacher, virtue retained a gendered, hierarchical meaning. Masculine rationality and self-control preserved public harmony, while charity, modesty, and tenderness provided female domestic stability. Most important, the Protestant (Puritan) notion of Providence or faith as the source of virtue competed with Enlightenment secular conventions of self-control and independence expressed in property holding and balanced government.[3]

By focusing on narrow secular concepts of virtue, historians ignore the diverse ethnic and spiritual challenges inherent in postrevolutionary moral formation that encouraged new bourgeois cultural and moral configurations. To apply the values of "Republican Motherhood" to an entire generation of postrevolutionary women obscures the fierce generational conflict that produced religiously orthodox Victorian daughters determined to break from Enlightenment maternal intellectual and moral strictures.[4] Critical method created a spiritual dialectic among young women who questioned Enlightenment models of common sense and discovered instead the rich resources of interiority.

The extent to which religio-ethnic minorities identified with or resisted bourgeois female ideology remains an open question in contemporary scholarship. A greater understanding of the minority Jewish population, however, offers a unique perspective on the issue of adaptation or rejection of white middle-class Protestant moral ideology. Studying pedagogy, one important gauge of assimilation, helps us interpret what "Republican motherhood" meant to German Jews, a small but culturally significant group in the Early Republican South. Pedagogy refers to the process of meaning-making between teacher and student; it is through this instructive dialogue that the definition of power relations emerges. Once established, the politics of pedagogy represents the social relations of family, community, and culture.[5] German Jews who experienced the shattering of traditional religious, intellectual, and family life in the European Enlightenment found common cause with the Enlightenment American experiment. Nonetheless, Enlightenment notions of egalitarian family relationships that prepared children for independence and the acceptance of secular values challenged Jewish norms of patriarchy and religious practice.[6] Tensions between traditional Jewish and Enlightenment ways existed in the educational and cultural dialogues of the Early Republic.

The German Enlightenment profoundly affected Orthodox Jewish women. Exempted from religious responsibilities so that they could tend to domestic needs, Orthodox women remained segregated in their homes and synagogues. Women commanded a lesser status than men, because they fulfilled fewer communal obligations and received an inferior education. Clearly, Orthodox Judaism defined religious practice according to gender. However, when late eighteenth-century modernization in Ger-

many opened secular education and social opportunities to Jews, successful Jewish merchants and professionals educated their daughters as ornaments to their newly achieved status. Eventually, educated German
women joined literary circles, hosted salons, and participated in school
organizations as parents and teachers. With the advent of Enlightenment
education, however, assimilation undermined Jewish community. Home
education then remained vital among German Jews so that Jewish values
could be preserved. Religious leaders blamed women in their role as
primary educators for assimilation and loss of faith among men and
children.[7] Despite criticism, German Jewish women achieved a certain
intellectual and social status that expanded and developed in America.

Jews, including German Jews, participated in a mercantile network in
Europe and America that supported the growth and development of their
communities. Often Jewish business efforts included a husband and wife
partnership. The Jewish population during the Early Republic doubled in
size, from a few thousand to six thousand; rapid growth and the concentration of the population in the cities resulted in the establishment of
synagogues that further enhanced the stability of the Jewish community.
In eastern coastal cities like New York, Philadelphia, Newport, and
Charleston, German Jews modified their distinctive rituals, dietary habits,
language, architecture, and dress, thus compartmentalizing their religion
to conform to American culture. Less is known about Jewish populations
in the small cities and villages, but studies reveal even greater pressures
for assimilation and fewer opportunities for association and community.[8]
Thus traditional Jewish life centered in the family experienced decisive
shifts in moral values and family hierarchy.

The Jacob Mordecai family, of German Jewish descent, established a
renowned school, the Warrenton Female Academy in Warrenton, North
Carolina. Mordecai entered into the family business after his mercantile
career collapsed. Rachel, Mordecai's eldest daughter, contended that Jewish identity made little difference in a small town. She wrote of herself in
a letter to British novelist Maria Edgeworth, "Living in a small village,
her father's the only family of Israelites who reside in or near it, all her
juvenile friendships and attachments have been formed with those of
persuasions different from her own; yet each has looked upon the variations of the other as things of course—differences which take place in
every society."[9] Despite Rachel's disclaimer, evangelicals attempted to
proselytize her father and her cousin Henrietta Marx.[10] Nonetheless, Ra-

chel's pedagogical experiment provides a reliable measure of adaptation and resistance to Anglo-American cultural hegemony.

Rachel Mordecai taught in her father's school, an extension of the Mordecai household. Family members taught, administered, and supervised the young women. The school bridged the distance between Enlightenment ideology and Jewish Orthodoxy, since the Warrenton Female Academy offered progressive method while the Mordecais kept an Orthodox household. In addition to her regular teaching duties, Rachel experimented with progressive Edgeworthian pedagogy, tested on her beloved young stepsister, Eliza. *Practical Education,* or "education of the heart," written by the Anglo-Irish educators Richard Lovell Edgeworth and Maria Edgeworth, offered the inducement of "useful and agreeable habits, well regulated sympathy and benevolent affections,"[11] in short, a warm yet disciplined heart, devoted to the practice of virtue. The experiment carried out in an Orthodox Jewish household, however, subtly transformed the sisters as it transformed the method. Enlightenment notions of "goodness" gave way to more expansive concerns for "holiness."

Rachel Mordecai's experiment imbricated Jewish pietism in Enlightenment method. Traditional Jewish literature, the Bible and the Talmud, does not recognize ethics outside the notion of holiness. Holiness, according to classical Jewish scholars, is more inclusive than the Enlightenment value of "goodness." Full and free assent to the will of God enjoins the individual in social action for God's sake. The call to holiness, in the context of a choice between good and evil, is a call to intimacy with the Divine. Human response is measured in the depth of compassion an individual might have for the marginal, the poor. In the struggle to respond willingly is a hidden desire to become what Divinity intended.[12] In contrast to Orthodox "holiness," the Enlightenment precept of "goodness" ascribes no inner godly response to external behavior; outward behavior manifests inner virtue, conformity to natural law or God's laws. Leniency, not severity or fear, governs the manner of Enlightenment discipline. And rather than a covenant responsibility for others' welfare, Enlightenment ethics prescribe natural concern for social harmony and welfare. The aim of Enlightenment education is the development of a "free and intelligent agent."[13] However, in the Enlightenment tradition free agency did not apply to women, who were identified as inseparable from families or marriages and therefore dependent.[14]

Both Enlightenment method and religious consciousness pervade the initial effort in Rachel's experiment. On a Sunday, May 19, 1816, Rachel wrote her intention "to commence writing juvenile, . . . nursery anecdotes" about Eliza. Rachel borrowed from the Edgeworths the didactic technique of recording her teaching dialogue. Her expectations also mark the progressive Lockean teacher; she wished to observe Eliza's growth through childhood's successive stages. Metaphorically, she wrote, "I wish to see if the tender bud which promises so fair, will bloom into a fragrant, lovely, and unfading flower." However, her expectation took the form of a covenant. She prayed to shape Eliza's character according to divine purpose:

> Should it seem good to the Most High to suffer *it* [the experiment], and *me,* to continue on this great theatre of existence, I will watch over, and mark its [Eliza's character] daily progress, I will endeavor to destroy each canker that would enter its bosom to render it less sweet and lovely. And O! may I be rendered capable of forming the materials which nature has bountifully placed in my hands; may reason, combined with virtue, and nourished by education, form a character eminently fitted to discharge every duty of this life, and when called from this transitory state of being, worthy to repose eternally in the presence of its Creator.[15]

The elder sister directed the voice of authority, of God's law, to the child's heart. Development of character involved a *conscious* moral choice on the part of the individual. Thus Rachel endeavored to remove each "canker," or obstacle to virtue. Jewish tradition stressed that in the proper fulfillment of its precepts, the obedient individual became a partner with the Almighty in the work of creation.[16] Rachel's own obedience to God's will allowed her to participate in the creation of Eliza's character. The education of reason and virtue aimed at a responsible life rewarded with eternal divine presence.

In her journal Rachel introduces Eliza as a "good girl," a "Rosamund" figure. Rosamund, a character in Maria Edgeworth's children's fiction, makes impulsive choices but learns through painful experience the necessity of obligation and the pleasures of benevolence. But within the historical reality represented in the diary, Eliza challenges authority, thereby defying the literary norm. In the "strawberries anecdote," Eliza is offered some strawberries through the kindness of her sister Caroline. But a servant mistakenly removes them and Rachel decides not to pursue the matter. Eliza, momentarily disappointed, recovers her composure and is just as satisfied with her sister's alternative, "playing with" but not eating filberts. When Caroline returns the strawberries, Eliza is given her share and Rachel remarks that Eliza receives the strawberries because "goodness is always rewarded." But Eliza evades literary expectations when she qualifies her sister's assertion and replies, "No sister R[achel] not *always* you know." In the cool tones of a mentor Rachel replies that virtue is its own reward.[17]

Edgeworthian literary convention breaks down under the spontaneous challenge of the child; Eliza, the "good girl," questions authority. Here is a seven-year-old child who typically enjoys arguing or challenging the rules of a game. Eliza's confidence is based on trust in her own observation; she speaks from a new self-contained stage as a thinking child. But, like the parent in Edgeworthian children's fiction, Rachel maintains authority. When she argues that virtue is its own reward, Rachel establishes a clear hierarchy—first, that she is the authority, and second, that a principle exists that can be grasped only by children older than Eliza. Eliza accepts the rule because it is from her older sister and reveals her good nature as well as her submission by offering some strawberries to Rachel.

Eliza's resistance and submission suggest something beyond literary convention and didactic assumptions, namely, the development of a self out of inner conflict. Literary convention illustrates the "good girl"; historical observation records the fact of resistance. The question is how to interpret resistance in the midst of didactic language that generally devalues, circumvents, and transforms resistance. What is significant is the pattern of resistance. Eliza ultimately rejected Enlightenment values— reason, good sense, orderliness, shaming techniques. Nonetheless, she used critical method and differentiation to construct her own talented, religious, social, and emotional self. Eliza confronted the human struggle—the will to do good or evil—and chose family harmony. Additionally, since Eliza caused Rachel some anxiety by her challenge, she offered a kind of restitution. She shared her strawberries. The offer appeased her sister but did not quite cancel out Eliza's criticism of the idea of a beneficent world where goodness is always rewarded. Her recognition of a more ambivalent world originated in her awareness that goodness was not a simple choice. Eliza admitted that at times she felt she couldn't help being good.[18] Eliza's quandary may have been provoked by the depth of her internalization of "good" and her aversion to antisocial behavior. Yet Eliza's socialization came at a cost. Rachel equated goodness with docility; she compared "good girl" to "good servant."[19] Mentors reminded a critical child of her place in the family hierarchy.

Eliza's internal struggle for self-control and a sense of self created a crisis within the Mordecai household, a crisis that propelled Eliza toward greater self-affirmation, yet firmly implanted her within the familial hierarchy. The unstated but compelling issue remained the power struggle between child and mentor. At stake, according to Rachel, was not simply her own but divine authority. Rachel invoked a potent dual parental authority—a maternal teaching authority and a paternal, religiously sanctioned authority.

Rachel relates the incident of a temper tantrum that occurred while she was teaching Eliza a lesson in "recollective memory." According to Rachel, Eliza tended toward heedlessness, the unconsciousness of a seven-year-old. Determined to instill motivation, Rachel promised to finish a story of Peter the Great's marriage only if Eliza reminded Rachel of it before bedtime. When Eliza requested the story after being put to bed, Rachel refused. Eliza hadn't remembered to request the story at the proper time. Humiliation and disappointment fueled Eliza's tantrum—she railed at having to remember everything in order to have any pleasure and insisted that she had remembered to request the story but not at the precise moment Rachel required. Rachel denied more than Eliza's impulse to have a story told; she denied Eliza's very self. Seven-year-olds are governed by the need for immediate gratification and expect punishment in a world of rules and reciprocity, but they are still creatures of impulse with an inability to mediate between self and object. The denial of an object is also a denial of self. A tantrum, according to psychologist Robert Kegan, is the result of a conflict of impulses when the impulse is the self.[20] Eliza "would not *listen to reason*," Rachel wrote in despair.[21] In Kegan's terms, Eliza rejected Rachel's insistence on reason because reason contravened Eliza's impulsive self. Shut off from the family and miserable, Eliza eventually apologized to Rachel and "prayed to God to make her a better girl." Rachel reassured her that "God would assist her."[22] Reasonable instruction and discipline had limits that only divine intervention could remedy. Divinity had the power to reshape and redirect character and animate a true self, according to religious instruction.

The crisis left Eliza pale and thin, enervated, depressed.[23] Here she may have rethought her earlier truce with Rachel, her earlier pattern of behavior as the pliant, apologetic child. A more defined sense of self may have suggested to Eliza a different relationship with Rachel. Such a relationship, however, is not clearly perceived by the reader of the journal. A crisis theoretically could evoke a radical change in a child's outlook, but in Rachel's journal Eliza's private thoughts are not recorded. Rachel observes listless, depressed behavior, but it is unlikely that Eliza redefined her relationship with Rachel, because she is still, at age seven, so embedded in family life and is caught between separation and integration, independence and compliance.

Eliza experienced such a crisis and probable ensuing imbalance in the middle of her seventh year. In subsequent entries in the diary Rachel records that Eliza misrepresented the amount of work she had done in her grammar exercise and her poetry and French lessons and evaded responsibility in the care of her dew plant. Rachel severely reprimanded Eliza for her lies and shamed her in front of family and playmates. Rachel instilled further measures of shame by depriving Eliza of a good night kiss and threatened her with the loss of God's love.[24]

Eliza's behavior may have been connected to her anger over the "Peter the Great" incident and the feeling that Rachel acted precipitously and harshly. The Edgeworths observed that lying resulted from servility, often practiced in the presence of masters. In contrast, they note honor and truth-telling among children and their peers. Here, the Edgeworths' class-bound notion that only servants lie fit well with master-slave relations in the southern Mordecai household. As a female, however, Eliza is included but not fully accepted into the world of white male values. Nonetheless, such class notions support Eliza's emerging sense of self.[25] In addition, the Edgeworths stated that if a preceptor is unjust, the child will conceal his or her thoughts and deceive.[26] Certainly, children respond more honestly to adult discipline if it is developed in an atmosphere of reason and affection.[27] According to the Edgeworths, family context determined children's integrity:

> [I]n families where sincerity has been encouraged by the voice of praise and affection, a generous freedom of conversation and countenance appears, and the young people talk to each other, and to their parents, without distinction or reserve; without any distinction but such as superior esteem and respect dictate. These are feelings totally distinct from servile fear: these feelings inspire the love of truth, the ambition to acquire and to preserve character.[28]

Trust and affection among siblings pervaded the relationships in the Mordecai household; however, the distinctions of "superior esteem and respect" may have been overplayed in the tutoring process, especially in the "Peter the Great" incident. Thus the limitations of hierarchy proved subversive of the relationship between Rachel and Eliza.

Thereafter, Eliza obeyed but criticized rules, giving Rachel evidence for inferring independent reflection. Rachel had a name for Eliza's habit of criticizing, namely, Eliza's "criticising cap." Eliza questioned the use of singular and plural and the nature of poetic license. Her confidence stemmed from her ability to apply rules and to question those rules.[29] Rachel observed that Eliza, on the eve of her eighth birthday, was both conscientious in admitting her faults and heedless in listening to commands, as if Eliza were reserving her energy to formulate and invent a self.

If identity, as Henry Louis Gates says, is influenced not only by the past but by the objects with which one identifies, one's liveliest attachments,[30] then Eliza's new ties to other family members shaped her identity. A trip to Richmond presented Eliza with novel possibilities of engagement and relationship. In Richmond she met her cousins and her friend Louisa, whom she dearly loved, and she experienced the excitement of a city. The allurements of Richmond society captured Eliza's imagination. Her uncle Samuel Myers owned a thriving mercantile business and provided for his family in style. Most important, the Myers cousins gave Eliza the sense of belonging to a group beyond Jacob Mordecai's household; Eliza found an extensive Jewish community in Richmond. In addition to the prominent and extended Myers family, the Mordecais connected their families through marriage to the mercantile Marx-Myers-Hays family of New York, Petersburg, Richmond, and Norfolk and to the Cohens of Philadelphia, Baltimore, and Richmond.[31]

Growing awareness of a context larger than the family encouraged an understanding of democratic order. During a grammar lesson that considered the pronoun "I," Eliza said, "I don't think it ought to be the *first* person to speak of *ourselves,* because we ought not to think of ourselves, before we do of any body else; ought we?"[32] Social responsibility formed a precept, an "ought." By the age of ten Eliza had begun to grasp the social cohesion that the rules supported. Her understanding emerged in the context of the Jewish faith. When Eliza first encountered anti-Semitism while reading James Riley's *Authentic Narrative of the Loss of the American Brig Commerce,*[33] she questioned the reason for such prejudice. Rachel repeated the commonplace narrative of the time: that Europe persecuted Jews, depriving them of rights or employment or education and thus making them a marginal, despised lot, but that in America, where each individual was judged by merit, Jews were treated with toleration. Eliza might not have been aware of evangelical proselytization attempts and the family's intellectual and religious isolation; she accepted Rachel's word and formed an enduring loyalty to Judaism and to American democracy. She said, "there are two things sister Rachel that I love better than anything else in the world ... my *religion* and my *country*." She perceived herself as Jewish American; faith took precedence over nationality. Eliza proclaimed her belief with all the vision of a ten-year-old who suddenly understands that she belongs to and has a special standing in a larger world of faith and civic responsibility.[34]

Eliza's moral development culminated in civic identification, a direction clearly delineated in Enlightenment children's fiction. With the help of a story, Thomas Day's *Sanford and Merton*,[35] Eliza easily identified the consequences of a lack of reciprocity. Squire Chase unmercifully beat Harry Sanford, but the boy subsequently saved his life. Eliza proposed that the squire must have been ashamed "when he found that it was Harry, who had helped him, and that such a little boy, was so much better than he was."[36]

Children's literature established the didactic principles of the "Golden Rule" and set them in conventional form, a type-scene familiar to biblical and classical (Homeric) stories. The story of Harry suggests such type-scenes, in which the character experiences various crises and develops from each a moral lesson. Although children's stories lack the portentiousness of events found in Scripture, still they show that choice has devastating consequences.[37] For Eliza, Squire Chase's comeuppance appears so complete because his vanquisher is "a little boy." The prosaic event resonates with religious meaning, divine judgment, as moral constancy uproots caste or established order.

One of Eliza's observations, which Rachel described as the "Jacob at the Well" incident, fused Enlightenment perception and biblical meaning. Rachel recounted the anecdote as an ironic type-scene: "Eliza saw one day at the well, two old negro women, a black boy [Robin], who was drawing water for them, and several dogs. 'Look sister ... , said she, there is *Jacob* drawing water for the *maidens*; and the dogs, you see, are *for* the sheep.' "[38] Eliza saw only a representation of a biblical tableau; but the fact that she elevated her subjects to biblical archetypes dignifies an otherwise ordinary scene of servility. Rachel's emphasis in the narrative suggests caste-like condescension; her subsequent observations on slavery taught Eliza to distinguish slave and mistress.

When Rachel complimented a considerate slave, Eliza mistakenly believed that Rachel praised Lucy as a "good servant" and proceeded to give Rachel this observation: "Sister R[achel] when any of the servants do any thing for me I never say, you are a good *servant* or any thing like that, because it seems as if it would make them feel bad, to put them in mind that they were our servants, would not it[?]" Rachel replied, "No my dear I believe not, they have always been servants, and do not feel their situation, a disgrace as they might do if they had ever been in different circumstances."[39] Eliza identified with the slave and felt as Lucy must have felt. Eliza reasoned that if the practice of reciprocity extended to all in a democracy, why not slaves? Rachel, with disciplined sensibility and conformity to household authority, placed slaves in a discrete category beyond the reach of equalitarian sympathy. In a southern family, justice accommodated the pursuit of harmony and order. Reciprocity applied to external behavior that preserved peace in families, their social and economic independence and well-being.[40] According to southern patriarchal ideology, slaves' dependent status limited their rational understanding; slaves, like children, needed supervision and secure placement in the household hierarchy.

A patriarchal predisposition, however, did not eradicate progressive education. Rachel fostered progressive method and sustained patriarchal authority, an anomaly that gave way under criticism and negotiation. Democratic alterations in family governance, namely, the family conference, paved the way for negotiations in educational practice. When Moses Mordecai, Jacob Mordecai's eldest son, announced his intention to marry Margaret Lane, a Christian, he defended his actions against the pleas of Jacob and Rachel to reconsider. However, Moses expressed doubts about his choice and opened the way for a family conference in October 1817. At the family meeting members spoke "freely and honestly"; but Moses determined not to break his engagement, a connection he said he would not have formed had he known how the family felt.[41] Moses's engagement surely created a model for consensual governance and prepared Rachel for participatory instruction, her ticket experiment.

In the hopes of providing stimulation and competition in her private tutoring, Rachel devised a ticket system, rewarding good behavior ("Early rising . . . bad habits overcome") and punishing bad habits ("Carelessness, heedlessness").[42] Faults incurred the penalty of forfeiting two good tickets. Seven good tickets obtained a reward—something the child viewed as pleasure, such as reading a book. Eliza's initial enthusiasm with the system pleased the family, but her sense of its fairness began to break down as the system grew more complicated. Eliza earned a reward and chose to have a story read the next night. In the meantime she misbehaved, thus postponing her reward. But Rachel assigned an exercise designed to make up for Eliza's deficit so that she might receive her reward more immediately. Nonetheless, Eliza considered the burden too heavy; for her impatience, Rachel postponed the story even longer. Fortunately, Rachel regretted her decision, admitted her misgivings, and asked Eliza exactly what she thought. Eliza replied with the candor to which she had been trained,

> Why, sister Rachel, I will tell you, I thought it was not quite *just* for you to deny me my reward, for what I did today, because you know I had *earned* it three days ago, & if I had chosen something else, I should have had it then, so it does not seem right that I should lose it for not being attentive today.[43]

Rachel readily agreed and promised to read the story that night. Thus the fixed system of rewards and punishments existed only with Eliza's free consent, and she was able to challenge and change the rules. The rules are no longer arbitrary, at the will of authority; they conform to Eliza's notion of independence.

The politics of pedagogy as practiced by Rachel and Eliza Mordecai reveals the contested nature of moral formation in the Early Republic. Rachel initially wished to establish hegemony through the enforcement of strict disciplinary rules. Eliza, hardly a passive child, challenged the rules by the use of rational discourse and subverted the patriarchal authority implicit in Rachel's definition of family hierarchy. Eliza's resistance changed both teacher and student and each approached a more independent self. Eliza's goal, however, remained the retention of Jewish Orthodoxy and identity. Enlightenment method created the medium for emergence of an Early Republican independent self, yet Jewish concepts of holiness defined the boundaries of self-creation, the safe areas for expression and action. Eliza resolved her early conflicted notions of self through prayer and family negotiation. Moreover, Eliza went beyond conventional notions of "goodness" when she expressed compassion for slaves and elevated their actions to biblical proportions. Covenant responsibility evolved from Eliza's deep sense of Jewish community and her attachment to her Richmond family. Yet Eliza undermined Rachel's insistence on patriarchal notions of family authority by adherence to the method of reasoning and negotiation. Eliza's creation of a self conformed to Enlightenment ideas of free agency and Orthodox concerns that precepts freely chosen lead to holiness.[44]

Eliza translated Enlightenment pedagogical practice into a regard for holiness and a search for Jewish community. She married her Orthodox Richmond cousin Samuel Myers and retained her loyalty to Judaism. At the same time, she pursued intellectual, musical, and literary interests. In effect, Eliza resisted secularization but adapted Enlightenment methods to her religio-ethnic familial values. The precepts of "holiness" led Rachel, steeped in rational dialogue and faith in Providence, to religious conversion. Rachel converted to Christianity on her deathbed after a tortuous ten-year investigation of evangelical Episcopal Protestantism.

The politics of pedagogy recorded in Rachel Mordecai's journal demonstrates that ethnic and religious identities are a process—contested and negotiated in intergenerational teaching dialogue. In the case of the Mordecais, assimilation does not wholly describe their experience. Rather, the Mordecais assimilated the element of Enlightenment dialogic method, transformed the element of goodness, and resisted wholly secular values.[45] For them, religio-ethnic identification followed a less linear pattern than persistent assimilation allowed. Both Rachel and Eliza invented themselves in the process of rational dialogue, displacing patriarchal authority with a more democratic pedagogy. Nonetheless, the traditional German Jewish culture that encouraged women's education and nurtured the call for holiness remained, providentially, in the cross-stitching of Rachel and Eliza's lives.[46] "Republican Motherhood," then, offered the Jewish minority an avenue for moral choice that led to the self Divinity intended.

NOTES

1. Rachel Mordecai Lazarus, diary, Myers Family Papers, Virginia Historical Society.

2. Mary Beth Norton, *Liberty's Daughters: The Revolutionary Experience of American Women, 1750–1800* (Glenview, IL: Scott, Foresman, 1980), 245, 247–49, 298; Linda K. Kerber, *Women of the Republic: Intellect and Ideology in Revolutionary America* (New York: Norton, 1980), 11, 199–200, 228–29, 235, 269.

3. Norton, *Liberty's Daughters*, 3–5, 111–17, 243–49, 256; Kerber, *Women of the Republic*, 11, 15–32; idem, "The Republican Mother: Women and the Enlightenment—An American Perspective," *American Quarterly* 28 (1976): 187–285; Jan Lewis, "The Republican Wife: Virtue and Seduction in the Early Republic," *William and Mary Quarterly* 44, no. 4 (October 1987): 689–721; Ruth H. Bloch, "The Gendered Meanings of Virtue in Revolutionary America," *Signs* 13, no. 1 (autumn

1987): 37–58; Kenneth A. Lockridge, *On the Sources of Patriarchal Rage: The Commonplace Books of William Byrd and Thomas Jefferson and the Gendering of Power in the Eighteenth Century* (New York: New York University Press, 1992), 39, 84–86.

4. For a comparison with daughters of eighteenth-century *salonnieres*, see Dena Goodman, "Filial Rebellion in the Salon: Madame Geoffrin and Her Daughter," *French Historical Studies* 16, no. 1 (spring 1989): 28–47.

5. See Peter McLaren, *Critical Pedagogy and Predatory Culture: Oppositional Politics in a Postmodern Era* (London: Routledge, 1995), 34.

6. Jay Fliegelman, *Prodigals and Pilgrims: The American Revolution against Patriarchial Authority, 1750–1800* (Cambridge: Cambridge University Press, 1982), 1–2.

7. Charlotte Baum, Paula Hyman, and Sonya Michel, *The Jewish Woman in America* (New York: Dial Press, 1976), 4–22; Rudolf Glanz, *The Jewish Woman in America: Two Female Immigrant Generations, 1820–1929* (New York: KTAV, 1976), ix, 25, 109, 114, 118.

8. Eli Faber, "The Formative Era of American Jewish History," *American Jewish History* 81, no. 1 (1993): 10–21; Ira Rosenwaike, "Characteristics of Baltimore's Jewish Population in a Nineteenth-Century Census," *American Jewish History* 82, nos. 1–4 (1994): 123–39; Louis Schmier, "Jews and Gentiles in a South Georgia Town," in *Jews of the South*, ed. Samuel Proctor, Louis Schmier, and Malcolm Stern (Macon, GA: Mercer University Press, 1984), 1–6; Henry L. Feingold, *Zion in America: The Jewish Experience from Colonial Times to the Present* (New York: Twayne, 1974), 68–71; Stuart E. Rosenberg, *The New Jewish Identity in America* (New York: Hippocrene, 1985), 44–48.

9. Edgar E. MacDonald, *The Education of the Heart: The Correspondence of Rachel Mordecai Lazarus and Maria Edgeworth* (Chapel Hill: University of North Carolina Press, 1977), 6.

10. Rachel Mordecai to Samuel Mordecai, 24 September 1810, Patti Mordecai Collection, North Carolina Archives. Jacob Mordecai to Samuel Mordecai, 29 November 1810; Rachel Mordecai to Ellen Mordecai, 30 January 1814; Rachel Mordecai to Samuel Mordecai, 30 January 1814; Samuel Mordecai to Rachel Mordecai, 16 February 1817, 22 February 1818, Mordecai Family Papers, Southern Historical Collection, University of North Carolina.

11. Richard Lovell Edgeworth and Maria Edgeworth, *Practical Education* (Boston: T. B. Wait and Sons, 1815), iv.

12. Eugene B. Borowitz, *Exploring Jewish Ethics: Papers on Covenant Responsibility* (Detroit: Wayne State University Press, 1990), 17–22.

13. John Locke, *Some Thoughts Concerning Education*, ed. John W. Yolton and Jean S. Yolton (Oxford: Clarendon, 1989), 23–28.

14. Norton, *Liberty's Daughters*, 5, 125; Kerber, *Women of the Republic*, 27; Carole Pateman, *The Disorder of Women* (Stanford: Stanford University Press, 1989), 71–84.

15. Myers Family Papers, Virginia Historical Society.

16. Ephraim E. Urbach, *The Sages: The World and Wisdom of the Rabbis of the Talmud* (Cambridge: Harvard University Press, 1979), 326.

17. Lazarus, diary, 19 May 1816.

18. Lazarus, diary, 3 February 1818.

19. Lazarus, diary, 15 March 1818.

20. Robert Kegan, *The Evolving Self: Problem and Process in Human Development* (Cambridge: Harvard University Press, 1982), 88.

21. Lazarus, diary, 27 October 1816.

22. Ibid.

23. Lazarus, diary, 9 February 1817.

24. Lazarus, diary, 9 February 1817, 20 February 1817.

25. I am indebted to Grace Elizabeth Hale for this observation.

26. Edgeworth and Edgeworth, *Practical Education*, 185–87.

27. See Ross D. Parke, "Some Effects of Punishment on Children's Behavior," in *Influences on Human Development*, 2d ed., ed. Urie Bronfenbrenner and Maureen Mahoney (Hinsdale, IL: Dryden Press, 1975), 257–59; Lynne Vallone, *Disciplines of Virtue: Girls' Culture in the Eighteenth and Nineteenth Centuries* (New Haven: Yale University Press, 1995), 11; Steven Schlossman and Robert B. Cairns, "Problem Girls: Observations on Past and Present," in *Children in Time and Place: Developmental and Historical Insights*, ed. Glen H. Elder, Jr., John Modell, and Ross D. Parke (Cambridge: Cambridge University Press, 1993), 110–11.

28. Edgeworth and Edgeworth, *Practical Education*, 187.

29. Lazarus, diary, 3 May 1817.

30. Henry Louis Gates, *Identities* (Chicago: University of Chicago Press, 1995), 3; idem, *Black Literature and Literary Theory* (New York: Methuen, 1984), 24.

31. Lazarus, diary, 15 January 1818. See also *Richmond's Jewry, 1769–1976: Shabbat in Shockoe* (Charlottesville: University Press of Virginia), 1969–72.

32. Lazarus, diary, 30 April 1817.

33. James Riley, *An Authentic Narrative of the Loss of the American Brig Commerce* (New York, 1817).

34. Lazarus, diary, September 1819.

35. Thomas Day, *The History of Sanford and Merton* (London: John Kendrick, n.d.), 60–64.

36. Lazarus, diary, 30 August 1817.

37. Robert Alter, *The Art of Biblical Narrative* (New York: Basic Books, 1981), 47–52.

38. Lazarus, diary, 30 August 1816.

39. Lazarus, diary, 15 February 1818.

40. Jan Lewis, *The Pursuit of Happiness: Family Values in Jefferson's Virginia* (Cambridge: Cambridge University Press, 1983), xiv, 11, 15, 21–22, 30.

41. Solomon Mordecai to Ellen Mordecai, 4 October 1817; Ellen Mordecai, diary, 22 October 1817, Mordecai Family Papers.

42. Lazarus, diary, 26 October 1819.

43. Ibid.

44. Urbach, *The Sages*, 272, 367–69.

45. Rosenberg, *The New Jewish Identity in America*, xi.

46. For a discussion of interpretations of ethnicity, see Kathleen Neils Conzen, David A. Gerber, Ewa Morawska, George E. Pozzetta, and Rudolph J. Vecoli, "The Invention of Ethnicity: A Perspective from the U.S.A.," *Journal of Ethnic History*, fall 1992, 3–41; Herbert Gans, "Comment: Ethnic Invention and Acculturation, A Bumpy Line Approach," *Journal of Ethnic History*, fall 1992, 53–58; David A. Gerber, Ewa Morawska, and George E. Pozzetta, "Response," *Journal of Ethnic History*, fall 1992, 59–63.

Chapter Six

Equality Deferred, Opportunity Pursued
The Sisters of Wachovia

Johanna Miller Lewis

EDITOR'S NOTE: *Maryland was founded as a refuge for English Catholics. The French brought Catholicism to Louisiana and the Mississippi valley and the Spaniards Catholicism to Florida, but the vast majority of the South's Christians were Protestants. The early development of Protestantism along national lines initially tied people to their ethnic identities. The English upper classes were often Anglicans, the Scots-Irish who spread across the backcountry brought their Presbyterian Church with them, and the Germans their Lutheran and Reformed Churches. In the mid-eighteenth century the emotional religious movement known as Pietism arrived from Europe. It emphasized moral behavior and dependence on God over theological dogma and resulted in a proliferation of denominations and sects.*

John Wesley, the English founder of Methodism, had been influenced by Moravian Pietists in Georgia; his disciple George Whitefield used the emotionalism of Pietism to counter the weak churchgoing tradition he found in the South when he led revivals from Georgia to Massachusetts in the mid-eighteenth century. Evangelical revivals energized many Presbyterians and also led to the establishment of the Baptist and Methodist denominations. Evangelical religion gained momentum with the Cane Ridge camp meeting in Kentucky in 1801 and became ubiquitous by the antebellum period. As a consequence, biblical literalism formed the basis of southern religion and conversion was its focus.

The gentry initially resisted the evangelicals, using armed bands to break up services, for they posed a threat to planter culture and authority. Evangelical leaders attacked the planters' lifestyle by opposing dancing, gambling, drinking, racing, whoring, and cockfighting. In addition, evangelical ministers organized their churches more democratically. They preached that all — even women and slaves — are equal in the sight of God, initiating the first large-scale conversion of slaves to Christianity.

Although the evangelicals began as critics of the establishment, their continuing success in the nineteenth century turned them into defenders of the status quo, as the Baptists and Methodists became numerically dominant and inclusive of all classes — even the planters. Support for slavery resulted in a religion that focused on personal vices, unlike northern revivalism, which spurred social reform. This privatized, individualistic religious outlook became a central aspect of southern culture and remains so today.

Fearing that conversion would emancipate slaves despite legislation to the contrary, planters initially had refused to proselytize, and African Americans resisted out of commitment to their traditional religions or, in some cases, Islam. Revivalism, however, brought entire families with their slaves to camp meetings, thereby exposing African Americans to the evangelical message and shrinking the cultural gulf between the two races. Slaves began to join white churches and to exhort others of both races. By the antebellum period, denominations were sending missionaries to the Black Belt. Black Christianity, however, looked beyond the self-serving homilies on the dutiful servant directed to them at interracial services. African Americans developed their own Christian rituals in an "invisible church" of secret services, where aspects of West African religious practices, especially in music and preaching styles, were retained.

Despite their many differences, Jews, Muslims, Catholics, and Protestants conceptualized religious authority in male terms and decreed a gender system in which women's roles were largely confined to bearing and raising children and accepting the authority of men. Yet after 1800 more women than men were church members. Evangelicalism's emphasis on an individual relationship with a loving God may have appealed to dependent and vulnerable women. In addition, organized religion provided opportunities for sociability to a largely rural and therefore isolated population whose women were not permitted to socialize at the courthouse and tavern, where men met together.

Biblical literalism lent itself to many interpretations of the same texts. Consequently, some groups offered women a larger role. The most influential were Quakers, who denied the need for ministers and believed that anyone could receive the "inner light." Women as well as men could speak at services and travel around the country doing so, and they also exercised leadership over women's activities, including education. For example, they ran a school for girls in Guilford, North Carolina. Two former Charlestonians, Angelina and Sarah Grimké, toured New England and New York antislavery societies in 1837. In the debate that followed, Sarah argued that Jesus made no gender distinctions when defining the duties of his followers. The Shakers went still further, believing that God was both male and female. Although their communities maintained a traditional division of labor, in religion and economics the genders were equal. Believing the end was near and that sin entered the world through sexual intercourse, they required celibacy. Spreading from New England, their communities reached to Kentucky. Unlike the Shakers, the Moravians did not believe in the dual nature of Jesus, but their practices provided some unique opportunities for women.

. . .

Among the myriad groups that populated the antebellum North Carolina backcountry, members of the *Unitas Fratrum* (United Brethren), or Moravian Church, stand apart from the rest. The Moravians participated in the mid-eighteenth-century migration from Pennsylvania down the Great Wagon Road, and they helped settle the western North Carolina frontier, creating what Carl Bridenbaugh called "Greater Pennsylvania."[1] In many ways they appeared to blend into the crowd: they had left Pennsylvania to relocate in North Carolina, they were Protestants (of a sort; see below), and they shared an ethnic heritage and reputation as hard workers with other Germanic peoples. However, the ways the Moravians in the main town of Salem worshipped God, devoted their lives to doing his work, and organized and documented their efforts to that end made them atypical. These differences, which included a semicommunal lifestyle and unusual theology, held some interesting possibilities for unmarried Moravian women, or Single Sisters, including gender and economic equality with the Moravian Brothers. This essay will explore how the promise of gender equality for women in Salem was deferred, while economic equality became reality.

Life on the North Carolina frontier was not easy, especially for women. As the wives, daughters, sisters, servants, and slaves of the male landowners, they were responsible for cooking, child care, gardening, butchering, farming, sewing, and milking and other dairy production. Most women's lives were defined by their personal and legal relationships with men. Married women's inability to own property, control their income, or possess credit, for example, made them financially dependent on their husbands. Conversely, while single women could own property and control their income, their lack of social respectability (usually provided to women through marriage) consigned them to a life spent in someone else's (usually a male relative's) household or on the fringes of polite society.[2]

The Moravians joined the migration to North Carolina in 1753, bringing with them a new role for unmarried women as Single Sisters. They had lived in Pennsylvania since 1740, after having abandoned their first New World settlement at Savannah, Georgia, when their pacifist views came into conflict with the colony trustees' desire to participate in England's war against Spain. They belonged to a Christian sect called the Brethren of the Law of Christ, which originated in 1456 in what is now eastern Germany. Followers of the martyred Bohemian priest Johann Huss, who was put to the stake in 1415 for advocating the reform of the church in Rome, the Brethren agreed with Huss that individuals could understand and correctly interpret the Bible themselves. They believed in a "heart religion," which expressed itself by action rather than by dogma. Fearing persecution by the church in Rome prior to the Reformation and suffering Catholic abuse during the Counter Reformation (1624–28), the Brethren went "underground" until only the idea, or "hidden seed," of the society remained a well-kept secret among the families that fled the Holy Roman Empire during this time. The "hidden seed" did not flower again until 1727, when a group of these refugees (many of whom originated in Moravia) living on the estate of Count Nicholas Von Zinzendorf, a Lutheran minister, renewed the teachings of the ancient *Unitas Fratrum* with his help. Unlike other Protestant denominations of the time, the Moravians did not consider themselves a separate or distinct denomination or church but a society that practiced day-to-day Christian living.[3]

The renewed society grew quickly. After establishing planned communities in eastern Europe, the Moravians came to the New World in 1734. They earned a reputation as thrifty and industrious settlers, establishing three large towns in Pennsylvania—Bethlehem, Nazareth, and Lititz—and as a consequence were highly sought after as colonists. However, Count Zinzendorf's intense desire to bring *all* Christians, despite their denomination, to the Moravian understanding of "heart religion" set the Moravians apart from other Protestants and made Zinzendorf and his followers targets of hostility.[4]

The Moravians came to North Carolina for reasons of mutual accommodation: they wanted to expand into the southern colonies, and the last lord proprietor of the Carolinas wanted more settlers on his land.[5] In 1753 the Brethren concluded lengthy negotiations to purchase a large tract of land. Directed to "the back of the colony," a scouting party of Brethren found an acceptable tract of more than ninety-eight thousand acres in the Piedmont section of North Carolina.[6] On November 17, 1753, a chosen group of male settlers arrived on the Wachovia tract. In their main settlement, Bethabara, and later in Salem, the Moravians replicated the pattern of life that had characterized Herrnhut, their first congregation town on Zinzendorf's estate in Europe. The founding principles behind the organization of the towns as well as their congregations and the church boards that governed the towns are found in Moravian theology. This "renewed" theology, developed under Zinzendorf's leadership at Herrnhut in the 1730s, centered around Christ as the mediator between an exalted God and his degraded people. As the Son of God, Jesus was both God and human being; and by sacrificing his life for their sins, he saved their souls from death. Consequently, Christ offered humans a way out of their disgraced state, and in return they owed him their unending gratitude.[7] The Father-Son relationship between God and Christ, as understood within the Trinity, was the model for all relationships in the Moravian Church. Count Zinzendorf saw the Trinity as a family: God as father, the Holy Ghost as mother, and Christ as the son; the relationship between Christ and the church and the relationship between Christ and the souls of individual Moravians (perceived as female because of Christ being male) were described as marriage. This was a structure easily understood and replicated on earth. A Moravian family, therefore, held multiple and overlapping religious meanings.[8]

Despite the importance of family symbolism to church theology, church leaders did not necessarily see the biological family unit as the most effective organization for promoting an individual's relationship with Christ. The use of dormitory-like housing at Herrnhut for economic purposes divided church members for a time by age, sex, and marital status. When church leaders realized that within each group some members had clearly advanced in their Christian growth and activity, they initiated the "choir system," in which all members belonged to choirs for worship. Under the choir system, the congregation (composed of choirs) was considered a family; the governing bodies of the church acted as patriarch, thereby maintaining the paradigm of the family.[9]

Most Moravian towns followed the model that developed out of the Herrnhut experience: everyone belonged to a choir, but the choirs lived together only if it was in their economic, as well as spiritual, best interest. Consequently, the family continued to be the best way to care for children;

but single adults (when there were enough of them) could create a productive economic and spiritual unit. Only in Bethlehem did all the choirs
live together in their own choir houses, where they worked, ate, and slept
together. An individual's life was marked by progress through this choir
system: infants; little boys and little girls; older boys and older girls;
Single Brothers and Single Sisters; Married Couples; Widows and Widow-
ers. The choir system, along with governance from the church boards,
provided the basis for the communal lifestyle in which each church member contributed according to ability and shared according to need. In
Bethlehem, the eradication of the nuclear family and separation of the
sexes that resulted from the totally inclusive choir system had a trans-
forming effect on Moravian women. Because of the communal living
arrangements, gender roles were more symmetrical than in any other
colonial society, and church leaders allowed women to participate in
encouraging spiritual growth (the Moravians' prime directive) in the same
way men did. In addition, the Single Sisters, like the Single Brothers, were
totally responsible for their own physical as well as spiritual needs.[10]

Salem was the largest town in Wachovia; because of its size, it had a
more developed choir system than Bethabara and Bethania. Throughout
the rest of Wachovia, in the country congregations of Friedland,
Friedburg, and Hope, church control was not as strict, no groups lived
communally, and the choirs functioned more as social organizations than
anything else. In essence, the country congregations, which accounted for
the majority of Moravians in Wachovia, lived more like the backcountry
population generally.

The choir system, then, still existed in Wachovia, but the Single Brothers, Single Sisters, and Widows lived together only in Salem. Church
governance guidelines for Salem as articulated in the Statutes of 1773
considered both the Single Brothers and the Single Sisters so important,
however, that leaders from those choirs joined the congregation ministers
and their wives, and various church officials in sitting on all but one
church board.[11] Consequently, both married and single women participated in important church decision making. During Wachovia's early
years, women were a major element on church committees, constituting
one-third of this leadership pool and frequently the majority of leaders
present in Wachovia at any particular time.[12]

Despite the possibility for equality offered by the choir system and
female presence on church boards, the church's "renewed" theology and
its emphasis on family roles ultimately undercut it, for the Christ-human

relationship model was a man-woman relationship, and the male embodied the superior role. The following passage describes some of the "principles" or rules that Married People were expected to follow:

> The husband is the head of the wife, just as Christ of the Gemeine; and just
> as Christ loves the Gemeine, so he should love, nourish, and care for his
> wife. . . . The wife is entrusted to his care in spiritual and physical matters.
> He must treat her with understanding, in order to give her respect as the
> weaker part, and to show her love, sincerity, and patience in accordance
> with Christ.[13]

Consequently, although women could be spiritual leaders for other
women, as acolytes and deacons, they could not be ordained as presbyters
or bishops of the church. In addition, women's appearance on church
boards may have been more show than reality; meticulously kept records
from Wachovia reveal that women board members rarely spoke and that
the Single Sisters had a male financial advisor.[14]

While the possibilities for advancement in the church may not have
been the same, all Wachovia residents shared an equal devotion to work.
In their perpetual effort to pattern their lives after Christ, virtues of
diligence, simplicity, frugality, punctuality, conscientiousness, and self-
control were not just highly desirable attributes but essential qualities.
Work, though not causing or guaranteeing salvation, became imperative
to maintaining a state of grace; labor thus provided a powerful ethical
justification and impetus to the vast enterprises of the church. To Zinzendorf, each individual's work should become the goal in life. In 1738 the
count wrote, "One does not only work in order to live, but one lives for
the sake of one's work, and if there is no more work to do one suffers or
goes to sleep [dies]."[15]

Not surprisingly, most work opportunities for women in Wachovia
were highly gendered. Women were not even allowed to settle in Wachovia its first two years, for church leaders expected life on the frontier
to be rough and therefore too difficult for women to survive. When they
finally sent for women in 1755, part of the reason was the need for gender-
specific work—men thought such jobs could be performed better by
women. Bishop Spangenberg wrote that females were necessary so that
"laundry, mending, sewing, and the like could be attended to properly."[16]
Once women arrived in Wachovia the gendered division of labor became
even more important: when Bishop Spangenberg asked the Brothers to
help the Sisters with the spinning, he was ignored. Having survived in

the backwoods of North Carolina for three years without spinning, the Brothers were not about to take up such a quintessential female task after the arrival of the Sisters.[17]

Another reason women were called to Wachovia was theological: quite simply, women were essential to a proper Moravian congregation, because the Trinity could not be replicated without marriage and procreation. Most Moravian women married, and their work was primarily domestic. Although a wife might help her husband with his work, only rarely was she recognized for her efforts. Among the Moravians, ministers' wives were a prominent exception. The expectation was that they would be spiritual counterparts to their husbands, and church leaders frequently recognized their service by allowing them to remain on committees after their husbands had died.[18]

The domestic workload for Moravian women is another characteristic they shared with women in the rest of the North Carolina backcountry. In preindustrial America, cooking, cleaning, spinning, weaving, sewing, and child care could easily keep a woman busy "from sun to sun." The women of Wachovia, especially those who lived in the country congregations, undoubtedly participated in some version of the "underground economy" that was common to women of the backcountry, trading various domestic products with others to satisfy household needs.[19] However, married women also shouldered an additional burden as a result of the separation of the sexes in Salem. Married women could have contact (i.e., be in the same physical space) with men, but single women could not. Consequently, any "female" tasks that needed to be fulfilled in a public venue, such as the tavern, had to be carried out by married women.

As Wachovia developed and grew, especially after the "official" opening of Salem in 1772, the labor load for married women with public duties became unmanageable. Rather than ignore the choir system and end the separation of single adults by sex, the Moravians followed the example of their backcountry neighbors and turned to slave labor. At first, because of the high cost of slaves and a concern that slaves might endanger the spiritual health of the community, slaves were leased. A female slave worked in the tavern, and a male slave worked in the cow yard. This arrangement apparently worked so well that in 1769, when a slave who had been leased for the past three years asked "to know the Savior," the congregation purchased him and allowed him admission into the church two years later.[20]

Slavery became more prominent in Salem in the nineteenth century, as it did throughout the backcountry, when the price dropped. The Moravian philosophy concerning slavery evolved over time. It had always acknowledged the existence of slavery, but at first it rationalized slavery as a means to support the welfare of the whole community; later, the use of slave labor merely as a means of economic advancement was deemed acceptable. Even though individual slave ownership was technically forbidden in favor of congregational ownership, church boards repeatedly issued permissions for individuals to purchase slaves to lighten their workload. By 1823, enough slaves and free blacks lived in and around Salem that St. Philip's Church was built for their worship.[21]

While the married women of Wachovia shared much in common with the backcountry housewife, the Single Sisters of Salem enjoyed a far different existence than the average single woman on the frontier. First, by living together to stimulate Christian growth and activity, the Single Sisters developed their own female culture with its own requisite power structure, leading to spiritual and financial self-reliance. In Wachovia, as on the rest of the southern frontier, women were expected to marry, and most women did so. However, those women who chose to live full-time as Single Sisters in Salem were perceived not as aberrations but as individuals fulfilling their obligations in a different way.[22]

Some of the opportunities offered by the Single Sisters came in the form of work. Because the church required choirs to be self-supporting, the Sisters were responsible for procuring and paying for everything they needed that they could not produce themselves. In Salem, this generally meant that some Sisters worked as domestics, cleaning and cooking for other Sisters who were involved in the traditional female trades of sewing, spinning, weaving, or serving in leadership positions in their choir. Leadership among the Sisters allowed women to advance further in their service to the Lord on their own terms and find more opportunities for individual fulfillment than even marriage to a minister or church official (on which the woman's spiritual status in the community depended) might provide. In short, the Single Sisters choir not only gave women the option of remaining single, but also provided these normal, active, and healthy women with the chance to lead rich and useful lives.[23] Such an alternative for women was important in a society with a sex ratio in which men outnumbered women (especially among single adults) throughout its first quarter century of existence.[24]

In Salem, the Single Sisters lived on the east side of the town square in a brick house in traditional Moravian style, built in 1786. The Single

Brothers House, built in 1768 of half-timbered construction, was located safely on the west side of the square, so the two groups would not come into contact. The Sisters' function within the community was to provide such trades as sewing, spinning, weaving, and glovemaking and services such as laundry and cooking.

The Sisters, like other working women on the southern frontier, did not shy away from entrepreneurship as inappropriate behavior for women. Only two years after moving into their house, they asked the board of supervisors for permission to use the vacant lot directly north of them as a bleaching green, to spread out and dry their laundry.[25] While church planners originally intended the "bleaching green" for the church, in 1797 the Elders' Conference decided to reconsider when it became apparent that a large church structure would cramp the Sisters' yard space.[26] The economic viability of the Sisters was so important to church officials that they changed the town plan.

Meanwhile, another successful enterprise of the Single Sisters concerned educating the town's daughters. Like many other religious groups in early America, the Moravians shared the belief that the ability to read and interpret the Bible was necessary for a full comprehension of the book's teachings. Unlike many such groups, however, the Moravians also inherited a tradition of education for women. The seventeenth-century theologian and Moravian bishop Johann Amos Comenius believed that learning should be fun and that students should be taught what they were capable of learning instead of a prescribed, traditional curriculum instilled by memorization. In extending this liberal philosophy to the realm of female education, Comenius was expressing a revolutionary idea. Unlike his contemporaries, Comenius believed that women had just as much intelligence as men, and therefore he could not find any reason to prevent females from acquiring knowledge. In the introduction to *The Analytical Didactic of Comenius*, he asked, "Are we afraid of their meddling? The more we introduce them to mental occupations, the less time they will find for meddling, which comes from an emptiness of mind."[27]

Education was a strong component of the Moravians' heritage, which led to the Single Sisters founding a school for young girls in Salem. In April 1772 Single Sister Elisabeth Osterlein opened the school in the meeting house, two lots north of the Single Sisters' house.[28] The "little girls' school" was intended only for the daughters of congregation members, but two factors changed the school's future. First, opportunities for formal education for young girls in the eighteenth-century South were rare. Not only did the geographical distance between plantations make organizing any type of school difficult, southern communities (unlike New England) did not consider educating children an obligation, so the burden fell to the parents. For those families with limited resources, funding an education for their sons took priority over daughters. Second, because Salem was a center of trade and manufacture, offering a wide variety of stores and artisan shops for backcountry clientele, the church received requests almost immediately from non-Moravian parents to enroll their daughters. In the early years of the nineteenth century, the minister of Salem recorded the hopes of many travelers coming through Salem that the Moravians would open a school for girls from the region.[29]

The Single Sisters responded to such requests with enthusiasm, in part because a boarding school for non-Moravians had the potential to generate increased income. Unfortunately, the Brethren were initially unconvinced of such a need or the ability of the Single Sisters to run such an operation. The Sisters eventually convinced the Brethren that they had enough education and experience to warrant opening a school. Lot approval was finally granted in the fall of 1802.[30] This decision marked an important change in policy for the church. Although the communities created on the Wachovia tract had all come in contact with outsiders, called "strangers" by the Moravians, this would be the first time strangers would be allowed to live in a congregation town. This was possible because young girls did not pose a threat to the church's control over the community or the church hierarchy, and the boarding school could be viewed as a form of missionary work.

The Moravians' conception of males as authority figures within the family meant that the Single Sisters' school would be headed by a man. On October 31, 1802, the Elders' Conference called Samuel Kramsch, a Moravian minister who had previously headed Nazareth Hall and taught at the Moravian boarding school for boys in Bethlehem, Pennsylvania, to be principal of the new school.[31] In January 1803, the Elders' Conference further decided that, since no space for dormitories or classrooms existed in any community buildings, a new structure to house the school was necessary.[32] For the convenience of the Single Sisters, the location selected was just north of their choir house on the former bleaching green.

No one in Salem had any firsthand knowledge of how to organize a girls' boarding school; nevertheless, the various committees of the church forged ahead, creating a wealth of plans for the new building and copying the organization of the Girls' Boarding School in Bethlehem.[33] Prices for tuition were the same as Bethlehem's, twenty dollars a quarter. Course work included reading, writing, arithmetic, grammar, history, geography, German, and plain needlework. For an extra two dollars a quarter, the Sisters also offered lessons in drawing, music, and fancy needlework.[34]

Always interested in boosting their income, the Single Sisters agreed to do the laundry and cooking for the school, setting the meal menu and prices for boarding the same as Bethlehem's. Laundry cost three dollars per quarter for pupils under twelve years, and four dollars for those above that age. For food the Sisters charged six shillings, six pence per week to serve the girls milk, bread, and butter for breakfast; meat, vegetables, bread, and occasionally soup for dinner (served at midday); bread and butter at Vespers; and milk, warmed-up items, pancakes, mush, and chocolate for supper.[35]

As soon as the doors to the new Federal-style brick structure opened on July 16, 1805, the Girls' Boarding School was an immediate and overwhelming success. Close supervision of small groups of students by the Sisters ensured a homelike environment for the students. Because of what was then a curriculum of high level, as taught by the Sisters, and the personal attention they paid to the students, the boarding school's popularity soared.[36]

The Girls' Boarding School was a continued educational success throughout the nineteenth century and into the twentieth. By 1850 it had become known as Salem Female Academy, attracting daughters of the planter elite throughout the South. In the early twentieth century it split into Salem Academy and Salem College. Supplying the teachers and most of the support staff for the school permitted the Sisters to achieve their economic goal of generating a reliable income. In fact, their operation of the Girls' Boarding School was more successful than the Single Brothers' short-lived attempt to run a Boys' Boarding School. With time, however, the income generated by the school lessened, as increasing enrollment brought the need for new facilities and additional faculty, which diminished the Sisters' profits.

More important, as the nineteenth century wore on, the semicommunal ways of the church died out. Not only did the church's control over the congregation scale back dramatically, separating the sexes no longer seemed appropriate. Even in Salem the nuclear family eventually replaced the choirs as grown children went off to live and work on their own. As the population of Single Sisters aged and dwindled and the educational requirements of the teachers increased, they could no longer staff the school themselves. By the end of the nineteenth century, the Single Sisters' stake in the school had vanished.

The Single Sisters of Salem were a true exception to the condition of women in the North Carolina backcountry. While Moravian theology and their unusual choir system set Wachovia apart from the backcountry, these elements also made them unique in colonial and early national America. Rarely was so much economic and personal autonomy granted to "the weaker sex" as the Single Sisters had in Salem. Even the attendance and minor participation of married and single women at church board meetings was unusual for this period.

Moravian women filled many roles in their personal and spiritual lives; Moravian theology and the choir system not only allowed women to choose the type of life they wanted, but made it possible for them to live their lives in a fulfilling manner. The church's encouragement of personal autonomy, coupled with the Single Sisters' philosophy of independence for their sex, helped all Moravian women develop a sense of spirituality and self-esteem.

NOTES

1. Carl Bridenbaugh, *Myths and Realities: Societies of the Colonial South* (Baton Rouge: Louisiana State University Press, 1954), 127. For more information on the settlement of the North Carolina backcountry, see Robert W. Ramsey, *Carolina Cradle: Settlement of the Northwest Carolina Frontier, 1747–1762* (Chapel Hill: University of North Carolina Press, 1964); Johanna Miller Lewis, *Artisans in the North Carolina Backcountry* (Lexington: University Press of Kentucky, 1995), 17–33.

2. Johanna Miller Lewis, "Women and Economic Opportunity in the Colonial North Carolina Backcountry," in *Women and Freedom in Early America*, ed. Larry Eldridge (New York: New York University Press, 1996), 191–208.

3. Chester S. Davis, *Hidden Seed and Harvest: A History of the Moravians* (Winston-Salem: Wachovia Historical Society, 1973), 2–14.

4. Vernon Nelson, "The Moravian Church in America," in Mari P. Van Buigtenen, Cornelius Dekker, and Huib Leeuwenberg, eds., *Unitas Fratrum: Moravian Studies* (Utrecht: Rijksarchief, 1975), 145–46; see also Adelaide L. Fries, *The Moravians in Georgia, 1735–1740* (Winston-Salem: n.p., 1945). For an in-depth perspective of the Moravians and Zinzendorf's actions in Pennsylvania, see Sally Schwartz, *"A Mixed Multitude": The Struggle for Toleration in Colonial Pennsylvania* (New York: New York University Press, 1987), 120–21, 127–42.

5. In 1728 seven of the eight proprietors of the Carolinas sold their interest in

the colony back to the Crown. The eighth, John, Lord Carteret (later Lord Granville), declined to sell, and in 1744 George II granted Granville all the territory lying between the Virginia line on the north and the parallel of 35°34′ on the south to settle the matter. This tract of land, sixty miles wide and including approximately two-thirds of the colony's population, became known as the Granville District.

6. Nelson, 150; John Henry Clewell, *History of Wachovia in North Carolina: The Unitas Fratrum or Moravian Church in North Carolina during a Century and a Half, 1752–1902* (New York: Doubleday, Page, 1902), 2, 6–8; Hugh Talmage Lefler and Albert Ray Newsome, *North Carolina: The History of a Southern State,* 3d ed. (Chapel Hill: University of North Carolina Press, 1973), 86.

7. Beverly Smaby, *The Transformation of Moravian Bethlehem* (Philadelphia: University of Pennsylvania Press, 1988), 8. Christ's sacrifice became almost an obsession for them. According to what was sometimes called "Blood and Wounds Theology," constant and graphic depictions of Christ's suffering would remind people of their debt to him.

8. Daniel Thorp, *The Moravian Community in Colonial North Carolina* (Knoxville: University of Tennessee Press, 1989), 50.

As father and husband, a man represented both God and Christ and was, himself, a bride of Christ, because in Zinzendorf's theology all souls were female and married to their Savior. Women were brides of Christ in their own right, but as mothers and wives they also symbolized His mother—the Holy Ghost—and the whole Moravian Church in its capacity as the Bride of Christ. The marriage itself between earthly husband and wife not only embodied the loving relationship that existed between Christ and His church . . . but was also strongly identified with the eternal union between Christ and the souls of individual believers. . . . And when children arrived, they not only represented the purity and innocence of Christ but completed a domestic version of the Trinity.

9. Smaby, 10–11, 24; Frances Griffin, *Less Time for Meddling: A History of Salem Academy and College, 1772–1886* (Winston-Salem: John F. Blair, 1979), 11.

10. Smaby, 13.

11. S. Scott Rohrer, "Backcountry Haven: Community, Religion, and Society in the Moravian Settlement of Wachovia, N.C., 1750–1820" (paper presented at Cultural Adaptation in the Southern Colonial Backcountry Conference, October 1996). 1773 Salem Statutes, translated by Elisabeth Somer, Moravian Archives-Southern Province. In Wachovia four committees governed the Moravian Church (although their names, composition, and member selection varied over the years), and women sat on all but the Board of Supervisors.

12. Thorp, 82–83.

13. *Verlass der vier Synoden . . . von den Jahren 1764, 1769, 1775, 1782,* 113:11, 13, as quoted in Smaby, 168.

14. Smaby, 13; Thorp, 83.

15. Gillian L. Gollin, *Moravians in Two Worlds: A Study of Changing Communities* (New York: Columbia University Press, 1967), 17–18.

16. Bishop August Spangenberg to the Brothers in Wachovia, June 29, 1755, as quoted in Thorp, 44.

17. Lewis, *Artisans*, 37.

18. Smaby, 10, 185–86; Thorp, 83.

19. Lewis, "Women and Economic Opportunity."

20. Thorp, 55–56.

21. Philip Africa, "Slave Holding in the Salem Community, 1771–1851," *North Carolina Historical Review* 54 (July 1977): 271, 290; Griffin, 156. The community concern that governed the initial use of slaves in Wachovia gradually disappeared with the growing popularity of slave labor in the nineteenth century. However, the Moravians' unusual approach to dealing with slaves in the earlier years has given rise to a myth that Moravians did not really believe in slavery and used slaves only because there was no other source of labor. On the contrary, historian Jon Sensbach has shown that in the nineteenth century Moravians acted like other southerners in their procurement and treatment of slaves. See "'A Separate Canaan': The Making of an Afro-Moravian World in North Carolina, 1763–1856" (Ph.D. diss., Duke University, 1991).

22. In Salem, as the main congregation in Wachovia, most marriages were arranged by church leaders (including female leaders). Marriage was never forced on unwilling participants, however, and the Single Sisters (even though most of them did marry eventually) offered a lifelong alternative to women who did not wish to marry. In the country congregations, individuals married whom they wished; after a certain age the infrequent "old maid" would relocate to Salem and join the Sisters.

23. Smaby, 180–85.

24. The adult sex ratio in Wachovia moved from 100:0, or all male, in 1754 when Bethabara was settled, to 114:100 in 1771, the year Salem was settled. Among single adults, however, the ratio was more skewed, moving from 100:0 in 1754 to 152:100 in 1771. See Thorp, 47–52.

25. Unpublished minutes of the *Aufseher Collegium*, August 5, 1788, Archives of the Moravian Church in America, Southern Province, Winston-Salem, NC, on file at Old Salem, Inc. The translations of these unpublished minutes of the various governing bodies are courtesy of the Archives of the Moravian Church, Southern Province (MA-SP).

26. *Aeltesten Conferenz* minutes, April 19, 1979, MA-SP.

27. Quoted in Davis, 8; and Griffin, 7–8.

28. The exact date of the founding of the little girls' school is unknown. The first rent payment on the meeting house was recorded in the account book of the church, April 30, 1772, MA-SP.

29. Salem Diary, August 31, 1802; Adelaide L. Fries et al., eds., *Records of the Moravians in North Carolina* (Raleigh: North Carolina Historical Commission, 11 vols. 1922–1969), 5:2235, 2350, 2370. According to Mary Beth Norton in *Liberty's Daughters: The Revolutionary Experience of American Women, 1750–1800* (Boston: Little, Brown, 1980), North Carolina Congressman John Steele (who lived in Salisbury, across the Yadkin River from Salem) asked the Moravian Girls' School in Bethlehem to open to non-Moravians in the early 1780s (283–87). See also Christie Anne Farnham, *The Education of the Southern Belle: Higher Education in the Antebellum South* (New York: New York University Press, 1994), 36, 40, 89–90, 108, 121, 124, 144, 156, 182; Linda K. Kerber, *Women of the Republic* (New York: Norton, 1986), 190; Elizabeth Fox-Genovese, *Within the Plantation Household* (Chapel Hill: University of North Carolina Press, 1988), 46; Griffin, 5; Johanna Miller Lewis, "The Social and Architectural History of the Girls' Boarding School at Salem, N.C.," *North Carolina Historical Review* 66 (April 1989): 129.

30. Griffin, 34.

31. *Aeltesten Conferenz* minutes, November 1, 1802.

32. *Aeltesten Conferenz* minutes, January 20, 1803.

33. *Aeltesten Conferenz* minutes, January 25, 1803.

34. *Aeltesten Conferenz* minutes, February 1, 1804; Samuel Kramsch, "Terms and Conditions of the Boarding School for Female Education in Salem, N.C." [May 20, 1804], Siewers Room Collection, Gramley Library, Salem College, Winston-Salem, NC.

35. Kramsch; minutes of the *Aeltesten Conferenz*, April 4, 1804.

36. In *The Plantation Mistress*, Catherine Clinton described Salem Academy as "[p]erhaps the most famous and widely praised institution during this era" (New York: Pantheon, 1982), 126–28.

Chapter Seven

According to His Wish and Desire
Female Kin and Female Slaves in Planter Wills

Joan E. Cashin

EDITOR'S NOTE: *Women at the top of southern society lived in close proximity to women at the bottom. By 1860 Maryland was no longer a tobacco-based economy and almost half of its blacks were free. But about three-fourths of the white families in the richest cotton-growing areas of the South were still slaveholders. Yet in the South as a whole only one-fourth of whites owned slaves, and most of these held fewer than six. The census defined a planter as one owning twenty or more slaves; according to that definition, there were only 46,264 plantations in a white population of over eight million in 1860.*

Perhaps because African women, like Native American women, did most of the farming, Africans sold more men than women to Europeans. Of the estimated ten to twelve million slaves introduced into the New World, only 6 percent went to North America, and only there did the population grow by natural increase. For example, between 1700 and 1780, 850,000 slaves were imported into the British West Indies, compared to 250,000 to North America. However, by 1780 the former had a population of only 350,000, compared to North America's 575,000. Absentee landlords, the availability of low-cost slaves, and the greater profits to be had from using almost all arable land for sugar cultivation rather than food led to deadly conditions in the West Indies. Continuous importation of fresh slaves from Africa replaced those who had died. This replenishment resulted in Latin slavery retaining stronger cultural connections to Africa than was the case in British North America. Long before the slave trade in the United States became illegal in 1808, balanced sex ratios had been attained. Consequently, family formation could take place, and African American culture developed as an amalgam of various African ethnic traditions with adaptations from European and Indian cultures.

Slavery had been widespread in human societies from ancient times, perhaps arriving with agriculture, for more laborers meant more produce. Slavery among the Aztecs, Greeks, and Romans is well known. Indeed, slavery was not tied to race, even in colonial America. Charleston merchants encouraged Cherokees and Creeks to attack other Native American peoples to gain captives. In 1708 Charleston's population included 1,400 Indian slaves among 1,000 white families. Deadly diseases that diminished Indian populations and led to their dispersal resulted in the development of a biracial society in the South in which all Africans were deemed slaves unless they could show otherwise.

Arab Muslims had long traded for slaves in sub-Saharan Africa, and the continent was crisscrossed with slave trading networks for local consumption. However, slavery could take many forms. Some male slaves rose to positions of power, because the slaveholder could rely on the slave's loyalty not being compromised by ties to a lineage or family, and some women became wives, because their husbands could control their children, unlike other fathers in matrilineal societies. Slave children or their progeny eventually became accepted members of African societies.

Historically, female slaves have always and everywhere been subject to sexual exploitation. Evangelical religion prevented open relationships with slave women like those found in Latin America, but miscegenation was not uncommon. Because the economy of the middle and New England colonies was not based on large-scale production of staple crops, there was no interest sufficiently powerful to stop the egalitarian ethos of the American Revolution from abolishing slavery in the North. Northern evangelism of the 1830s promoted reform movements. One of these, abolition, painted the South as a brothel in its propaganda.

The South met such attacks by elaborating an ideology of planter paternalism in which the slaveholder was viewed as the head of a large family that included slaves. Placing white women on pedestals was a central strategy of this ideology, for slavery followed the status of the mother. If a biracial society is to be maintained, white women must remain faithful wives and exhibit cultural characteristics distinguishing them from slave women. Thus, they were idealized as pure, fragile flowers that could bloom only under the protection of white men. Slave women were stereotyped as the obverse — as strong as oxen and therefore natural field laborers and as wanton seducers of white men.

Despite paternalism, slave marriages had no legal validity, and the certitude of death ensured the breakup of many slave families upon the owner's decease. Access to control of economic resources was denied to planter mistresses, so planters' deaths marked major changes in their fortunes as well. Not only did

southern women of the highest and the lowest orders live in close proximity, but
their fates were determined to a large degree by the same men — the planters.

•   •   •

Virginia Woolf once remarked that old men caused a lot of heartache with
their wills, and the same could be said about planters in the antebellum
South.[1] Historians agree that inheritance can tell us much about family
relationships throughout the Western world. In the United States, scholars
have concentrated on the end of primogeniture and entail. Both practices
were outlawed throughout the country by the end of the eighteenth
century for intestates (men who died without valid wills) as inappropriate
for a republican society. But the movement toward equal treatment of
sons and daughters was slow; equitable distribution of property appeared
in parts of the South by the dawn of the nineteenth century, while discrimination against female heirs persisted in other sections of the region into
the late antebellum era. We know little about the treatment of widows in
planter wills and even less about slave women.[2]

The most comprehensive work on southern inheritance practices, Suzanne Lebsock's study of Petersburg, Virginia, posits fundamental differences in the ways that the sexes divided their estates. Lebsock argues that
most white men of all social classes gave equal shares to their children,
while most white women did not. Instead they rewarded their favorites,
usually their daughters, or helped out relatives in financial distress. They
also excluded heirs who had evidently displeased them in some way.
Lebsock calls this outlook "personalism" and believes that it is evidence
of a distinctive female culture. Furthermore, she finds a "special relationship" between white women and slave women. White women were more
likely than white men to free slaves in their wills, to try to prevent slaves
from being sold, or to give cash payments or lifetime support for slaves.
In general, they more often than white men expressed "particular attachments" for individual slaves in their wills.[3]

This essay explores how inheritance practices among antebellum planters affected white and black women and what those practices reveal about
gender and race relations on the plantation. It addresses a series of related
questions: Did planter widows serve as executors? Could they remarry if
they wished? Did they receive the dower that the law suggested? Did
daughters receive shares equal with sons? How were slave women treated
in wills? Our discussion is based on 102 wills written by planter men who

lived in six states from the Virginia Piedmont to the Texas frontier.[4] They wrote their last testaments between 1820 and 1860, with a median date of 1841. They had an average of six children, typically three daughters and three sons. These were large families by national standards, for the average American household in 1860 contained five persons (two parents and three children), and by regional standards, for most white southern families included five to seven persons. These planters were quite rich, too: the average slaveholding, forty-two, was well above the median of twenty-three for the entire South in 1860. Most of the authors were probably in poor health when they wrote their wills, for they typically wrote their last testaments about a year and a half before death.[5]

As we will see, most of these men saw themselves as patriarchs with the duty to provide for their dependents and the right to punish heirs as they saw fit. These men often buttressed their decisions by such emphatic statements as "I wish it distinctly understood that it is my wish" or "it is my will and desire that it remains So." What is more, the law made little difference in how these men divided their estates, for they frequently disregarded the spirit of legal reforms. Nor did urban residence make any difference; those planters were just as high-handed as men living in the countryside. Contrary to the findings in Petersburg, Virginia, most planter men throughout the South paid close attention to the particulars of family relationships and divvied up estates in highly "personalistic," inequitable ways. These wills provide the last chapter in a narrative of family relationships as the patriarchs perceived it, and most fathers calibrated their bequests to reflect that history.[6]

There is little evidence here of companionate marriage, the equitable partnership between peers that was becoming the ideal in the antebellum North. Nor do we see much evidence of the desire to treat all children fairly, male and female, that ordinarily characterizes the modern family. These men, rather, saw the family as a hierarchy with themselves at its head; most of them firmly believed that they knew what was best for their dependents. Nor is there much "paternalism" visible in how masters treated female slaves. Readers may recoil from the contents of many of these wills, for these testaments were about revenge as well as bounty, about power as well as love. As to how these testaments shaped the inner lives of white and black women and their relationships with each other, we can only hazard informed guesses. But the dynamics visible in these wills surely left their mark on them.[7]

The provisions for widows show that most planters did not think that women could manage a lot of property by themselves. Of the seventy-eight planters whose spouses were living when they wrote their wills, only a third (twenty-six) included the widow as an executor, considerably lower than in other American communities. Only six planters made their wives sole executor with complete freedom to dispose of the estate. The six wills were evenly distributed across the period; half were written before 1841, the median date for all wills. These planters owned fewer slaves than the average planter in this sample (twenty-eight), which confirms the findings of other scholars that the less valuable the estate, the more likely the widow was to be named executor. Several men also directed their sons to reside with the widow and manage her business affairs for the rest of her life.[8]

On the subject of the widow's remarriage, planters may have been guided largely by concern for their minor children. Remarriage penalties dated back to early modern England, but they seem to have been declining in much of antebellum America. Three-quarters of the men whose wives were living when they wrote their wills (fifty-eight) permitted widows to remarry without losing property, but nineteen penalized their wives, and they meant business: ten of them stipulated that their spouses would lose all of their property if they wed again. The others promised to hold back significant amounts of property, such as the house or a tract of land. Planters' views on the issue did not change over time; about half of each group of testators died before 1841. Those men who let their widows remarry without penalty owned close to the average number of slaves (forty-one), while the naysayers were richer, owning forty-nine slaves. Family size per se was not germane; the average number of offspring was six for each group, but the ages of those children may have been decisive. Among the men who permitted remarriage without penalty, only a third (34 percent) mentioned underage children, while half of the testators who penalized remarriage (53 percent) referred to children under twenty-one.[9]

The few men who explained these provisions underscored the supreme importance of providing for their young offspring. Blair Bolling of Virginia stated that he gave his estate to his wife, Penelope, so that she could support their children, but if she remarried, she would lose all of it except for income from some bondsmen. Another planter reminded his widow to use her property to support their underage children; if she remarried, her portion would be reduced from twenty-six slaves to nine. Very few of the testators mentioned their ages or that of their wives, but life expectancy for American men in this generation was the late forties. Since the typical plantation mistress was five or six years younger than her husband, many of these women were in middle age with several young children to raise as their husbands began pondering their wills. These men probably distrusted the motives of stepfathers who might waste the estate or mistreat the children, and they may have felt jealous about another man taking their place.[10]

Regarding the size of the widows' shares, the picture is decidedly mixed. Only about half got dower or more, and the richer the household, the worse the widows did. Under common law, all women lost control of their property when they married; if their husbands died intestate they received dower, which is one third of the real estate and the personal estate for life. The common law portrayed this as compensation for the wife's loss of property upon marriage and her contributions to the household's welfare. The widow's third had the force of tradition behind it, for this concept of dower reached back several centuries in English law. In America, it had the imprimatur of none other than Thomas Jefferson, who wrote this definition of dower into the Northwest Ordinance for men who died intestate. Furthermore, all six of the southern states under examination allowed widows to dissent from wills that did not give them dower.[11]

But in the early nineteenth century widows' rights were eroding all over the country. In order to facilitate trade, some states allowed dower to be converted into cash, and in 1818 the Supreme Court denied widows their traditional third in "unimproved" or uncultivated lands. The lawmakers in the six states under discussion may have intended to discourage widows' challenges, for some asked women to dissent within six months of the will's probate, even though it often took much longer to put a planter's estate in order, and other states made the process cumbersome. Alabama, for instance, required widows to submit a petition to five male commissioners. But most important, men who wrote wills could do whatever they wished with their property; in no state were they *required* to give dower. Tradition advised it, and the law suggested it with the example for intestates, but testamentary freedom was the foundation of property law, and planter men, like male property owners all over the United States, could devise their property however they wanted when they composed their wills.[12]

Savvy women could protect their property with a marriage settlement, roughly equivalent to today's prenuptial agreement, but settlements were rare among these families. Only one woman, Lucinda Easley of Perry County, Alabama, drew up a settlement before she wed, and her husband, Edward, the owner of twenty-seven slaves, honored that agreement when he died three years later. Unfortunately, he did not describe the terms of the settlement. Nor did any of the women in this study make use of the courts of equity, a parallel legal system originating in Tudor-Stuart England, as some women did in colonial and early national South Carolina.[13]

Most women instead had to rely on their husbands' largesse, and, paradoxically, their concern for the children. Even though almost all of these planters left their wives some property, most of them seemed to be primarily concerned with providing for their underage children. Seventy-eight men had spouses living when they wrote their wills, sixteen of which had to be dropped because they did not describe the widow's share clearly; this left sixty-two men whose wills can be examined. Slightly less than a third of these men (nineteen, or 31 percent) provided the traditional widow's dower. (Throughout these calculations, I took advancements of property—also called intervivos gifts—into account when figuring the widow's share.) Their widows typically got the dwelling, the furniture, and a third of the rest of the estate, in these families an average of eleven slaves. Some planters made it clear that they had chosen to follow traditional ideas about dower, such as the Virginian who gave his wife seven "dower negroes" (see table 1). Dower may well have served an important additional purpose of giving young children a secure home. The average number of children in these households was six, and well over a third of these household heads (eight, or 42 percent) mentioned underage children. The average number of slaves owned by these testators was thirty-six. Planters' views on dower did not change much over time; nine of the wills date before the median year, 1841.[14]

Meanwhile, slightly more than a quarter of the widows (seventeen, or 28 percent) received more than dower, an average of twenty-seven slaves (fifteen "extra" slaves above the widow's third). Some planters, obviously,

TABLE 1
Planter Widows and Dower

	Children	Slaves owned by testator	Slaves received
Dower	6	36	11
More than dower	6	37	27
Less than dower	5	57	9

N = 62 wills

could be quite generous. Henry Beverly of Virginia gave most of his ample estate to his wife, Frances, and appointed her sole executor. If she married again, he wanted the slave property to remain under her control "as though she were a femme sole," or single woman. (Since this clause infringed on the second husband's legal rights, and that state granted no property rights to married women, it could have been challenged in court.) William Venable was just as generous, giving his wife, Margaret, joint ownership of the plantation, sole ownership of seventeen slaves, the crops, livestock, and furniture, all of which she could dispose of "as she thinks best" among the children and grandchildren. These households contained an average of six children, and the planters owned an average of thirty-seven slaves. These wills are evenly distributed across time, with eight before 1841 and nine after that date. Again, these men may have intended the wife's share chiefly to provide for young children, since 42 percent (seven fathers) alluded to minors.[15]

A plurality of widows (twenty-six, or 42 percent) received less than dower, on average only nine slaves, ten fewer than the traditional widows' third. Testator attitudes did not change over time; half of these wills dated before 1841. A few planters were explicit about their actions: Samuel McGovern of Polk County, Texas, gave his wife sixteen bondsmen "in lieu of her dower," which would have given her twenty. He and the other men said nothing about why they devised these amounts, but demographics yield some clues. These families were smaller (an average of five children) and older (nine, or 35 percent, alluded to minors) than other households. They were also richer, holding an average of fifty-seven slaves, which supports the hypothesis of other scholars that the richer the family, the worse the widows do. Finally, we cannot discount more private motives, such as in the case of William Hootsall of Adams County, Mississippi, who alone among the 102 men lived apart from his spouse. He gave his wife, Polly, less than dower—part ownership in some slaves and the plantation she lived on in Louisiana. Then he made sure that she would never become executor by methodically setting up a line of succession among male friends and relatives in both states.[16]

What is particularly striking, two of these planters left their wives absolutely no property, and another threatened to do so, all three of them Virginians. William Higginbotham of Amherst County gave his entire estate to his children and grandchildren and simply asked a son to provide for his widow, Mary. John Hatcher of Cumberland County allowed his wife to have the profits generated by his estate but divided the rest of the property among his children. Higginbotham wrote his will in 1832 and Hatcher five years later, and both were less wealthy than the typical planter in this study, for Higginbotham owned thirty-two slaves and Hatcher twenty-three. The private history of these relationships is concealed from view, but Higginbotham referred to his wife as "beloved," implying, perhaps, that he was not reacting to some perceived wrong but had simply decided that she could not manage property of her own. Hatcher did not even mention his wife's name, which may suggest that he did not feel much affection for her. William Warwick of Amherst County informed his wife, Frances, that she would receive nothing from his estate if she tried to claim any property beyond what his will provided for her. He too was comparatively less wealthy (he owned twenty-five slaves), but offered no explanation for his actions.[17]

Widows in those states with Married Woman's Property Acts did not benefit very much when it came to their right to dispose of property after their husbands' deaths. In the wake of the panic of 1837, Mississippi passed the nation's first Married Woman's Property Act in 1839. Lawmakers designed the bill primarily to allow men to shelter their property from creditors in hard times, not to enhance women's rights, but it did concede to widows the right to devise property as they wished. Other southwestern states passed similar laws, Texas in 1846 and Alabama in 1848, while Virginia and the Carolinas did not extend these property rights to married women until the Reconstruction era. Among the twenty-nine planters from southwestern states who had wives living when they composed their wills, only seven granted them the right to bequeath property in their own wills as they wanted.[18]

Even more surprising, three of the seven planters wrote their wills *before* the laws changed. Philip Pitman of Montgomery County, Alabama, one such man ahead of his time, left much of his estate to his wife, Phereba, in 1820 and said that she could distribute it "as she by her last will and testament may direct." These seven men were unremarkable in other respects, raising an average of five children and owning an average of forty slaves. Among the twenty-two men who did not grant their widows the right to dispose of property as they wished, eleven wrote their wills *after* the reforms. When Abner Mardis of Adams County, Mississippi, divided his estate in 1850, eleven years after the passage of the state's Married Woman's Property Act, he stipulated how her share (a plantation, furniture, livestock, and nine slaves) should be apportioned among three of their six children upon her death. Just as in the case with dower, attitudes among planter men seem to have operated more or less independently of changes in law codes.[19]

The picture for daughters is also mixed, although daughters from the richest families tended to do better, in contrast to how their mothers did. Since the beginning of the nineteenth century, all six of the states under consideration required that the property of intestates be divided equally among daughters and sons, but, just as in the case of the widow's dower, the law did not require men who wrote their wills to partition their estates in equal shares.[20] Once again, planter behavior lagged behind changes in intestacy law. Among the 102 wills, twenty-three had to be dropped because the size of the shares was unclear; in the remaining seventy-nine wills, only seventeen provided for roughly equal distribution of property among daughters and sons. On average these daughters received thirteen slaves each. (Again, I included all property advancements when calculating the shares.) These attitudes toward equity among children represented the vanguard of change, since eleven of these wills were written after 1841. The fathers had small families, an average of five children, and they were extremely rich, the owners on average of seventy slaves, more than half again as many as the typical planter in this sample (see table 2).[21]

Several of these fair-minded planters stated their intentions with unmistakable clarity. John Dennis declared that his five sons and only daughter should receive shares of exactly the same size. Others took deliberate steps to eliminate any possible inequity. George Shackleford gave land to his four sons and cash payments to his four daughters to make their shares equal to those of their brothers. It may be instructive that the richest man of them all, Benjamin Roach of Adams County, Mississippi, wanted his vast estate dispensed equally among his five children. When he distributed over four hundred slaves and forty-five

TABLE 2
Childrens' Shares in Planter Wills

	Children	Slaves owned by testators	Slaves received by daughters
Equitable wills	5	70	13
Crudely inequitable wills	5	37	4
No gender pattern	7	33	1–16
Adult children singled out	7	37	4+/-6

N = 79 wills

thousand acres of land, he gave his daughter, Mary, a share equal to those of her four brothers. Roach added that she, not her husband, should have full control over her share.[22]

Most adult daughters nevertheless learned that unequal division of property was the norm. Sixty-two planters, over three-quarters of the seventy-nine men, wrote wills that were inequitable in some fashion, but the inequities took some unexpected forms. Crude gender discrimination was rare. Only nine blatantly favored sons over daughters, and their attitudes trailed those of their peers, for seven of these men wrote wills before 1841. The average number of children for these families was five, and these men were less affluent than most planters in this study, owning thirty-seven slaves on average. Among the nine fathers, four men bequeathed only slaves to their daughters while giving sizable tracts of land, slaves, and other property to their sons. Four other men gave both land and slaves to their children but divided the property in openly inequitable ways; the daughters in these wills received an average of four slaves each. A ninth father, James Dozier, lent shares of his estate to his two daughters but gave shares outright to his three sons, noting in passing that he wanted to be "just" to his sons.[23]

Another set of fathers, eighteen in number, favored some groups of children over others, with no gender pattern apparent. Aside from the above-average family size (seven children) and below-average slaveholdings (thirty-three), it is hard to generalize about these men. Nine wrote their wills before 1841, so there is no change over time. Some daughters came out ahead of their siblings, while others received less property than their brothers and sisters, in what seem to be highly idiosyncratic outcomes. Fathers kept silent on the reasons for their decisions, even though the property differentials could be large, ranging from one to sixteen slaves per heir. William Falconer, one of two men giving precise dollar amounts for all the shares, left his unmarried daughter Henrietta the smallest cash gift of his eleven children ($2,200) but bequeathed the largest cash gift to his daughter Martha Henry ($4,215), with amounts for his remaining five daughters and three sons spread out in between. William Archer gave his two daughters $5,000 each, while his four sons received amounts ranging from $1,500 to $12,000.[24]

Most of the men who wrote inequitable wills, thirty-five in all, set apart individual children of either sex to be favored or punished. They gave extra property to adult sons and daughters who pleased them and withheld property, either the entire share or most of it, from offspring who had somehow disappointed them. William Davenport, a South Carolinian, gave his five offspring *"Equal"* shares when he drafted his will in 1840, but then changed his mind. He added a codicil two years later that gave two children less valuable chattel, implying that they had quarreled with the family. The average number of children in these families was seven, which may have helped fathers rationalize these decisions, and the average slaveholding was thirty-seven. Such men were bringing up the rear, so to speak, for twenty-one of these wills were written in or before 1841.[25]

All of these planters and their adult children appear to have engaged in some intense dialogues over what kind of behavior one generation owed another. These exchanges must have happened more often between generations of men than between fathers and daughters, for more sons are singled out for rewards (thirteen sons, seven daughters) or punishments (fourteen sons, three daughters). The fathers were more generous with "good" sons, giving them eight extra slaves on average, while "good" daughters received only four extra bondsmen. They dealt more harshly with "bad" daughters, leaving them six fewer slaves than the other children, while the "bad" sons received four fewer bondsmen. These fathers may have believed that their daughters' husbands would provide for them, or they may have been more angry with their daughters, whom they may have expected to conform readily to their wishes.

When planters favored adult sons, they picked out one or on rare occasions two for extra gifts of property. They apparently did not reward oldest sons; only four men even mentioned birth order, and just one, John Harmon of Newberry County, South Carolina, favored his firstborn by giving the home plantation to him and his sons after him, for life. Most fathers did not explain their motives, but the few who did rewarded sons who helped them with business affairs. William Gaines left his sons Richard and Robert an extra thousand dollars each because they provided "valuable services" in managing his property. Hodijah Meade gave his son William a plantation in Amelia County, Virginia, and made him sole executor with authority to distribute the rest of the estate as he saw fit. He asked his son to "stand in the place of a parent to my other children" and added that William was worthy of this responsibility.[26]

Fathers who punished sons singled out one or sometimes two, but their displeasure rarely cost the scions a great deal of property. Most planters did not elaborate on their motives, probably because these provisions were not unusual or because family members knew something of the reasons. Fleming Palmore denied two of his four sons ownership of their shares and asked friends to manage the property for them, declaring that his property should be partitioned as he deemed "desirable." He noted that the executors, which included a third son, would understand his motives. A few planters hinted that a kind of "black sheep" syndrome was at work. Martin Hancock excluded his "unfortunate" namesake from the estate and asked two sons to support him with investment income, implying that young Martin was incompetent or perhaps incapacitated. Other fathers attempted to rein in the profligate. Joseph Binford stated in a codicil that all of the property he had originally presented to his son Thomas should go to his son John instead, that John was to support his brother but would not be liable for his debts, and that if Thomas died without "children lawfully begotten," his share would go to Binford's nine other offspring.[27]

Similarly, when fathers rewarded their adult daughters, they singled out one or on occasion two favorites who had behaved well by patriarchal standards. William Branch Giles gave his place of residence to his unmarried daughter Harriet because she had managed his "domestic interior affairs" for some years "much to my satisfaction." Giles did not say why he bequeathed another daughter, Ann Conway, a plantation that he described as "probably" more valuable than the land he gave his other offspring, but it may have been for similar reasons. In the few cases in which the planter described the partition of land, the differentials could be sizable. Ophelia Williford, daughter of John Williford, received three tracts of land in Bertie County, North Carolina, while one of her brothers received one tract and another brother and five sisters received none.[28]

When fathers elected to punish individual daughters, they gave no explanations at all. Gabriel Jones bequeathed his daughter Sally Tunstall the grand sum of five dollars, but gave three other daughters and a son several slaves and large tracts of land. For good measure, he excluded Tunstall's children from ever receiving any slaves or land. William Elliott left his daughter Mary J. Gillespie whatever cash might be on hand when the will was executed, which was to stand "in the place and stead of other property"; if there was no cash on hand, she received nothing. By contrast, he gave his six sons and two other daughters several slaves each, livestock, and furniture, plus a hefty tract of land for one son. Something had gone wrong between these fathers and daughters, but exactly what is occluded from our sight.[29]

Many inequitable wills also contained special clauses that gave property to heirs on condition that they behaved in a certain way. Planters designed some clauses to meddle in the lives of the heirs, others to protect them, and still others to threaten them, but all reflected the assumption that father knew best. Three men wrote clauses requiring that slaves belonging to their spinster daughters stay on the home plantation as long as the women remained unmarried, thereby preventing their daughters from exercising their rights as femme soles, to whom the law granted the capacity to dispose of property as they wished. One planter added for emphasis that this was his "will and desire." John Ashurst tried to control the residence of his five minor children (two daughters and three sons), for he stipulated that they could not live with his two married children. His wife had already passed away, and he had not remarried, yet Ashurst did not state exactly what he expected the young people to do—go to boarding school, perhaps? He also interfered with the rights of his adult children, who were "settled to themselves," to decide for themselves whether any of their siblings might live with them.[30]

Several other adult women discovered that their fathers were keenly interested in controlling their behavior. William Winans of Wilkinson County, Mississippi, promised his daughter Ann tha   e named one of her sons after him, the infant son would receive a   who would be hers to manage until he came of age. John Brooch,   ter from Charlotte County, Virginia, attempted to intervene in an   ore significant part of his daughter's life. If Ann Brooch married   y to my well known wishes," she would receive a legacy of exac   dollar, but if she married the man he had selected for her, she   tain thirty-eight slaves and some land. Brooch did not provide i   on either suitor, and the will does not throw any more light   asse between father and daughter. No other daughter and   of the sons in any other will were subjected to such pressure on the choice of a mate.[31]

William Glenn of Cumberland County, Virginia, made a truly extraordinary attempt to intervene in his daughter's marriage. He added a codicil to his will giving Ann Harris one dozen slaves on the condition that she have "heirs of her body" with her spouse, Henry St. George Harris. To make sure that his intent was clear, he appointed his son-in-law an executor, along with Ann's brother William, Jr., and a male friend. Glenn took this step upon some deliberation, attaching the codicil five months after he penned the will in March 1844. The implication is that she could choose to bear children, and the further implication is that Ann Harris had either ceased sexual relations with her husband or was using some kind of birth control. Whatever the specifics of the case, William Glenn exerted the utmost financial pressure on his daughter to have children, surely one of the most intimate aspects of a married woman's life.[32]

The patriarchs could protect their female heirs, of course, as well as bully them. Eight men set up trusts to shield them from wayward sons-in-law or, in a few families, for daughters-in-law to safeguard them from the writer's own sons. That the motives in these wills was protective is evident from the language in William Tigner's testament. This planter from Wilkinson County, Mississippi, left ten slaves, 375 acres of land, and $1,000 in trust for his daughter Sarah J. Womack. Tigner added that if Womack's marriage ended by death "or otherwise," the property would go to the Womack children or to Sarah's siblings, not to his son-in-law. Three of these eight fathers set up trusts to benefit their daughters-in-law and grandchildren. Pascal Leigh created a trust of six slaves for the wife and children of his son Pascal, Jr., placed another son in charge of the trust, and then sealed it off so that it could not be used to pay his son's debts. The trusts usually contained some combination of slaves, land, and cash, ranging from six to twenty-four slaves, the large amounts of property suggesting that the sons-in-law and sons had major deficiencies in the fathers' eyes. In these families, some women benefited from the patriarchal ideal.[33]

If all else failed to persuade legatees to follow the fathers' wishes, the patriarchs resorted to threats. Ten planters threatened to disinherit their heirs, as the law allowed all testators to do. Six leveled threats against their female legatees, with Isham Harvey qualifying as the most egregious. If any one of his ten children, including his four daughters, objected to the will, that child would receive a total of five dollars. James McDade was just as blunt, telling his four daughters and three sons that the local probate court would apportion his estate for them if they could not accept the terms of his will. In the same spirit, William Branch Giles promised to strip two daughters and a son of their shares if they disputed his decision to sell a particular tract of land.[34]

Some of these threatening wills contain clauses that are truly repellent to modern readers. Henry Beverly admitted that he had hired out the slaves that his mother-in-law had bequeathed to his young daughter Mary, keeping the proceeds himself. He warned his daughter, now an adult, that she would receive nothing from his estate if she asked for the money. Otherwise she could have the slaves. Martin Hancock lent his daughter-in-law Sally, widow of John, a tract of land and four slaves but threatened to pass her share to his grandson if she remarried. (Strangely enough, he did not threaten his own wife with disinheritance if she remarried.) These men are atypically nasty, but they laid open the power dynamics within the planter family in frank language.[35]

When planters devised their female slaves, the patriarchal values of duty and privilege appear again but in exaggerated form. When a slaveowner died, it was customary for a member of the white family to read the will aloud to the assembled slaves, so most of them knew its contents. A tiny number of slaves benefited from the master's approval: planters named twelve women (2 percent of the 4,283 slaves in this study) for preferential treatment. Only three planters liberated any slaves, one each. The infinitesimal number of emancipations is probably due to the economic value of slave property and the fact that the antebellum law codes made it difficult, or in some states, impossible, to free slaves. These men owned the average number of bondsmen (forty-two) and wrote their wills on widely dispersed dates; there was no discernible trend over time.

But they did have very small numbers of white children (an average of three), which may have made it easier for them to part with some of their estate—even though two of these freed slaves may have been blood relations. Tarlton Woodson of Virginia stated in his will of 1855 that a bondsman named Henry Milton was to be freed, but only after Woodson's wife Elizabeth died, maybe to spare her having to confront the nature of Henry's relationship with the master. Woodson asked one of his white sons to "treat him kindly" and help Henry leave the state if he wished. He made no provisions for Henry's mother, a slave identified as Louisa, or her other children. In 1860 David Pitts required that William, son of Lucinda, be apprenticed to a blacksmith, hired out, emancipated, and sent away from Alabama to a free state. He too made no provisions for the boy's mother, but he and Woodson were both likely providing for their mulatto sons.[36]

Joseph Johnson of Mississippi made a similar provision for a slave woman, but added a distinctive twist. In his will of 1832 he freed a woman called Eady, but also required his wife, Rachael, to support her. After his wife's death, his white son had to support Eady with the labor of five "first rate" slaves. These provisions, unique among all the wills examined in this article, suggest that Eady was either Johnson's daughter or sexual partner and that she was some years younger than Johnson's wife. Rachael Johnson's reactions are impossible to discern, but she may have suspected something after the will was probated, if she did not already, or she may have exhibited that capacity for not seeing that white southern women could demonstrate when evidence of miscegenation appeared on their own plantations. Joseph Johnson may have relied on her blindness to such implications, or perhaps he hoped for forgiveness, or maybe he intended to humiliate his wife. The will says nothing about his motives, which may have been a mix of conflicting emotions, a mystery even to himself. Nor does the document say anything about how the five other slaves felt about laboring to support Eady, or what she may have thought about being tethered to the Johnson family as an ostensibly free woman for the rest of her days.[37]

Personal intimacy with the master obviously did not result in freedom for many slave women, but it may have brought significant improvements in their living conditions after his death. One Virginian, Pascal Leigh, provided for the lifetime support of a bondswoman, asking that Isabel be given a "comfortable home." Four other planters allowed slaves to choose their owners, and they permitted more females than males to do so, probably because these women had some kind of private relationship with the master, either as sexual partner, daughter, or nurse to his white offspring. Joseph Russell let "My old woman Milly" select her owner, and William Winans of Mississippi allowed the "old female servants" Dolly and Milly to pick their owners among his four white children. Arthur Barrett, a South Carolinian, directed that the slave Lawesa choose her owner among the writer's seven white offspring, but only after his wife died. Just one master, Blair Bolling, allowed a man to select his owner.[38]

A mere half dozen planters made some reference to preserving slave families, yet again they favored women over men, six to five. Planters evidently perceived the slave "family" as the mother-child dyad, with the slave father left out, almost as if they believed themselves to be the head of the slave family. Benjamin Palmore, for example, dictated that Phebe, her children, and her grandchildren be kept together and given to the writer's wife and children, but said nothing about the fathers. John Sims declared that Milly and her daughters could not be sold, although he too kept silent about the father. Two planters seemed to be intent on preserving individual families, one who wanted three slaves, including Jane, to live together with the writer's wife, and another insisted that a trio of slaves, including Caroline, remain together after his death. Other planters gave a nod to the paternalistic ethos and made more general provisions without naming names. Isham Harvey directed that all his slaves should be kept in Virginia and added that "having raised them principally in families it is my desire that they should remain so as much as circum-stances will admit." An Alabaman asked that his slaves be divided by families "as much as possible," and a Texan bequeathed slaves to his heirs in family groups. But the majority of owners, knowing that some or all slave families would be split up by their deaths, did not even try to conform to the paternalistic ideal.[39]

The master's favor could turn to disapproval, as some slave women realized. When planters went out of their way to destroy slave families, they singled out six women by name and not one man, suggesting that their relationships with slave women had a more volatile, unpredictable quality than those with slave men. William Sandidge declared that Alcey and her three children had to be divided among his white grandchildren, and Benjamin Palmore, who protected Phebe and her children from being split up, required that Angelina, Peggy, and their children be distributed among his six white children. Samuel Woodfin insisted that Jane and her children be divided between his white children and their heirs. Some planters robbed individual bondswomen of their children, such as the man who dictated that Bridget's daughter Mary go to his white daughter, or the one who decreed that the first living child born to Fanny would go to one of his white grandchildren. Of course many other masters broke up slave families without bothering to name names, such as the planter who wanted his slaves divvied up by lot among his seven white children. All of these divisions must have terrified slaves, as they may have been intended to do.[40]

When white men sold individual slaves, however, they were more likely to name males. They kept their counsel on the reasons, which may have included pure economics, because males often brought higher prices, or efforts to get rid of unruly men, who usually posed a greater threat than rebellious women. In any case, four planters directed that individual slaves had to be sold, a total of five men, two women, and several children of unknown gender. Thomas Barton, for one, demanded that the slave Sam be sold. Another planter broadcast an all-purpose threat: if a slave of either gender became "unmanageable," the executor was to sell that slave. Planters' views of chattel of both sexes may best be summed up by Blair Bolling, who told his executors to sell any slave if necessary to purchase other property that was "better suited to the use of my [white] family or farm."[41]

Like Squire Bolling, most planters were mainly interested in meeting the needs of their white families when they devised their slaves. They followed the sexual division of labor and matched up most of their slave bequests by gender. These men wrote seventy-one bequests involving eighty-four slaves mentioned by name, and the majority (fifty-seven) provided that female slaves go to female heirs and male slaves to male heirs. James McDade, for instance, asked his executors to provide a male carpenter for his son Richard. Planters sometimes matched bequests by age as well as gender, giving young slaves to young heirs. Robert Harris left a young female slave to each white daughter and a young male slave to each white son as they married or came of age. These provisions may have reflected the gendered worldview of planter men and reinforced a gendered worldview among slaves.[42]

Individual black women could be yoked to white women in other ways, most often via wills that tied their fates to events in the lives of the mistress or her daughters. William Elliott did so when he told his wife, Sally, that seventeen of her slaves (gender unknown) would be divided among his nine children if she remarried. Another planter declared that the eight slaves (gender also unknown) he left to his wife would be dispersed among his white children if she remarried. In other cases, masters linked the fates of African American women to the fertility of white women. Daniel Rudd bequeathed nine slaves, including five females, to his daughter Sallie and dictated that they be divided among his five other children if Sallie died without issue. Jonathan Davenport left eight slaves, including three females, to his daughter Aimy and declared that they would be divided among Aimy's three siblings if she died childless. These clauses, so menacing from the perspective of the slave quarters, probably made black women acutely aware of events in the white family.[43]

In a few instances, planters put the destinies of slave women directly into the hands of white women. One man left the slave woman Rosah to his widow to "dispose of as she thinks proper," and another gave his wife a slave woman Eliza and her three youngest children, plus the slave Esther and her three children, to do with as she wished. (He made no reference to Eliza's older children.) Sometimes white women could choose among the slaves, deciding their fates after the will was probated. A Texan allowed his daughter to select one of two slave girls, Rean or Elisa, and a Virginian permitted his wife to choose four of the fourteen slaves he bequeathed to her. These provisions no doubt affected relations between slaves and white women in ways that we can only speculate about. If a black woman wanted to stay on the plantation, it would have been in her interest to cultivate the mistress's approval; if not, it would have been in her interest to provoke a sale. If the slave was also the master's daughter or sexual partner, the potential for resentments, even hatreds, on both sides was great.[44]

In light of these patterns, we might ask, did planter attitudes on race bear any relationship to their attitudes on gender? In other words, did white men who had egalitarian attitudes on gender in the white family also demonstrate any concern for slaves? The evidence in these wills suggests that any connection was tenuous at best. Among the six planters who made wives sole executor, only one, Joseph Johnson, took any kind of beneficial action by freeing a slave woman, and this gesture is somewhat ambiguous. Planters who treated their white daughters fairly proved to be no more likely to take steps to free, support, or assist slaves in any way. Among the seventeen egalitarian fathers, only one, John Sims, took protective steps of any kind toward slaves by stipulating that three individuals could not be sold. The white family apparently belonged to one universe, and the slaves to another.[45]

These wills address another long-standing issue, the relationship between legal change and behavior patterns. Did the law codify existing behavior, or did changes in the law provoke changes in behavior? These planter men, born in the late eighteenth century or early nineteenth century, constituted the first post-primogeniture generation, yet they were slow to adopt the egalitarian outlook that Thomas Jefferson and other lawmakers tried to promote when they abolished the old practices. The carapace of habit, custom, and ingrained belief took much longer to break. Only in the 1840s and 1850s did some of them begin to practice the equitable inheritance among their daughters and sons that law codes in the older states had suggested in the late eighteenth century. Yet another generation may have had to pass before white elites in the South embraced the practice. In the antebellum South, testamentary freedom may have had the inadvertent effect of strengthening the patriarchal family, for it permitted men to reward and punish children at will or give widows whatever they deemed proper.[46]

We might also ask, how did these high-handed men and their arbitrary wills affect the emotional lives of women on the plantation? We can only conjecture, but all of these wills, both the generous and the punitive, may have had the effect of binding white women to powerful men. A few individuals must have balked, as Ann Brooch did when she refused to marry the man her father selected, but more women may have decided to accept inequity, to resign themselves to it. If a white woman wanted to inherit a sizable share of the estate, it would be prudent to try to avoid challenging the patriarch.[47] Most black women had the resources of the slave community to draw upon in resisting the master, and some no doubt rebelled against his authority. Yet female slaves remained the ultimate hostages to patriarchal favor, because the master could destroy their families with a stroke of the pen. Some may have decided that it was wiser under these cruel circumstances to win the master's approval, or at the minimum try to avoid provoking his wrath, if only to keep their loved ones nearby. More research is necessary on this topic, but these wills suggest that the statute books did not matter very much when a planter wrote his last testament. Any woman, black or white, who questioned the wishes of the patriarch could pay dearly for it. He was a law unto himself.

NOTES

1. Virginia Woolf, *Three Guineas* (New York: Harcourt Brace Jovanovich, 1966), 67–68. The author thanks Kenneth Lockridge, Lynn Lyerly, and Thomas Price for their trenchant criticisms of drafts of this article.

2. Jack Goody, introduction to *Family and Inheritance: Rural Society in Western Europe, 1200–1800,* ed. Jack Goody, Joan Thirsk, and E. P. Thompson (Cambridge: Cambridge University Press, 1976), 1–9; Carole Shammas, Marylynn Salmon, and Michel Dahlin, *Inheritance in America: From Colonial Times to the Present* (New Brunswick: Rutgers University Press, 1987), 30–35, 64–65, 108; Michael Grossberg, *Governing the Hearth: Law and the Family in Nineteenth-Century America* (Chapel Hill: University of North Carolina Press, 1985), 4–30. See John E. Crowley, "Family Relations and Inheritance in Early South Carolina," *Histoire Social/Social History* 17 (May 1984): 35–57; J. W. Deen, Jr., "Patterns of Testation: Four Tidewater Counties in Colonial Virginia," *American Journal of Legal History* 16 (1972): 154–76; C. Ray Keim, "Primogeniture and Entail in Colonial Virginia," *William and Mary Quarterly,* 3d ser., 25 (1968): 550–57; Daniel Blake Smith, *Inside the Great House: Planter Family Life in Eighteenth-Century Chesapeake Society* (Ithaca: Cornell University Press, 1980), 231–48; Jonathan M. Wiener, *Social Origins of the New South: Alabama, 1860–1885* (Baton Rouge: Louisiana State University Press, 1978), 236; Steven Hahn, *The Roots of Southern Populism: Yeomen Farmers and the Transformation of the Georgia Upcountry, 1850–1890* (New York: Oxford University Press, 1983), 78–80; Jane Turner Censer, *North Carolina Planters and Their Children, 1800–1860* (Baton Rouge: Louisiana State University Press, 1984), 105–8, 117; Orville Vernon Burton, *In My Father's House Are Many Mansions: Family and Community in Edgefield, South Carolina* (Chapel Hill:

executors usually asked a son to serve with her; the average number of executors was two people. Most planters were loath to include women as witnesses to their wills, for only 5 women appeared among the 287 witnesses for the 102 documents.

In the colonial era, men in all regions more frequently appointed women as executors, from 40 percent of male testators to over 90 percent; see Linda E. Speth, "More Than Her 'Thirds': Wives and Widows in Colonial Virginia," *Women and History* 4 (winter 1982): 23; Narrett, *Inheritance*, 107; Crowley, "Family Relations and Inheritance," 45; Kulikoff, *Tobacco and Slaves*, 190; Lois Green Carr and Lorena S. Walsh, "The Planter's Wife: The Experience of White Women in Seventeenth-Century Maryland," *William and Mary Quarterly*, 3d ser., 34, no. 4 (1977): 556. Speth (23) and Crowley (46) point out that the percentage of females who were sole executor declined over time, and Lebsock, *Free Women*, 37–38, finds that none of the very rich appointed widows as executors.

9. Shammas et al., *Inheritance in America*, 28–29. Joan R. Gundersen and Gwen Victor Gampel, "Married Women's Legal Status in Eighteenth-Century New York and Virginia," *William and Mary Quarterly*, 3d ser., 39 (January 1982): 122, discover that 6 percent of colonial Virginians penalized remarriage; Pease and Pease, *Ladies, Wenches, and Women*, 106, find that five of sixty-nine men of all social classes in antebellum Charleston punished remarriage of widows; Lebsock, *Free Women*, 272 n. 39, discovers that 15 percent of men who wrote wills between 1831 and 1860 penalized remarriage.

10. Will of Blair Bolling, probated 5 August 1839, Will Book 11, Powhatan Co., Va.; Will of William Elliott, probated 16 June 1856, Will Book 10, Prince Edward Co., Va.; Censer, *Planters and Children*, 91–92; Burton, *In My Father's House*, 118; Jonathan M. Wiener, "Female Planters and Planters' Wives in Civil War and Reconstruction: Alabama, 1850–1870," *Alabama Review* 30 (April 1977): 145; Wells, *Revolutions in Americans' Lives*, 126–27. The only planter who gave his age was sixty-five; see Will of William Tigner, written 9 May 1854, Record of Wills, Wilkinson Co., Miss. This overriding concern for minor children may explain why only four planters left bequests for relatives beyond the nuclear family.

11. *Abridgment of the Public Permanent Laws of Virginia* (Richmond: Augustine Davis, 1796), 83; Hen. Potter, J. L. Taylor, and Bart. Yancey, eds., *Laws of the State of North Carolina*, 2 vols., rev. ed. (Raleigh: J. Gales, 1821), 1:469–70; John G. Aiken, ed., *Statutes at Large of South Carolina*, vol. 2; *A Digest of the Laws of the State of Alabama* (Philadelphia: Alexander Towar, 1833), 129; A. Hutchinson, ed., *Code of Mississippi* (Jackson: A. Hutchinson, 1848), 620–22; H. P. N. Gammel, ed., *The Laws of Texas, 1822–1897*, 5 vols., intro. C. W. Raines (Austin: Gammel Book Company, 1898), 2:149–51. The law defined dower as either the absolute ownership of a third of the property (called fee simple or absolute estate), or the use of a third of the property (called a life estate), or some combination of both. Gundersen and Gampel, "Married Women's Legal Status," 121, note that Virginians rarely challenged their husbands' wills.

12. Marlene Stein Wortman, ed., *Women in American Law*, 2 vols. (New York: Holmes and Meier, 1985), 1:18; Pease and Pease, *Ladies, Wenches, and Women*, 91; Morton J. Horwitz, *The Transformation of American Law, 1780–1860* (Cambridge: Harvard University Press, 1977), 56–58; Hutchinson, *Code of Mississippi*, 623, 621; Harry Toulmin, ed., *A Digest of the Laws of the State of Alabama* (Cahawba, Ala.: Ginn and Curtis, 1823), 382, 259; Shammas et al., *Inheritance in America*, 12, 22, 22–26.

13. Will of Edward Easley, appraised 6 December 1844, Estate Records of Perry Co., Ala.; Marylynn Salmon, "Women and Property in South Carolina: The Evidence from Marriage Settlements, 1730 to 1830," *William and Mary Quarterly*, 3d ser., 39 (October 1982): 655–85; Shammas et al., *Inheritance in America*, 34. Lebsock, *Free Women*, 72, and Censer, *Planters and Children*, 74–76, find that marriage settlements were rare. See also Thomas Price, "Palmettos and Property: Historical Memory and Political Culture in Early National South Carolina" (Ph.D. diss., University of Illinois at Chicago, 1995).

14. Will of Benjamin Palmore; Salmon, "Women and Property," 655–85. Most of the land was located in the testator's home state, much of it in their home counties; unfortunately most planters did not give exact acreage. Crowley, "Family Relations and Inheritance," 44, finds that three-fifths of the widows received dower in eighteenth-century South Carolina; Kulikoff, *Tobacco and Slaves*, 191, discovers that between 17 percent and 32 percent of wills in colonial Chesapeake counties provided for dower or less than dower. In some states, the law considered slaves to be part of realty, and in other states, part of personalty, and in yet others, it was left up to the testator.

15. Will of Henry S. Beverly, probated 2 March 1837, Will Book 7, Nottaway Co., Va.; Will of William H. Venable, probated 15 September 1856, Will Book 10, Prince Edward Co., Va. Speth, "More Than Her 'Thirds,' " 17–20, suggests that testators in colonial Virginia exceeded dower when they had young children. Carr and Walsh, "The Planter's Wife," 568, find that 24 percent of men in eighteenth-century St. Mary's County, Maryland, gave widows more than dower; Speth (16–17) discovers three-quarters of testators in eighteenth-century Virginia counties; Kulikoff, *Tobacco and Slaves*, 191, finds between 11 percent and 24 percent of wills in selected Chesapeake counties; Lebsock, *Free Women*, 272 n. 39, estimates two-thirds of men.

16. Will of Samuel McGovern, probated 26 January 1853, Wills and Probate Records, Polk Co., Tx.; Will of William Hootsall, written 17 July 1823, Will Record, Adams Co., Miss. Crowley, "Family Relations and Inheritance," 45, finds that the wealthiest testators usually gave their wives less than dower, and Carr and Walsh, "The Planter's Wife," 568, assert that 31 percent of men in St. Mary's County, Maryland, in the eighteenth century gave their wives dower or less.

17. Will of William Higginbotham, written 2 January 1832, Will Book 8, Amherst Co., Va.; Will of John Hatcher, probated 28 August 1837, Will Book 10,

Cumberland Co., Va.; Will of William Warwick, probated 20 August 1832, Will Book 8, Amherst Co., Va. Apparently neither Higginbotham nor Hatcher had any minor children; Warwick had three sons under twenty-one and asked his adult sons to pay for their education.

18. John J. Ormond, Arthur P. Bagby, and George Goldthwaite, eds., *The Code of Alabama* (Montgomery: Brittan and De Wolf, 1852), 381; Hutchinson, *Code of Mississippi*, 496–97; Gammel, *Laws of Texas, 1822–1897*, 2:1459; Shammas et al., *Inheritance in America*, 83, 86–88; Suzanne D. Lebsock, "Radical Reconstruction and the Property Rights of Southern Women," *Journal of Southern History* 43 (May 1977): 196, 200; Sandra Moncrief, "The Mississippi Married Women's Property Act of 1839," *Journal of Mississippi History* 47 (May 1985): 110–25.

19. Will of Philip Pitman, written 29 June 1820, vol. 1, Record of Wills, Montgomery Co., Ala.; Will of Abner Mardis, written 16 February 1850, Will Record, Adams Co., Miss. Nor did southwestern courts always uphold the reforms; see Maxwell Bloomfield, *American Lawyers in a Changing Society, 1776–1876* (Cambridge: Harvard University Press, 1976), 115. Five of the Mississippians who denied widows freedom of testation wrote wills after 1839; two of the Texans after 1846; and four of the Alabamans after 1848.

20. John V. Orth, "After the Revolution: 'Reform' of the Law of Inheritance," *Law and History Review* 10 (1992): 40; *Abridgment of the Public Permanent Laws of Virginia*, 80; Potter, Taylor, and Yancey, *Laws of North Carolina*, 1:465; Thomas Cooper, ed., *The Statutes at Large of South Carolina*, 10 vols. (Columbia: A. S. Johnston, 1837), 5:572; Aiken, *Digest of the Laws of the State of Alabama*, 128–29; William L. Sharkey, Henry T. Ellett, and William L. Harris, eds., *The Revised Code of the Statute Laws of the State of Mississippi* (Jackson: E. Barksdale, 1857), 15; Gammel, *Laws of Texas, 1822–1897*, 3:129. Daughters in the southwest did better than seaboard daughters, for almost a quarter of those planters (eight out of thirty-seven men) divided their estates equitably, while fewer seaboard men did so (nine out of sixty-five men). Seaboard widows did better than southwestern widows, for almost half of them received dower or better (twenty-five out of fifty-six).

21. Equitable wills affected forty-three daughters. Linda Speth finds that the wealthiest fathers were the most egalitarian in eighteenth-century Virginia; see "More Than Her 'Thirds,' " 16. On the dilemmas of fathers who divided estates among sons, see Jan Lewis, *The Pursuit of Happiness: Family and Values in Jefferson's Virginia* (Cambridge: Cambridge University Press, 1983), 106–68; Michael P. Johnson, "Planters and Patriarchy: Charleston, 1800–1860," *Journal of Southern History* 46 (February 1980): 55–57. Six of the seventeen men who wrote egalitarian wills for their children included their wives as executors, and one of those six made his wife sole executor.

22. Will of John Dennis, probated 7 April 1835, Will Book 7, Charlotte Co., Va.; Will of George Shackleford, written 23 April 1853, vol. 3, Record of Wills, Montgomery Co., Ala.; Will of Benjamin Roach, written 20 February 1847, Will Record,

Adams Co., Miss. Censer, *Planters and Children*, finds that planters who owned at least seventy slaves divided their estates equitably among their sons and daughters. Kulikoff, *Tobacco and Slaves*, 201, discovers that between 26 percent and 44 percent of wills in the colonial Chesapeake divided land among all children, although not necessarily in equal shares.

23. Will of James Dozier, probated October term 1844, Estate Records, Perry Co., Ala. Crudely inequitable wills affected twenty-one daughters. Censer, *Planters and Children*, 111, discovers more equity in wills written after 1840. Nineteen planters left bequests to grandchildren, usually a single slave or a cash gift, and they tended to leave more valuable property to grandsons.

24. Will of William Archer, probated 27 November 1851, Will Book 17, Amelia Co., Va.; Will of William Falconer, written 18 May 1840, vol. 2, Record of Wills, Montgomery Co., Ala. Wills with no gender pattern affected fifty-nine daughters.

25. Will of William Davenport, probated 7 November 1842, vol. 2, Wills of Greenville Co., S.C. Wills that singled out individual children affected 107 daughters.

26. Shammas et al., *Inheritance in America*, 56; Will of John Harmon, written 23 April 1849, vol. 4, Wills of Newberry Co., S.C.; Will of William Gaines, probated 5 January 1852, Will Book 10, Charlotte Co., Va.; Will of Hodijah Meade, probated 27 January 1842, Will Book 15, Amelia Co., Va. For other men who mention birth order, see Will of Jacob Fouts, probated May term 1835, vol. 6, Record of Wills, Randolph Co., N.C.; Will of Robert Dunbar, written 10 January 1826, Will Record, Adams Co., Miss.; and Will of James McKnight, probated November term 1852, Record of Wills, Nacogdoches Co., Tx.

27. Will of Fleming Palmore, probated 24 August 1835, Will Book 9, Cumberland Co., Va; Will of Martin Hancock, probated 1 October 1838, Will Book 8, Charlotte Co., Va.; Will of Joseph Binford. Disinheritance was rare in other American communities; see Narrett, *Inheritance*, 163, 165; Censer, *Planters and Children*, 114. Crowley, "Family Relations and Inheritance," 44, finds few complex intergenerational obligations and few restrictions on the heir's right to dispose of property.

28. Will of William Branch Giles, probated 23 December 1830, Will Book 12, Amelia Co., Va; Will of John Williford, probated August term 1833, vol. G, Record of Wills, Bertie Co., N.C.

29. Will of Gabriel Jones, probated 23 June 1836, Will Book 13, Amelia Co., Va.; Will of William Elliott.

30. Will of Benjamin Ward (quoted), probated 3 December 1840, Will Book 7, Nottoway Co., Va; Will of Samuel McGovern; Will of George Shackleford; Will of John Ashurst, written 2 July 1830, vol. 2, Record of Wills, Montgomery Co., Ala. Among the sixty-three inequitable wills, twenty-four contained conditional clauses, all discussed below.

31. Will of William Winans, written 13 January 1854, Record of Wills, Wilkinson Co., Miss; Will of John Brooch, probated 3 July 1854, Will Book 11, Charlotte Co.,

Va. See also Guion Griffis Johnson, "Courtship and Marriage Customs in Ante-Bellum North Carolina," *North Carolina Historical Review* 8 (October 1931): 396.

32. Will of William Glenn, probated 26 May 1845, Will Book 11, Cumberland Co., Va. On the rare use of birth control, see Sally G. McMillen, *Motherhood in the Old South: Pregnancy, Childbirth, and Infant Rearing* (Baton Rouge: Louisiana State University Press, 1990), 35, 107–8, 122.

33. Will of William Tigner; Will of Pascal Leigh, probated 21 January 1856, Will Book 10, Prince Edward Co., Va. Sons or male friends usually served as trustees. Censer, *Planters and Children*, 116–17; Salmon, "Women and Property," 657, 673; Friedman, "Patterns of Testation," 45, note that many trusts were designed to protect wives or daughters.

34. Will of Isham Harvey; Will of James McDade, dated 25 May 1850, vol. 3, Record of Wills, Montgomery Co., Ala.; Will of William Branch Giles.

35. Will of Henry S. Beverly; Will of Martin Hancock. William Warwick also threatened his stepson, while James Anderson threatened a son-in-law and William Tigner and Benjamin Palmore, their sons.

36. Peter Kolchin, *American Slavery, 1619–1877* (New York: Hill and Wang, 1993), 89–90; Will of Tarlton Woodson, probated 26 January 1857, Will Book 12, Cumberland Co., Va.; Will of David Pitts, written 5 May 1860, Estate Records, Perry Co., Ala. Lebsock, *Free Women*, 94–95, finds that whites who freed slaves were more likely to free men. White heirs sometimes blocked emancipations; see Judith K. Schafer, "'Open and Notorious Concubinage': The Emancipation of Slave Mistresses by Will and the Supreme Court in Antebellum Louisiana," *Louisiana History* 28 (spring 1987): 165–87.

37. Will of Joseph Johnson, written 6 September 1832, Record of Wills, Wilkinson Co., Miss. Lebsock, *Free Women*, 96–97, finds that few emancipated slaves received financial support, and that most of them were men. On the capacity for denial among white southern women, see C. Vann Woodward, ed., *Mary Chesnut's Civil War* (New Haven: Yale University Press, 1981), 29.

38. Will of Pascal Leigh; Will of Joseph Russell, probated 19 September 1836, Will Book 7, Prince Edward Co., Va.; Will of William Winans; Will of Arthur Barrett, probated 19 September 1845, vol. 1, Wills of Greenville Co., S.C.; Will of Blair Bolling.

39. Will of Benjamin Palmore; Will of John Sims, written 23 March 1857, Record of Wills, Wilkinson Co., Miss.; Will of Dennis Morgan, probated 1 January 1855, Charlotte Co., Va.; Will of Jordan Flournoy, probated 5 August 1833, Will Book 9, Powhatan Co., Va.; Will of Isham Harvey; Will of Robert Ware, written 6 January 1827, vol. 2, Record of Wills, Montgomery Co., Ala.; Will of Samuel McGovern. Censer, *Planters and Children*, 62, 140–41, finds that only 9 percent of planters asked that slave families be kept together and that the entire family was not necessarily protected. Paul Escott estimates that slave families were broken up by sale far more frequently (over half of the cases he studied) than by inheritance (9 percent);

see *Slavery Remembered: A Record of Twentieth-Century Slave Narratives* (Chapel Hill: University of North Carolina Press, 1979), 48. On the destruction of families through sale or inheritance, see Cashin, *A Family Venture*, 49–51, 76–77; White, *Ar'n't I a Woman*, 148–50; Eugene D. Genovese, *Roll, Jordan, Roll: The World the Slaves Made* (New York: Vintage Books, 1976), 492–93, 520, 650.

40. Will of William Sandidge, written 26 June 1830, Amherst Co., Va.; Will of Benjamin Palmore; Will of Samuel Woodfin, probated 18 January 1832, Will Book 9, Powhatan Co., Va.; Will of Mickleborough Montague, probated 20 December 1827, Will Book 7, Powhatan Co., Va.; Will of Samuel Ingram, written 13 November 1839, vol. 2, Record of Wills, Montgomery Co., Ala.; Will of James McKnight. Sometimes heirs sued over the ownership of slave mothers and children; see Margaret Burnham, "An Impossible Marriage: Slave Law and Family Law," *Law and Inequality* 5 (July 1987): 217–18. For other slaves chosen by lot, see George P. Rawick, ed., *The American Slave: A Composite Autobiography* (Westport, Conn.: Greenwood, 1977), *Mississippi* 7: 169–70.

41. Will of Thomas Barton, written 6 October 1825, Record of Wills, vol. 2, Montgomery Co., Ala.; Will of Robert Harris, probated 16 January 1831, Will Book 8, Powhatan Co., Va; Will of Blair Bolling. See also Will of Zadock Mitchell, probated February term 1834, vol. G, Record of Wills, Bertie Co., N.C.; Will of Arthur Barrett; Will of Jonathan Davenport, written 18 May 1842, vol. 4, Wills of Newberry Co., S.C.; Will of Jordan Flournoy. Most of the masters who either let slaves choose their owners, tried to preserve or destroy specific slave families, or required individual slaves to be sold came from the seaboard, suggesting that the nature of the master-slave relationship was somehow different there.

42. Will of James McDade; Will of Robert Harris. Planters gave slaves to thirty-two white female heirs and thirty-nine white male heirs.

43. Will of William Elliott; Will of William Blassingame, written 13 March 1841, Estate Records, Perry Co., Ala.; Will of Daniel Rudd, written 22 March 1856, vol. 4, Wills of Newberry Co., S.C.; Will of Jonathan Davenport.

44. Will of Arthur Barrett; Will of John J. Simpson, written 28 May 1855, Record of Wills, Nacogdoches Co., Tx; Will of James McKnight; Will of William H. Venable.

45. Censer, *Planters and Children*, 135–49, underscores the gulf between whites and blacks but also emphasizes the affectionate, democratic side of planter life.

46. Wortman, *Women in American Law*, 1:5–6; Norma Basch, *In the Eyes of the Law: Women, Marriage, and Property in Nineteenth-Century New York* (Ithaca: Cornell University Press, 1982), 113–35, 224–32; Mark V. Tushnet, *The American Law of Slavery, 1810–1860: Considerations of Humanity and Interest* (Princeton: Princeton University Press, 1981), 17, 27–37. Gundersen and Gampel, "Married Women's Legal Status," 134, argue that the actual working of the legal system was less restrictive than tenets of the common law.

47. On the "culture of resignation" among white southern women, see Joan E. Cashin, *Our Common Affairs: Texts from Women in the Old South* (Baltimore: Johns

Hopkins University Press, 1996), 1–41. On inheritance disputes, see Herbert Weaver and William G. Eidson, "The James K. Polk Home," *Tennessee Historical Quarterly* 24 (spring 1965): 5; Helen Tunicliff Catterall, ed., *Judicial Cases Concerning American Slavery and the Negro*, 5 vols. (Washington, D.C.: Carnegie Institute, 1926–37).

Chapter Eight

The Northern Myth of the Rebel Girl

Nina Silber

EDITOR'S NOTE: *Americans who moved to what is today Texas wanted to bring slaves and grow cotton. This desire led them to strike for independence from Mexico and to adopt a constitution legalizing slavery in 1836. Texas became a southern state, with its annexation in 1845, but the question of slavery in the West continued to be a national issue with the acquisition of land following the Mexican War. The resulting Compromise of 1850 satisfied no one. By the election of 1860 the Democrats had split along sectional lines, and the Republicans gained the presidency. That outcome convinced the South that slavery could not be preserved if it remained in the Union. The Deep South used force to support its decision to secede, precipitating a conflict that became a total war unsurpassed in the loss of lives and resources. Lincoln moved aggressively to keep parts of the Upper South — Delaware, Maryland, Kentucky, Missouri, and what became West Virginia — in the Union; but the rest of the South followed the Confederacy into war.*

The South's strong military tradition encouraged women initially to romanticize war, which in any case was assumed would be short. White women stitched regimental banners and wrapped bandages and kissed their menfolks good-bye after dances and parades in their honor. Early victories stimulated Confederate nationalism. However, advances in weapons technology quickly removed the romance. As early as 1862 the South suffered from shortages of food and medicine. Women led bread riots in the Confederate capital; many encouraged soldiers to desert, at least until the plowing was done. Women filled positions in the postal service and other government bureaucracies and managed farms and slaves.

As the war dragged on, slave discipline broke down. Anytime Union forces drew near, slaves, including women with their children, fled to their camps, forcing Lincoln and Congress to address the issue of slavery. The Emancipation Proclamation, although it freed no slaves in the Union, referring only to areas under Confederate control, nonetheless signified that the conclusion of the conflict would bring an end to the institution.

The long and bloody war frayed the terms implicit in the white South's gender contract whereby men provided for and protected ladies in return for their deference and domesticity. The war brought suffering on such a scale that it required more than the sacrifices white women had been socialized to make.

• • •

The Civil War, perhaps more than any other period in American history, generated a veritable minefield of mythology. Many of these myths took shape in the late nineteenth century, during the white South's celebration of its so-called Lost Cause, a celebration that significantly blunted and distorted the racial edge of Confederate history. In creating the Lost Cause legend, elite southerners promoted images of faithful black slaves willing to risk life and limb to save the master's china from Yankee invaders. Few spoke of the atmosphere of tension on most plantations that were within spitting distance of the Union army. In the same light, Confederate commanders became noble and heroic leaders wrestling with constitutional dilemmas, rarely white men defending the right to keep black people in bondage.

In addition to these whitewashed legends, gender has also figured prominently in Civil War mythology. Coming at a point in American history when gender roles were more rigidly circumscribed than they had been before, the American Civil War prompted a tremendous amount of conflict over masculine and feminine activity. Women especially were often required to go beyond or even violate traditional norms of behavior. While women's wartime actions were codified into a few noteworthy myths, it also became possible to portray this activity as highly irregular and unusual—the message was that these were dramatic sacrifices made in wartime, not acceptable actions for ordinary circumstances. Southern white women have often been the focus of Civil War myths, perhaps because of the extreme refinement and gentility associated with the mid-nineteenth-century image of Southern ladyhood, but also because of the extreme demands the war placed on Dixie's females.

In this regard, one of the most enduring legends to emerge from the Civil War was the myth of the fiery and spirited rebel "girl," the white southern woman who would do anything for her beloved Dixie. According to the myth, not only did the rebel girl struggle valiantly for the Confederacy, but she also took the cause more closely to heart than did most men. Historians, both northern and southern, repeated many of these ideas soon after the war had ended and well into the twentieth century. Certainly Margaret Mitchell appropriated more than just a hint of this myth in her portrait of the tempestuous Scarlett O'Hara. More recently, scholars such as Drew Faust and George Rable have challenged some of the central tenets of this image. Hardly the spirited defenders of southern independence, southern women, according to Faust and Rable, became increasingly angry and embittered toward the men of the Confederacy. Nonetheless, the myth endured and in fact flourished during the late nineteenth century. It became a staple of wartime and postwar ideology, not just among southerners (where we might expect to find it), but especially among northerners.[1]

When the Civil War began, Confederate propaganda assigned women a role that was anything but tempestuous. Urged to send men willingly, even cheerfully, off to war, white southern women were then expected to wait silently and patiently at home, finding appropriate and refined ways to boost army morale. Given southern society's conception of women's patriarchal subservience to men, Confederate literature generally did not allow for a more active and aggressive part for its females. But in light of the fact that southern women would often find themselves in direct contact with enemy troops (much more so than northern women), the frustration of being part of the fight but circumscribed in their actions undoubtedly intensified the wartime anguish of Confederate ladies. "What is the use," wondered a thwarted Sarah Morgan, "of all these worthless women in war times?"[2] This sense of frustration seems to have played a significant part in pushing some southern women into a role that northerners would later see as typical of all southern womanhood. Unable to respond with force, some women, especially those in Union-occupied areas, turned to whatever means they had at their disposal to show their opposition to the Union army—their skirts, their words, their manner of walking, their handkerchiefs, even their chamberpots. In this way, some southern females managed to make a fine art out of rudeness and insolence.

Still, even these types of actions forced southern women to walk a thin line between acceptable and unacceptable forms of behavior. Blurring the distinction between ladylike and unladylike activity could create a dangerous predicament for southern women immersed in a tradition of feminine refinement; it could also provide excellent fodder for enemy propaganda. Here was a picture of a society that had placed women in a position where they no longer acted the way women should. In a world in which societies were often judged by the gender distinctions that were or were not respected, enemies could easily be made to appear "uncivilized" when women were shown to behave in masculine ways. Northerners seized on the image of angry, defiant southern women and used it toward a number of political and military ends.

The war, in fact, had scarcely begun before images of defiant, if not savage, southern women began to spread through the Union army. As early as June 1861, stories began to circulate among northern troops that women in Richmond were wearing ornaments made from the bones of Union soldiers. New Yorker Maria Daly heard, in July 1862, of a southern lady who claimed to wear a brooch made from a Federal soldier's skull. "I lose all patience," Daly wrote, "when I think of these demoniac Southern women, whose pride and arrogance have had so much to do with this fearful state of things." By the time the war had ended in 1865, Republican Carl Schurz could write, "We have heard so much of the bitter resentment of the Southern ladies that the tale becomes stale by frequent repetition." Clearly, as Schurz suggested, northerners relished the chance to expound on the rebelliousness of southern females. But they also did more than simply recount a few truthful anecdotes about angry Confederate women. Rather, northern soldiers and citizens took something that was undoubtedly rooted in some degree of truth and developed an image that placed southern women beyond the pale of civilized behavior, an image that could make them extremely unfeminine and at times even freakish. It was also an image that was meant to offer a blanket appraisal of all the white women of Dixie, and by extension it became a comment on the Confederacy itself.[3]

Such an image was significant from the standpoint of Union propaganda as it helped to discourage feelings of concern and sympathy for southern white women who might be and often were the victims of war. With women so hostile and defiant, they had ceased to be innocent and deserving ladies; hence, despite their desperate circumstances, the standard courtesies could be ignored. It would not be necessary to give them assistance or comfort in wartime; it might, in fact, be necessary to treat them as potentially dangerous enemies.

The most dramatic incident in this regard may well have been Benjamin Butler's confrontation with the women of New Orleans. The details of this well-known tale need not be repeated here, other than to note that the insults heaped upon occupying Federal troops by some of the ladies of the Crescent City (especially the dumping of a chamberpot on a Union officer's head) prompted General Butler to issue his famous "Woman Order," which likened this defiant feminine behavior to prostitution. Butler's order was nothing if not controversial, but it translated southern women's spitefulness into something the Union army could take action against—in a few extreme cases New Orleans women were placed under arrest. Perhaps even more significantly, as historian Mary Ryan notes, Butler's order made a number of proper southern ladies reconsider their insults against Union officers as they came to dread this most public and unladylike form of humiliation. In either case, whether through arrest or humiliation, Butler's order managed to silence feminine hostility.[4]

The notion of southern women's bitter and angry defiance assumed even greater importance as the Civil War increasingly became total war, that is, a war that did not just pit armies against armies but made civilians feel the brutal and direct effects of the conflict. As a large percentage of the at-home population, southern white women might have undermined the northern soldiers' willingness to destroy the southern home front had it not been for all the talk of southern women's extreme intransigence. After all, it would be hard to maintain the manly and heroic image of the soldier if one were constantly compelled to subjugate helpless female victims. Captain Charles Wills of the 103rd Illinois Infantry, for example, was forced to defend himself against rumors circulating at home that he had been cruel to southern women and children. "I do take a little private satisfaction," Wills wrote to his sister from Alabama in February 1864, "in knowing that I have never said a word, except respectfully, to any woman in the Confederacy."[5] Nonetheless, the implication remained in Wills's comments that Confederate women may not have always been deserving of respectful treatment. Soldiers like Wills may have taken pride in their own chivalric deportment, but many Union soldiers became convinced that enemy women as a whole were some of the most vicious defenders of the Confederacy that they would encounter.

Not surprisingly, soldiers in Sherman's army often depicted southern women as bitter and vindictive representatives of the South. These soldiers, who were enmeshed in this new style of total warfare, often magnified the role of southern women in the sectional conflict. Their hyperbole, in part, may have helped them justify their own brutal actions against a domestic population. Some of Sherman's soldiers, for example, made southern women the focus of their class hostility toward the South. All the females of Dixie, they suggested, regardless of their specific social standing, symbolized the aristocratic style of the South, an attitude that was revealed in the arrogance they displayed toward hardworking northerners. Referring to a Georgia woman of moderate means, one of Sherman's soldiers explained, "I did not much pity her. She was a regular secesh and spit out her spite and venom against the dirty Yanks and mudsills of the North."[6] The image of the rebel girl was thus embellished amid the fury of Sherman's destruction: she was not just an enemy in the path of war but a symbol of the South's snobbish contempt for the North.

Moreover, in the context of Sherman's campaign, the rebel girl appeared not just as another spiteful female but as a principal player in the sectional conflict. "I have often (also) felt that even in the case of women— Southern ladies," explained Henry Hitchcock, a major in Sherman's army, "what they received was but a just retribution for the large share they personally had had in bringing on and keeping up this war."[7] In Hitchcock's view, southern women were hardly helpless victims and were, in fact, more than just bitter enemies—they were principal factors in causing the war in the first place and therefore legitimate targets of Sherman's campaign.

Not that Hitchcock was advocating a policy of wholesale attack against the South's feminine population; his comments spoke more to the general destruction and upheaval to which women were subjected. Nonetheless, there were times when northern soldiers' feelings of contempt for southern white women took the form of aggression and abuse, when political and sexual hostility merged. Although there were few reported cases of Union soldiers raping southern white women (there were a greater number of cases in which black women were raped by both northern and southern troops), it was not unusual for northern soldiers to express their contempt for Confederate women in sexual terms. One soldier, for example, stationed in an island town off the Gulf Coast of Mississippi in August 1865, reportedly told a group of local women that "he would Bayonet them in [the] abdomen, [as this was the] best thing he knew of for traitors." In this case, sexual threats may have offered this soldier a way to vent his desire for greater military and political authority in occupied territory. Even more significantly, Union officials apparently allowed a certain amount of leeway for this type of offensive action against enemy women. This particular soldier did not receive any serious punishment for his behavior and was, in the words of another soldier, "only reprimanded." More common than this type of aggressive posture was probably the sentiment of Mathew Woodruff, also stationed on the

Gulf, who fantasized about his conquest of the local females, although he seemed somewhat more secure about his position as military conqueror. Woodruff, who apparently enjoyed playing the part of the military commander romancing the ladies, wrote in his diary about some "lovely Females" and noted, "feel like possessing their charms, but resolve not to do it."[8]

The desire for a sexual and political triumph over rambunctious southern women emerged as a dominant theme in one popular postwar novel, written by one of the era's most well-known authors, William T. Adams, also known as Oliver Optic. In *Fighting Joe*, published in 1865, Optic created the ultimate rebel girl in the figure of Maud Hasbrouk, "a majestic and haughty young lady" of the South who assisted a band of Confederates in capturing a young Union officer, Captain Thomas Somers. Somers, who had at one point been impressed with Hasbrouk's beauty, hurls the ultimate insult at her after his capture. "You are one of those feminine Don Quixotes," says Somers, "who have unsexed themselves in the cause of treason and slavery." Somers eventually gains the upper hand over his captors, but it is his conquest of Hasbrouk that provides the most dramatic moment in the plot. "It was something," wrote Optic, "to see a brawling rebel woman, the most pestilent and inveterate enemy the government had in the contest, in a pleading posture." Somers claimed that Hasbrouk had "unsexed" herself, in part to justify his own willingness to use his gun on her. Yet clearly, Somers achieves not only a political conquest over the Confederates but a sexual conquest as well. The Union soldier is here able to prove his worth and his manliness, not just in military battle, but also in a type of sexual victory over dangerous and deceiving female rebels.[9]

The image of Maud Hasbrouk, especially the notion of her as "the most pestilent and inveterate enemy" of the Union, echoed throughout northern postwar writing. The extent to which the South's feminine intransigence became such a prominent and exaggerated image in northern postwar writing suggests that the image came to serve a new and larger purpose in this period. White women were often singled out as the most vociferous defenders of the Confederacy, as the ones who became the lifeblood of the southern cause. Northern journalist Sidney Andrews, writing from the South in 1866, made southern women central to the Confederate cause when he referred to those "bitter, spiteful women whose passionate hearts nursed the Rebellion." Northern relief worker Annie Wittenmyer echoed the sentiments expressed by Major Hitchcock when she reflected on the intensity of southern women's opposition to the Union. "There is no question about the matter," she wrote in her Civil War memoirs, "the Southern women, in their blind, partisan fury, prolonged the contest to the last extreme of desperation. They could not believe defeat possible."[10]

Given that military hostilities had ceased, what was the meaning of this type of talk for postwar northerners? In a period when many southern whites continued to express loyalty to the Confederacy, these attitudes called into question the legitimacy of the whole Confederate enterprise. The Confederacy, in effect, had promoted a cause that only a woman could love—it had aroused feminine, more than masculine, passion and had produced feelings that were irrational and uncontrollable. A commitment to the Union, many suggested, was the product of sober and mature reflection. The commitment to the Confederacy, however, was rooted in impulsive and excitable behavior, behavior that was certainly more feminine than masculine. Some suggested that men who abandoned the Union in favor of the Confederacy had given in to unhealthy feminine emotions. Writing in 1866, one northern textbook writer thus characterized the position of Robert E. Lee: "He seems to have been easily seduced from his allegiance to his flag by the dazzling offers of the Virginia conspirators." By siding with Virginia, Lee had gone the way of "men of easy political virtue," according to this writer. Others challenged the validity of the Confederate cause by suggesting not only that men had given in to their own feminine urges but also that southern women played too prominent a role. Carl Schurz advanced the view that young southern men who remained "unconquered" in July 1865 had been duped by women. This group of men, he wrote, consists mainly "of individuals that are apt to be influenced by silly women," women who provided the spirit without which "the rebellion would have broken down long ago."[11]

Such talk also seems to have played a part in shaping the political agenda of the Reconstruction period. This is not to say that northerners undertook Reconstruction in order to punish southern women; but northerners may have at times used the image of unreconstructed southern women as a way to justify the need for further Yankee reforms. Northerners made it clear that they did not remain in the South in order to rub the Confederate soldier's nose in his own defeat. The combatants, many explained, had already been convinced of northern superiority, and Yankees were too magnanimous to make these poor men suffer any further. No, the opposition now came from noncombatants, many of whom were women. Or, as one former Union soldier told northern traveler Mary Dodge in 1867, "I think the men are rather more inclined to reconstruction than the women." The presence of men in some of the most violent and hostile anti-Reconstruction activities belies this attempt to make support or opposition to Reconstruction an issue that centered on gender. Yet, in expressing this attitude northerners tried to establish a certain generosity for their former foes even as they continued to point out the problem of the South's social and political disorder, disorder that could be seen in the defiant activity of southern women.[12]

In fact, for some northerners, southern white women became an especially fitting target for their Reconstruction objectives. Southern women seemed to epitomize many of the problems of plantation society; like the soldiers in Sherman's army, many postwar northerners again called attention to southern females' attitude of aristocratic superiority. "It was aristocratic to keep aloof from Yankees," explained Union officer John DeForest in reference to his own encounters with southern ladies during Reconstruction, "and what woman does not desire to have the tone of grand society?" Because of her assumed aristocratic inclinations (and perhaps also because southern white women were rarely found in positions of paid labor), the southern white woman could serve as a symbol of northern reform goals, especially the desire to instill in the white South an appreciation for good, old-fashioned work. Northern journalist Sidney Andrews commented in 1866 on the importance of teaching all southerners about the nobility of hard work but noted that it was especially important "to teach the women of the South that labor is not degrading."[13]

As the Reconstruction process got under way, lazy and haughty southern ladies offered a useful counterpoint to a reform agenda that stressed Yankee uplift and enterprise. In a June 1865 cartoon entitled "Richmond Ladies Going to Receive Government Rations," *Harper's Weekly* depicted the humbling of southern arrogance in gendered terms. The caption conveyed the words of one Richmond woman who remarked to a fellow recipient, "Don't you think that Yankee must feel like shrinking into his boots before such high-toned Southern ladies as we?" In this depiction, southern women's hostility to the Union and their arrogant nature were inextricably linked. Moreover, the word "high-toned" is clearly meant to be ironic, considering the Confederacy's defeat and congressional Reconstruction's effect of humbling the South. Finding himself in precisely the same circumstances as the *Harper's* cartoon, northern lawyer and Sanitary Commission administrator George Templeton Strong also commented on the desire to rein in southern arrogance. Strong traveled to Richmond three weeks after Appomattox, where he oversaw the work of local Sanitary Commission agents. "The office was crowded with applicants, mostly women, in black, with baskets," Strong explained in his diary.

> They were receiving Northern charity with little show of gratitude. . . . The women were arrogant and sour. . . . We decided to stop these issues. . . . It seems hard and cruel, but providing tea and sugar for sick rebels is no part of our legitimate work, and it strengthens Southerners in their delusions about their own supreme dignity and the duty of Yankees to take care of them.

For Strong, the image of defiant and arrogant rebel girls offered an object lesson in Reconstruction strategy—they became symbols not only of the southern aristocracy but of all white southerners' supposed reluctance to work for themselves. In refusing to give aid to these Richmond women, Strong hoped that the South's dissolute ways might slowly be reformed.[14]

Some northern men who imagined this submission of angry southern females to northern agents continued to take pleasure in the sexual and political triumph the conquest implied. While visiting New Orleans in 1869, former Union soldier Russell Conwell recalled the fire and passion of the New Orleans ladies, but he added his own ending to the story. "This host of armed Amazons," wrote Conwell in reference to the events of 1862, charged through the city's streets, trying to stir up "the spirit of chivalry and rebellion." The men, however, having seen the approaching Federal troops, were not to be stirred. And so "the sweet dears went home to comb their hair and fix up to receive the Yankees."[15]

Ultimately, as Conwell himself suggested, these "sweet dears" could be won over to the northern point of view through courtship and love, although Conwell also took pleasure in hinting that these "armed Amazons" might not be good enough for Union boys. By the 1870s, this was an oft-repeated theme: the marital triumph of a northern man over an initially spiteful but ultimately submissive rebel girl. Indeed, few travel accounts that appeared in the late 1860s and 1870s (mostly written by northerners) failed to mention the preponderance of southern white women who were searching for love and marriage, even if it came in the form of a Yankee husband. Describing the atmosphere at the exclusive

Virginia springs, an 1877 correspondent to the *Nation* magazine was explicit about the romantic possibilities. "The Springs, too," he wrote, "became very early, and are now, a great marrying place. . . . widows abound at the Springs just now—by which I mean widows who would not object to trying the chances of matrimony again." The wartime deaths of so many southern white men undoubtedly did create a situation in which many southern ladies were anxious to wed. Yet this situation also helped to develop the image of the rebel girl in a way that added further ammunition to northerners' postwar political agenda. Here was an opportunity for Yankees, including some who may have missed the chance to serve in the army, to conquer the South once again—only this time with romance. At the White Sulphur Springs, explained northern journalist Edward King, one could find beautiful southern ladies who "twirl their fans and frown defiance at Northern beaux," thus describing a scene that was ripe for romantic conquest.[16]

Here, also, as presented in countless novels and plays that began to appear in the 1870s and 1880s, was an image of national reunification—an image that codified southern subservience through the southern bride's submission to her northern husband. A reviewer of one such reconciliation drama, *The Heart of Maryland*, observed how widespread the formula was: "As is usual in plays of this sort," he wrote, "the heroine is a loyal southern girl, and the hero a soldier of the North." In this incarnation, the rebel girl was still fiery and spirited, but the Yankee soldier, now sure of his military and political authority, could find that spirit more alluring than repulsive. By the 1880s, the female rebel was no longer a political viper but a flirtatious belle. She was, explained a northern reviewer, "(an) impulsive, passionate, coquettish, tender, and high-spirited, Southern girl."[17]

Thus, as the twentieth century began, the image of the spirited rebel girl lived on—ever dedicated to the memories of a glorious Confederate past, ever compulsive in spirit. It was an image that drew on stories and accounts of vicious southern women who abused Yankee soldiers, but it blossomed into a more romantic image that allowed northern men the chance to tame and subdue the white southern woman's willful defiance. Ultimately, it fed into a gendered vision of postwar reunion, a vision in which national harmony was nurtured by men who made women (and the South) their conquered and occasionally resistant partners in the arrangement.

NOTES

1. For an example of a historical work that portrays southern white women as diehard supporters of the Confederacy, see H. E. Sterkx, *Partners in Rebellion: Alabama Women in the Civil War* (Rutherford, 1970). Drew Faust, *Mothers of Invention: Women of the Slaveholding South in the American Civil War* (Chapel Hill, 1996); and George Rable, "'Missing in Action': Women of the Confederacy," in *Divided Houses: Gender and the Civil War*, ed. Catherine Clinton and Nina Silber (New York, 1992), 134–46.

2. Sarah Morgan quoted in Rable, "'Missing in Action,' " 136.

3. Reid Mitchell, *Civil War Soldiers* (New York, 1988), 25; Maria Lydig Daly, *Diary of a Union Lady, 1861–65*, ed. Harold Earl Hammond (New York, 1962), 158; Joseph H. Mahaffey, ed., "Carl Schurz's Letters from the South," *Georgia Historical Quarterly* 35 (September 1951): 246.

4. For insightful accounts of the New Orleans incident, see Rable, "'Missing in Action,' " 134–46; and Mary P. Ryan, *Women in Public: Between Banners and Ballots* (Baltimore, 1990), 143–45.

5. Charles W. Wills, *Army Life of an Illinois Soldier* (Washington, D.C., 1906), 214.

6. Soldier quoted in Charles Royster, *Destructive War: William Tecumseh Sherman, Stonewall Jackson, and the Americans* (New York, 1991), 86.

7. Henry Hitchcock, *Marching with Sherman: Passages from Letters and Diaries* (New Haven, 1927), 287–88.

8. According to Joseph Glatthaar, there were only two soldiers who were prosecuted for rape during Sherman's march. Michael Fellman has also observed that the guerrilla war in Missouri generated few reported cases of the rape of white women by either Yankee or Confederate men; black women and Native American women, he finds, were more frequently victims. See Joseph Glatthaar, *The March to the Sea and Beyond* (New York, 1985); and Michael Fellman, "Women and Guerrilla Warfare," in *Divided Houses*, ed. Clinton and Silber, 147–65. On the other hand, Catherine Clinton, who has begun to compile evidence for a study on rape during the Civil War, suggests that rape was much more widespread than what has so far been revealed by historians. Both Gulf Coast soldiers quoted in F. N. Boney, ed., *A Union Soldier in the Land of the Vanquished: The Diary of Sergeant Mathew Woodruff, June–December, 1865* (University, Ala., 1969), 32, 40.

9. William T. Adams [Oliver Optic], *Fighting Joe* (New York, 1865), 29, 64, 134.

10. Sidney Andrews, *The South since the War, as Shown by Fourteen Weeks of Travel and Observation in Georgia and the Carolinas* (Boston, 1866), 187; Annie Wittenmyer, *Under the Guns: A Woman's Reminiscences of the Civil War* (Boston, 1895), 137.

11. Benson J. Lossing, *Pictorial History of the Civil War in the United States of America*, 3 vols. (Philadelphia, 1866–68), 1:420–21; Mahaffey, "Carl Schurz's Letters," 247.

12. Mary Abigail Dodge [Gail Hamilton], *Wool-Gathering* (Boston, 1867), 302.

13. John DeForest, *A Union Officer in the Reconstruction* (New Haven, 1948), 198; Andrews, *The South*, 348.

14. *Harper's Weekly*, June 3, 1865, 340; Allan Nevins and Milton H. Thomas, eds., *The Diary of George Templeton Strong*, 4 vols. (New York, 1952), 3:592.

15. Russell Conwell, *Magnolia Journey: A Union Veteran Revisits the Former Confederate States* (University, Ala., 1974), 115–16.

16. "The Virginia Springs," *Nation*, September 13, 1877, 178; Edward King, *The Great South* (Baton Rouge, 1972), 674.

17. Undated review, *The Heart of Maryland* clippings file, Theater Collection, New York Public Library; undated review, *Barbara Frietchie* clippings file, Theater Collection, NYPL.

Chapter Nine

"Stand by Your Man"
The Ladies Memorial Association and the Reconstruction of Southern White Manhood

LeeAnn Whites

EDITOR'S NOTE: *White southerners accepted the end of slavery but not the idea of racial equality. The Civil War ended, but the conflict over the position of African Americans in southern society continued throughout Reconstruction and beyond.*

Slaveholding families, having accepted the paternalistic ideology that painted slaves as happy children, were shocked at the exodus of former slaves, interpreting their departure as evidence of ingratitude for years of "care." White women scoffed at black women for substituting fashionable dress for their former home-spun garments, considered them insolent when they refused to step into the gutter to let white ladies pass, and struggled to find deferential domestic help. Believing slaves to be lazy, whites interpreted their travel across the countryside and into towns as a form of vagrancy. Blacks, however, knew that their movement prevented whites from taking emancipation for granted. In addition, many freed-people were seeking the protection and provisions Union forces in the towns could provide. They were also trying to locate relatives. Sales and wills had ended many slave marriages and separated parents from children and adults from their elderly relatives, especially as a result of the domestic slave trade, which took excess slaves from older areas of the southeastern seaboard to newer areas of cotton and sugar cultivation.

Whites were particularly concerned about the loss of agricultural labor. Even if arrangements could be made with freedmen, black women, who represented half of this labor force, initially withdrew from field work. They were generations removed from African societies where agriculture was largely women's work and had accepted the prevailing view that women's work was domestic. But blacks were set free with nothing but the clothes on their backs. The land was owned by whites and there was little work to be done outside agriculture. Refusing to remain on large plantations but unable to rent or purchase farms, most freedpeople became sharecroppers. Dividing plantations into small farms in which they worked for a share of the crop provided a modicum of autonomy and allowed fewer opportunities for sexual exploitation of black women by white men. However, white creditors on whom they depended for supplies insisted on the production of staple crops, despite falling prices caused by worldwide overproduction; and even when women returned to the fields to increase production, they often found themselves reduced to a peonage only slightly better than slavery.

Whites categorized blacks exclusively by race rather than class. Not all black women were agriculturalists or domestics, however. Leaders emerged from a small upper class, whose members consisted of antebellum free black families and blacks who had gained material resources through relationships with whites and from an educated elite who had studied at the many black colleges founded after the war. These leaders worked to establish institutions to build a viable community life in a South segregated by race.

Sharing political power with blacks was anathema to the white South, because whites believed them to be inherently inferior. When the Black Codes passed by moderate white southern state legislators during President Johnson's administration turned out to be similar to former slave codes, Congress wrested control of the reunification process from the presidency and gave black men the vote, opening the way to black officeholders. These men were overwhelmingly literate and represented the interests of their constituents. But the very existence of black officials infuriated the white South, and perhaps as many as 10 percent were victims of white violence. Guerrilla warfare raged for decades, as white nightriders whipped and massacred blacks and their white Republican supporters. As a result of election chicanery and violence and the failure of the North to intervene, all the Confederate states had been returned to white rule by 1877. A long and bloody war to keep one race enslaved, its labor exploited for the benefit of the other, and a peace that succeeded in maintaining this exploitation in another guise were bare facts too harsh to face. They had to be rationalized in myth.

•   •   •

Two days after Robert E. Lee signed the armistice with Ulysses S. Grant at Appomattox, signifying the end of the long and bitter Civil War, the *Augusta Chronicle*, a major southern newspaper, published an editorial entitled "Female Influence and Energy." The author argued that women were much better suited to withstand life's failures and defeats than men:

"Those disasters which break down the spirit of man and prostrate him in the dust seem to call forth all the energies of the softer sex." While single men who encountered defeat in life were apt to descend into "waste and self neglect," the spirits of married men were sustained by the influence of this positive "female energy." "Relieved by domestic endearments and self respect," defeated men could be "kept alive by finding that, though abroad may be all darkness and humiliation, yet there is still a little world at home of which he is monarch."[1]

Historians of southern women have taken widely differing positions on the impact that the defeat of the Confederacy and the accompanying emancipation of the slaves had on white women and white gender roles. Over twenty years ago, in her pathbreaking work *The Southern Lady*, Anne Firor Scott argued that the war "opened every door for women." She attributed this outcome to the combined effect of white women's independent activities during the war and the blow that emancipation and defeat presented to patriarchal power. More recently, historians have been less sanguine about the emancipatory possibilities that the postwar social order offered to southern white women. The gains that women made during the war in forming autonomous public organizations, entering wage labor, and directing their own households are viewed as temporary expedients that evaporated at war's end, as rapidly as the cause that generated them in the first place.[2]

Regardless of which position historians espouse, they share the underlying assumption that improvement in women's status was based on their ability to become more independent. The war created this opportunity for women, if only because it required a massive departure of men to the front. As a consequence, Confederate women were forced to become autonomous, as heads of households or wage earners, for instance, if only to guarantee their own and their children's survival. It is this aspect of the war, the way it structurally drew women out of their dependent status into the independent place previously occupied by their men, that has absorbed much of the attention of historians. From this perspective, the end of the war and the return of the men home would naturally lead to a decline, if not an outright reversal, in women's independence.

It is not surprising, then, that historians have given little consideration to the role that "female influence," as depicted by the Augusta editorial, might have played in the postwar empowerment of southern white women.[3] Yet it is precisely in the arena of postwar gender relations that the possibility for a new form of postwar empowerment among southern white women existed. Indeed, the editor concludes his analysis of the war's impact on postwar gender relations with a classic antebellum gender analogy. Before the war, southern white men were like the "towering oak," while southern white women were the "clinging vine." In these "happier days" the vine "twined its graceful foliage about the oak and has been lifted by him into the sunshine." The Civil War passed over this southern landscape like a violent storm, however, and the oak was "riven by a thunderbolt," its spine cracked. The once clinging ivy now had the possibility of a new role to play. It could hold the splintered oak erect, if it would only "cling around with its caressing tendrils and bind up its shattered brow."[4]

White southern men had indeed suffered multiple defeats with the fall of the Confederacy, in relation to northern men as well as in relation to the southern slave population. Even those white southerners who had never supported the war effort were left to confront the economic devastation and dislocation that the Confederate defeat brought to all white men, regardless of political affiliation. Confronted with a myriad of military, political, and economic defeats, their women certainly found themselves in a critical position. Would they continue to pursue the apparently independent roles the war had opened to them? Or would they "stand by their men," and in that way play a critical role in the reconstruction, rather than the further deconstruction, of southern white manhood?

The Ladies Memorial Associations that were formed in the South in the war's immediate aftermath were clearly dedicated to the reconstruction of southern white men. These associations took as their first charge the care of the most defeated of Confederate men—those who actually fell in the conflict, the Confederate dead. They saw to it that these men received a decent burial, that the sacrifice of their lives was honored at least once a year on Confederate Memorial Day, and that their story was emblazoned on monuments to the Confederate soldier that are to be found to this day in every southern town of any size.[5]

This organization has been almost universally overlooked by historians to this day; perhaps no better testimony exists as to its success in subordinating its own identity to the salvation of southern white manhood. And this despite the fact that besides women's church auxiliaries, the Ladies Memorial Associations had by far the largest membership of any women's organizations in the South, certainly through the 1870s and perhaps into the 1880s. Its influence outside its immediate membership was also substantial. The Augusta, Georgia, association, for example, regularly organized hundreds of schoolchildren to decorate the graves of the Confederate dead on Memorial Day. The ceremony to lay the cornerstone of the town's Confederate Monument drew a huge crowd, the largest in the town's history, and the actual unveiling of the monument in 1878 was even larger, estimated by the local press to exceed twenty thousand.[6]

What explains historians' neglect of this organization? Perhaps it is because the subject is gender as a *relationship*, that is to say the proposition that men are *made* in relation to women, and women are *made* in relation to men, a deeply contested proposition. For historians of women, who view the establishment of women's voluntary organizations in the nineteenth century as the beginning of the women's rights struggle as a mass movement, organizations like the Ladies Memorial Associations, which were overtly dedicated to the rehabilitation of their men, are something of an embarrassment. For historians of the Confederate memorial tradition and veterans' organizations, the recognition that the apparently manly pursuit of telling old war stories, of being "real" men, was initially constructed by the postwar activities of their mothers and wives is also perhaps best overlooked.[7]

Perhaps the hesitancy of historians to explore this form of "female energy" goes even deeper to the blind, unreasoning love that binds us one to the other. Historians are perhaps more comfortable discussing less subjective forces that bind men and women together, such as the excesses of patriarchal authority, the benefits of paternalistic benevolence, or the pressure of economic necessity. The Ladies Memorial Association, however, had no such hesitation. Out of the raw, abraded ends of their attachment to their fallen husbands, fathers, and sons, out of the massive carnage that the Civil War represented for them, they committed themselves to perpetuate what they, at least, still had the power to perpetuate, the binding tie of "mother love." Frequently, the pattern of officeholding in the organization was explained by the extent of maternal loss these women experienced as a result of the war. Presidents, for instance, would have lost the most sons, vice presidents would just have one unclaimed on some unknown battlefield.[8]

Whereas historians of women have been inclined to view women's voluntary associations as a basis for women's struggle for independence, they can just as easily be viewed as an extension of women's "dependent" domestic role as mothers of men. Indeed, "mother love" was with Confederate men at the war's outset, for while the soldiers' aid societies sprang up across the South in the first months of the war to meet the basic structural need for women's labor in order to properly outfit the soldiers, it was frequently the very depth of their domestic attachment to their husbands and sons that inspired this labor. As one soldiers' aid society explained in its initial call for volunteers, "We will in this small offering of service secure to ourselves the heartfelt satisfaction that patriotism always inspires, and this will serve as solace to each of us for the absence of those whose lives are so dear to us."[9] As the soldiers began returning from the front, wounded and diseased, these women transformed their labor to match the soldiers' new needs. They set up hospitals and Wayside Homes to hopefully nurse these men back to health. Here, perhaps even more forcefully than in the initial construction of uniforms, Confederate women's labor was infused with their own desire to preserve their own particular domestic ties. As they labored over men otherwise unknown to them, they prayed fervently that their own sons and husbands might be spared a similar fate, or that if they should be wounded they might receive the same loving care at the hands of some other woman.

It was in this context of wartime hospital and nursing work that Confederate women first took up the task of caring for the Confederate dead. When men died under their care, the women were the ones who laid them out, saw to it that they received a fitting burial, and took care of their graves. After the war, it was these soldiers' aid societies that transformed themselves into the Ladies Memorial Associations. As they had clothed, fed, nursed, and buried soldiers in the war, so now would they care for their graves and for their memory.[10]

As in the case of the wartime aid societies, part of the reason for the continued existence of Ladies Memorial Associations was purely practical. The immediate physical problems of the Confederate dead went far beyond simply tending the graves of those men who had died unknown or unclaimed by their kindred during the war. The poor condition of war cemeteries everywhere begged for attention. Burial sites were frequently in a deplorable state, and poorly marked graves threatened to lose their identity altogether. Even more daunting was the problem of the battlefields themselves, where soldiers had been buried in mass graves or simply covered over in shallow trenches where they fell. The work of bringing home the Confederate dead, establishing special sections in graveyards for their remains, and raising the funds for standardized grave markers frequently took these organizations years of work.[11]

A proper burial, however, was not the end of these women's postwar activity but the beginning. For as much as the plight of the Confederate dead continued to call forth the labor of southern white women, even more did it call forth the underlying attachment between mothers and sons, husbands and wives, brothers and sisters that had inspired that labor from the war's outset. Here is where the defeat of the Confederacy and its soldiers came to play a critical role, for if the Confederacy had been successful, women undoubtedly would have cared for the graves of their own men, but the responsibility for somehow "memorializing" or honoring and recognizing the Confederate cause would not have fallen upon this normally private and individualized act of mourning. The victorious soldier is honored by his nation. Even a defeated nation can still honor its dead, but in the case of the Confederacy there was no nation, so the domestic tie between these women and their lost men bore the weight of that political burden.[12]

This politicization of domestic relations is perhaps most visible in the establishment of that central Confederate memorial tradition, Confederate Memorial Day, by the Ladies Memorial Associations in the year following the war. In March 1866, the Columbus Ladies Memorial Association issued a call published widely in the southern press for women throughout the South to "aid us in the effort to set apart a certain day to be observed, from the Potomac to the Rio Grande, and to be handed down through time as a religious custom of the South, to wreathe the graves of our martyred dead with flowers." In its initial call, the association went on to elaborate the day's larger meaning, a meaning that would become a standard explanation not only for Confederate Memorial Day but for the Confederate memorial tradition and ultimately for the war itself: because they "all did their duty. . . . They died for their country." The association argued that the larger issues of right and wrong, of victory or defeat, were irrelevant in the face of the basic sacrifice these men had made. For these women *as* women, the larger issues of why the South fought were irrelevant. They loved these men regardless of the war's rationale and outcome.[13]

From the perspective of the Columbus Ladies Memorial Association, it was more than simply convenient that Confederate defeat had occurred in the spring, when flowers were readily available for grave decoration. As they noted in their history of the origins of Confederate Memorial Day some thirty years later, in settling on April 26 they had hoped to encourage the citizenry to draw the connection between their own Confederate dead and the resurrection and ascension of Christ. "Like the hope that spread over the earth on the morning of the Resurrection," they recorded, "so the soft light of this sentiment shone over Dixie, and when April came, love wreathed her roses where the soldiers sleep." Wrapping themselves in this domesticized Christian rhetoric, these women went on to assert the primacy of their own role in this resurrection of the war dead. "Whose task," they queried, "had this been even in Biblical times?" "When the smoke cleared away, where do we find the devoted women? Where were Mary Magdalene and the other Mary after the crucifixion?" [14] According to the Columbus Ladies Memorial Association, it was "mother love" that would raise the Confederate dead, if only on monuments of stone.

Their own relationship to these men provided the ideological as well as material basis for the memorialization. The Confederate dead deserved to be honored, not for the cause they had lost—not for political power or racial hegemony—but simply because they had done their "duty" and "sacrificed" their lives for the defense of southern women and children. "For what did the South fight?" the Ladies Memorial Associations queried. "Not," they answered, "for the institution of slavery." "That," they asserted, "was a mere incident in the great drama. Let the true answer ring from the lips of every Memorial orator for generations to come." The "true answer" was that Confederate men fought not to preserve slavery, but to preserve their *own* "liberties" as free men, liberties that were embodied in their position as heads of their own households that allowed them to "protect" their dependents in the antebellum South and during the war itself.[15]

Of course this perspective overlooked the fact that it was precisely the position of African Americans as slaves in white households that supported these men's "liberties" before the war. In the face of the emancipation of the slaves, white southern men were rendered more dependent on those household dependents that remained to them. They turned to their women and their children to validate them, to create out of their own continued subordination the basis for their reconstruction as honorable men, even in the face of their defeat in relation to northern men and the southern freedpeople. For their part the Ladies Memorial Associations rose to the occasion by moving white women to the very center of the war's causality. "No one," they asserted, "could refuse us the simple privilege of paying honor to those who died defending the life, honor and happiness of southern women." [16]

The expanded public role that the Ladies Memorial Associations assumed for the purpose of valorizing their men put them potentially at cross-purposes in this effort to "stand by their men." The problem was how to provide a means for the reconstruction of their men's self-image without reconstructing themselves in the process—or at least without appearing to do so. As a result, the Ladies Memorial Associations worked hard to maintain the conventional forms of public gender subordination even as they eroded its underlying substance. They gave over conventionally "male" aspects of public organizational activities—public speech making, managing the construction finances for monuments, reordering graveyards, and negotiating with building contractors—to prominent men. They asserted their commitment to male representation forthrightly and perhaps somewhat defensively in the local press. "Southern women," one association wrote, "frankly acknowledge their dependence on Southern men and waiving women's rights and parliamentary usages, they claim the privilege of having their public announcements made by gentlemen." They claimed that this behavior was only to be expected, because "Southern ladies naturally shrink from contact with the outside world."[17]

This association explained the meaning of its memorial activities in the most gender-conservative frame possible. Theirs was a defensive movement, a response to the incursions that the war had made into the domestic arena. The war had essentially turned domestic life inside out. The Ladies Memorial Associations continued to be active in a public world, now rendered structurally domestic as a result. This constituted no assertion of women's individual rights, autonomy, or equality with men. Quite the contrary, this constituted a continued attachment to domesticity—albeit a domesticity that, because of unforeseen circumstances, had been compelled to assume a public and even a political face. As the Augusta Ladies Memorial Association expressed it, rather than being committed to "women's rights," its organization was based on domestic loss, a loss that began with the Confederate dead, but radiated out to include a militarily, economically, and politically defeated white southern manhood in general.[18]

What did it mean for the larger southern social order that, despite the defeat of southern white men and the enlarged public role that their women continued to occupy as a result, these women continued to eschew direct responsibility for their actions and instead turned their postwar public empowerment toward undergirding a social construction of white manhood that had otherwise lost its material moorings with the emancipation of the slaves and the economic devastation of the war? An argument can be made that this strategy of "standing by your man" served to ease the transition to a society in which white women would increasingly be called upon to stand by themselves or stand with the aid of other women. This is perhaps most clearly evident in the establishment of homes for Confederate widows and orphans in the war's aftermath.

As the Ladies Memorial Associations took up "protecting" the Confederate dead, so too did they assume the responsibility for "protecting" their widows and orphans by establishing public homes for the most destitute. In Charleston, the Home for Mothers, Widows and Daughters of Confederate Soldiers was established through the efforts of Mrs. Mary Amarintha Snowden, who was also one of the founding members of the Charleston Ladies Memorial Association and its president during her lifetime. Within six months of its establishment, the home had seventy inmates, fifty of whom attended the home's school. In educating the younger generation to become "self helping and self respecting working women," such homes assisted in moving some of the younger generation of white women into a more autonomous position.[19]

Neither the establishment of these public homes nor the increased employment of white women that they facilitated was understood to be a response to the systemic decline of white men's ability to "protect" their women and children that the war had set in motion; instead, these women were able to wrap their activity in the reassuring mantle of the Confederate dead, insisting that the last wish of the dying soldier was that his family be provided for, even if it fell to women to do so. Far from undermining the position of postwar white manhood, these women presented themselves as actually contributing to it through the medium of the Confederate dead and their continuing needs. This connection between elite women's increased voluntary activity and the needs of the Confederate widows and orphans became a standard line of argument for such women in the years following the war.[20]

Nonetheless, a case can be made for the roots of white women's progressive reform activity in the postwar South in the establishment of these homes for needy Confederate widows and their children. Some of the women who began their public organizational work in these Confederate widows' homes of the 1860s and 1870s went on to form the King's Daughters, the Women's Exchanges, and the Woman's Christian Temperance Unions of the 1880s.[21] Unfortunately, no such positive construction can be placed on the racial politics created by the continued subordination of white women to the task of the reconstruction of white manhood. Perhaps the clearest illustration of this is the Ku Klux Klan.

The Klan was formed ostensibly as a social club on 24 December 1866 by six young Confederate veterans in Pulaski, Tennessee, who dressed up in sheets and rode through the streets. According to one early Klan history, African Americans "thought they had seen ghosts from the nearby battlefields, and had with haste gone back to their former masters, only too willing to work."[22] From this day forward, Klansmen appeared in their ghostly attire, demanding buckets of water, as men on battlefields were known to be in great thirst. Whether the freedpeople or their white supporters believed this ruse or not, the larger point is that the Klan carried their attachment to the Confederate dead one step further than the Ladies Memorial Associations. They made the dead ride again.[23] Who better to maintain the old social and racial order than the Confederate dead themselves? Who better to make war on black Reconstruction than those men who had given their lives to the preservation of the antebellum southern social order and white men's position in it?

In 1867 the Klan held a convention in Nashville, Tennessee, to form a united organization. Before this convention, some Klan representatives asked Robert E. Lee to lead this newly unified regional order. Here the parallel to the Confederacy is clear, for as the Klan represented the Confederate soldier reborn, who better to lead them than their old commander in chief? Lee, in declining this honor, was reputed to have advised the Klan to "keep it as you have it, a protective organization." The statement of organizational purpose adopted at the Nashville convention in 1867 reflected this advice, with its commitment to "protect the weak, the innocent, the defenseless from indignities, wrongs and outrages of the lawless, the violent and the brutal; to relieve the injured and oppressed, succor the suffering, especially the widows and orphans of the Confederate soldiers."[24]

The Klan's mission of protecting the "weak" and the "innocent," especially the widows and orphans of the Confederate dead, closely parallels the Ladies Memorial Associations' vision of what the war was all about. The preservation of the institution of slavery became a mere "incident" in the war, an adjunct of the "real" reason Confederate men went to war— to protect their homes, especially their women. Similarly, the racial terrorism of the Klan was viewed not from the position of its African American victims, over whom southern whites had lost control with the demise of slavery, but rather from the position of those whose allegiance they continued to hold, the loyal white women of the South.

The first histories of the Klan were generally written by the participants themselves or their descendants. These works perpetuated this vision of the Klan as an organization primarily committed to the protection of the white population.[25] Several of these histories were written by women who were the daughters of original Klansmen. In 1924, for instance, Susan Lawrence Davis published *The Authentic History of the KKK, 1865–1877*. Her father was one of the founding members of the Athens, Alabama, Klan, and she claimed to have known much of the KKK leadership personally. She dedicated her work, however, to "her mother, Sarah Ann (McClelland) Davis and the other southern women who designed and manufactured with their Own fingers the Regalia of the Ku Klux Klansmen and the trappings for their horses." Another Klan history coauthored by a woman, Mrs. W. B. Romine, placed a similar emphasis on the critical role women played in providing uniforms for the Klan. The Romines claimed that ex-Confederate women designed and made more than four hundred thousand Klan robes for both rider and horse and that "not a word was said by these women to anyone about them and not one single secret concerning them was ever revealed."[26]

Why is so much significance attributed in these histories to Klan robes? The parallel to the Civil War is apparent. As southern white women "stood by their men" by forming soldiers' aid societies to make their uniforms, so southern white women "stood by their men" in this reincarnation of the Confederate dead. The differences in the uniforms are instructive, however, because they point to a substantive reconstruction of white male identity. Although initially Klan uniforms varied widely, a standard uniform eventually emerged. The white sheet with the red cross on the upper right shoulder undoubtedly symbolized many things to the wearers—it was clearly "ghostly," it represented "white supremacy," but in the Romines' and Davis's explanation, it was white primarily to symbolize the central aim of the Klan, the "purity and preservation of the home." Indeed, Davis went so far as to portray the Klan as being a woman's organization, arguing that while "southern men and women supported the Civil War, southern women and men supported the Klan." Here the order is significant; while white men lost the Civil War, Davis argued that white women, acting indirectly through the Klan, finally won the war for "home rule," redeeming the South from Radical Reconstruction.[27]

While white southern men may have been redeemed by 1877 from Radical Reconstruction, that is, from a racial or regional reconstruction, the basis for that redemption was a gendered one. Consider, for instance,

Davis's description of the Klan's Grand Wizard, General Nathan Bedford Forrest. During the war, Davis tells us, Forrest never drank, he always held religious services in his tent on Sundays, and he prayed before battle. He also had a "profound respect" for womanhood and was a "devoted husband." Indeed, his wife, Mary Montgomery Forrest, was his "inspiration." Whether Forrest actually exhibited these qualities, Davis holds him up as the exemplar of the characteristics that postwar white men should embody. Like the "White Life for Two" advocated by the WCTU, Davis was proposing the "white sheet for two."[28]

This vision of the Klan as an organization of "self sacrificing" men simply doing their duty to protect their women and children from an African American population rendered threatening by the influence of rapacious northern white carpetbaggers was not seriously revised by historians until the 1960s. At that point the original Klan histories written from the gendered perspective of the early participants were dismissed out of hand. As William Randall argued in his work, *The KKK: A Century of Infamy*, the 1867 Nashville statement of principle was "high sounding and innocuous," a mere rationale for the racial terrorism that was the Klan's real purpose.[29]

In 1898, Charlotte Perkins Gilman wrote what was arguably the nineteenth century's most devastating indictment of indirect female influence. In *Women and Economics*, Gilman argued that the ills of the capitalist social order—poverty, class exploitation, and violence—could be attributed directly to the subordinate status of women and the domestic realm as a whole. Because women in their roles as mothers and wives were essentially the servants of men, they raised sons and affirmed husbands in the belief that men's needs were the only valid ones. Through their loving service, they taught their men to be greedy and self-centered in relation to the larger world. Because these self-centered men needed to "support" such women, they took this greedy and self-centered construction of themselves out into the larger social order, doing whatever was necessary—robbing, oppressing, and exploiting others—to meet their women's domestic needs. Gilman argued, therefore, that the truly radical solution to problems of poverty, conflict, and oppression in industrial capitalist society is the destruction of women's indirect influence. When women were directly integrated into public life, motherhood would be freed from its need to serve; the result would be a more humane manhood.[30]

Gilman would have done well to turn her attention to the situation of the postwar South. Like so many northerners of New England extraction, she apparently assumed that there were no lessons for her there. If, however, she had considered the social trajectory of this region in the late nineteenth century, she would have found a striking affirmation of her argument for the connection between the continued subordination of women, particularly elite white women, and the violence and exploitation of the working classes by the KKK. However, she also would have confronted a devastating refutation of her proposed solution to this problem: the integration of women's previously privatized domestic labor into public life. In the postwar South this step toward the integration of white women and white domestic relations into the public arena not only failed to undercut white male domination, it in fact served to reinforce it.

NOTES

1. *Augusta Chronicle and Sentinel*, April 14, 1865.

2. Anne Firor Scott, *The Southern Lady: From Pedestal to Politics, 1830–1930* (Chicago, 1971). For a different view on this issue, see, Jean Friedman, *The Enclosed Garden: Women and Community in the Evangelical South, 1830–1900* (Chapel Hill, 1985); Jean Bethe Eltshain, *Women and War* (New York, 1987); and George Rable, *Civil Wars: Women and the Crisis of Southern Nationalism* (Chicago, 1989).

3. One notable exception is Suzanne Lebsock, whose *Free Women of Petersburg: Status and Culture in a Southern Town, 1784–1860* (New York, 1984) points to the way white women gained power indirectly, through the economic difficulties of their husbands, which led to the establishment of separate estates for their wives.

4. Historians of gender roles have now begun to consider how the war affected southern white men. See, for example, Nina Silber, "Intemperate Men, Spiteful Women, and Jefferson Davis," and Victoria Bynum, "Reshaping the Bonds of Womanhood: Divorce in Reconstruction North Carolina," in *Divided Houses: Gender and the Civil War*, ed. Clinton and Silber (Oxford, 1992), 283–305, 320–34; and LeeAnn Whites, *The Civil War as a Crisis in Gender: Augusta, Georgia, 1860–1890* (Athens, GA, 1995).

5. For an extensive discussion of the history of Confederate monuments, see Gaines Foster, *Ghosts of the Confederacy: Defeat, the Lost Cause and the Emergence of the New South* (New York, 1987).

6. Augusta Ladies Memorial Association minutes, April 5, 1873, Richmond County Historical Society Collection, Augusta, GA. *Augusta Chronicle and Sentinel*, November 1, 1878. According to this account, ten thousand gathered for the cornerstone laying for the monument on April 26, 1875, and twenty thousand three years later for the unveiling. The city's population was under thirty thousand.

7. Among historians of southern women, Jean Friedman contends that in the postwar period white women's wartime organizations disappeared entirely. Historians of the Confederate memorial tradition are similarly inclined to ignore the very existence of the Ladies Memorial Association. See Gerald Linderman, *Embattled Courage: The Experience of Combat in the American Civil War* (New York, 1987), 266–97; and Charles Reagan Wilson, *Baptized in Blood: Religion of the Lost Cause, 1865–1920* (Athens, GA, 1980). Foster's, *Ghosts of the Confederacy,* an exception to this pattern, includes a chapter on the organization; however, he concludes that because the Ladies Memorial Association was "within the realm of sentiment," it had few "ideological or political implications" and "did not offer a coherent historical interpretation of the war and therefore did little to define the Confederate Tradition" (46).

8. See, for example, "A History of the Origin of Memorial Day as Adopted by the Ladies Memorial Association of Columbus, Georgia" (Columbus, 1898); Marielou Armstrong Cory, "The Ladies Memorial Association of Montgomery, Alabama: Its Origin and Organization, 1860–1870" (Montgomery, AL, 1902), 57–58.

9. *Augusta Chronicle and Sentinel,* June 7, 1861.

10. Anne Firor Scott notes the connection between the soldiers' aid societies and the Ladies Memorial Associations in *Natural Allies: Women's Associations in American History* (Chicago, 1991). The Augusta, GA, Columbus, GA, Charleston, SC, Montgomery, AL, and Raleigh, NC associations all follow this pattern. For a further discussion of these cases, see Charles Colcock Jones and Salem Dutcher, *Memorial History of Augusta, Georgia* (Syracuse, NY, 1890), 181; Cory, "The Ladies Memorial Association of Montgomery, Alabama"; P. F. Pescud, "A Sketch of the Ladies Memorial Association of Raleigh, NC: Its Origin and History (Raleigh, NC, 1882); James G. Holmes, ed., "Memorials to the Memory of Mrs. Mary Amarintha Snowden" (Charleston, SC, 1898); and "History of the Origin of Memorial Day."

11. For a graphic discussion of the difficulties of disinterring and burying decaying bodies in leaky, hastily constructed coffins, see Pescud, "Sketch of the Ladies Memorial Association," 5. For a discussion of the difficulties of returning the soldiers to their place of origin, see "Confederate Memorial Day at Charleston, SC: Reinterment of the Carolina Dead from Gettysburg" (Charleston, SC, 1871). In the Charleston case it was not until six years after the war that the bodies were reclaimed from Gettysburg.

12. Not only did women assert this politicized view of their domestic labors as a result of the demise of the Confederacy, the local press and prominent spokesmen for the Confederate memorial tradition did as well. See, for example, the speeches of Charles Colcock Jones, "Annual Addresses Delivered before the Confederate Survivors Association in Augusta, Georgia" (Augusta, 1879–91). Jones was the lifetime president and founder of the Augusta Confederate Survivors Association.

13. "History of the Origin of Memorial Day," 24–25.

14. Ibid., 6.

15. For a further discussion of the relationship between southern white men's position as heads of household and their "liberties" in the antebellum South, see Elizabeth Fox-Genovese, *Within the Plantation Household: Black and White Women of the Old South* (Chapel Hill, 1988), 37–99; and Stephanie McCurry, *Masters of Small Worlds: Yeoman Households, Gender Relations, and the Political Culture of the South Carolina Low Country* (New York, 1995), 37–91. For a discussion of the way the Civil War and Reconstruction transformed that relationship, see Whites, *Civil War as a Crisis in Gender*, esp. chap. 5.

16. Whites, *Civil War*, 30, 25.

17. *Augusta Chronicle and Sentinel*, April 2, 1873.

18. The association between the Confederate dead and the war's "survivors" was a frequent topic of memorializing speeches. See, for example, the speeches of one prominent Georgia Confederate Memorial Day speaker, Joseph B. Cumming, in Occasional Addresses (Augusta, GA, n.d.).

19. Holmes, "Memorials to the Memory of Mrs. Mary Amarintha Snowden," 22–25. Mrs. Snowden's career is archetypal. Wife of a prominent Charleston doctor, she took up hospital work during the war. Widowed and impoverished after the war with a family to support, she mortgaged her only asset, her home, to finance the establishment of a home for Confederate widows and orphans, simultaneously employing herself and her sister.

20. For example, see Rebecca Latimer Felton, *Country Life in the Days of My Youth* (Atlanta, 1919), 95–107, 270–72.

21. A study of the officers of the Ladies Memorial Association of Augusta indicated that of the twenty-five officers of the organization who could be identified, more than half held positions as officers in other organizations, the most common being the widows' home, but other organizations included the King's Daughters, the Women's Exchange, the United Daughters of the Confederacy, and the Woman's Christian Temperance Union. The organizational work of some of these women over their lifetimes is truly staggering. Take, for instance, the case of Catherine Rowland, who was the wife of a cotton commission merchant in the town and a young matron at the time of the Civil War. In the war's aftermath, she held the position of president of the Ladies Memorial Association, director of the Widows' Home, member of the executive committee of the Women's Exchange, president of the King's Daughters, and vice president of the United Daughters of the Confederacy, although not all at the same time. Ella Gertrude Clanton Thomas, young wife of a substantial planter, followed a similarly prodigious postwar organizational career: vice president of the Ladies Memorial Association, officer of the WCTU, recording secretary of the UDC, and finally president of the Atlanta woman s suffrage association.

22. Susan Lawrence Davis, *Authentic History of the Ku Klux Klan, 1865–1877* (New York, 1924), 8. The story of the origins of the KKK has been told repeatedly. See also John C. Lester and Daniel L. Wilson, *KKK: Its Origin, Growth and Dis-*

bandment (Nashville, 1884); Stanley F. Horn, *Invisible Empire* (Boston, 1939); Walter L. Fleming, *The Sequel of Appomattox* (New Haven, 1919); and more recently, William Randall, *The Ku Klux Klan: A Century of Infamy* (New York, 1965); and Allen Trelease, *White Terror: The Ku Klux Klan Conspiracy and Southern Reconstruction* (Westport, CT, 1971).

23. H. Grady McWhiney and Francis B. Simkins make a strong case, using interviews with Klan victims from the U.S. congressional investigation conducted in 1871, that the black population was not taken in by this "ghostly" attire but rather feared the violence employed by the Klan against them. See McWhiney and Simkins, "The Ghostly Legend of the KKK," *Negro History Bulletin* 16 (1950–51): 109–11. See also Gladys-Marie Fry, *Night Riders in Black Folk History* (Athens, GA, 1975).

24. Davis, *Authentic History of the Ku Klux Klan*, 88.

25. Lester and Wilson, *KKK: Its Origin, Growth and Disbandment* and John C. Reed, *The Brothers' War* (Boston, 1905) were both participant accounts. Mr. and Mrs. W. B. Romine, *History of the Original Ku Klux Klan* (Pulaski, TN, 1924) and Davis, *Authentic History of the Ku Klux Klan* were written by descendants of Klan members. They all present the organization as grounded in domestic defense.

26. Romine and Romine, *History of the Original KKK*, 15.

27. Davis, *Authentic History of the KKK*, 310.

28. Ibid., 90. As in the "White Life for Two" advocated by the WCTU. Ted Ownby, *Subduing Satan: Religion, Recreation and Manhood in the Rural South, 1865–1920* (Chapel Hill, 1990), discusses this postwar "domestication" of southern white men.

29. Randall, *The Ku Klux Klan*, 14. See also Trelease, *White Terror*, xii.

30. For a further discussion of this theory, see Charlotte Perkins Gilman, *Women and Economics* (New York, 1898), esp. 99–145.

Chapter Ten

Susannah and the Elders or Potiphar's Wife? Allegations of Sexual Misconduct at Booker T. Washington's Tuskegee Institute

Adele Logan Alexander

EDITOR'S NOTE: *The white South had not completely eliminated the votes of black men in its successful effort to end Reconstruction, but it had rendered them ineffective. However, the elimination of the threat of "Negro domination" exposed the class fissures that divided the poor farmers from the businessmen who dominated political office. Continued overproduction and soil exhaustion worsened the plight of farmers of both races. The Populist Party began to court the black vote on the basis of their commonality of interests as farmers and the desire to garner sufficient votes to defeat the Democrats. Fusion governments of Populists and old Republicans were successful in North Carolina, resulting in widespread black officeholding. Recognition that blacks held the balance of power, a situation that would lead to continuing election chicanery, prompted renewed efforts by both Populists and Democrats to remove them from politics, this time legally rather than through fraud and intimidation.*

In the 1890s southern states revised their constitutions, incorporating literacy tests, poll taxes, and other means to legally remove the black vote without contravening the Fourteenth and Fifteenth Amendments to the Constitution. Legislatures passed additional laws to segregate society, and in 1896 the Supreme Court upheld the concept of a color line in Plessy v. Ferguson.

These changes in voting laws also disfranchised large numbers of white males who were impoverished and illiterate. Their removal from the voting rolls would have been impossible without intensifying the racist rhetoric to obscure class interests. As a consequence, race riots erupted in cities like Atlanta and lynchings

increased dramatically, becoming spectator events that whites of both sexes at-
tended in large numbers. The antebellum stereotype of the black male slave as
Sambo, loyal and faithful retainer of the planter's family, was superseded by the
myth of the black rapist who lusted after white women. Just as the ideology of the
southern lady functioned to uphold slavery, the ideal of pure, white womanhood
was the rationale on which white supremacy rested at the turn of the century.

It was during this turbulent period that Booker T. Washington, born a slave,
built Tuskegee Institute in Alabama into a prominent coeducational institution
for blacks. It provided vocational education in the belief that, by establishing an
economic and propertied base through self-reliance, African Americans would
eventually win acceptance in mainstream society. Washington's speech at the
Atlanta Cotton Exposition in 1895, arguing that "in all things that are purely
social we can be as separate as the five fingers," brought him to the attention of
northern philanthropists, who made him the broker for much of their gifts to black
institutions. Thus, he became a national spokesperson for African Americans,
although his views were eventually challenged, especially by W. E. B. Du Bois, a
Massachusetts native who received graduate training in Berlin and a Ph.D. from
Harvard. Du Bois argued for a liberal arts education to train leaders and a frontal
assault on disfranchisement, in contrast to Washington's advocacy of industrial
education and secret legal challenges to white supremacy.

Because of Washington's and Tuskegee's high national profile, its chaplain was
pressured to leave because of charges of sexual harassment and assault detailed
below. Washington and other black leaders and white sympathizers of both
genders were engaged in attempts at "racial uplift," although for different rea-
sons. Blacks urged racial uplift primarily as a vehicle to gain acceptance in
mainstream society, whereas whites saw it as a means of raising a formerly
enslaved people to civilized (i.e., white) standards. The core of racial uplift was
the Puritan work ethic combined with Victorian sexual ideology; and it was the
latter that necessitated the removal of both the chaplain and his accuser to protect
Tuskegee from scandal.

Victorians considered sex to be unspeakable. Women were required to be
virgins at marriage and faithful thereafter. Although unfaithfulness was immoral
for men as well as women, it was thought to be a failing inherent in men, because
of the strength of their sexual urges. Therefore, such lapses could be overlooked in
men but made women social outcasts. Societies differ profoundly in their sexual
ideologies. In that respect, precolonial West Africans were more like Native
Americans than Victorians. Expressiveness regarding sexual matters was ac-
cepted, for sex was seen as natural and normal. In many societies premarital sex
was permitted but adultery condemned. This pattern was repeated under slavery,

although Victorian views began to influence African American culture through evangelical religion.

However, racism continued to leave African American girls and women vulnerable to sexual exploitation. Legally, there was no such thing as rape of a slave by the owner, for she was his private property. The stereotype of slave as seducer blamed the victim. The Jezebel image carried over into the next century, as did the custom of white males seeking out black women for their first sexual encounters. Black women were left vulnerable in the black community as well. The judicial system was harsh on black-on-white crime but largely ignored black-on-black offenses. Often black females were left with only their wits and the possible threat to the reputations of those who had designs on them for protection. In such a situation the young were particularly at risk, for they often lacked knowledge as well as resources and were more easily intimidated by older and more powerful figures.

• • •

The brief but agonizing drama recounted here, which unfolded in early twentieth-century Alabama, included six major players. They were Flavia Ridley, a black fifteen-year-old student from New Orleans; her white hometown physician, Dr. Bush; the Reverend Edgar Penney, dean of the Phelps Bible School at the famed Tuskegee Institute; Jane Clark, the dean of women; Booker T. Washington, Tuskegee's founder and principal and the country's most renowned African American; and his wife, Margaret Murray Washington, "Lady Principal" and primary enforcer of the institute's moral and behavioral codes.[1]

The central subject here is sexual harassment, perhaps even sexual assault. Despite increasing attention to such issues in contemporary society, little historiography exists for earlier eras, especially in instances when both the accuser and accused have been African Americans.[2] Although similar stories permeate modern newspapers, magazines, campus records, and conversation, these matters generally have been ignored or overlooked by historians, at least in part because sexual harassment only recently has been designated a criminal offense, because institutional records usually are closely guarded, and because any discussion of sexual behavior made most people in Victorian America feel so squeamish. The latter circumstance, of course, remains somewhat true even today.

This particular cautionary southern story may be considered in splendid (or tawdry) isolation as an intriguing but inconclusively resolved morality play. Even better, perhaps, we can look at it in the complex context of race, gender, age, and power relationships in the period of American history that for much of the country has been called the Age of Reform, but which esteemed black historians like Rayford Logan more often—and probably more accurately—have labeled the Nadir.

In the winter of 1907, Flavia Ridley had been at Tuskegee Institute only since the previous September. She was a small, physically frail girl who recently had endured several extended hospital stays following surgery to correct an unspecified malady. The operation resulted in some temporary paralysis of one leg, but that condition ameliorated over time. She also experienced ongoing bladder pain and intense menstrual discomfort. Because of her chronic poor health, she had come to board at the home of the Reverend Edgar Penney, his wife, Estelle, and their two children, Van Buren and Emma (Ridley's contemporary), rather than living in one of the dormitories at Tuskegee. Ridley's closest school friend was a girl named Florence, who often visited her at the Penneys'.

In January 1907, Flavia Ridley reported to several institute officials that Edgar Penney had made a number of unwelcome and improper sexual overtures toward her the previous month. During the official investigation into these charges, an unidentified person associated with the school also searched Ridley's bedroom and found several letters written to her by a physician in New Orleans named Bush.[3] This correspondence, suggesting some sort of clandestine interactions with erotic overtones between Bush and Ridley the previous year, promptly was turned over to institute authorities.

According to Ridley, the incidents (about a half dozen) that constituted Penney's alleged misconduct started shortly before Christmas 1906, and continued through early January. She made her formal complaints the following week, and subsequently was interrogated twice, first by Dean Jane Clark, then, several days later, by Margaret Murray Washington.

Ridley charged that the first episode occurred the Saturday before Christmas, when Penney kissed her in a manner that she considered inappropriate. "My father doesn't do it that way and I don't want you to," she told him. She slapped Penney's face, she said, and asserted that his kiss was not the sort that should be bestowed on "a little girl," as he had claimed. The day after Christmas, her account continued, Penney summoned her to his study, closed the door, and forcibly tried to pull her onto his lap. Later that week, Ridley asserted, he urged her to participate in some "gymnastics" with him, then hugged and kissed her. She tried to get away, but he just "would laugh and go on" when she protested. Soon thereafter, she said, he attempted to maneuver her into his bedroom, but was interrupted by his wife's unexpected arrival. One evening Penney, without invitation, entered Ridley's room, and again tried to embrace her, saying, "Don't you see you want me as bad as I want you? See how red your face is." Another afternoon, the girl declared, Penney insisted that she come to his study to pick up a letter. He teasingly withheld it from her, then told her to retrieve it from the sofa. When she did, he threw her onto the couch. She wanted to get up but he held her down. "I am not going to hurt you," he insisted. She struggled and cried out, but no one, she believed, could hear her. Ridley was a small girl and the chaplain was a large man in his early fifties; she was not strong enough to deter him. She told him not to touch her, but he started "fooling with my clothes," and felt around inside her dress and undergarments with his hand. He ceased fondling her, she stated, only when he discovered she was menstruating, saying, "Oh, I did not know that you were unwell, I will let you go."

Flavia Ridley detailed these charges during the interview conducted by Dean Clark. Prior to that time, she had told the story to no one but Florence, her school chum, and Dr. John Kenney, Tuskegee Institute's physician. Kenney neither confirmed nor denied the conversation, though Ridley asserted that when she confided in him, she thought the doctor believed her account. Ridley never told Penney's daughter about the unwelcome incidents because it concerned "her father . . . she would not believe it . . . she says I am crazy." "I thought," Ridley said during the interrogation, "I would wait and see if he would stop." As the first round of questioning concluded, she swore that she could "stand by this [her testimony] in the sight of God."

A few days after the session with Dean Clark, Ridley was again called to the institute's offices and questioned on that second occasion by Margaret Murray Washington, the school's Lady Principal and Booker T. Washington's wife. As was common in such schools, personal as well as professional associations linked the ranking administrators with one another, and the Penneys and Washingtons had been friends for more than fifteen years. Estelle Penney, the chaplain's spouse, often cared for the Washington children and had nursed them and Margaret Washington herself through several illnesses. Margaret Murray Washington certainly would have been predisposed to believe Edgar Penney and doubt his young accuser. In addition, establishing his innocence and casting doubt on Flavia Ridley's honesty clearly would be in the institute's best interests. A troublemaking student could be dismissed with far less furor and explanation than the school's longtime chaplain.

During a follow-up interrogation session, Ridley verified and duplicated much of her prior testimony, but this time the questioning also delved into her medical history, exploring several strange incidents when Dr. Bush, her physician in Louisiana, hypnotized her, treated her while she was "asleep," then trained her in self-hypnosis—supposedly to help alleviate her menstrual cramps.

Margaret Washington based most of her questions on the contents of the letters from Bush that were taken from Ridley's room. Midway through this second interview Flavia Ridley protested, "where did my letters come from?" but received only Margaret Washington's blunt retort: "I am asking questions now." Because the student was in their "charge," the Lady Principal asserted, the school, serving *in loco parentis,* had a "perfect right to have" her personal correspondence, though Ridley complained that even her father "never reads any of my letters."

In excruciating detail, Margaret Washington explored a statement from one of the doctor's letters, in which he wrote that he wanted Ridley to "let me massage the neck of your bladder." The girl denied that the physician had "massaged" her in that fashion, although she admitted that because of the hypnosis, she could not confirm exactly what "treatment" he might have administered. Ridley further said that she no longer believed that Dr. Bush was "a good man," although others—including her own family— certainly did. Over the course of the previous autumn she had come to conclude that he was a "dishonourable husband," because of the improprieties suggested throughout his correspondence. She never answered Bush's letters, she said, and in any case, probably would not have been mature or assertive enough to challenge his conduct. In closing, Margaret Washington asked Ridley, "You know so much about hypnotism, don't you think that these things [her accusations against Penney] are just in your mind?" Flavia Ridley answered, "No." "Have you told all the truth about this matter?" Washington continued. "Yes," replied Ridley. "Nothing but the truth?" "No ma'am," she insisted.

The purloined letters from Ridley's physician were brought to bear as evidence against her and used to reflect adversely on her judgment, "purity," and mental stability. The correspondence indicated that in the previous year, when the girl had been Bush's patient, the doctor had treated both her urinary tract problems and menstrual disorders, but it also suggested that a nonprofessional relationship had developed between them—although perhaps not one of mutual consent. Bush had even persuaded her to spend some recuperative time as a houseguest (with him and his wife) in the Louisiana country town where he conducted some of his practice.

Writing to Booker T. Washington at the time of this debacle, one of Penney's staunch defenders argued that Bush's letters to Ridley completely "invalidated . . . her character . . . [and] render[ed] her testimony worthless." They were written, it was asserted, by "a married man, apparently white, who mingles medical advice with love-making." The extraordinary presumption was that most of the blame for these alleged interracial improprieties lay with the girl.

Throughout the summer of 1906, Bush had written often and intemperately to his young patient, on one occasion saying, "you see, Flavia, I am selfish. I want *you* . . . I long to have you." "Ever since I first hypnotized you, you have seemed to belong to me—to be a part of me," he went on. He further directed that "you will refuse to let anyone but me give you local treatment." Additional massage (erotic manual stimulation, it would seem), he assured her, "would do your bladder good. . . . I know you would like to be treated that way again." He obsessively ordered Ridley to send him a letter "right from your heart and soul," adding, in what must be presumed to be posthypnotic suggestion, "*when you have read this you will . . . get into your bed, . . . you will see my eyes . . .* [and] dream of what was best last May." "Be my obedient child," he commanded, "no one else shall have you." "Write to me, Baby," he continued. "I know letter-writing is hard for you, but not when you are writing your love to me."

In response to Flavia Ridley's charges against him, Edgar Penney declared both orally and in writing that most of the girl's accusations were total fabrications. He said that he had neither hugged and stroked her, pulled her into his study, pushed her onto a couch, nor "drew her up to me." He characterized the purported comment about discovering that she had her menstrual period when he probed inside her clothing as "absolutely untrue," adding, it "makes me blush with shame to have to write the word." He stated that she never slapped his face, "there being no occasion for such action." He did ask her to come upstairs on one occasion to retrieve a letter but said that he remained at his desk when she came to get it. He had suggested some "gymnastics" but argued that those activities included both his own son and Ridley. Penney further stated that his wife, not Ridley, objected to the strenuousness of the proposed exercises.

"Never, never," the chaplain insisted, did he, or would he, say that he "wanted her as bad as she wanted me."

Booker T. Washington quickly decided (and so wrote Penney on January 19, 1907) that "there is nothing left for me to do but to suggest that it will be better for all concerned for you to present your resignation." "It is practically impossible," Washington continued, "for you to render any further service to the institution." "This latter view," he concluded, "represents not only the attitude of teachers but students" as well. There is, however, no evidence suggesting that Tuskegee's students had any involvement whatsoever in Washington's actions regarding this case. He added that his decision did "not in any degree attempt to pass judgment upon your guilt or innocence, upon your discretion or lack of discretion." "In the long run," Washington concluded, Edgar Penney would "be happier and more useful elsewhere."

The chaplain strenuously resisted resigning, but ultimately had no choice but to leave "under pressure." He negotiated a favorable settlement with the institute by which he and his family remained in their school-owned home for some months, while he continued to receive half his usual salary, although he was relieved of all official duties. With the termination agreement in place, Penney submitted his resignation, admitting no culpability, and continued to protest the loss not only of his work but of his "good name" as well. "You have treated me," he wrote his old friend Booker T. Washington, "as though I had had a fair trial and had been found guilty and dismissed in disgrace." "You could not have planned better to do me and my family the greatest human injury," he continued. In spite of this alleged mistreatment, Penney asserted, "I shall always love Tuskegee Institute. It is our school; we helped to make it. I would not, willingly, lift a finger to harm it."

It soon became known, however, that on at least two previous occasions other young women had made similar accusations against Penney. The first incident supposedly took place at Atlanta University, possibly while the chaplain was a student there during the 1870s, but no description of that purported event has been found. Rumors about those early charges of misconduct against Penney may have been passed on by another graduate of Atlanta University who lived and worked at Tuskegee Institute.[4] The second episode when a female student complained about his behavior occurred at the institute itself around 1895. On that occasion, the chaplain was "exonerated and retained, and the girl sent away." The devious student who had divulged this "mischievous tale" ultimately "acknowledged that she had . . . only brought the charges that she might force her parents to take her home." In both prior cases, Penney's defenders in the Ridley situation flatly asserted, "the word of the girl has been impeached in such a way as to show her testimony to be worthless."

One of the school's most persistent and racist detractors, however, had already written about Tuskegee's "faculty scandals" involving a "Negro Clergyman . . . all of which is too indelicate for divulgation." He added, "It is so difficult for a modest, virtuous Negro girl . . . to preserve her chastity athwart the smooth allurement of some Negro Parson or Educator." [5]

Undeterred by such inflammatory claims, Penney's supporter soundly berated Booker T. Washington for his handling of the 1907 Penney-Ridley matter, asking whether the school was "not bound to be governed, in dealing with him, by the ordinary laws of evidence which prevail among men even outside the courts?" "Does a school owe nothing to a teacher in the way of protection from the calumnies of irresponsible students?" Penney's dogged champion continued, never suggesting that the school might "owe" something to one of its students as well "in the way of protection" from an "irresponsible" teacher. He further argued that Washington had "done Mr. Penney a grievous wrong, besmirching his character and injuring him financially . . . upon insufficient grounds." The letter condemned the institute's apparent disregard of proper "legal" procedures in respect to Penney's "rights." Edgar James Penney, the writer declared, had no opportunity to "be confronted with the girl who made the charges—a claim which even a guilty man should hardly be denied." And what did Penney's persistent advocate suggest that Washington might have done in light of the supplemental "evidence" provided by Dr. Bush's letters to Ridley? Should Washington have used his considerable moral and administrative authority to exonerate the chaplain? "It is never too late to rectify a mistake like this," the stalwart defense concluded. No one, it seems, spoke up for Flavia Ridley.

Although no formal charges were brought against her and no records detail her dismissal, Ridley was promptly expelled and sent home to New Orleans. But she found little comfort or support there either. Both her father and aunt (her mother was deceased) evidently "disbelieve[d] the charges she has made, and have written letters of regret and sympathy to the Penneys."

Much to their distress, Tuskegee Institute officials could not keep this matter, with its lurid implications, out of the press. The *Birmingham Ledger* and the *Montgomery Advertiser* (both white-owned Alabama newspapers) ran articles about the unfolding scandal at the famous black school. The *Ledger* sent a reporter, who obtained an interview with Booker T. Washington—certainly the principal's attempt at "damage control."

In the *Ledger's* account, Washington confirmed the "rumors," which, he said, had brought Penney's "usefulness as a member of the Tuskegee Institute faculty to an end." He showed the reporter much of the relevant correspondence, including a letter from the chaplain's wife "appealing to Dr. Washington to retain Penn[e]y." Washington told the newsman that "Rev. Penn[e]y has been with Tuskegee Institute for fifteen years [and] has made a splendid record," although, he somewhat cryptically added, "he is naturally of a nervous temperament." Further, Washington asserted, "gossip" suggested that "Penn[e]y had acted very imprudently and that he had overstepped the bounds of propriety in that he had kissed his ward and boarder." "I, with the advice and consent of some of the trustees," continued Washington, "asked for Penn[e]y's resignation, which request has been complied with."

The *Montgomery Advertiser's* account added that "Penn[e]y threatens to sue the college authorities because of his dismissal, but . . . no concern is felt at the school over his threats." "Washington," this second report also confirmed, "was not convinced of either the truth or the falsity of the charge." If the institute had been able to substantiate the charges, the later article concluded, "criminal proceedings would be instituted against the former chaplain." This never happened, and, in fact, no documentation concerning this incident substantiates any threatened legal actions.

Flavia Ridley's accusations against Penney never were proved or disproved; nonetheless, both parties ultimately left Tuskegee Institute under a cloud. Their names surely had been tarnished. Penney, however, was not so seriously damaged that he was deprived of his livelihood. Possibly he even received circumspect letters of recommendation from the institute. Almost certainly Washington, as influential as he was, never cautioned any potential employers about the suspected proclivities of Tuskegee's former chaplain and his own longtime friend. Nothing has been discovered about Ridley's life after she was sent home in disgrace to New Orleans. Despite the impact on the two central players in this drama, Washington's halo may have been knocked slightly askew, but his personal reputation and that of his renowned industrial school remained basically unsullied.[6]

Many present-day comparisons can be made to this case.[7] Young women remain reluctant to tell about how men in positions of power and respect may manipulate and sexually abuse, or even assault them. Like Flavia Ridley, they may have good reason to fear that institutional officials—and sometimes even their own families—may disbelieve, condemn, and punish them. Often charges cannot be substantiated, especially when the perpetrators are trusted, influential citizens. Usually there are no witnesses. It is extremely difficult to prove such allegations against physicians, teachers, members of the clergy, and other "elders" possessing that sort of rarely challenged authority and prestige.

On the other hand, particularly at a school like Tuskegee—and similar incidents have occurred at virtually every academic establishment—officials concluded that they must go to great lengths to protect the *institution's* reputation against any unsavory innuendo. Most of the white community also remained (and remains) ready to believe any and all such stories about sexual improprieties attributed to African Americans, both male and female. And men of otherwise honorable reputations easily *can* be maligned unfairly. Black men especially have always been vulnerable to irresponsible accusations concerning sexual misconduct.

In the South, however, lynchings and other acts of violence perpetuated against African Americans have occurred almost exclusively when allegations of sexual improprieties have been made concerning nonwhite men and white women. Unlawful actions or subsequent legal proceedings *never* resulted when white men like Bush sexually abused black females and rarely happened when African American men were suspected of taking unwelcome sexual liberties with women of their own race.[8] At Tuskegee Institute, however, where officials always perceived such a pressing need to defend the school's reputation, someone like Edgar Penney could and did lose his position on the faculty as a result of the charges brought by a young African American female. Although he left Tuskegee under a cloud, Penney nonetheless soon found appropriate work. He went on to other black schools and, somewhat surprisingly, ultimately became the minister at an all-white church, where he served for a number of years prior to his death in 1935.

The Penney-Ridley case was not the only documented case of this sort during Tuskegee Institute's early years. A similar episode concerning a different member of the faculty had transpired a decade earlier. On that occasion, school officials discharged the head academic teacher, William Jenkins, following accusations of "sexual advances" made by two "girl students." At the time of this earlier case Washington asserted that "it would not be best for you [Jenkins] nor for the school for you to longer remain connected with it," adding, with apparently genuine sorrow, that the dismissal was "the most painful duty that I have been called upon to perform during my connection with the institution." Twenty-six professors and administrators rallied to Jenkins's defense, as did some students, but Washington cast aside their expressions of support, arguing that he did not wish to "have students meddling in such affairs." Not all faculty members, however, championed their possibly errant colleague. One influential teacher told Washington that although she was "deeply pained at the Jenkins incident," she nonetheless wished to "express to you my hearty approval of your investigation," adding that it was important to "impress the students that we stand here for purity among men and women."[9]

William Jenkins understandably decried "the ruin of my reputation," which was, he said, "a matter of life & death to me." He did, however, plead "guilty, in part, to indiscretion," but further asserted that "no immorality was intended or shown." "As matters now stand," he protested, "the impression has gone forth that I attempted to commit rape." This, Jenkins argued, was a "great wrong." Washington replied that the school's executive council had "not declared you guilty of the charge . . . but we find that your name and the reputation of the school were so connected with the charges that to keep you here meant the ruin of all that we are trying to do." "You cannot," he continued, "class this case as a court case . . . [when] a charge must be proven."[10]

"I still maintain that whenever a teacher or preacher becomes involved in a scandal," Jenkins somewhat prophetically responded at that time, "his or her usefulness is impaired . . . and he or she should seek new fields of labor, whether guilty or innocent." "I do not," he asserted, "belong to that class of despoilers of homes that prey upon the virtue of our young girls." "But," he concluded, "the action of your committee [the school's executive council] has placed me thus."[11]

Yet just as it would come to pass ten years later in the Penney-Ridley case, William Jenkins's career, in fact, was not ruined. He moved on to a job at his alma mater, Fisk College in Nashville, Tennessee. He later became a federal civil servant in Washington, D.C. and then in Montgomery, Alabama (positions almost certainly acquired with the help of references from the politically influential Booker T. Washington). He died a few years before the new round of accusations of sexual misconduct surfaced against Penney. Ironically, Washington recalled that the errant Jenkins himself often had "reminded him [Washington] of the harm that has been done the school by the retaining of Mr. Penney," when the prior charges were brought against the chaplain in 1895.[12]

The Reverend Edgar Penney was an ordained minister and an established scriptural scholar who would have been familiar with early versions of the Bible that included the story of Susannah and the elders. Susannah was an appealing young woman who, while bathing one day, was spied on and lewdly taunted by a group of lascivious and voyeuristic elderly judges. This account has been portrayed by a number of Renaissance painters, but it "didn't make the cut" and does not appear in the Bible's more commonly used modern editions.[13]

Another brief anecdote appearing in virtually every translation of the Old Testament is that of Potiphar's wife, an otherwise unidentified woman who, reportedly, unsuccessfully tried to seduce Joseph—he of the many-colored coat. According to the Scriptures, when Joseph rejected her advances, Potiphar's wife retaliated by accusing him of taking improper sexual liberties with her. Although no one else witnessed that incident, Joseph's protestations of innocence were accepted, and he was fully exonerated of any wrongdoing.

Which leads us to ask whether Flavia Ridley was Susannah, lusted after and victimized by various "elders" in her life: first her physician, Dr. Bush, next Penney, her Tuskegee guardian (a cleric and teacher), then ultimately betrayed by institute authorities, who expressed their official and personal regrets over the chaplain's unwilling departure but apparently had no concerns about a troublesome, quickly expelled student and her future. Or was she more akin to Potiphar's wife, who, for whatever reasons (personal antipathy, adolescent rebellion against authority, or retaliation following a rejection of her own romantic overtures) made up a story, lied, and thereby cast aspersions on the reputation of an honorable man?

Was Edgar James Penney wrongly accused? If he did behave as Flavia Ridley asserted, was this a case of inappropriate and unintentionally offensive conduct, or should it be characterized (in our contemporary frame of reference) as sexual harassment, abuse, even assault? After the passage of almost a century, probably nothing more about the accuracy and intricacies of this particular story will ever be known. Also, in 1907, few legal definitions had been established or statutes instituted dealing with sexual misconduct other than rape or attempted rape.[14]

It confirms, however, that nothing really is new under the sun, and young women have always been (and remain) vulnerable to this kind of exploitation. Often they feel shamed, intimidated, or both, and cannot deal with behavior of this sort, especially when it is initiated by older men whom they are taught to trust, respect, and obey. Usually the girls are reluctant to speak out. On the other hand, their charges, true or false, can severely (sometimes wrongly) damage those whom they accuse. Generally, however, little attention is paid to the pain and suffering that the young women may endure or the long-term effects on their lives. Thus it often remains, even now, in so many situations that only recently have been legally defined and declared unlawful. The whole truth is difficult to come by. Frequently there is no "hard," irrefutable evidence. In most cases, there are no witnesses. It's her word against his. Whom should we believe?

Like Tuskegee Institute at the turn of the century, schools, churches, and other institutions usually still have much to gain and nothing to lose by trying to sweep these sorts of unpleasant circumstances under their proverbial rugs. Only rarely, however, is it asked or ascertained what reasons these young women might have to make up such destructive stories. Unlike the men whom they accuse and who strenuously protest their innocence, it would seem that, in most instances, they have very little to profit from telling such sorry tales.

NOTES

1. Except where otherwise indicated, all documentation concerning the Penney-Ridley case has been gleaned from the 1907 folder for Tuskegee Institute's Phelps Bible School, Booker T. Washington Papers, Manuscript Division, Library of Congress (hereafter BTW Papers). This incident was called to my attention by Louis R. Harlan. It is briefly detailed (with a somewhat different slant and conclusion) in Harlan, *Booker T. Washington: The Wizard of Tuskegee, 1901–1915* (New York, 1983), 159–61. Some of the relevant documents in this case are reprinted in Louis R. Harlan and Raymond W. Smock, eds., *The Booker T. Washington Papers*, vol. 9, *1906–8* (Urbana, 1980), 187–90, 194–96, 203–4, 212–13, 214–16, 220–22, and 234–35. I especially thank Professor Harlan for his frank and helpful conversations. Comments concerning this paper at the 1994 American Historical Association convention, the "Black Women in the Academy" conference that same year, and the Association for the Study of Afro-American Life and History convention in 1995 have helped me refine my arguments.

2. One exception that provides an overview and theoretical framework is Darlene Clark Hine, "Rape and the Inner Lives of Southern Black Women: Thoughts on the Culture of Dissemblance," *Signs: Journal of Women in Culture and Society* 14, 4 (summer 1989): 912–20.

3. I have been unable to learn Dr. Bush's given name.

4. Although Atlanta University subscribed to the Du Boisian philosophy of providing a classical academic education for the "Talented Tenth," Tuskegee Institute recruited a number of very able faculty members from that institution. It seems possible, though no hard evidence supports it, that Adella Hunt Logan—a longtime Tuskegee teacher, the Washingtons' next-door neighbor, and wife of Booker T.'s second in command, Warren Logan—passed on this story. She had attended Atlanta University at roughly the same time as Edgar Penney.

5. Ruperth Fehnstroke, *Letters from Tuskegee, Being the Confessions of a Yankee* (Birmingham, 1905), 15.

6. Persistent though unsubstantiated rumors suggest that Booker T. Washington himself engaged in questionable sexual activities. Harlan briefly discusses these whispered scandals in his Washington biographies, especially *Wizard of Tuskegee*, 399–401.

7. Professor Anita Hill's widely discussed 1991 testimony concerning the actions of Justice Clarence Thomas stimulated this paper, and the controversies surrounding Professor C. Eric Lincoln, poet and teacher Derek Walcott, and of course Senator Bob Packwood raise comparable issues.

8. See, for example, the work of Ida B. Wells-Barnett, such as "Lynch Law," reprinted in Mildred I. Thompson, *Ida B. Wells-Barnett: An Exploratory Study of an American Black Woman, 1893–1930* (Brooklyn, 1990).

9. Harlan and Smock, *Washington Papers*, vol. 9; and Adella Hunt Logan to Booker T. Washington, December 1895, BTW Papers.

10. Harlan and Smock, eds., *Washington Papers*, vol. 9.

11. Ibid.

12. Ibid.

13. I thank Professor Alice Bellis of Howard University's Divinity School for her knowledge of and perspectives on stories about sexual misconduct in the Old Testament.

14. Professor Anita Faye Hill is currently working on a history of sexual harassment law.

Chapter Eleven

Waiting for the Millennium, Remembering the Past

Appalachian Women in Time and Place

Margaret Ripley Wolfe

EDITOR'S NOTE: *Until the second half of the twentieth century, the South was the most homogeneous region of the nation, being largely a biracial society of British and West African descent. Nevertheless, there was great variety within such homogeneity, and this variety produced a corresponding diversity of myths and stereotypes. For example, both the southern belle and the Appalachian hillbilly were thought to be examples of a noble Anglo-Saxon heritage, but whereas the former was supposed to be the natural product of aristocratic breeding, the latter belonged to a people trapped in time, living like their Anglo-Saxon forebears.*

The southern highlands had remained a part of the antebellum backcountry, ill adapted to staple crops. Large families and subsistence agriculture continued to characterize the region in the postwar period. The textile mills, which were in part an attempt to address rural white poverty, siphoned off some women and their families but provided only a pittance. Railroad construction in the early twentieth century opened up the coal fields at the same time that the national press discovered Appalachia, describing it as both a place and a problem. But instead of bringing prosperity to the region, the mines paid starvation wages, leading to violent strikes in the 1930s, when a county in Kentucky got the name "Bloody Harlan."

The industrial boom initiated by World War II created opportunities for those willing to leave Appalachia for Detroit, Chicago, and other midwestern cities. In retrospect, the 1940s were a watershed decade for the entire South, because the region was able to become increasingly modernized as a consequence of the war effort and was able to share in the prosperity that followed. Improved communications, especially television, brought the rest of the nation and indeed the world into the homes of southerners who heretofore had been characterized as closed-minded.

Nevertheless, the exodus continued. Hillbillies were not the only ones to leave the South. Attracted by higher wages and more urbane lifestyles, southerners migrated both north and west. There was a "brain drain" of the highly educated. African Americans, whose Great Migration had begun when jobs opened up in the North during World War I, continued to leave in large numbers. As a consequence of blacks changing from a rural people to an urban one, concentrated in all the nation's major cities, racism became a national, not just a regional, problem. All these groups took aspects of their southern culture with them, as the spectacular growth of the Southern Baptist denomination and the spread of jazz and country and western music attest.

With the end of segregation and the spread of air conditioning to cars and homes as well as public buildings, the South had by the 1960s become more like the rest of the country. By the 1970s its low wages and nonunion workforce became increasingly attractive to national corporations competing with the low wages of developing nations. The recession of the early 1980s, in which many factories in the "Rust Belt" of the Midwest closed or cut back, sent workers to the Sun Belt. With them came management-level and service personnel, bringing ethnic diversity that contrasted sharply with the largely British and African origins of southerners. Florida in particular seemed increasingly less southern over the course of the twentieth century. Its milder winters made it attractive to northern retirees, especially Jews from the Northeast; and problems in Latin America increased migration from the Southern Hemisphere. Cubans fleeing Castro built a prosperous community in Miami, while refugees from Haiti struggled for acceptance. The Vietnam War added to the numbers of Asian Americans sprinkled across the South.

The in-migration of such diverse cultures raises the question of southern distinctiveness. The post–Civil War South had been a region set apart: more overtly racist, less educated, poorer, less industrialized and urbanized, more violent, and more attached to religious fundamentalism and social conservatism than the rest of the nation. Yet it was also believed to be friendlier, more mannerly, slow-paced, and traditional. Has this in-migration diluted southern distinctiveness to the point where the region is more a geographical than a cultural entity, or have the newcomers adopted the attitudes and values of the South, causing it to endure as a distinctive culture? Even Appalachian women, long isolated from mainstream culture, have experienced significant social change, especially in the latter half of the twentieth century.

· · ·

The fast-breaking social, economic, and political changes of the twentieth century have maneuvered the great majority of Appalachian women into the American mainstream. The advent of suffrage and the enactment of more enlightened state laws pertaining to divorce and the status of married females in tandem with federal antidiscrimination legislation have lifted most of the statutory restrictions that once virtually guaranteed the subordinate status of the nation's women. Furthermore, industrialization, urbanization, and technology have relieved rural isolation; educational opportunities and better medical care have improved the standard of living.[1] Nonetheless, with a new century dawning, considerable confusion still surrounds Appalachian women. Homespun grannies, "yarb" doctors, "fotched-on" women, Dogpatch cuties, and coal miners' daughters capture the popular imagination.[2] Indeed, examples of all of these can be identified in the southern mountains. Yet categorical use of such images tends to reduce the vast majority of flesh-and-blood women to stereotypes and consigns them to a time and a place that defy contemporary reality.

Appalachian distinctiveness seems to be a recurring theme in American culture, and the aberrant behavior of the minority garners far more attention from the media than the normal conduct of the majority. A fundamental ambivalence likewise runs through much of the music and many of the fictional works, historical accounts, and sociological studies that focus on the Appalachian region. Contemporary treatments by natives as well as outsiders often seem to resonate with the theme of "yesterday's people."[3] In a 1996 paean to a lifelong resident of Avery County, North Carolina, who had just celebrated her hundredth birthday, a writer for *Blue Ridge Country* declared, "The greatest masterpiece I have ever seen is a stately mountain woman, tall and proud. With a back as straight as a hickory chair, a wit sharper than an ax, and a penchant for gardening, storytelling, needlework, and home remedies, she's a classic." Tennessee state historian Wilma Dykeman, a native of Asheville, North Carolina, and resident of Newport, Tennessee, adopted this bit of wisdom for the title and theme of her 1962 novel, *The Tall Woman*, which features the isolated but resilient Lydia McQueen. In *The Dollmaker*, first published in 1954, writer Harriette Simpson Arnow, herself a native of the Cumberlands, had introduced a powerful mountain female. Arnow told a story of alienated Appalachian migrants in World War II–era Detroit through the character Gertie Nevels.[4]

Fond memories of a world never experienced are a force to be reckoned with among the common folk, and the temptation to relegate mountain women to a nostalgic past looms almost as large with the literati. Yet some of Appalachia's feminine voices have proved to be astute observers of the contemporary scene. The coal miner's daughter, eastern Kentucky's Loretta Lynn, expresses the liberating effects of birth control in "The Pill," which became a hit record for her in 1975. "Well, they didn't have none of them pills when I was younger, or I'd have been swallowing 'em like popcorn," Lynn explains in her autobiography. "See, the men who run some of the radio stations, they banned the record because they didn't like what I was saying. But the women knew. Like I say, I know what it's like to be pregnant and nervous and poor." Loretta Lynn's recordings "The Pill" and "Rated X" speak openly to women's issues.[5]

Dolly Parton, a superstar from Sevierville, Tennessee, has hardly been reticent about her modern views. An astute businesswoman and a millionaire many times over, she is the embodiment of the "rags to riches" story. Parton is particularly noted for the song "Nine to Five" as well as the like-named film that depicts the lives of working women in metropolitan America. Remembering the onset of adolescence in the Great Smokies, Parton writes, "Womanhood was a difficult thing to get a grip on in those hills, unless you were a man. My sister and I used to cling desperately to anything halfway feminine." Sin, sex, and salvation seemed to mesh in traditional mountain communities. "I guess it wasn't unmasculine for the men to get their religion in these short, intense doses," observes Parton. "I suppose also that most of the women had relationships with God that were more constant and committed, much like their relationships with their spouses." Describing her own baptism, she remembers, "When I was twelve, those body parts that were destined to become my calling card in life and the reference point for many a joke by late-night talk-show hosts were already well in evidence." After being fully immersed, Dolly's "white cotton dress became somewhat transparent in the rushing water, and the boys on the bank were moved to shout 'Hallelujah!' "[6]

Both Lynn and Parton have not only followed in the footsteps of pioneering performer Patsy Cline but have also ventured into new frontiers. When Cline, from Winchester, Virginia, went "Walking after Midnight," her sultry voice conveyed a sensuous message. Whether she was belting out "San Antonio Rose" or remembering "Faded Love," she hardly concealed her raw sexuality. While some of the more recent female entertainers from the Appalachian region have placed themselves on the cutting edge of social issues and experimental styles, a few of their predecessors had managed to carve out nontraditional careers for themselves by embracing and perpetuating traditional musical styles and performing songs that incorporated age-old themes. For example, "No group better embodied the mood and style of the family parlor and country church than the Carters," according to Bill C. Malone, an authority on country music. The original Carter Family, with Maybelle Addington Carter, Sara Doughterty Carter, and A. P. ("Doc") Carter, provided "three-part harmony, Maybelle's unique guitar style, and their large collection of vintage songs (such as 'Wildwood Flower' and 'Will the Circle Be Unbroken') [which] still influence country singers today." Nonetheless, for Maybelle and Sara, touring extensively and making records represented a dramatic departure from the usual conduct of mountain women in and around Maces Spring, Virginia. Along the way, A. P. and Sara's marriage broke up (they divorced in 1939); and Maybelle left her husband at home on the farm when she renewed her career and took her daughters on the road with her as Mother Maybelle and the Carter Sisters. Many years later, Naomi Judd of Ashland, Kentucky, and her daughter Wynonna launched their highly successful mother-daughter act with traditional music, but in their personal lives they have exhibited a liberated, free-wheeling attitude.[7]

Just as the country music entertainers from the Appalachians have sometimes blended the traditional and the contemporary in their music and their lifestyles, so too have recent fiction writers. Lee Smith, a native of Grundy, Virginia, revisits the worlds of her relatives and her own youthful haunts in such works as *Oral History, Fair and Tender Ladies, Family Linen, The Devil's Dream,* and *Saving Grace.* Sharyn McCrumb, who also claims an Appalachian heritage, has become one of the most acclaimed female mystery writers in America. *If Ever I Return, Pretty Peggy-O, The Hangman's Beautiful Daughter, She Walks These Hills,* and *The Rosewood Casket* are all set along the Tennessee-North Carolina border. A relatively new voice on the literary scene, Elaine Fowler Palencia, writes of the denizens of "Blue Valley" in her collected stories published as *Small Caucasian Woman.* One of her characters, a resident of a nursing home, nostalgically opines, "Although we were no longer living in Blue Valley, Blue Valley still lived in us." Palencia grew up in Kentucky and Tennessee;

she no longer lives in Appalachia, but Appalachia lives on in her fiction.[8]

Yet another female writer sounded a somewhat more adventuresome and futuristic note in 1985. The internationally acclaimed poet Nikki Giovanni, an African American from Knoxville, Tennessee, declared that she would like to be "the first poet in space." "There should be a black woman in space," she explained, "and if it couldn't be a black woman, it should be a woman from Appalachia. We need somebody in space who would recognize life if they saw it." More chauvinistically than defensively, the actress Park Overall, a native of Greeneville, Tennessee, and the nurse on television's long-running sitcom *Empty Nest*, makes no secret of being proud of her heritage or her desire to bring integrity to southern characters. "We often aren't portrayed with the rich folk humor and wisdom that we have," she observes.[9]

Collectively, mountain women represent the full range of feminine experience, a spectrum that reflects both saints and sinners and all garden varieties in between. In an imaginary place that J. W. Williamson, editor of the *Appalachian Journal,* has dubbed "Hillbillyland," there reposes "extraordinary equality [for] women," including "the democracy of violence" and "the democracy of sexuality." The 1989 film *Blaze Starr*, for example, provides a Hollywood rendition of the romance between a voluptuous real-life stripper, born Fanny Belle Fleming of Mingo County, West Virginia, and Governor Earl Long of Louisiana. "'I must say, you look like a democrat to me,' Old Earl later says to her in his mating dance, but he doesn't know the half of it," according to Williamson. "Blaze forces her full equality on him, won't settle for anything less."[10]

Pitcher Nolan Ryan just had signed with the New York Mets, and the organization had sent him to Marion, Virginia, to join one of the teams in the Appalachian League. On the road he roomed with Roger Hennington. "One night," Ryan recalled, "we were in Harlan, Kentucky, staying in a room on the bottom floor of the hotel. Our room faced the alley and the hotel wasn't air-conditioned, so we kept the windows wide open." The youngsters heard a knock on the screen about midnight. "Two hookers were out there. They explained that the house security was in the lobby of the hotel and wouldn't let them come in." The "working girls" merely sought access to the hotel through the ballplayers' room. "Roger and I helped those gals crawl in through the window. . . . Then about two o'clock in the morning the hookers knocked on our door. They went through our room and exited from the hotel by crawling back out through the window."[11]

Despite the sometimes humorous aspects of human foibles—and the Appalachian region produces a wellspring of them—such tragic problems as rural poverty, inadequate medical and educational facilities, and the environmental devastation wrought by strip mining continued to stalk portions of the region as late as the 1960s. These realities were hardly lost on serious students of the region, but too often many of them spurned the present and retreated to the past. Harriette Simpson Arnow, for example, in 1960 and again in 1963 revisited her origins in two nonfiction works, *Seedtime on the Cumberland* and *Flowering of the Cumberland,* which were deeply rooted in her mountain heritage. "It was not until I was eighteen years old, away from home in a remote place," she explained, "that I made my first note ... realizing ... that when the great storytellers died and mice and rats and time had their way, many little things of the ordinary people would be lost."[12] Nonetheless, from her vantage in Ann Arbor, Michigan, Arnow remained a caustic observer of the perennial drama in the southern mountains. "I must get down to Kentucky and renew my laughter," Arnow wrote.

> I go down about twice a year; last fall there was this story of a fiercely fought nomination—it was decided to discredit the opposition by proving he was not a "good family man"; they hired a "Scarlet Woman," took the usual photographs in a hotel room, etc. The stubborn man took the case to court; testimony revealed the Scarlet woman was also a Kentucky Colonel.[13]

A sense of humor—and the ability to laugh at themselves and each other—remains an invaluable asset for Appalachians, both male and female. Not only does it sustain them in their daily lives, but it also serves them well in dealing with their critics. Casting aspersions on the region's residents may not qualify as a national diversion, but it has provided an undue amount of comic relief. Appalachians remain beyond the pale of the protected, and derogatory statements about mountain people are hardly confined to the distant past. Apparently it is still open season on hillbillies. The national media have an uncanny ability to ferret out Appalachian aberrations. Tragic tales of child brides and reports of snake-handling rituals gone awry make their way from the mountains into metropolitan America. Indeed, the license to disparage Appalachians extends into the halls of Congress as well. In a newspaper interview in July 1995, U.S. Representative Mark Souder, a Republican from Indiana, criticized the federal government for its raid on cult leader David Koresh's headquarters and the siege that followed at Waco. Said Representative

Souder, "The only law that [the FBI] clearly established [David Koresh] broke that I can see so far is he had sex with consenting minors. Do you send tanks and government troops into the large sections of Kentucky and Tennessee and other places where such things occur?" *Time* magazine titled its sidebar "The Dogpatch Defense."[14]

Regional authors, too, have been known to lace their fiction with references to incest, and seamy jokes still lurk about in the grass-roots mind. There is, for example, the tale of the only girl in fifth grade who is still a virgin; the punch line: "She's the one who can outrun her brothers." Rumors of incest and restricted gene pools continue to hover over the Appalachian populace, and popular culture has given rise to stereotypes that depict mountain women as Daisy Mae Yokum of Dogpatch, U.S.A.; Aunt Loweezy, the wife of moonshiner Snuffy Smith; or the irascible Granny and tomboy nymph Ellie Mae Clampett of *The Beverly Hillbillies*.[15]

In terms of class, ethnicity, education, vocation, and aspiration, Appalachian women have been and remain diverse. Geography, however, has served as the defining factor as well as the common denominator. *Appalachia* remains as much a state of mind as a specific place. As defined by the Appalachian Regional Commission, it encompasses thirteen states or portions thereof, stretching from the Deep South to New England; but prevailing imagery centers largely on what is known in contemporary parlance as Central Appalachia or to earlier writers and observers as Southern Appalachia and the southern highlands.[16] The region's most recent rediscovery occurred during the 1960s and 1970s. Spawned in a society fractured by civil rights crusades, rising ethnic consciousness, the Vietnam War, and women's demands for equality, the renewed interest in Appalachia brought a few national politicians to glimpse the ravages of strip mining, troops of VISTA (Volunteers in Service to America) workers, and waves of photographers and journalists. Collectively, they focused national attention on Appalachian poverty and environmental problems.

Out of this era came the writings of Harry M. Caudill as a voice crying in the wilderness. Indeed, it was the Whitesburg, Kentucky, lawyer who had been largely responsible for piquing America's renewed interest in Appalachia. His books, articles, and speeches—particularly *Night Comes to the Cumberlands: A Biography of a Depressed Area* (1963)—focused the nation's attention on the region's problems. Caudill and his wife, Anne, found themselves caught up in what she later termed "the grand poverty tour." During the 1960s, she "kept the coffee pot perking for the flow of journalists, professors, government officials and others who came to call in great numbers." By 1970 the Caudills reported, "It's a younger group these days, mostly college students." The youth movement of the 1960s and 1970s was not without its humorous aspects. "It's a great time for ladies and gentlemen to travel together in Volkswagens," Harry Caudill observed. There is "one thing you can always count on with these college students—they're invariably hungry," which distinguishes them from "most newspaper and TV men, who are drought-stricken."[17]

Two hundred years separated the youthful visitors of the 1970s from the first white settlers in Appalachia. Bisecting eastern North America, the Appalachian Mountains first represented an impediment but then became an important milestone of the westward movement. The frontier process created Appalachian women. Indeed, some of the first white women to be carried across the Appalachians were captives of Indian braves. When the first significant numbers of European females trekked into the Appalachian South, some accompanied by African American slaves of their own sex, other women already awaited them. Their Native American sisters had preceded them by thousands of years. "Inasmuch as the Cherokees had emerged by the late seventeenth century as the largest indigenous people within the Appalachians and a powerful player in the geopolitics of the eighteenth-century South," writes historian Thomas Hatley, "their story must be included in any history of the southern Appalachians."[18]

Interaction surely occurred between the white, black, and native women of this era, though it may have been limited. The record is sketchy, for as Hatley observes, "The experience of native American women is written on the faded margin of the documents we have inherited from the colonial period." Cherokee females and a few of European descent must have come in contact with each other at Fort Loudoun, which was established in 1756 on the Little Tennessee River, then the westernmost English outpost in America. Later, in 1776, Nancy Ward, "War Woman of the Cherokee," born Nanye'hi of the Wolf clan at Chota in present-day Tennessee, intervened to spare the life of Mrs. William Bean, who had been taken captive. According to oral tradition, Mrs. Bean taught her savior how to make butter.[19]

Matrilocal residence patterns and matrilineal kinship among the southeastern Indians proved bewildering to the English as well as other Western Europeans. By the early nineteenth century, however, the "Five Civilized Tribes" of the Southeast, so called because of the alacrity with which they had adapted themselves to transplanted European culture, had moved toward a redefinition of gender roles. Perennial contact with the whites affected the status of Native American women, including the Cherokee. Historian Theda Perdue notes that Indian women "began to fade from economic and political life in the early nineteenth century." Nonetheless, as cultural stresses of the eighteenth century had impacted their society, the Cherokee women farmers continued to make important economic contributions; but they could not thwart the consequences of depopulation, warfare, and colonial trade relations. Nor could they avert the removal of the 1830s, although as early as 1818, a Cherokee women's council had resisted the idea "because it appears to us that we, by this removal, shall be brought to a savage state again; for we have . . . become too much enlightened to throw aside, the privileges of a civilized life." In the late twentieth century, Native American women have reclaimed and even exceeded their former status. Wilma Mankiller ended her tenure as principal chief of the Cherokee Nation in Oklahoma in August 1995; the Eastern Band of the Cherokee Indians went to the polls the next month and elected Joyce Dugan to their highest office.[20]

As the advancing frontier and the presence of males of European descent in the backcountry undermined the status of Native American women, it reinforced the subordination of white females. It also introduced and reinforced the enslavement of their black counterparts, for the institution of slavery existed in the mountains. In 1860, for example, on the eve of the Civil War, some fifteen thousand black slaves worked in agricultural as well as nonagricultural pursuits in southwestern Virginia; another thousand or so free blacks lived in the same vicinity. Men expected women to perform the most grueling tasks associated with clearing forests, breaking ground, raising crops, and tending livestock, but that was about the extent of sharing and equality. "That the frontier created a spirit of equality among the sexes could not be farther from the truth," writes historian David Hackett Fischer. Following wandering husbands also often meant separation from parents, siblings, relatives, and friends. For most frontier women, isolation and loneliness exacerbated an already difficult existence.[21]

European newcomers had carried with them a patriarchal family structure and other common cultural attributes. Nonetheless, as early as the late eighteenth century, a class system emerged in the southern mountains, and different religious, ethnic, and racial groups coexisted.[22] Decades of relative isolation and economic retardation placed the region and its people in the backwash of civilization, although not to the exaggerated degree that the media have often suggested. In the late nineteenth and

early twentieth centuries, preindustrial society gave way to the moderniz-
ing effects of industrialization. Class structure became even more clearly
defined and cultural pluralism even more pronounced, urban areas increased in number and size, and the traditional family lost ground.

While the world of nineteenth-century Appalachian women was not
stagnant, neither was it dynamic. Indeed, from the settlement of the late
eighteenth century until the "rediscovery" almost a hundred years later,
development languished. The region included not only the rough rural
edges of society but also the cultivated lifestyles of such valley towns as
Roanoke, Virginia, Asheville, North Carolina, and Knoxville, Tennessee,
and scattered villages and county seats that were not immune to human
pretentiousness. Likewise, Appalachians as well as other relatively isolated rural Americans sometimes felt the impact of technological changes
and the powerful forces of national history.

Just as gender, class, and race affected the existence of mountain
women, so too did the patriarchal folkways transplanted from Europe
and redefined in the American wilderness. Furthermore, over time the
ideal of the southern lady—the finer points of which seem to have been
extrapolated from seventeenth-century aristocratic codes of conduct—
took hold. By the antebellum era, this model of feminine conduct had
become well entrenched. It transcended class lines to influence middle-
and lower-class women, for it was not and is not necessarily restricted to
the highborn.[23] Vestiges of this ideal, especially suffering in silence and
deferring to men, have carried over into the twentieth century and continue to impinge on the lives of Appalachian women.

"At times of peak labor demand," writes sociologist Shaunna L. Scott
in a study of agricultural life in Harlan and Letcher Counties in Kentucky,
"the entire conjugal family, extended kin, and neighbors often worked
together. Mixed-sex work teams commonly hoed corn together. There
seemed to be few job taboos for either men or women, and little stigma
attached to doing 'opposite sex work,' particularly during childhood."
Scott observes, however, that "trading work across gender boundaries
functioned primarily in one direction: that is, women were routinely
deployed in 'men's' field activities but men rarely did housework."
"Helping out," a phrase used by Appalachian men to characterize the
field work done by their women, diminished the significance of the female
contribution and maintained the centrality of males. This attitude seems
to be in keeping with the "androcentric pattern" that often has been found
in American farm families.[24] In tattered clothes and worn-out shoes,

sometimes using mattocks to hoe the hard ground of hillside tobacco patches when neither tractors nor animals have been available to pull plows, an element of twentieth-century Appalachian women have continued to feel the impact of "southern chivalry" and the "southern lady."

The Civil War served as an important watershed for Southern Appalachians as well as all southerners, displacing people and disrupting traditional roles. Temporarily at least it fractured the male dominance of daily life. Internal schisms seem to have plagued Appalachia more than other parts of the South during these troubled years. Although significant portions of the highlands remained relatively unscathed by major battles, they witnessed deep local divisions and harsh conflicts between Union and Confederate sympathizers. Some Appalachian women helped their men avoid the draft and the deserters elude apprehension. Most of them probably behaved more conventionally, sewing for the troops and corresponding with their loved ones.[25]

Because of the importance of the East Tennessee–Southwest Virginia corridor as a transportation and communication link between the Upper and Lower South, the war came to this particular area. The genuine deprivation of a people torn by their own factionalism and set upon by foraging parties from both armies contributed to the national image of Appalachians as needy and the southern mountains as a legitimate missionary field. These troubled times disrupted agricultural production, virtually halted construction of housing and other buildings, undermined the traditional connections between the small market towns and their isolated hinterlands, and gave rise to rampant inflation. The region's population knew what it meant to be hungry. Starvation stalked the residents of Cades Cove, a small mountain community in the Great Smoky Mountains, for example, as persistently as the guerrillas along the North Carolina-Tennessee border. As for the wartime experience of Appalachian women, many of them did nothing more remarkable than survive, although there were exceptions. Belle Boyd of Martinsburg, West Virginia, gathered intelligence for the likes of J. E. B. Stuart and "Stonewall" Jackson in the Shenandoah Valley.[26]

In addition to the misery that it wrought, the Civil War also served to renew the nation's interest in the resources of the Appalachian region. Before the nineteenth century had run its course, American and British capitalists had begun their systematic exploitation. "Stand at Cumberland Gap and watch the procession of civilization, marching single file," wrote the eminent historian Frederick Jackson Turner of the eighteenth-century

Trans-Allegheny frontier; "the buffalo following the trail to the salt springs, the Indian, the fur-trader, and hunter, the cattle-raiser, the pioneer farmer—and the frontier is passed." "Stand at Cumberland Gap" in the late nineteenth century and again "watch the procession of civilization, marching single file"—surveyors, geologists, railroad men, coal operators; journalists, moonshiners, Catholic priests, and Protestant missionaries; southern blacks, the native mountain whites, and the foreign-born; and "fotched-on" women.[27]

Females in the United States, particularly in the American South, had been conditioned to speak not of their rights but of their responsibilities. "During the Nineteenth Century," according to the historian Paula Baker, "women expanded their ascribed sphere into community service and care of dependents, areas not fully within men's or women's politics," an approach she labels "domestic politics." Within the conundrum of reform and reaction, Progressive philosophy and "New South" propaganda, religiosity and racism, and ambition and altruism, "domestic politics" arrived in Dixie during the latter part of the nineteenth century. As a new century dawned, southern women not only continued to perform their duties but also expanded their own opportunities. Those who had gained access to higher education, either in the women's colleges or in the increasing number of coeducational institutions, discerned the personal possibilities that reform held: to influence the world in which they lived, to carve out a public role, to find legitimate careers for themselves. Such women, according to the historian Allen F. Davis, embraced the social settlements and other Progressive-era reforms because they felt a "sense of uselessness" that "rested most heavily upon the growing number of college women—who felt they had to prove their right to higher education by doing something important."[28]

During this era, Appalachia appealed to female reformers from some European countries as well as those from the northern and southern United States, and it served as an outlet for the energies of educated, socially conscious women who ministered to the mountaineers. Katherine Pettit, May Stone, Ethel de Long Zande, Mary Breckinridge, Marguerite Butler, and Alice Lloyd joined dozens of lesser-known females in mountain mission work. Religious zeal served as the inspiration for some of these female reformers, but social consciousness of a secular nature motivated still others. Elizabeth Collins, an English woman, worked among immigrant and American-born miners and their families in southwestern Virginia during the early twentieth century. Known as the "Angel of

Happy Hollow," she centered her Methodist mission work around the coal camp of Roda, visiting from home to home and teaching girls to sew. An elderly physician wanted to marry her; when she refused him, legend has it, he committed suicide. During roughly the same time frame, Ellen Bergen, a Swede, established Kermit Mission in Scott County, Virginia, and provided a home for missionaries of different denominations. A talented artist, she painted murals on the walls of her dwelling and opened her doors to the residents of the surrounding farming and logging community. Another female at the Kermit Mission taught young girls how to do needlework. German-born Wilhelmina ("Minnie") Baer conducted an Assembly of God mission at Mendota, Virginia, commencing her work in 1937 and continuing until the early 1950s, when her health failed.[29]

Those who made their living from the fertile valley fields or who managed an existence on hillside farms represented a more homogeneous population than the denizens of coal towns. Although Appalachian mining camps of the late nineteenth and early twentieth centuries hardly qualified as melting pots, they clearly resembled double-gendered cultural smorgasbords. Novelist Denise Giardina made these environments the setting for her 1987 fictional account of labor unrest in the coal fields, *Storming Heaven*. The populations of these enclaves included not only native-born mountain whites but also "new" immigrants and American blacks from the Deep South. Referring to the various national groups, a Catholic clergyman at St. Bernard's Abbey in Cullman, Alabama, wrote during the 1920s that "while their church attendance would admit of improvement, still they cling faithfully to the faith of their fathers and at occasions like First Communion, Confirmation or dedication of a new church, the outpouring of Catholics is quite a revelation and one would imagine to live for the time in a village of the former Austrian-Hungarian Empire."[30]

According to the Dillingham Commission, established by Congress to study immigration, foreign-born workers represented three-tenths of the labor force in Alabama, Virginia, and West Virginia during the first decade of the twentieth century. Southern Italians constituted the largest ethnic group, over 30 percent of the foreign-born and more than 8 percent of the total number of employees. The Italian men often proved to be transient workers, and only a small proportion had families with them. Nonetheless, Catholic church records indicate that those immigrant men who regularly attended services had brought wives with them from the old countries or had married among their own ethnic or national groups after arriving in the United States. In some instances, Italian men as well as those from other immigrant groups married native-born Appalachian women. The outbreak of World War I in Europe and subsequent U.S. involvement virtually halted emigration while at the same time requiring the buildup of American armed forces. Consequently, such operations as the Stonega Coal and Coke Company in Wise County, Virginia, actively recruited blacks from Alabama, increasing the African American population in the Appalachian region.[31]

As the coal industry experienced one of its boom-bust cycles during the post–World War I years, most of the immigrants left the region to pursue economic opportunities elsewhere. So too did hundreds, even thousands, of native-born whites. Indeed, Appalachia's Cumberland Plateau was anything but prosperous from the 1920s through the 1950s. A Benedictine priest, Father Clarence Meyer, who did mission work in the mountains of Kentucky and Tennessee from 1926 to 1932, reported seeing "miners with their families living in burlap tents on the top of a mountain in the dead of winter rooting in the wilds for something to eat." A report from Clay County, Kentucky, during the Great Depression of the 1930s claimed that when men and boys passed one cabin, they "pulled their caps down over their eyes"; the reason, as they explained, was, "Well, you see the women folks in that thar place hain't got no clothes at all. Even their rags is clean wore out and gone!" From this milieu came great fictional literature. James Still's *River of Earth* provides an account of the mining camps of Appalachia during the Great Depression and a family confronting starvation that rivals John Steinbeck's *Grapes of Wrath*.[32]

The coal culture, with which Appalachia has so often been identified, represents merely one facet, albeit an important one, of a complicated regional history. Within that milieu, women have had their roles; generally, as miners' wives they have been supporting actresses. There have also been heroines; the most noted was Mary Harris "Mother" Jones, who had a long career as a labor agitator. In March 1913, when she was eighty-one, "Mother" Jones and forty-seven other civilians were tried by a military court in West Virginia on charges of murder and conspiracy to murder. The charges stemmed from violence during the long coal miners' strike around Paint Creek and Cabin Creek in Kanawha County. Jones's subsequent imprisonment led the U.S. Senate to establish a subcommittee to investigate the circumstances. Public pressure came to bear, resulting in settlement of the strike and the release of the prisoners.[33]

Appalachian women have also labored in the mines. Indeed, accounts of rare instances of female miners date from the early twentieth century, but significant numbers of them did not gain employment until the 1970s. Nearly eight hundred women worked underground in the Appalachian region by 1978. As they crossed traditional lines, these females faced considerable discrimination and a hostile work environment in what heretofore had been a rigidly sex-segregated, all-male occupation. Organized in 1977, the Coal Employment Project has attempted to assist women actually working as miners as well as those seeking such employment. The CEP commenced operations with a $5,000 research grant from the *Ms.* Foundation and subsequently established itself in 1978 as a nonprofit corporation with a regional office at Oak Ridge, Tennessee, and a national office in Washington, D.C.[34]

As New South advocates of the late nineteenth and early twentieth centuries touted industrialization, cheap labor became their clarion call; cutting costs and raising profits, their motto. At the same time, some residents of the highlands, both landowners and tenants, lured by the prospect of regular cash income, abandoned farming and took up mill work. Subsistence agriculture had always been more common than large commercial ventures in Southern Appalachia, and the size of families sometimes outstripped the land's capacity to accommodate all of those who might have chosen to remain farmers. The advent of industrialization offered an alternative. In such a milieu, harshness tended to characterize the work culture of the Southern Appalachians; such matters as a living wage and safety often received short shrift. To challenge owners and operators and the prevailing order required a rare fortitude. In 1929, Margaret Bowen led a walkout of some 340 women at a German-owned rayon plant in northeast Tennessee, which set off a general strike. The unrest at Elizabethton marked the first of a series of labor disturbances across the Upper South that challenged New South claims of docile workers.[35]

In an environment hostile to union organizing specifically and labor assertiveness in general, reformers during the 1920s and 1930s attempted to build an alliance with workers to create a new social order. Western North Carolina most often sheltered the monthlong camps of the Southern Summer School for Women Workers and the weeklong Young Women's Christian Association Industrial Conferences. A native of the region, Eleanor Copenhaver Anderson of Marion, Virginia, first served as the southern secretary for the YWCA Industrial Department and later as its executive director. Labor education, as practiced by the SSS and the YWCA, represented a thinly disguised attempt at labor organizing. Courses in personal hygiene included instruction in feminine health care and access to birth control information.[36]

Well into the twentieth century, the persistence of a high birthrate in some sections of the southern highlands severely limited women's options. As Martha W. Griffiths, a former congresswoman and Michigan lieutenant governor, once observed, "This nation was not born in Philadelphia but in wigwams, log cabins, and places of every description across America out of the agony of women." In the words of Harry M. Caudill, one of Appalachia's most eloquent and sympathetic masculine voices, "We men often forget that the most important people in our lives are women." Extolling women as life-givers, Caudill explained, "We men owe so very much in so many ways to our womenfolks that our kindnesses to them can be, at best, only affectionate tokens of our appreciation whenever and however we can."[37] For Appalachian women as well as females across America, biology has, to a considerable extent, been destiny.

"Next to China's, the American population growth rate in the nineteenth and early twentieth centuries ranks as a major phenomenon of modern history." Southerners "gave birth most often," according to the historian Jack Temple Kirby, "with whites of the Appalachian highlands and blacks throughout Dixie in the lead." The Frontier Nursing Service, established by Mary Breckinridge in 1925, provided midwifery and general nursing care to some ten thousand people in a three-hundred-square-mile area in eastern Kentucky, where passable roads were virtually nonexistent and no licensed physicians practiced. Breckinridge subsequently established a graduate school of midwifery at Hyden, which was expanded to include a family nursing program in 1970. J. Huston Westover, who served as medical director for the FNS during the 1970s, recalled that the graduate nurses "were among the most committed health workers I had ever seen." As he explained, they "no longer made their county-wide rounds on horseback but used jeeps on the rough, difficult roads." Still, "travel was hard, there was some danger at the midwifery end, nurse practitioner studies were difficult, and they were virtually isolated from the world at large."[38]

Around 1940, Dr. Louise Hutchins, the wife of Berea College's president and herself a physician, had become actively involved in the work of the Mountain Maternal Health League, which was then about three years old. Still affiliated with the program in 1976, Hutchins reported that it had not been unusual for her to meet a nurse and drive two hours to Hazard or Breathitt in eastern Kentucky, where sometimes as many as eighty female patients awaited her at the clinics. The women she initially encountered knew nothing of family planning and were delighted to learn about contraception. "We 'bootlegged' supplies" into eastern Kentucky counties, she confessed, before the general distribution of birth control information and devices became legitimate. As long as physicians and nurses did not talk about their family planning activities and kept news of them out of the press, the sponsors raised no objections. Patients ran the gamut from a thirteen-year-old who came to Hutchins for birth control assistance to a forty-five-year-old who had borne her fifteenth child several months earlier.[39]

As the twentieth century nears its end, circumstances described by Dr. Hutchins represent exceptions. To an inordinate degree, however, homespun nostalgia and coal-culture disasters continue to dominate perceptions of Appalachia. Yet the region also includes the prosperous Tennessee-Virginia corridor, transportation links, and significant towns, cities, and resorts. It claims a striking amount of agriculture, industry, and commerce; educational and cultural opportunities abound. Most women share in the amenities associated with contemporary American life and enjoy a satisfactory standard of living. Just as their counterparts elsewhere, some of them look to the future, others look to the past, and still others merely mark time.

NOTES

1. For a discussion of southern women and twentieth-century developments and related matters, see Margaret Ripley Wolfe, *Daughters of Canaan: A Saga of Southern Women* (Lexington: University Press of Kentucky, 1995), 145–204; see also idem, "Reflections of an Appalachian Historian: A Personal Odyssey," *Register of the Kentucky Historical Society* 83 (autumn 1985): 299–314.

2. A "yarb" doctor is an individual who uses herbs to practice healing; "'fotched-on' woman" is an eastern Kentucky reference to women from elsewhere in the state or country who came into the mountains as missionaries and social workers.

3. A familiar phrase employed by the local colorists of the late nineteenth and early twentieth centuries to describe Southern Appalachians, this particular appellation is actually used in Jack E. Weller, *Yesterday's People: Life in Contemporary*

Appalachia (Lexington: University of Kentucky Press, 1965). More recently, Robert Schenkkan's Pulitzer Prize–winning play *The Kentucky Cycle*, a six-and-a-half-hour melodrama, has perpetuated a singular view of an Appalachia lost in time and beset by violence. When the play opened at Washington's Kennedy Center in 1993, Schenkkan, who apparently had made only one visit into eastern Kentucky, observed, "The problems of the Cumberland are not simply political or economic or social; they lie somewhere in the bewildering maelstrom of corrupting legacies that has trapped the people and the region in recurring cycles in a poverty that is as much spiritual as physical." See Miriam Horn, "The Malignancies of History," *U.S. News and World Report,* 20 September 1993, 72, 74.

4. Jean Taylor-Todd, "Cozie Tales," *Blue Ridge Country,* July–August 1996, 21; see also Wilma Dykeman, *The Tall Woman* (New York: Holt, Rinehart and Winston, 1962); and Harriette Arnow, *The Dollmaker,* with afterword by Joyce Carol Oates (New York: Macmillan, 1954; reprint, New York: Avon Books, 1974).

5. Loretta Lynn with George Vecsey, *Loretta Lynn: Coal Miner's Daughter* (Chicago: Henry Regnery, 1976), x, 97.

6. See Dolly Parton, *Dolly: My Life and Other Unfinished Business* (New York: HarperCollins, 1994), 58, 73–74, 79.

7. See Ellis Nassour, *Honky Tonk Angel: The Intimate Story of Patsy Cline* (New York: St. Martin's, 1993); Bill C. Malone, "Country Music," in *Encyclopedia of Southern Culture,* ed. Charles Reagan Wilson and William Ferris (Chapel Hill: University of North Carolina Press for the Center for the Study of Southern Culture at the University of Mississippi, 1989), 1004; June Carter Cash, *From the Heart* (New York: Prentice Hall, 1987); Mary A. Bufwack and Robert K. Oermann, *Finding Her Voice: The Saga of Women in Country Music* (New York: Crown, 1993), 52–58; and Naomi Judd, *Love Can Build a Bridge* (New York: Villard, 1993).

8. Lee Smith's novels include *Oral History* (New York: Putnam, 1983); *Family Linen* (New York: Putnam, 1985); *Fair and Tender Ladies* (New York: Putnam, 1988); *The Devil's Dream* (New York: Putnam, 1992); and *Saving Grace* (New York: Putnam, 1995). Sharyn McCrumb's novels include, *If Ever I Return, Pretty Peggy-O* (New York: Scribner's, 1989); *The Hangman's Beautiful Daughter* (New York: Scribner's, 1992); *She Walks These Hills* (New York: Scribner's, 1994); and *The Rosewood Casket* (New York: Dutton, 1996). See also Elaine Fowler Palencia, *Small Caucasian Woman* (Columbia: University of Missouri Press, 1993), 53.

9. Quoted in Bill Williams, "Giovanni: Opinionated Poet, Author," *Kingsport (Tennessee) Times-News,* 18 October 1985; and "Who's News," *USA Weekend,* 24–26 February 1989, 2.

10. J. W. Williamson, *Hillbillyland: What the Movies Did to the Mountains and What the Mountains Did to the Movies* (Chapel Hill: University of North Carolina Press, 1995), 255–58; quotations from 225–26 and 256.

11. Nolan Ryan with Harvey Fromme, *Throwing Heat: The Autobiography of Nolan Ryan* (New York: Doubleday, 1988), 32–33.

12. Harriette Simpson Arnow, *Seedtime on the Cumberland*, introduction by Margaret Ripley Wolfe (New York: Macmillan, 1960; reprint, Lincoln: University of Nebraska Press, Bison Books, 1995), xiii; idem, *Flowering of the Cumberland*, introduction by Margaret Ripley Wolfe (New York: Macmillan, 1963; reprint, Lincoln: University of Nebraska Press, 1996).

13. Harriette Simpson Arnow to Harry M. Caudill, 5 March 1963, Harry M. and Anne Frye Caudill Collections (unnumbered box labeled Publications—Correspondence, April 19, 1960–October 31, 1963), Margaret I. King Library, University of Kentucky, Lexington. "Kentucky Colonel" is an honorary title bestowed by the governors of the commonwealth.

14. *Time*, 14 August 1995, 18. A United Press International story, which appeared in the *Kingsport (Tennessee) Times-News*, 9 August 1985, detailed the marriage and divorce of a thirteen-year-old child bride in Cocke County, Tennessee. An Associated Press report in 1995 provided an account of the tragic outcome of snake handling. A Parrotsville, Tennessee, woman, twenty-eight-year-old Melinda Francine Duvall Brown, died after being bitten by a poisonous reptile during a religious service at Full Gospel Tabernacle in Jesus' Name at Middlesboro, Kentucky; *Kingsport (Tennessee) Times-News*, 2 September 1995. For more on such religious practices, see Thomas Burton, *Serpent-Handling Believers* (Knoxville: University of Tennessee Press, 1993); see also Dennis Covington, *Salvation on Sand Mountain: A Snake Handling and Redemption in Southern Appalachia* (Reading, Mass.: Addison-Wesley, 1995); and David L. Kimbrough, *Taking Up Serpents: Snake Handlers of Eastern Kentucky* (Chapel Hill: University of North Carolina Press, 1995).

15. For a contemporary regional author who has dealt with incest, see Smith, *Saving Grace*. For a discussion of perceptions of the region and its people, see Williamson, *Hillbillyland*; Henry David Shapiro, *Appalachia on Our Mind: The Southern Mountains and Mountaineers in the American Consciousness, 1870–1920* (Chapel Hill: University of North Carolina Press, 1978); David E. Whisnant, *All That Is Native and Fine: The Politics of Culture in an American Region* (Chapel Hill: University of North Carolina Press, 1983); and James C. Klotter, "The Black South and White Appalachia," *Journal of American History* 66 (March 1980): 832–49.

16. Margaret Ripley Wolfe, "The Appalachian Reality: Ethnic and Class Diversity," East Tennessee Historical Society's *Publications*, nos. 52–53 (1981–1982): 40–60; see also Michael Bradshaw, *The Appalachian Regional Commission: Twenty-Five Years of Government Policy*, with foreword by Senator John D. Rockefeller IV (Lexington: University Press of Kentucky, 1992).

17. Carol Sutton, "Youth Is a Welcome Guest in the Caudills' Environment," *(Louisville, Kentucky) Courier-Journal*, 1 February 1970.

18. See, for example, Thomas D. Clark, *Kentucky: Land of Contrast* (New York: Harper and Row, 1968), 9–10, which mentions Mary Ingles, who with her children had been taken on 8 July 1755 by the Shawnee at Draper's Meadow on the Virginia

frontier. Subsequently, at Big Bone Lick in Kentucky, where her captors had brought her to make salt, Ingles encountered an aged Pennsylvania German woman who like herself had been the victim of a border raid. Leaving her baby behind, the only child still in her possession, Ingles and the older female, armed with tomahawks and knives, escaped and made their way to the relative safety of Virginia. Harry M. Caudill, *Dark Hills to Westward: The Saga of Jennie Wiley* (Boston: Little, Brown, 1969), recounts the legend of another captive who was taken by Indians at a disputed location somewhere along the eastern Kentucky–southwestern Virginia border. See also Thomas Hatley, "Cherokee Women Farmers," in *Appalachian Frontiers: Settlement, Society, and Development in the Preindustrial Era*, ed. Robert D. Mitchell (Lexington: University Press of Kentucky, 1991), 37.

19. Hatley, "Cherokee Women Farmers," 50; Stanley J. Folmsbee, Robert E. Corlew, and Enoch L. Mitchell, *Tennessee: A Short History* (Knoxville: University of Tennessee Press, 1969), 39–46; Stuart O. Stumpf, "Fort Loudoun, Tennessee," in *Tennessee in American History*, ed. Larry H. Whiteaker and W. Calvin Dickinson (Needham Heights, Mass.: Ginn Press, 1991), 1–6; J. G. M. Ramsey, *The Annals of Tennessee to the End of the Eighteenth Century* (Charleston, S.C.: Walker and Jones, 1853; reprint, Knoxville: East Tennessee Historical Society, 1967), 51–61; and Theda Perdue, "Nancy Ward (1738?–1822)," in *Portraits of American Women: From Settlement to the Civil War*, ed. C. J. Barker-Benfield and Catherine Clinton (New York: St. Martin's, 1991), 83–100.

20. Theda Perdue, "Southern Women and the Cult of True Womanhood," in *The Web of Southern Social Relations: Women, Family, and Education*, ed. Walter J. Fraser, Jr., R. Frank Saunders, Jr., and Jon L. Wakelyn (Athens: University of Georgia Press, 1985), 47–48; Hatley, "Cherokee Women Farmers," 50; quoted in Joan M. Jensen, *With These Hands: Women Working on the Land*, Women's Lives Women's Work Series, ed. Sue Davidson (Old Westbury, N.Y., and New York: Feminist Press and McGraw-Hill, 1981), 28–29; Wilma Mankiller and Michael Wallis, *Mankiller: A Chief and Her People* (New York: St. Martin's, 1993); Associated Press wire story in *Kingsport (Tennessee) Times-News*, 8 September 1995.

21. Cathy Carlson Reynolds, "The Civil War in Southwest Virginia," unpublished manuscript in the possession of the author; David Hackett Fischer, *Albion's Seed: Four British Folkways in America* (New York: Oxford University Press, 1989), 676; see also Joan E. Cashin, *A Family Venture: Men and Women on the Southern Frontier* (New York: Oxford University Press, 1991); and Wolfe, *Daughters of Canaan*, 66–70.

22. Wolfe, "Appalachian Reality," 40–60; see also Mary Beth Pudup, "Social Class and Economic Development in Southeastern Kentucky, 1820–1880," in *Appalachian Frontiers*, ed. Mitchell, 235–60.

23. For a discussion of the "southern lady," see Wolfe, *Daughters of Canaan*, 8–9, 60–64.

24. Shaunna L. Scott, "Gender among Appalachian Kentucky Farm Families: The Kentucky Farm Family Oral History Project and Beyond," *Journal of Appalachian Studies* 2 (spring 1996): 104–5.

25. Reynolds, "Civil War."

26. See Daniel Ellis, *The Thrilling Adventures of Daniel Ellis* (New York: Harper and Brothers, 1867); Ellis guided East Tennesseans with Unionist sentiments through the mountains into Kentucky where they could join up with Federal forces. See also James Welch Patton, *Unionism and Reconstruction in East Tennessee* (Chapel Hill: University of North Carolina Press, 1934); and Durwood Dunn, *Cades Cove: The Life and Death of a Southern Appalachian Community, 1818–1937* (Knoxville: University of Tennessee Press, 1988). For information on Belle Boyd, see Katharine M. Jones, *Heroines of Dixie* (Indianapolis: Bobbs-Merrill, 1955), 172–75; and Mary Elizabeth Massey, *Bonnet Brigades* (New York: Knopf, 1966), 96–98.

27. Frederick Jackson Turner, *The Frontier in American History*, with a foreword by Ray Allen Billington, reprint ed. (Huntington, N.Y.: Robert E. Krieger, 1976), 12; see also Margaret Ripley Wolfe, "Aliens in Southern Appalachia: Catholics in the Coal Camps," *Appalachian Heritage* 6 (winter 1978): 43–56; idem, "Aliens in Southern Appalachia, 1900–1920: The Italian Experience in Wise County, Virginia," *Virginia Magazine of History and Biography* 87 (October 1979): 455–72; idem, "Catholicism and Community: Mountain Missions and 'New' Immigrants in Appalachia," *Border States*, no. 10 (1995): 16–23.

28. Paula Baker, "The Domestication of Politics: Women and the American Political Society, 1780–1920," *American Historical Review* 89 (June 1984): 625; Allen F. Davis, *Spearheads for Reform: The Social Settlements and the Progressive Movement, 1890–1941*, Urban Life in America, ed. Richard Wade (New York: Oxford University Press, 1968; paperback ed., 1970), 37.

29. See David E. Whisnant, "Second-Level Appalachian History: Another Look at Some Fotched-On Women," *Appalachian Journal* 9 (winter–spring 1982): 115–23; Lucy Furman, "Katherine Pettit: Pioneer Mountain Worker," *Register of the Kentucky Historical Society* 35 (January 1937): 75–80; Carol Crowe-Carraco, "Mary Breckinridge and the Frontier Nursing Service," *Register of the Kentucky Historical Society* 82 (summer 1984): 257–76; and Nancy K. Forderhase, "Eve Returns to the Garden: Women Reformers in Appalachian Kentucky in the Early Twentieth Century," *Register of the Kentucky Historical Society* 85 (summer 1987): 237–61; P. David Searles, *A College for Appalachia: Alice Lloyd on Caney Creek* (Lexington: University Press of Kentucky, 1995); interview with Helen Johns, a Magyar (Hungarian) immigrant who lived for many years in southeastern Kentucky and southwestern Virginia, 29 August 1975, Kingsport, Tenn. (notes in the possession of the author); conversations with Gertrude Blessing Ripley, a native of Scott County, Va., who resided in the Kermit area during her youth, Church Hill, Tenn. (notes in the possession of the author); report prepared by Greg Wallace, September 1995, WCYB-TV, Bristol, Va.; telephone conversation with Greg Wallace, 22 September 1995.

30. Denise Giardina, *Storming Heaven: A Novel* (New York: Norton, 1987); Crandall Shifflett, *Coal Towns: Life, Work and Culture in Company Towns of Southern Appalachia, 1880–1960* (Knoxville: University of Tennessee Press, 1991); "Sacred Heart Church of Stonega and Missions," 4, Archives of St. Bernard's Abbey, Cullman, Ala. Benedictine priests from St. Bernard's conducted mission work in the Southern Appalachians from around 1900 to 1940.

31. U.S. Senate, *Reports of the Immigration Commission*, S. Doc. 633, 61st Cong., 2d sess., 1909–10, *Immigrants in Industry: The Bituminous Coal Mining Industry in the South*, vol. 5, 136–40; see also Wolfe, "Aliens in Southern Appalachia: Catholics," 43–56; idem, "Aliens in Southern Appalachia, 1900–1920: The Italian Experience," 455–72; Stonega Coal and Coke Company, *Annual Report, 1920*, 4, in the possession of Westmoreland Coal Company, Big Stone Gap, Va.

32. The Reverend Clarence Meyer to the author, 25 September 1974; quotation in Thomas H. Coode and John F. Bauman, " 'Dear Mr. Hopkins': A New Dealer Reports from Eastern Kentucky," *Register of the Kentucky Historical Society* 78 (winter 1980): 59; James Still, *River of Earth* (New York: Viking, 1940; reprint, New York: Popular Library, 1968).

33. Carol A. B. Giesen, *Coal Miners' Wives: Portraits of Endurance* (Lexington: University Press of Kentucky, 1995); see also "Miners' Wives in the Coal Strike," *Century Magazine*, November 1922, 82–90; and Edward M. Steel, ed., *The Court-Martial of Mother Jones* (Lexington: University Press of Kentucky, 1995).

34. Melanie Greer Storie, "Digging through Tradition: Women in the Appalachian Coal Mines, 1930–1990" (M.A. thesis, East Tennessee State University, 1994); Collection Guide, Coal Employment Project Records, Archives of Appalachia, Sherrod Library, East Tennessee State University, Johnson City, Tenn.

35. James A. Hodges, "Challenge to the New South: The Great Textile Strike in Elizabethton, Tennessee, 1929," *Tennessee Historical Quarterly* 23 (December 1964): 343–57; and Jacquelyn Dowd Hall, "Disorderly Women: Gender and Labor Militancy in the Appalachian South," *Journal of American History* 73 (September 1986): 354–82.

36. The papers of the National Board of the Young Women's Christian Association at the organization's headquarters in New York City and in the Sophia Smith Collection at Smith College, Northampton, Mass., and the Southern Summer School Papers, Labor-Management Documentation Center, Martin P. Catherwood Library, Cornell University, Ithaca, N.Y., detail the labor-education activities. See also Mary Evans Frederickson, "A Place to Speak Our Minds: The Southern Summer School for Women Workers" (Ph.D. diss., University of North Carolina, Chapel Hill, 1981); and Margaret Ripley Wolfe, "Eleanor Copenhaver Anderson of the National Board of the YWCA: Appalachian Feminist and Author's Wife," *Winesburg Eagle: The Official Publication of the Sherwood Anderson Society* 38 (summer 1993): 2–9.

37. Martha Griffiths, speech at symposium on "Women and the Constitution:

A Bicentennial Perspective," sponsored by the Carter Center at Emory University, Georgia State University, and the Jimmy Carter Library, February 1988 (author's notes); Sally G. McMillen, *Motherhood in the Old South: Pregnancy, Childbirth, and Infant Rearing* (Baton Rouge: Louisiana State University Press, 1990); Harry M. Caudill to Diana Ellen Caudill Grace, 17 January 1983, in the possession of Mrs. Harry M. (Anne Frye) Caudill, New Albany, Ind.

38. Jack Temple Kirby, *Rural Worlds Lost: The American South, 1920–1960* (Baton Rouge: Louisiana State University Press, 1987), 163; Carol Crowe-Carraco, "Mary Breckinridge (1881–1965): Nurse," in *Encyclopedia of Southern Culture*, ed. Wilson and Ferris, 1364–65; J. Huston Westover, "From Korea to the Kentucky Coalfields: My Life as a Quaker Physician," unpublished manuscript, copy in the possession of Anne Frye Caudill, New Albany, Ind.

39. Interview by Barry Bingham, Sr., of Dr. Francis Hutchins and Dr. Louise Hutchins in "Distinguished Kentuckians," Kentucky Educational Television, 1976 (videotape).

Chapter Twelve

"Most Sacrificing" Service
The Educational Leadership of Lucy Craft Laney and Mary McLeod Bethune

Audrey Thomas McCluskey

EDITOR'S NOTE: *Education is monumentally important to women, because education is power. The Reformation's insistence on the "priesthood of all believers" led to the idea that everyone, including women, should become literate in order to enhance opportunities for salvation by reading the Bible, even though this idea collided with the commonly held view that women's intellects are inferior to men's. In the colonial period even a few slave girls were taught at missionary schools of the Anglican Church.*

Unlike the Puritans, however, who required settlements of any size to support public schools, southerners believed that schooling was the parents' responsibility. Wealthy whites hired tutors for their families and permitted relatives and neighbors to join their classes; groups of parents built schools and hired teachers who were paid out of student tuition; and some husband-wife teams opened their homes to boarders for the purpose of teaching them music, dancing, sewing, and crafts in addition to the three Rs. A few schools for free blacks managed precarious existences in antebellum southern cities, and individual owners and their families sometimes taught slaves despite laws making instruction illegal. But because education was not supported by the state and was even illegal for blacks, southern literacy levels lagged far behind the rest of the nation in 1860.

Advancement beyond the fundamentals for women was largely the result of the idea of "Republican Motherhood," which became prevalent after the American Revolution. Arguing that mothers were the first teachers of small children, that education was primarily for the purpose of building character, and that the new and highly experimental Republic might fail if there were not a majority of virtuous citizens to vote and hold office, educators in the North insisted that women needed education themselves if they were to be able to successfully teach their children, the future citizens of the Republic. The acceptance of this argument led to the spread of academies, initially in towns along the Atlantic seaboard.

The belief in the mental inferiority of females was challenged by the achievements of academy girls to such a degree that it was superseded by the view that male and female intelligence was equal — but different. This emphasis on bipolar gender differences was basic to Victorian notions of masculinity and femininity and was encapsulated in the "cult of true womanhood," which defined women as pious, pure, submissive, domestic, and charitable by nature. This ideal had the historically anomalous consequence of conceptualizing women as morally superior to men. Such rhetoric also advanced female education, for the connection between education and character building remained strong.

The cult of true womanhood intersected with the ideal of the southern lady in its emphasis on refinement and gentility. As a consequence, the South led the nation in the founding of antebellum female colleges. Whereas higher education threatened northern gender systems by challenging men's exclusive access to occupations and fueling the rise of feminism, in the South such an education was primarily emblematic of high social standing.

This overriding emphasis on education as a marker of gentility, combined with postbellum poverty, prevented the South from keeping up with advances in women's education in the late nineteenth century at northern colleges like Wellesley and Bryn Mawr. However, black women found in this emphasis on gentility a tool with which to counter racist conceptions of African American inferiority, which underpinned white supremacy.

Following the Civil War the Freedmen's Bureau and northern religious and philanthropic organizations established all levels of schools for blacks in the South, including colleges like Hampton, Howard, and Atlanta University. Teachers were mostly northerners, many of them single white women for whom training in the tenets of the cult of true womanhood rivaled their devotion to teaching more traditional educational subjects. Southern whites were hostile to education for the freedpeople. Northern whites were determined to use education as the means for "raising up" and civilizing a benighted population. Blacks themselves were strong advocates of education, not only for upward mobility (a traditional rationale among both native-born and immigrant whites) but also in the hopes of gaining social acceptance.

The end of Reconstruction obliterated the political gains blacks had made and stifled their economic and social opportunities, leaving education as one of the few avenues by which an improvement in status could be sought. Black women recognized this prospect and utilized aspects of the nation's contemporary gender ideology to construct a rationale for the entrance of black Americans into the mainstream of American life.

• • •

Despite a generational divide, Lucy Craft Laney (1854–1933) and Mary McLeod Bethune (1875–1955) held similar beliefs and values that informed their educational work. These women, born a generation apart and nurtured in the racially segregated, gender-stratified South, were among a group of black women who founded schools and organizations that represented female achievement and racial pride under circumstances that were hostile to both. Education was the foundation of their rise to prominence between the late 1880s and the first decades of the twentieth century, during an era when the primary vehicle of professional status for black women was teaching. Laney and Bethune's relationship as mentor and mentee was anchored in a shared sense of purpose as educational pioneers and "race women." Faced with the contrasting educational ideologies of Booker T. Washington and W. E. B. Du Bois, they utilized, to different degrees, salient aspects of the utilitarianism of Washington's industrial training and the progressive bent of Du Bois's focus on liberal education.

Laney devoted her life entirely to education, remaining principal of the school that she founded—Haines Institute in Augusta, Georgia—until her death in 1933. Bethune expanded her leadership role from that of founder and principal of a school for girls to the presidency of what became Bethune-Cookman College in Daytona Beach, Florida, into the presidency of national women's organizations and a directorship of a federal program in the New Deal administration of Franklin Delano Roosevelt. Yet like Laney, she never relinquished the title of educator. The work of both women reflected an ideology of female service and self-sacrifice that they construed as the path to equality and opportunity for African Americans.

Exposure to the "cult of true womanhood" in their own Protestant mission-sponsored schooling emphasized women's moral and spiritual superiority and provided Laney and Bethune with a standard for female conduct and duty.[1] As members of the first and second generation of post-emancipation black women, they received an education encoded with messages of self-help and racial redemption that became the driving force in a campaign for respectability and racial uplift. This agenda inspired the formation of the National Association of Colored Women with its motto,

"Lifting as we climb." Their redemptive work was launched against the backdrop of severe social, economic, and political repression that denigrated all blacks as inferior and black women as moral outcasts.

In identifying themselves as a special group of women uplifters, Laney and Bethune were in league with such notables such as Dr. Anna Julia Cooper, longtime teacher at Washington, D.C.'s premier black high school, the M Street School, whose protofeminist text *A Voice from the South* (1892) called black women the force for "a regenerative womanhood"; Mary Church Terrell, first president of the National Association of Colored Women; and activist-educator Nannie Helen Burroughs, founder of a "training" school for black women and girls in Washington, D.C. These "representative"[2] women formed a loosely connected cadre of social reformers intent on using their own exemplary lives as evidence of the possibilities within their race and gender.

Historians came late to the study of their role as leaders, in part because their emphasis on service and the lingering imprint of the "cult of true womanhood" inscribed their work with the diminutive label of "female duty" and "natural" women's roles. Yet they established a counternarrative to the idea of black inferiority that declared black women as virtuous and responsible in an era when the opposite message resonated throughout American popular culture.[3] This gendered dimension of Laney and Bethune's service-inspired leadership is the subject of this essay.

Laney and Bethune had much in common. Daughters of the South, they were socialized by the experience and memory of slavery. The upbringing they received in large, close-knit, religious families and communities permitted their intelligence and leadership abilities to surface. Both women also had very strong mother figures who encouraged their daughters to get an education, although that was not a likely option for most black children of their day. They were tutored in the philosophy of black self-help and the need for moral redemption, and their views on the role of black women and the centrality of education in racial uplift can be traced to their similar backgrounds and social environments, including the influence of their own missionary-based schooling.[4]

Bethune served a one-year apprenticeship with Laney in 1896–97, shortly after completing her formal schooling at Scotia Seminary for Negro Girls in North Carolina and Moody Bible Institute in Chicago. Bethune's career path in education was also influenced by other notable black women, including her first teacher in Mayesville, South Carolina,

Emma Wilson, and the interracial staff at Scotia. It is Laney whom she credits with giving her "a new vision" of the possibilities for racial uplift in America, which replaced her earlier goal of becoming a missionary in Africa.[5] Laney also awakened her to the special needs of black girls and inspired her decision to open a school especially for them. Bethune said of Laney, "I was impressed with her fearlessness, her amazing touch in every respect, an energy that seemed inexhaustible and her mighty power to command respect and admiration from her students and all who knew her. She handled her domain with the art of a master."[6] Laney's former students felt the same way. They organized "Lucy Laney Leagues" in various cities to support the school. Laney's combination of charismatic leadership and generosity (she reportedly owned only one good dress, which she covered with a multi-pocketed apron from which she dispensed nickels and dimes to needy children)[7] earned the never-married educator the sobriquet of "mother of a race."[8]

Laney began life as a slave in Macon, Georgia, but her father, a minister and carpenter, managed to buy the family's freedom and reunite them. Laney's parents as well as her mother's white employer nurtured her love of learning.[9] After completing the curriculum of the local missionary school and Lewis High School for blacks, Laney entered the American Missionary Association (AMA) affiliated Atlanta University at age fifteen.[10] She excelled in the school's liberal arts curriculum and received high academic honors in the first graduating class of 1873. In later years she pursued an advanced degree at the University of Chicago during the summer months.

In 1886 Laney chartered Haines Normal and Industrial School in Augusta, Georgia, with a mostly liberal arts curriculum. Meanwhile in Alabama, Tuskegee Institute principal Booker T. Washington used the support of northern white industrial philanthropy to activate the "Tuskegee machine," which spread the gospel of industrial education and conservative politics throughout the southern Black Belt. Although she favored liberal education, Laney showed rational pragmatism in naming her school the Haines Normal and Industrial School. It paid tribute to a generous white woman supporter, while the inclusion of "industrial" in the title positioned Laney for appeals to northern white philanthropists who supported industrial education.[11]

Despite such appeals, her friendship with Washington, and the obvious financial success of his industrial education program, Laney exhorted her students to "learn Greek and Latin and take every course that will im-

prove your opportunity to become better educated and better prepared."[12] Like W. E. B. Du Bois, Laney urged students to serve their
communities by becoming doctors, lawyers, teachers, and other professionals. She believed, also like Du Bois, that education should be broadly
based, not only teaching trades and skills, but instilling a higher purpose
and goals. For part of its history Haines Institute was the only school in
the state to offer high school–level courses for black students.

In addition to liberal arts, the curriculum emphasized religious and
moral training, themes closely associated with industrial education.
Haines Institute offered what Laney believed was missing in the mini-
mally funded public schools for blacks—"a complete education for the
child," which included character building and academic competence.[13]
Although she soon admitted boys, her original idea was to open a school
for girls. Reflecting her missionary education and the tenets of "true
womanhood," Laney believed that it was women's spiritual nature to
serve humanity and to mold the character of children: "Only [women] of
character and culture can do successful [up]lifting; for she who would
mold character must herself possess it."[14]

In 1892 her service orientation and emphasis on economic self-sufficiency led her to organize the first nurses' training course for black
women in the state of Georgia, which later became the LeMar Training
School for Nurses.[15] Laney's other educational firsts in Augusta included
opening a kindergarten, dressing girls in uniforms, and organizing ath-
letic teams.[16] Her programs for the surrounding black community made
use of the school's facilities year-round. Because of this she was remembered as the "saint of social service."[17] Laney was concerned about society's negative perception of the black race, and the shame that slavery
and its aftermath created among black people. Laney believed that educated black women, particularly those in Christian mission schools, were
best suited to lead the race in counteracting the effects of that legacy of
"shame and crime."[18] Her leadership emanated from her own example of
strong religious beliefs and allegiance to traditional notions of the educated woman's "burden" to be the moral leader in the family and for the
black race. Laney, who never married, expressed these views in a speech
at Hampton Institute in 1899: "Women are by nature fitted for teaching
very young children. . . . Negro women of culture . . . have a rare opportunity to the lifting of these burdens . . . they may instill lessons of cleanliness, truthfulness, loving kindness . . . and love for Nature's God. [They
are] . . . the salvation of the race."[19]

Laney, a devout Christian, imbued her educational and social agenda with a strong moral message. Her crusade to purge "shame and crime" from the black community is reminiscent of the morality-tinged crusades of earlier groups of white "true women," such as educator Catharine Beecher, and later social reformers like Jane Addams and Frances Willard.[20] The dictates of social acceptability led Laney and other black women reformers to condemn certain activities and behaviors among the black working class. Celebrations like "Egypt walking," which she described as a "sacrilegious and unbecoming religious ceremony," engaged in on New Year's Day, were almost single-handedly stamped out by Laney.[21] Such displays, Laney and other uplifters believed, were used to stigmatize blacks as uncivilized and to rationalize repressive acts against the race.[22] Laney considered the adoption of aspects of middle-class conformity a strategy to *fight* racism. She counseled her students to overcome racial discrimination with hard work, self-respect, and faith in God. Although conservative in demeanor and dress, she was also known to speak out when blacks were being unfairly attacked. In a 1903 speech she criticized those whites who called blacks "shiftless" and "undeserving of an education" and dismissed the accusation as "a trumped-up charge" that, she said, "no real Christians believed, if they bothered to observe the tremendous accomplishments of blacks in education, ownership of businesses, homes, newspapers, in just forty years of freedom."[23]

During her long tenure, the Haines School expanded, becoming a junior college in 1930. As a model of black female achievement, it drew national attention that included a visit by W. E. B. Du Bois, and in 1908 a visit by president-elect William Howard Taft. Rising costs, unsteady leadership after Laney's death in 1933, and competition from public schools forced Haines to close in 1949.[24] Through her work as a school founder and teacher Lucy Craft Laney made her life an instrument of moral Christian living, self-sufficiency, and service that she believed was necessary for redeeming and uplifting the black race. In pursuing that work she inspired younger women like Mary McLeod Bethune, who emulated her service-inspired leadership and expanded its mandate.

Born one of seventeen children of former slaves, Bethune was given the opportunity—through divine intervention, she believed—to attend Emma Wilson's mission school near the farming community of Mayesville, South Carolina, and then on to Scotia and Moody. Her path led closer to home—to the Maysville Educational and Industrial Institute founded by her first teacher, Emma Wilson. At the outset of her teaching career Bethune borrowed liberally from the teaching philosophies of her mentors Scotia, Wilson, and Laney. She applied a version of the Scotia motto, "head, heart, and hand" to her mission of racial uplift. Scotia emphasized mental development, spiritual enrichment, and practical skills, and its graduates were expected to conduct themselves in ways that reflected positively on the entire race. They were encouraged to return to their communities and become exemplars of racial uplift and service to the masses of black people.[25]

The Daytona Educational and Industrial School for Negro Girls opened on October 4, 1904, eight years after Bethune completed her apprenticeship with Laney. She had married Albertus Bethune, given birth to a son, and moved from teaching positions in Savannah, Georgia, and Palatka, Florida to Daytona, Florida, the winter resort of northern millionaires, where prospects for fundraising were more favorable. Although now a wife and mother, Bethune admitted that she had no intention of letting motherhood interfere with the important work she had to do.[26]

While Bethune publicly agreed with Laney about the primacy of black women's role in uplifting their families, her own life revealed a contradiction. In 1907, Albertus Bethune left the family and returned to his Charleston, South Carolina, home. Although the couple never divorced, any semblance of a traditional woman's role ended for Mary Bethune. In the early years of her school she announced that she would teach her girls to cook and sew and improve their home lives, while preparing them for the available job market. Like her mentor Laney, Bethune emphasized home life and urged that black girls "be taught cleanliness, beauty, and thoughtfulness in making home life possible."[27] Although her school enshrined domesticity, Bethune steadily expanded her role in public affairs. She later advanced a more politically tinged message of female activism and empowerment than Laney. Bethune's school, however, was initially like Haines—a site for the reclamation and inculcation of social and cultural values meant to earn blacks middle-class status.

Bethune also included "industrial" in the name of her school as a nod to industrial philanthropists. She believed that themes associated with such a curriculum—morality and "practical" work—improved her ability to raise funds among the wealthy northern whites. In early letters to potential benefactors, Bethune touted her girls' school as a source of "wholesome training . . . in the midst of ignorance and vice."[28]

The early curriculum emphasized work, family, and religion, themes associated with industrial education. Like many other black educators, Bethune admired Booker T. Washington's success, particularly in attracting white benefactors. Yet her curriculum gradually moved beyond the strict Hampton-Tuskegee industrialism, and evolved toward Laney and Du Bois's idea of liberal education combined with moralistic social themes.[29] Washington visited Bethune's school in 1912 during a tour of southern black schools. He reportedly gave her advice on fundraising, but there is no evidence that Washington helped her obtain funding from influential white philanthropists. Correspondence shows that she wrote to Washington in 1914 soliciting a donation of $100 for her school. He responded with an encouraging letter, but declined to send money.[30] Bethune received no major support from Washington's allies in prominent philanthropic organizations such as the General Education Board (GEB) until well after Washington's death in 1915. In fact, her first major grant from a philanthropic agency was $55,000 from the GEB in 1934, which spawned an era of growth at the school.[31]

In her decision to concentrate on females, Bethune fulfilled Laney's original objective of focusing on the "special needs" of black girls. Bethune created an environment of Christian asceticism: each day began with Bible study, and activities were governed by the ringing of bells, beginning with the five-thirty a.m. "rising bell" and ending with the lights out bell at nine p.m. The strict code of conduct was intended to demonstrate that black women lived moral, Christian lives and were equal to white women and to everyone else.[32]

Also like Laney, Bethune built a hospital and nurses' training program that began offering services to the black community in 1911. Reminiscent of Laney's opposition to "Egypt-walking," Bethune's 1905 campaign to outlaw the sale of liquor in the county reflected her belief that alcohol had a deleterious effect on black family life. With the help of her students, she also launched evangelical campaigns among blacks who lived in lumber company work camps near Daytona, teaching reading and Bible study along with sanitary habits. Bethune's political activism was more extensive than Laney's and included voter registration.

One of her early strategies for fundraising was to invite wealthy Daytona Beach residents to visit her school, where she showcased her students' discipline, work habits, and desire to learn. The struggling institution was helped by their contributions, and she asked some of the donors to serve on her board of trustees. She also formed a women's advisory board of influential women in Daytona, usually wives of potential donors who helped Bethune with many of her projects. She continued to rely on the black community for various types of support. Black Daytonans were her first and main source of support when she began in 1904 with the fabled $1.50 in pocket change. Churches passed the collection plate, and their members helped her sell sandwiches and sweet potato pies and brought eggs and milk to help feed the girls. A group of regular volunteers assisted with school maintenance, and a local minister taught the Bible course.[33]

The curriculum gradually expanded to offer high school–level courses in mathematics, science, English, and foreign languages. Some members of the interracial board thought that Bethune was moving too fast in adding grade levels. With characteristic drama, she quieted the board by threatening to quit and start over. In 1923, to relieve mounting financial pressure, she reluctantly approved a merger with Jacksonville's Cookman Institute, under the auspices of the Board of Education of the Methodist Episcopal Church. The new coed Bethune-Cookman Collegiate Institute steadily evolved toward its present status as an accredited four-year liberal arts institution. There are indications, however, that Bethune had second thoughts about the change to coed status. In 1938 she wrote an "urgent" memo to her board outlining reasons the college should return to its original mission of educating black women, because of the "unique" contributions such an institution would make.[34] As the school grew, so did Bethune's reputation. In less than ten years her school had become a showplace of black female achievement, occupying a campus of over fifteen acres. By 1920 the physical plant was worth over $100,000 and gave Bethune high status in state and regional educational leadership.[35] She became active in the National Association of Teachers in Colored Schools, a primarily southern-based black teachers' association, and was elected president in 1924. Bethune's success as a school administrator and activist propelled her into the national spotlight and leadership of two black women's organizations—the National Association of Colored Women (she was elected to two consecutive two-year terms as president beginning in 1924) and the National Council of Negro Women, which she founded in 1935. As her national constituency increased, Bethune continued to characterize her work primarily as service to womanhood, her race, and the nation.[36]

In continuing to focus on women even as she expanded her mandate to include all black people, she exemplified what Laney called the "burden" of educated black women. Bethune envisioned and worked actively to realize black women as educated professionals and businesswomen, wielding power and influence to help their communities overcome the obstacles of race and gender. As president of NACW, and later NCNW, Bethune preached black women's solidarity and empowerment. She reached out to women outside the United States and in 1926 called for "a worldwide meeting of women of color" to chart a strategy for mutual progress.[37] Bethune viewed herself as both a representative and a symbol of black female achievement. Upon being awarded the Spingarn Medal of Freedom in 1935, by the National Association for the Advancement of Colored People for her activities in advancing the cause of black progress, she accepted it, as the first woman so honored, "in the name of the womanhood of America."[38]

The changing social and political climate for blacks—in particular the election of Franklin Roosevelt—increased Bethune's political influence, but it also forced her to loosen her control over her school. The self-sufficiency that was one of her goals for her students remained illusive for Bethune-Cookman College. Under her tutelage the college never became the financially solvent institution that she envisioned. Her pleading letters to a widening list of potential contributors and friends underscore that fact. By the time she relinquished the full-time presidency to join Roosevelt's "black cabinet" as director of the office of Negro Affairs in the National Youth Administration, her service to her race and to her country reflected a wider definition of political and economic empowerment for all black Americans.

Lucy Laney and Mary McLeod Bethune were educational activists with a social vision. Under the mantle of female-endowed service, their schools were a response to the yearning for education universally expressed among the disenfranchised, disempowered black peasantry. Their ability to traverse the ideological debates about black education that divided Washington and Du Bois shows their political savvy. Perhaps more important, it shows their understanding of the need for a multileveled approach to the daunting task of educating blacks in the post-Reconstruction era, including the importance of garnering the support of sympathetic whites. Although their service and uplift ideology reflected some aspects of white middle-class morality, they situated their goals and objectives firmly within authentic black aspirations for education and self-determination. They did not consider their uplift ideology an imitation of white people but simply the price of social acceptance and their hoped-for racial equality. Their unprecedented task was to embrace conventionality while undermining conventional wisdom about their race and gender. Bethune and Laney believed that in order to be equal, blacks had to disprove the slavery-generated myths of inferiority, while instilling in black women a sense of self-worth and accomplishment that would redound to the entire race. Their schools—as examples of service-inspired Christian leadership, producing self-reliant, achieving students—surmounted tremendous odds. To the extent that it was successful, the use of established conventions such as "true womanhood" represented an optimist effort to subvert their negative impact on black people. While the limitations of such a strategy are today quite obvious, Laney and Bethune were products of a time that bred such optimism. Only a few decades from slavery, their schools were monuments to possibility that defied troubling racial trends.

Yet there were obvious tensions between the idealized roles that Laney and Bethune advocated for black women and their own lives. Laney, in her untiring work to educate black children, was elevated to the role of the surrogate and saintly "mother of a race," exempted from the everyday toils of being a wife and mother. Similarly, Bethune found the singularity of her service and uplift mandate incompatible with the traditional domestic role of wife and mother she espoused. Yet she became for millions of black Americans the symbolic "Mother Bethune," who fought political and cultural battles on behalf of the black family. Through their acts of "most-sacrificing"[39] service, Laney and Bethune provided models of female leadership that need to be evaluated not only in terms of the educational institutions they founded and sustained, but also for the lessons they can provide as the struggle to empower present and future generations of African Americans continues.

NOTES

1. Linda M. Perkins, "The Impact of the 'Cult of True Womanhood,' " *Journal of Social Issues* 39, no. 3 (1983): 17–27. The term "cult of true womanhood" was introduced by Barbara Welter in a 1966 article, "The Cult of True Womanhood," *American Quarterly* 18 (winter 1966): 151–69. Welter described the idealized characteristics of nineteenth-century middle-class white women as piety, submissiveness, and domesticity. "Lifting as we climb" was the motto of the National Association of Colored Women, founded in 1896. The history of the NACW is documented in Linsley Davis, ed., *Lifting As We Climb* (Ann Arbor, 1979).

2. Black clubwomen referred to themselves as representatives of the race, especially when speaking before white audiences. See Paula Giddings, *When and Where I Enter: The Impact of Black Women on Race and Sex* (New York, 1984), chap. 6.

3. See George M. Frederickson, *The Black Image in the White Mind: The Debate on Afro-American Character and Destiny* (Middletown, CT, 1971), chap. 1.

4. Ronald Butchart, *Northern Schools, Southern Blacks, and Reconstruction: Freedman's Education* (Westport, CT, 1980), 24–25.

5. Mary McLeod Bethune, "Faith That Moved a Garbage Heap," *Who Magazine*, June 1941, box 3, folder 8, Amistad Research Center, New Orleans (hereafter, ARC).

6. Mary McLeod Bethune, "A Yearning and a Longing," n.d., Mary McLeod Bethune Foundation, Daytona (hereafter, MMBF).

7. "History of Haines Normal and Industrial School," n.d., Lucy C. Laney vertical file, Moorland-Spingarn Research Center, Howard University, Washington, DC (hereafter, M-SRC).

8. Tributes to the Founder, Golden Jubilee Program, 1936, p. 37, Laney vertical file, M-SRC.

9. "History of Haines Normal and Industrial School."

10. As one of the primary white mission societies involved in black higher education, the American Missionary Association established schools that promoted liberal education over the industrial education offered at Hampton and Tuskegee. For a fuller discussion, see James D. Anderson, *The Education of Blacks in the South, 1860–1935* (Chapel Hill, 1988), chaps. 2 and 3.

11. Laney named her school in honor of a white Minnesotan, Francine F. Haines, president of the woman's department of the Presbyterian Church, who gave Laney considerable support after the church rejected her first appeal for funds to start her school. Another white woman, Mrs. Marshall, also of Minneapolis, donated ten thousand dollars to build Marshall Hall, the first dormitory (Laney vertical file, M-SRC). In 1889 the Board of Missions, Colored Division of the Presbyterian Church became a major financial sponsor. Also, the practice of including "industrial" in the title of black schools in the South was a bow to northern industrial philanthropy and its interest in such a curriculum for blacks. However, Laney received most of her early funding from the efforts of the black citizenry of Augusta. See "History of Haines Normal and Industrial School."

12. Flora F. Low, "Hampton's Heroes," *Abbott's Monthly*, n.d. Laney vertical file, M-SRC.

13. Haines Institute's Golden Jubilee Programme, Laney vertical file, M-SRC.

14. Lucy Craft Laney, "The Burden of the Educated Colored Woman," Hampton Negro Conference, paper no. 3 (1899), Hampton Institute, 41.

15. Low, "Hampton's Heroes."

16. Lucy C. Laney, clippings in vertical file, n.d., M-SRC.

17. Historical Sketch of Haines Normal and Industrial School, n.d., 6, Laney vertical file, M-SRC.

18. Laney, "Burden of the Educated Colored Woman."

19. Ibid.

20. Beecher's immense popularity in the mid-1800s derived from her advocacy of a separate sphere for women, primarily domestic, in which they would enculturate and preserve the family. Her message was to middle-class white women only and excluded both poor women and women of other races. Frances Willard expressed patently racist sentiments in her comment that the black race "reproduces like locusts," Giddings, 91. These problematic positions made it difficult for black women to negotiate their stance between support for the ideas and goals of reformism and disavowal of racism. Bethune organized her own temperance group at her school. Audrey Thomas McCluskey, "Mary McLeod Bethune and the Education of Black Girls, 1904–1923" (Ph.D. diss., Indiana University, 1991), chap. 2.

21. Lucy Laney, untitled essay, n.d., vertical file, M-SRC.

22. Hazel Carby, "On the Threshold of the Woman's Era: Lynching, Empire, and Sexuality in Black Feminist Theory," *Critical Inquiry* 12 (autumn 1985): 262–76.

23. *Haines Journal*, no. 1 (1903), Laney vertical file, M-SRC.

24. Laney remained principal at Haines for fifty years. Her advanced age and the fact that she suffered a long period of declining health probably robbed Haines of the energetic leadership that Laney had once offered. The school had been the center of her life since her mid-twenties. This no doubt made it difficult for her to pass the torch to a new generation.

25. McCluskey, chap. 5.

26. Mary McLeod Bethune, interview by Charles S. Johnson, 1939, n.p., Oral History Project, MMBF.

27. Mary McLeod Bethune, "A Philosophy for Education for Negro Girls," n.d., ARC.

28. Letter to Dr. Wallace Buttrick, Secretary, General Education Board, January 22, 1906, MMBF.

29. Bethune told interviewer Charles S. Johnson of a dream that she had prior to opening her school in which Washington showed her a soiled handkerchief, removed a huge diamond, and said, "Here, take this and build your school." Also, Bethune wrote to Washington in 1902 while still teaching in Palatka, Florida, to solicit a contribution for her school. Letter to Washington, in Louis R. Harlan and Raymond W. Smock, eds., *The Booker T. Washington Papers*, vol. 6 (Chicago, 1984), 573. After receiving a scholarship from a white seamstress, Bethune attended Scotia Seminary in Concord, North Carolina, from 1887 to 1894. The Presbyterian Church–affiliated school for black girls was founded in 1867 and modeled after northern seminaries for white females. Its curriculum emphasized domestic arts and Christian virtues. Its "head, heart, and hand" motto reflected the emphasis on developing competent women who would serve their communities. See Louis R. Rubin, *Teach the Freedman: The Correspondence of Rutherford B. Hayes and the Slater Fund for Negro Education* (New York, 1890). Bethune also studied for one year at

Moody Bible Institute in Chicago with hopes of becoming a missionary in Africa. When the mission board turned her down because of her race, she returned home to teach and after one year, went to Augusta to work with Laney. See Rackman Holt, *Mary McLeod Bethune: A Biography* (New York, 1964).

30. Harlan and Smock, 297.

31. Elaine M. Smith, "Black Female Icon: Mary McLeod Bethune, 1875–1955," introduction to the Mary McLeod Bethune Papers, Bethune College Collection, (Washington, D.C.: University Publications of America, 1995), 9.

32. Clara Stillman, "A Tourist in Florida," *Crisis*, February 1924, 171–74.

33. Bethune, interview.

34. Mary McLeod Bethune, memo to the Board of Trustees, Bethune-Cookman College, November 26, 1938, Methodist Church Archives. The board discussed her request, but announced publicly that the school would remain coed. Sheila Y. Flemming, *Bethune-Cookman College, 1904–1994* (Daytona Beach, 1995), 62.

35. Benjamin Brawley, *Two Centuries of Methodist Concerns: Bondage, Freedom and the Education of Black People* (New York, 1974), 185.

36. Mary McLeod Bethune, "A Spiritual Autobiography," 1935, MMBF.

37. Mary McLeod Bethune, president's address to Fifteenth Biennial Convention, NACW, August 2, 1926, MMBF.

38. Mary McLeod Bethune, Spingarn Award acceptance speech, June 23, 1935, Bethune papers, ARC.

39. Bethune to Charlotte Hawkins Brown, October 29, 1927, MMBF.

Chapter Thirteen

Black Women's Culture of Resistance and the Right to Vote

Darlene Clark Hine and Christie Anne Farnham

EDITOR'S NOTE: *The right to vote is one of the essential elements of democracy — a right for which people having been willing to die. Yet from the first organized efforts at Seneca Falls in 1848, it took American women 72 years to win the vote and southern black women 117 years. Although politics was not considered the province of women, women have always been politically active. As early as 1774, fifty-one white women in Edenton, North Carolina, endorsed the Nonimportation Association's resolves prior to the American Revolution; they declared in their petition that they could not remain "indifferent on any occasion that appears nearly to affect the peace and happiness of our country." Such efforts were routinely quashed through ridicule, the strength of law and custom, and the notion that women's place was in the home and that blacks should "know their place."*

Evangelical religion and the cult of true womanhood, together with advances in women's education, however, allowed women to enter some public debates in the nineteenth century through women's clubs. The northern interest in reform inspired by revivalism led to earlier efforts than were made in the South, where evangelicalism focused on personal vices rather than social sins and where a more patriarchal social structure and rural isolation retarded the growth of women's organizations. The postbellum period, however, proved more auspicious for southern clubwomen. Initially, white women devoted their efforts to reading clubs for self-improvement and church missionary societies, whereas black women built a panoply of organizations necessitated by a segregated society. Club work for both races provided leadership training that impelled some women to widen the range of concerns to include public policy issues. They defended their involvement in public policy with arguments drawn from true womanhood's moral superiority and the idea that some issues, like sanitation and kindergartens, were simply an extension of women's domesticity. By the second decade of the twentieth century, women's participation in the public arena, though limited, was sufficiently widespread that woman suffrage was no longer a demand of the "radical fringe" but had become a social movement. Women's club work had served as the bridge to a wider acceptance of women's involvement in the public arena.

Black women's club work, evangelical commitment, and involvement in education were major factors in the final attainment of voting rights for black women through the Civil Rights Movement. It was Jo Ann Robinson of the Women's Political Council who set the Montgomery Bus Boycott in motion after Rosa Parks had deliberately refused to give up her seat to a white man in 1955. It was the black church, a majority of whose members were women, that formed the backbone of the movement. And it was black students like Diane Nash and Ruby Doris Smith who played significant leadership roles when students became the cutting edge of the movement. Despite the fact that black men exhibited many of the attitudes toward women pervasive in mainstream culture, the burdens of race overrode those of gender, and black women like Ella Baker, who organized the first meeting of what became the Student Nonviolent Coordinating Committee, endured sexism in the interest of ending racism.

• • •

It is a challenge to grasp fully the broad significance of black women's participation in the woman suffrage movement. It is important to begin with a roll call of their names to identify individuals and reclaim the history of their deeds. Who were these black suffragists? What did they do? Second, their efforts must be understood in the context of the origins and evolution of a distinct black women's culture and consciousness. From the outset, black women envisioned woman suffrage as necessary to the success of a larger political agenda. The biggest obstacle to understanding and reconstructing the history of black women and the suffrage movement stems from black women's need to juggle gender allegiances and race loyalty while simultaneously carving out a separate compounded identity for themselves. Third, it must be recognized that to answer the question, "When did women get the vote?" with 1920 and the Nineteenth Amendment is only partially true. For black women in the South, the answer is 1965 and the Voting Rights Act. The Jim Crow South was so violently opposed to suffrage for black women and society generally so sexist in privileging male voices and leadership that it is difficult for historians simply to retrieve the history of southern black women suffragists, for their efforts were often shrouded from the larger public. Some did achieve prominence, however, like Ida Wells-Barnett, but she is also an example of the many women who found it necessary to move north or to Washington, D.C. in order to carry on their reform campaigns. Even after the passage of the federal amendment, segregation prevented almost all southern black women from voting; only their participation and leadership in the Civil Rights Movement and the club movement that preceded it eventually succeeded in bringing them the vote.[1]

The compound nature of black women's identities—as blacks, women, Americans, and people who are often impoverished—increased their significance, though still largely unacknowledged, to the struggle for universal suffrage and first-class citizenship. Black women's multiple identities enabled them to improvise and manipulate a culture of resistance whose contingent strategies transcended time and place. Initially, slavery and resistance to it defined the birth of black women's oppositional consciousness and strengthened their resolve to resist dehumanization and to nurture and preserve, against overwhelming odds, a positive sense of self. Specific historical and material conditions dictated that black women develop an everyday arrangement of values, beliefs, customs, and behaviors that reflected an evolving tradition of persistent, nonconfrontational activism. The suffrage movement, therefore, is but one part of a century-long struggle for human dignity and universal rights.

This essay, then, argues that as women, black women engaged in the suffrage movement on many different levels. Unlike white women, black women found that the ratification of the suffrage amendment failed to alter their status, because a racial second-class citizenship remained the rule throughout the nation, especially in the South. Left with no recourse, southern black women retreated into a separate and distinct network of local-level political action groups and clubs. On the national level the most prominent organization of black women was the National Council of Negro Women, founded in 1935 by Florida educator and New Dealer Mary McLeod Bethune. Southern black women created their own private spaces where they nurtured a shared political consciousness, developed and sharpened mobilization and leadership skills, and plotted various activities and strategies subversive of segregation. In quick succession, black women acknowledged and retreated from the failure of the suffrage movement and increased their involvement in separate club work in the 1930s and 1940s. Then in the 1950s they submerged, or some would say sacrificed, their feminist identities on the altar of race. Black women became the most loyal supporters of black male charismatic leaders like Martin Luther King, Jr., and a score of others. Throughout the 1960s black women were tireless, if not invisible, workers or foot soldiers in numerous freedom rights organizations and campaigns. In 1965 their decades of hard and unrelenting work bore fruit with the enactment of the Voting Rights Act.[2]

Antebellum black women activists, like Sojourner Truth, Maria Stewart, Harriet Forten Purvis, Margaretta Forten, Sarah Remond, and Mary Ann Shadd Cary, were northerners. Most black women lived in the South, where they were enslaved; the few who were "free" were perforce constrained by southern society's conflation of suffrage with abolition. One "free" black woman, however, became a renowned activist by moving north. Frances Ellen Watkins Harper, poet, novelist, and journalist, was a free black born in Baltimore who moved to Ohio to teach at Union Seminary, the precursor of Wilberforce. An active agent of the Underground Railroad that helped escaping slaves, after the war she became a prominent black clubwoman, a national board member of the Woman's Christian Temperance Union, and a founder of the American Woman Suffrage Association in the post-Civil War period. After emancipation a new generation of black women activists emerged to continue the fight for suffrage and women's rights. Although not as well known as their northern counterparts, black southern women like Charlotte Rollin and her sisters Frances, Louisa, and Kate of Charleston, South Carolina, and Adella Hunt Logan of Tuskegee, Alabama, exhibited astute political engagement and consciousness. Still others were southerners who had fled the South, like anti-lynching crusader Ida Wells-Barnett, who moved to Chicago after whites destroyed her Memphis newspaper and threatened her life.

The black women's club movement of the late nineteenth century was launched by the first generation born after slavery. As leaders, these educated, middle-class women swung their personal and organizational support to the suffrage cause. Northern women like Gertrude Bustill Mossell of Philadelphia, Josephine St. Pierre Ruffin of Boston, and Fannie Barrier Williams of Chicago had achieved positions of leadership in their communities. However, southern black women suffragists faced a daunting situation: the South was moving away from suffrage in its hate-filled and frequently violent campaign to disfranchise black men and nullify the Fifteenth Amendment to the U.S. Constitution. Southern legislators revised state constitutions to incorporate such strategems as poll taxes and literacy tests to remove black men from the voter rolls. They segregated society by statute and reinforced it with lynch law. Yet somehow, some southern black women found space, largely within educational communities and large urban areas, especially in the Upper South, to raise their voices to support the suffrage cause.

Whether in the North or South, these women consistently subscribed to universal suffrage—not suffrage restricted to the educated—and to the idea that black women needed the vote for protection and in order to exercise power in their own interest and for the good of their communities. This rationale implicitly aimed at changing racial and gender hierarchies in the United States. Within black communities the struggle for woman suffrage drew its meaning from racialized conceptions of gender and class. Nannie Helen Burroughs, founder of the National Training School for Women and Girls in Washington, D.C. and catalyst for the establishment of the Women's Convention Auxiliary of the National Baptist Convention (then the largest black women's organization in the United States), called the ballot "a weapon of moral defense." She explained, "When she [a black woman] appears in court in defense of her virtue, she is looked upon with amused contempt. She needs the ballot to reckon with men who place no value upon her virtue."[3]

Black women activists fought the contemporary stereotype that painted all women of the race as unchaste.[4] Like white women, they believed in a woman's culture that was morally superior to that found in the public sphere, and they employed this sometimes essentialist notion of woman's nature in their arguments for the franchise. "Racial uplift" was a key component of the black women's club movement. Anna Julia Cooper, a North Carolina native who was an educator, author, scholar, feminist, lecturer, and force in the black women's club movement, epitomized this view when she wrote that African American women were "the fundamental agency under God in the regeneration . . . of the race, as well as the groundwork and starting point of its progress upward."[5]

The suffrage movement is instructive of women's way of struggle. The Nineteenth Amendment marked the achievement of a bloodless revolution, but it occurred only after long decades of agitation and conflict. Unraveling this process of social change exposes the ways sex, race, and class differences impeded women's efforts but also simultaneously motivated suffragists from time to time to build new boundary-crossing coalitions. It also reveals the strength of the antisuffrage forces and the compromises made in order to win the vote. Similarities and parallels between the modern Civil Rights Movement and the first wave of feminism abound. The unity among women, like that among black Americans, was fragile. Women and other excluded groups were unable to sustain a coherent movement that joined all races, religions, classes, and sexual identities equally. A closer look at the suffrage movement exposes these fissures.

The fight for the Fifteenth Amendment to give the vote to black men split the women suffragists in the late 1860s into two major umbrella organizations, each with its own leaders and ideological orientations: the National Woman Suffrage Association (NWSA) under Elizabeth Cady Stanton and Susan B. Anthony and the American Woman Suffrage Association (AWSA) led by Lucy Stone, Henry Blackwell, and other northeasterners. The NWSA resented the fact that the Fifteenth Amendment gave the vote to former male slaves but not to women; therefore, they advocated a constitutional amendment for woman suffrage. The AWSA supported the Fifteenth Amendment out of political expediency and advocated state and local campaigns to achieve the vote for women.

Black women were members of both groups, although fewer were attracted to the NWSA, which was a more radical organization that explored a range of other issues, like "free love." Some AWSA members were black southerners, like Charlotte Rollin of Charleston, who was an ex-officio member of their executive committee at the 1872 meeting in New York City. She had spoken in support of universal suffrage on the floor of the South Carolina House of Representatives in 1869 and had chaired the founding meeting of the interracial South Carolina Woman's Rights Association in 1870. Journalist Mary Ann Cary attended the NWSA convention in Washington in 1871 while she was a student at Howard University Law School. In 1876 she wrote to the NWSA on behalf of ninety-four black women from the District of Columbia, requesting that their names be included in an autograph book as signers of the NWSA's "Woman's Declaration of Rights."[6]

Black women were caught in the middle. Unable to disaggregate themselves, they fought for woman suffrage and black enfranchisement sequentially and simultaneously. Such complexity of struggle was necessary. As the suffrage movement gained momentum at the turn of the century, black women confronted the racism of white suffragists while simultaneously encouraging black men to support women's quest for the vote.[7] Black women had to straddle the racial and gender divide; to avoid slipping between the cracks they had to carve a distinct path that reflected their compounded identity as black women. Thus, black women engaged in the suffrage movement variously from the positions of African American, woman, and black woman.

Black men were aware of black women's double agency. In the March 1921 issue of *The Crisis*, editor W. E. B. Du Bois, an ardent supporter of woman suffrage, confessed that "a larger opportunity for the Negro during the past half-century has been carried on by colored women, although they have not always received the credit for it." In his 1903 book *The Souls of Black Folk*, he described the classic dilemma of double consciousness: "One ever feels his twoness—an American, a Negro; two souls, two thoughts, two unreconciled strivings; two warring ideals in one dark body, whose dogged strength alone keeps it from being torn asunder."[8] The difference between his male perspective on double consciousness and that of black women was that what he saw as a dilemma or weakness was for black women a source of strength and power. It is now clear that black women never enjoyed the luxury of a mere twoness. Indeed, multiple and compounded identities and consciousnesses became critical holdings in their arsenal of weapons to gain suffrage, black freedom, and personal empowerment. This very multiplicity, however, rendered black women enigmatic, on the one hand, and fostered their legendary perseverance, on the other.

Part of that perseverance was demonstrated in their commitment to woman suffrage despite the racism of white suffragists. Younger suffragists brought about the reunification of suffrage organizations in 1890 (National American Woman Suffrage Association or NAWSA), and the leadership began a campaign to recruit the South. Historically, woman suffrage and abolition had been connected, making it unacceptable to white southerners. Using a strategy first developed by Henry Blackwell, NAWSA turned away from universal suffrage in favor of literacy qualifications, excluded southern blacks from their organization, and argued that giving women the vote would restore white supremacy by enlarging the white voter base, making it impossible for blacks to gain a majority. Educational qualifications that would give most white women the vote would render the black women's vote too small to matter, as a consequence of their lower educational rates. In this way white supremacy could be maintained without dependence on the state constitutional changes and segregation laws then being put into place, which white southerners feared might be overridden at the federal level. Marjorie Spruill Wheeler suggests that "Though historians usually focus on the race issue as a prime obstacle to the suffragists' success, there is considerable evidence to indicate that the race issue was, in fact, a major causative factor in the emergence in the 1890s of the woman suffrage movement in the South."[9] It is, indeed, one of the ironies of history that racism was part of a move toward gender equality.

White southern suffragists born before 1865 and residing in states with large black populations, like Georgia's Rebecca Latimer Felton and Mississippi's Belle Kearney, were the most uncompromising racist suffragists. But even the national leadership moved in this direction. Frustrated by the large numbers of illiterate immigrant men arriving in the North who could vote by virtue of their sex, while native-born, educated women remained excluded, white suffragists moved from advocating universal suffrage to championing educational qualifications. Of the late nineteenth-century national leaders, Susan B. Anthony remained the least racist, but younger leaders like Carrie Chapman Catt shared many of the racist assumptions of the times that were widely held in the North as well as the South.[10]

Seeking to organize the South, the NAWSA held its 1895 convention in Atlanta. Anthony asked Frederick Douglass to stay away so as not to offend southern whites. Douglass, the most famous black American in the nation and a prominent woman suffragist, had seconded Elizabeth Cady Stanton's proposal for the ballot at the Seneca Falls Convention of 1848, which launched the woman's rights movement. The NAWSA continued to court white southern support by holding its 1903 convention in New Orleans. At this meeting, the board endorsed the right of individual states to set forth their own positions on suffrage—a policy reinforcing white supremacy by opening the door for whites-only provisions that would not have been acceptable to the North in a federal amendment. While in New Orleans Anthony visited the Phillis Wheatley Club, whose president, Sylvanie Williams, did not hesitate to point out in her welcome speech the discrimination black women experienced in the suffrage movement.[11]

Persisting in the face of such racist appeals was difficult, but many clubs, temperance unions, church auxiliaries, sororities, and educational groups began to add woman suffrage to their concerns. Activists like Cooper, Minnie Crosthwait, registrar at Fisk, and Lugenia Burns Hope of Atlanta University advocated woman suffrage in their speeches and writings. Memphis-born Mary Church Terrell, founder and first president of the National Association of Colored Women, was one of the leading black women activists. Speaking before the 1890 National Woman Suffrage Association convention in Washington, D.C., she argued that "a White Woman has only one handicap to overcome—a great one, true, her sex; a colored woman faces two—her sex and her race. A colored man has only one—that of race." Organizations devoted exclusively to attaining the vote appeared in such cities as Memphis, Washington, Charleston, and St. Louis. Mary Ann Cary, for example, founded the Colored Women's Progressive Franchise Association in Washington in 1880. Adella Hunt Logan, teacher and later wife of a Tuskegee Institute administrator, was a life member of the NAWSA and published articles in the *Woman's Journal* and *The Crisis*, yet she was deliberately excluded from suffrage conventions in the South even though she was active in the Alabama Federation of Colored Women's Clubs and the Southern Federation of Colored Women's Clubs, and headed the department of suffrage for the NACW.[12]

By the end of the century the Republican Party had abandoned its support of ballots for black men, Congress had refused to challenge the dubious constitutionality of southern stratagems, and the Supreme Court had permitted white supremacy to become legally entrenched in southern society. White southern suffragists' attempts to get woman suffrage into state constitutions also had been a failure.[13] Southern politicians thought that the same kind of violence used against black male voters could not be widely used against black females, and they did not want to have to face black women's persistence. Demagogues like J. K. Vardaman, a senator from Mississippi, insisted, "The negro woman will be more offensive, more difficult to handle at the polls than the negro man." South Carolina senator "Pitchfork" Ben Tillman argued, "Experience has taught us that negro women are much more aggressive in asserting the 'rights of the race' than the negro men are."[14] The NAWSA's southern strategy had failed, and the fledgling white suffrage societies in the South died or became inactive. The argument that enfranchising women would solve the "Negro problem" not only lost saliency but now appeared to be an argument threatening white dominance.

By 1910, however, the southern suffrage campaign had entered a new phase.[15] With white supremacy solidly ensconced, proponents now argued that there was no connection between the issues of woman suffrage and race. Instead, it was the Progressive movement that influenced strategy. Continued industrialization and urbanization had altered life for American women, increasing the size of the middle class and the number of college-educated women. The move into club work by women of both races, in part a consequence of these changes, led to the view even among antisuffragists that women had a role to play in public life in areas that were an extension of their domestic responsibilities, like education and sanitation.[16] In the North, Progressives thought that woman suffrage would enhance their prospects for legislative success. In the South a major opponent of suffrage was the textile industry, which feared women's objections to child labor.

Catt's secret "winning plan" emphasized intensive lobbying of congressmen, pushing for referenda in states likely to pass woman suffrage and avoiding such fights where they were likely to fail (which included all southern states), and keeping the issue of black woman suffrage in the background. Alice Paul, who broke from the NAWSA to form the National Woman's Party, used pickets and hunger strikes and a policy of holding the party in power responsible for failure to pass a suffrage amendment; but she too sought to keep black women out of the spotlight. In the NWP's 1913 parade in front of the White House, Wells-Barnett was told not to march with the white suffragists from Chicago, for fear of offending white southerners. This failure to publicly support black woman suffrage made their cause vulnerable to various attempts to change the language of the Anthony amendment (as the woman suffrage proposal was known) to exclude black women. Strong objections by the NACW and the National Association for the Advancement of Colored People, coupled with the realization in the North that the votes of black men would be significant in any ratification battle, prevented the success of this "states' rights" strategy.[17]

The Anthony amendment had been continuously before Congress since 1878, but it received little support until the second decade of the twentieth century. Finally, in 1919 the necessary two-thirds vote was attained. Before becoming part of the Constitution, however, the amendment needed the approval of thirty-six states. Texas became the ninth state in the Union and the first in the South to ratify the amendment, followed by Arkansas and Kentucky; however, Alabama, Georgia, South Carolina, Virginia, Maryland, Mississippi, Louisiana, and Delaware opposed it. Of the five states yet to take action, Connecticut, Vermont, and Florida failed to call special legislative sessions to address the issue, and North Carolina, which did so, did not pass the amendment. Attention then turned to Tennessee. The antis mounted a strong campaign, melting away support for the amendment, which finally passed by only one vote.[18] The Nineteenth Amendment was added to the Constitution on August 26, 1920, ending a campaign that had begun in 1848. Eventually, all of the southern states ratified; but some, clinging to the antebellum view of women as ladies too angelic and pure to be sullied by the evils of the political world, were incredibly slow to do so: Maryland (1941), Virginia (1952), Alabama (1953), Florida (1969), South Carolina (1969), Georgia (1970), Louisiana (1970), North Carolina (1971), and, finally, Mississippi (1984).

Initially, large numbers of black women registered throughout the South, especially in Georgia and Louisiana. They founded "colored women voters' leagues" to provide instructions to both men and women on how to qualify for registration. Southern whites, however, feared that black voters would bring back the two-party system by voting Republican, the party of Lincoln and Reconstruction. The example of Jacksonville, Florida, demonstrated the reality of such a threat. The NAWSA had changed its name to the League of Women Voters when success seemed assured. The Jacksonville branch, however, became the Duval County League of Democratic Women Voters when black women registered and voted in greater numbers than the white women. In fact, there is fragmentary evidence from cities where black women were not prevented from voting that they voted in greater proportions than white women and in about the same proportion as black men.[19]

Despite such interest in the ballot, the white registrars and politicians soon perfected ways to largely eliminate black women's vote, all the while explaining low voter turnout as a manifestation of black apathy. Columbia, South Carolina, for example, kept black women from the voter rolls by requiring them to have paid taxes on property valued at three hundred dollars and pass a literacy test judged by white registrars. No such requirements were made for white women. The NAACP testified before Congress in 1920 concerning such abuses, but to no avail. The League of Women Voters again compromised its principles for the sake of retaining white southerners: it permitted African American women to speak about these abuses before its 1921 convention in Cleveland but took no action. The NWP's record was no better. *The Crisis* reported that "Miss Paul was indifferent" to an appeal from a delegation to the annual convention of sixty black women from fourteen states, whose statement declared that "Five million women in the United States cannot be denied their rights without all the women of the United States feeling the effect of that denial. No women are free until all are free." But Paul insisted that black women's inability to enjoy the franchise was a "racial" and not a "feminist" issue.[20]

At this pivotal juncture the hopes of bridging the rift between black and white women vanished. Realizing that woman suffrage had failed to usher in a new era for African Americans, black women shifted their allegiance and altered their consciousness. By the mid-1930s black women became "race women." Burning from the dismissal of white suffragists, they reconcentrated activities and attention on dismantling American apartheid and white supremacy. From a high of two hundred thousand members, by 1930 the membership of the older NACW had dropped to approximately fifty thousand. Clearly, the always separate and distinct black women's culture needed revitalization in the Depression and World War II decades. By the 1930s, leading black political women had arrived at the conclusion that one massive political organization should be created through which they could make their collective voices heard. It is within this context that Mary McLeod Bethune founded the National Council of Negro Women in 1935.

In an initial press release, Bethune declared the purpose of the NCNW to be the development of "competent and courageous leadership among Negro women and [to] effect their integration and that of all Negro people into the political, economic, education, cultural, and social life of their communities and the nation." During the next twenty years black women's political consciousness and agency were mobilized to an impressive degree. As black women fought racial discrimination, Bethune confided to fellow clubwoman Mary Church Terrell that she intended for the NCNW to "insure greater cooperation among women in varied lines of endeavor." She thought it was time for "Negro women [to] . . . do some thinking on public questions." By the mid-1940s the NCNW had become the largest black women's organization in America, numbering eight hundred thousand members.[21]

In Montgomery, Alabama, under the leadership of an English professor at Alabama State, black women organized the Women's Political Council. Jo Ann Robinson and her colleagues were the women who started the Montgomery Bus Boycott and in so doing laid the basis for the retirement of Jim Crow's strange career.[22] The boycott ignited the modern Civil Rights Movement. Historian Sara Evans, commenting on the centrality of black women in the Movement, wrote, "In addition to their warmth and courage in taking in civil rights workers, these black women also furnished the backbone of leadership in local movements. Volunteers wrote home of 'Mama' doggedly attempting to register again and again or of a rural woman attending a precinct meeting. [And when] . . . no one showed up . . . with a neighbor as a witness, she called the meeting to order, elected herself a delegate and wrote up the minutes."[23]

Black women opened the floodgates of protest that drenched the country for the next two decades, resulting in the passage of the Twenty-fourth Amendment to the U.S. Constitution in 1964, outlawing poll taxes, and the passage of the Voting Rights Act of 1965. That African Americans now enjoy the franchise is a testament to the effectiveness of black women's quiet persistence and, most important, the significance of the compounded identities and multiple consciousness of generations of resourceful black women.

NOTES

1. The suffrage movement in the South has received less attention than other regions and within the South, black women have received less attention than white women. A. Elizabeth Taylor produced studies of individual states in the 1950s and 1960s, and Aileen S. Kraditor in *The Ideas of the Woman Suffrage Movement, 1890–1920* (1965; reprint, New York: Norton, 1981) and Anne Firor Scott in *The Southern Lady: From Pedestal to Politics, 1830–1930* (Chicago: University of Chicago Press, 1970) included chapters on suffrage in the South, but it was not until the nineties that the southern suffrage movement began to receive its due. Marjorie Spruill Wheeler is the most prominent of a new group of scholars examining the South, with *New Women of the New South: The Leaders of the Woman Suffrage Movement in the Southern States* (New York: Oxford University Press, 1993). All these studies, however, concentrate on white women. The leading scholar of black woman suffrage is Rosalyn Terborg-Penn. See "Discrimination against Afro-American Women in the Women's Movement, 1830–1920," in Sharon Harley and Rosalyn Terborg-Penn, eds., *The Afro-American Woman: Struggles and Images* (New York: Kennikat Press, 1978); idem, "Discontented Black Feminists: Prelude and Postscript to the Passage of the Nineteenth Amendment," in Lois Scharf and Joan M. Jensen, eds., *Decades of Discontent: The Woman's Movement, 1920–1940* (Westport, Conn.: Greenwood Press, 1983); and idem, "African American Women and the Woman Suffrage Movement," in Marjorie Spruill Wheeler, ed., *One Woman, One Vote: Rediscovering the Woman Suffrage Movement* (Troutdale, Or.: New Sage Press, 1995). Important work has also been done by Evelyn Brooks Higginbotham, "In Politics to Stay: Black Women Leaders and Party Politics in the 1920s," in Louise A. Tilly and Patricia Gurin, eds., *Women, Politics, and Change* (New York: Russell Sage Foundation, 1990); Jacqueline Jones, *Labor of Love, Labor of Sorrow: Black Women, Work and the Family from Slavery to the Present* (New York: Basic Books, 1985); and Paula Giddings, *When and Where I Enter: The Impact of Black Women on Race and Sex in*

America (New York: William Morrow, 1984). Not surprisingly, these works have a national focus; it has been much more difficult to uncover the southern record except for activists with a national reputation. However, the broad outlines of the southern black woman suffrage movement are coming into focus with the works of Cynthia Neverdon-Morton, *Afro-American Women of the South and the Advancement of the Race, 1895–1925* (Knoxville: University of Tennessee Press, 1989); and Adelle Logan Alexander, "African-Americans in the Woman Suffrage Movement and the Ladies from Tuskegee Institute," in Marjorie Spruill Wheeler, ed., *Votes for Women; The Woman Suffrage Movement in Tennessee, the South, and the Nation* (Knoxville: University of Tennessee Press, 1995); and idem, "How I Discovered My Grandmother . . . and the Truth about Black Women and the Suffrage Movement," *Ms.*, November 1983, reprinted in Darlene Clark Hine, ed., *Black Women in American History from Colonial Times through the Nineteenth Century*, vol. 1 (Brooklyn, NY: Carlson, 1990). For an overview of scholarship on woman suffrage, see Gayle Veronica Fischer, "The Seventy-Fifth Anniversary of Woman Suffrage in the United States: A Bibliographic Essay," *Journal of Women's History* 7 (fall 1995): 172–99.

2. There is a vast and growing body of work on the Civil Rights Movement, although most of the early scholarship focuses on men. Especially useful on the role of women are Giddings, *When and Where I Enter*; Sara M. Evans, *Personal Politics: The Roots of Women's Liberation in the Civil Rights Movement and the New Left* (New York: Vintage Books, 1979); Vicki L. Crawford, Jacqeline Anne Rouse, and Barbara Woods, *Women in the Civil Rights Movement: Trailblazers and Torchbearers, 1941–1965* (Bloomington: Indiana University Press, 1993). Also see Charles M. Payne, *I've Got the Light of Freedom: The Organizing Tradition and the Mississippi Freedom Struggle* (Berkeley: University of California Press, 1995), 265–83.

3. Nannie H. Burroughs, "Black Women and Reform," *The Crisis* 10 (August 1915): 187; see also Giddings, *When and Where I Enter*, 121–23; and Evelyn Brooks Higginbotham, "Nannie Helen Burroughs," in Darlene Clark Hine, ed., *Black Women in America: An Historical Encyclopedia* (New York: Carlson, 1993), 1:201–4.

4. The origins and ramifications of negative stereotypes of black women are explored in bell hooks, *Ain't I a Woman: Black Women and Feminism* (Boston: South End Press, 1981), 30–38; Beverly Guy-Sheftall, *Words of Fire: An Anthology of African-American Feminist Thought* (New York: New Press, 1995).

5. Anna Julia Cooper, *Voice of the South* (Xenia, OH: Aldine, 1892), 15.

6. Terborg-Penn, "African American Women," 140–41; Joel Williamson, *After Slavery: The Negro in South Carolina during Reconstruction, 1861–1877* (New York, 1975), 338. Rollin's work was done during Reconstruction when African American political participation was encouraged by the federal government. In 1900, about thirty years later, Virginia Young, president of the woman suffrage association in South Carolina, claimed that the movement in South Carolina began with the founding of her organization of white women in 1890. This is but one example in which whites define "southerner" as only white; all actions by black Americans

either become invisible to them or are represented as something "other." Terborg-Penn, "African American Women," n. 11.

7. In its November 1917 issue, the *Crisis* asserted that a majority of black men opposed suffrage for black women, claiming not only that they resented the racism of white suffragists but also that they "looked forward to the time when his wages will be large enough to support his wife and daughters in comparative idleness at home." Quoted in Neverdon-Morton, *Afro-American Women of the South*, 204. Paula Giddings, however, believes that not only did almost all black women support woman suffrage but that black men as a group, especially those in leadership positions, supported women, although there were some notable exceptions, especially among conservative Baptist clergy. *When and Where I Enter*, 119–21. Black women saw their enfranchisement as a wedge to win back the vote for black men in the South. As congressional passage of the amendment appeared increasingly likely, northerners looked to the black male vote in their region to pass it.

8. Quoted in Darlene Clark Hine, "'In the Kingdom of Culture': Black Women and the Intersection of Race, Gender and Class," in Gerald Early, ed., *Lure and Loathing; Essays on Race, Identity, and the Ambivalence of Assimilation* (New York: Allen Lane, 1993), 337–51.

9. Wheeler, *New Women of the New South*, 101.

10. The racism of white suffragists is widely documented. See especially the works of Terborg-Penn.

11. See, for example, Marjorie Spruill Wheeler, "A Short History of the Woman Suffrage Movement in America," in Wheeler, *One Woman, One Vote*, 13; Terborg-Penn, "African American Women," 149.

12. Quote from Beverly Jones, "Mary Eliza Church Terrell," in Hine, *Black Women in America*, 2:1157; Alexander, "African Americans in the Woman Suffrage Movement," 77, 89–90.

13. Kentucky, Louisiana, and Tennessee passed partial suffrage legislation permitting women to vote under special circumstances, like municipal elections.

14. Quoted in Giddings, *When and Where I Enter*, 123.

15. Wheeler, *New Women of the New South*, 125–32.

16. Anastacia Sims, "Beyond the Ballot: The Radical Vision of the Antisuffragists," in Marjorie Spruill Wheeler, *Votes for Women*, 105–28.

17. Terborg-Penn, "African American Women," 148–50. As the federal suffrage amendment gained momentum, Kate Gordon led in founding the Southern States Woman Suffrage Conference to oppose it out of a commitment to state sovereignty.

18. For a detailed discussion of the passage of the Anthony amendment in Tennessee, see A. Elizabeth Taylor, *The Woman Suffrage Movement in Tennessee* (New York: Bookman, 1957). See also Anastacia Sims, "Armageddon in Tennessee," in Wheeler, *One Woman, One Vote*, 333–52.

19. Terborg-Penn, "African American Women," 153; Nancy F. Cott, *The Grounding of Modern Feminism* (New Haven: Yale University Press, 1987), 104.

20. Quote from "Resolutions Re: National Woman's Party, February 15–18, 1921," NAACP files, Suffrage, Library of Congress, Washington, D.C. For a detailed description of the reactions of the League and the NWP to the prevention of black women's exercise of the franchise, see especially Giddings, *When and Where I Enter,* 164–70; Terborg-Penn, "African American Women," 151–53; and Higginbotham, "In Politics to Stay," 199–220.

21. "Purpose of NCNW-1935," press release, November 11, 1948, in the Papers of Mary Church Terrell, container 23, Library of Congress. Also see Mary Church Terrell, *A Colored Woman in a White World* (Washington, 1940); Mary McLeod Bethune to Mary Church Terrell, March 15, 1930, Mary Church Terrell Papers, Library of Congress; Bettye Collier-Thomas, "National Council of Negro Women," in Hine, *Black Women in America,* 2:853–64.

22. David J. Garrow, ed., *The Montgomery Bus Boycott and the Women Who Started It: The Memoir of Jo Ann Gibson Robinson* (1987). See also Mary Fair Burks, "Trailblazers: Women in the Montgomery Bus Boycott," in Crawford et al., *Women in the Civil Rights Movement,* 71–83.

23. Evans, *Personal Politics,* 76.

Chapter Fourteen

Renegotiating Liberty
Garveyism, Women, and Grassroots Organizing in Virginia

Barbara Bair

EDITOR'S NOTE: *Black southerners were unable to escape the poverty, disfranchisement, and segregation of the post-Reconstruction South, for racism permeated all ranks of white society. It now had a pseudoscientific underpinning in social Darwinism, which ranked "races" and claimed that in the struggle for "survival of the fittest," African Americans would invariably lose out. The Civil War had energized the industrialization of the North, creating thousands of new jobs. In the 1880s over five million immigrants came to the United States. The depression of the 1890s slowed the influx, but it increased again by eight million between 1900 and 1910. Native-born whites feared that their culture would be overwhelmed by these immigrants, who seldom spoke English and who adhered to Catholic, Orthodox, and Jewish faiths rather than Protestantism; nevertheless, immigrant labor was preferred to black, and most African Americans remained mired in the South.*

However, as a result of slowed immigration, army enlistments from the ranks of labor, and increased demand for manufactured goods, World War I resulted in labor shortages that opened hiring to blacks. Concurrently, southern agriculture suffered from depressed wages and devastation brought on by the boll weevil and floods. With the encouragement of the African American press, hundreds of thousands of black women and men turned their backs on the racist South and headed for the "land of promise" in what is known as the Great Migration. This was a watershed event in black history, for it transformed a rural peasantry into an urban proletariat. Movement slowed during the Depression but increased again with World War II, as blacks moved to cities in the West as well as the North. Large numbers of those remaining in the South also moved to cities.

Although the dense concentration of people in urban ghettos brought enormous social problems, it also resulted in some political gains. In 1928, for example, Oscar DePriest of Chicago became the first African American from the North to be sent to Congress. The large population of blacks in Harlem made it the capital of African Americans and the center of a literary renaissance as well as the New Negro movement, which was intent on confronting American racism.

Unfortunately, the North did not turn out to be the promised land, and the "New Freedom" promised by Woodrow Wilson was shown to be an illusion by the backlash following World War I. Seventy blacks were lynched in the first year after the war, eleven of whom were publicly burned alive. Twenty-five race riots in places like Longview, Texas, Knoxville, Tennessee, Elaine, Arkansas, and Chicago occurred in 1919 alone; and the Ku Klux Klan became a powerful national organization, especially in Indiana, Illinois, Michigan, New England, New York, and Oregon.

Marcus Garvey, a Jamaican of African descent, brought his Universal Negro Improvement Association to Harlem in 1916. Into the midst of a society that told blacks they were an inferior people from a continent that had never produced a civilization worthy of the term stepped Garvey with a message of race pride. He built the first mass movement of African Americans, forging a new identity out of black African nationalism that reflected the aspirations and discontent of the new urban dwellers.

Garvey hoped to drive European imperialists out of Africa and return some African Americans to the land of their forebears. For this purpose he set up the Empire of Africa as a government in exile, replete with nobility, civil servants, parades, international conventions, and a panoply of organizations like the Universal Black Cross Nurses, the Universal African Legion, and the Black Star Steamship Line. Garvey favored racial separation and opposed miscegenation on the grounds that justice could not be expected of whites, because racism was at the core of white civilization. W. E. B. Du Bois and other members of the black intelligentsia, many of whom were mulattoes working for integration, became his enemies. Influenced by Booker T. Washington, he encouraged self-reliance and black enterprise by setting up restaurants, laundries, groceries, and other small businesses, but it was his sale of stock in the steamship line that led to his imprisonment for mail fraud and subsequent deportation in 1927.

Garvey's Back-to-Africa plans held little appeal for the lower economic orders who followed him. What attracted them was his message of race pride. Garvey argued that peoples depict god in their own image; therefore, blacks should worship a black god. He was tolerant of Islam, and his ideas influenced Elijah Muhammad, future leader of the Black Muslims who had been a UNIA member in Detroit, and Timothy Drew, who included passages from Garvey in the Koran he devised for his Moorish Science Temple. Garvey's historical teachings described whites as living in caves at a time when Egypt and ancient African kingdoms were proud civilizations. Viewing history as cyclical, he looked forward to the time when blacks would again be dominant. Garveyites sold black dolls and held black beauty pageants, anticipating the "black is beautiful" slogan of the Black Power Movement.

Although the UNIA was strongest in northern cities, it was surprisingly widespread in the South, where Garvey's message of race pride and black nationalism also resonated. Indeed, his ideas permeated far beyond the UNIA and have regained their currency, if in somewhat modified form, in the Afrocentrism of the 1990s.

• • •

On an early fall day in 1926, excursion boats festooned with streamers arrived on the western shores of the James River and docked at the landing outside the small town of Claremont, Virginia. They were filled with celebrating African American families dressed in their Sunday best. As a Universal Negro Improvement Association (UNIA) band began to play, the sun glinted off the polished buttons of the uniforms of UNIA African Legion auxiliary members who lined up near the dock to greet the newcomers. The brightness of the day made the flowing white caftans of the UNIA's Black Cross Nurses seem to glow with light. Smiling mothers disembarked with their children and took their husbands proudly by the hand. They strode up the hill to the buildings of the UNIA's new school, called Liberty University, which was soon to open for its first session. UNIA members came to Virginia from the Northeast and mid-Atlantic states to gather together for the event. Many of them came from UNIA strongholds in Harlem and Philadelphia. Others came in dusty wagons or autos, by nearby train, or on horseback or small boat from the almost fifty local UNIA divisions located around the state in towns and cities large and small.[1]

One of the big draws of the day was the appearance of Amy Jacques Garvey, the wife of the UNIA's president general, Marcus Garvey, who was at that time incarcerated in Atlanta Federal Penitentiary. Amy Jacques Garvey was a strikingly beautiful and intelligent woman, dignified in bearing and elegant in word. When she rose to help dedicate the new school in front of the gathered witnesses, she was breaking new ground in more than one way. The UNIA was accustomed to the symbolic occupation of territory in the North. When they staged their famous UNIA parades through the streets of Harlem, they boldly claimed those streets as African American political territory.[2] The dedication of the grounds and buildings of Liberty University in Virginia was a similar kind of political action. It represented the reclaiming of land from white supremacist use and its conversion to the service of Afrocentric goals.[3] The trek of so many UNIA members to Claremont to honor the opening of the school shifted for a time the locus of UNIA activism from North to South. It also represented a shift in power that was going on within the organization from male to female. The opening of Liberty University and her presence on that day was a particular triumph for Amy Jacques Garvey, whose leadership within the UNIA was at the time being defiantly challenged by men.

The UNIA in Virginia

The trends that were epitomized in the September 1926 ceremonies on a hill above the James River had been developing for years. The UNIA was originally founded in Jamaica by Marcus Garvey and Amy Ashwood (who soon became Garvey's first wife). It is usually thought of as a northern movement, with membership concentrated in the urban and industrial centers of the Northeast. Although the movement was headquartered in New York and many of the largest divisions were in northern and midwestern cities that attracted black migration and immigration, the majority of local UNIA divisions were actually located in the South. North and South were also not fixed categories. There was considerable fluidity between northern and southern divisions, as black southerners migrated to work in the North, joined family members in northern cities, or came home to the South to see relatives who had been left behind. UNIA members in the South corresponded regularly with those in the North. The UNIA newspaper, the *Negro World*, regularly wound its way south through the mail. It was also passed in increasingly tattered form from hand to hand, making the transition from pristine condition in a print shop in New York to being read aloud at UNIA meetings in households, churches, and halls in Virginia. A woman who joined the Garvey movement outside Atlanta wrote to her sister in Cleveland about the experience, and soon the Cleveland UNIA division had a new member.[4] Railroad porters similarly served as conduits of UNIA news as they worked lines running between divisions in different parts of the country. In the mid-1920s UNIA organizer Laura Kofey, who first became involved in the UNIA in Detroit, became the most successful organizer of new UNIA divisions in Alabama and Florida, holding camp-style meetings that swept members into the UNIA by the hundreds in the spirit of a religious revival.[5] Visitors to New York from Richmond would write home excitedly about seeing Garvey in action at UNIA headquarters, building enthusiasm for the activities of the local division.[6] Amy Jacques Garvey and other UNIA organizers, male and female, who were headquartered in New York made frequent appearances as keynote speakers at mass meetings in Richmond, Norfolk, Atlanta, New Orleans, Memphis, and other urban UNIA strongholds in the South.

The grassroots divisions founded in Virginia were extremely varied. Located in places as different as Hampton Roads and Fairfax, Hopewell and Somerset, Portsmouth and Danville, they varied in both size (from seven members to hundreds) and composition. Their membership ranged from tiny groups of tobacco and cotton workers who lived in the extensive agricultural sections of the state, domestic servants and railroad employees who worked in white homes and railway stations in northern or central Virginia towns, and middle-class professionals and businesspeople as well as service workers and shipyard and dock workers who lived in the African American sections of the state's major eastern urban centers of Richmond, Norfolk, Berkeley, and Newport News.[7]

While the dramatic appeal of the Black Star Line[8] helped draw members into the UNIA, the Garveyites' commitment to the development of separate African American economic and educational institutions within the state also struck responsive chords among black Virginians. In Richmond, the site of one of the largest and most influential UNIA divisions in Virginia, one of the main meeting halls used by the UNIA for its large programs was around the corner from the Jackson Ward home of Maggie Lena Walker, whose study wall sported a large photograph of Marcus Garvey and a framed copy of his UNIA manifesto, *African Fundamentalism.*[9] Banker Maggie Lena Walker, along with Madam C. J. Walker of beauty product fame, were often held up to rank and file Garveyites as models of black business acumen. Indeed, many Garveyite women made their living in the beauty industry selling or applying Madam C. J. Walker's or a competitor's products, which were advertised for black women consumers in the *Negro World*. With Maggie Walker's Order of St. Luke in Richmond and Hampton Institute as local models of business and educational success, the UNIA sought to build similar enterprises in

Virginia and to incorporate commercialism and teaching/learning into the ongoing programs of the local divisions.[10]

The UNIA's function as a spiritual movement and the close conjunction of its rituals and ceremonies with those of church and fraternal organizations were bolstered by the fact that several of the leading theologians active in the Garvey movement were born or trained in Virginia, including those who studied at the Virginia Theological Seminary and College at Lynchburg. Most local divisions relied on the use of Baptist or African Methodist Episcopal churches for meeting space (known as Liberty Halls), and UNIA and church activism often overlapped. The gender structure of the church was replicated in the UNIA: male leaders tended to have the highest profile within local UNIA divisions, but women made up the backbone of active membership and oftentimes constituted the numerical majority of members. The large divisions like the ones in Norfolk and Richmond had two slates of officers, one male and one female; the president of the division, a man, was responsible for the activities of the division as a whole, but the Lady President and her assistants oversaw the women in what were called Ladies Divisions. These urban divisions also had (male) African Legion and (female) Black Cross Nurse auxiliaries, and a Juvenile Division for girls and boys, with classes usually taught by women. Women leaders were addressed by the title "Lady" or "Madame." In an era when some white members of Congress were trying to build a Black Mammy monument, romanticizing the "days of slavery," this manner of address was a sign of respect counteracting the white habit of referring to black people in overly familiar terms. It was also an appropriation of both the tradition of Anglo-Saxon nobility and the white southern practice of using the word *lady* to connote cultivation, dignity, and sexual purity. As in the church, music was an important part of UNIA gatherings, and women were frequent soloists at meetings. They also offered recitations, served as secretary-recorders, and, in their capacity as officers in the Ladies Division, gave addresses to the membership at large.[11]

Reported activities of UNIA divisions located near Claremont in August and September 1926 give an idea of the regular participation of women at the local level as well as the role of women in the interplay between North and South. Laura Johnson, Lady President of the Richmond division in the mid-1920s, regularly gave the introductory address at division meetings held at the Bethel A.M.E. Church or the Thirty-first Street Baptist Church, while Racilla W. S. Jones recorded the proceedings, and the "musical directress," Mrs. A. V. Davenport, "electrified the audiences with splendid renditions by the juveniles." In August 1926, the Berkeley division (the largest in the state) held a mass meeting "with religious services conducted by Miss Aleatha Reddick," and a regular Sunday night program in which Mrs. Sarah Mayo read Garvey's weekly front-page *Negro World* editorial aloud to the assembly, and Mrs. Annie C. Sykes, who had recently arrived home from a visit to New Jersey, "made an inspiring address." During this period, Mrs. Johnson, the Lady Vice-President of the UNIA's Philadelphia division, spoke at the Campostella, Virginia, division meeting, and UNIA international organizer Mme. M. L. T. De Mena of New York headlined mass meetings and oversaw the election of new male and female officers at the Norfolk division. In her talk at Campostella, Johnson "spoke directly to the women on cherishing our idealism and holding fast to the work. We were all uplifted by the inspiration left with us and by her charming personality." A few years earlier, in July 1922, when Marcus Garvey and Amy Jacques Garvey came to Richmond, "Mrs. Lillian Jackson Willis, formerly of Richmond, but now working for the UNIA in New York, made an impassioned address prior to the speech of Hon. Marcus Garvey and made a most favorable impression." In all the local UNIA divisions, women members brought organizing and speaking skills they had learned in their churches and activated circles of women they knew through religious worship into task forces that carried out UNIA programs in their neighborhoods and towns.[12]

The Black Cross Nurse auxiliary similarly built on existing networks of women to spread the word about good maternal and child health. In Richmond they offered literary and musical entertainment at meetings, including pageants about the history of nursing and the glories of Africa. They held meetings in women's homes to teach well-baby care techniques and share knowledge about birth control. They offered workshops and gave lectures at Ladies Division meetings to teach about nutrition and sanitation. And they appeared in emblematic form in UNIA pageants as black angels of mercy, ladies holding high a torch or lamp, shedding enlightenment and offering a counter of purity and nobility to white racist stereotypes of African American women as morally wanton. They urged UNIA women who sharecropped or were tenant farmers to plant vegetable gardens to supplement cash crops, and in the cities they helped organize UNIA supper kitchens and community gardens. In all their functions, they built on personal connections among friends and kin to institute public health services in black communities where no formal services existed. In bolstering black health and helping black families to better thrive, they directly countermanded what UNIA members saw as a white supremacist plan of genocide directed against African Americans. Their womanist efforts on behalf of insuring black health and survival were also laden with the politics of Pan-African liberation. In UNIA rhetoric, songs, and poems, the Black Cross Nurses were heralded as figures that would bring succor to male soldiers on the future battlefields in Africa, in the struggle to free Africa from colonial rule.[13]

A similar politics of liberation lay behind the push for the Black Star Line, the founding of Liberty University, and the UNIA's support for the antimiscegenation and repatriation legislation that was introduced in the Virginia General Assembly in the mid-1920s. In all these areas in which the UNIA was active in Virginia, women played key roles.

Gendered Organizing

In the first years of the UNIA's influence in Virginia, national organizers, including Amy Jacques Garvey, the Nicaraguan-born Mme. M. L. T. De Mena, and Henrietta Vinton Davis of Maryland, made repeated visits to the state. They helped build new divisions, settle internal disputes in existing ones, attract new members through mass meetings, and encourage investment in the Black Star Line and Black Cross Navigation and Trading Company shipping enterprises. In so doing, they drew on a long history in Virginia of support for African colonization and migration movements, as well as interest in the shipping industry. They also offered, through their high-profile participation, a reworking of Marcus Garvey's dominant rhetoric of liberation, whose gendered arguments about black power were offered within a framework of manhood and masculinity.

When Garvey spoke at a mass meeting about the Black Star Line in Newport News on 29 October 1919, he focused on the change that serving in World War I had wrought in the attitude of black men and the resulting emergence of the New Negro movement. "I have discovered that the Negro of the South is a new and different man to what he was prior to the war," he told his audience at the Newport News First Baptist Church. "The bloody war has left a new spirit in the world—it has created for all mankind a new idea of liberty and democracy, and the Southern Negro now feels that he too has a part to play in the affairs of the world." "The New Negro manhood movement is not confined to the North alone," he stated, "it has found its way far down South and there are millions of black folks here who mean to have all that is coming to them or they are going to die in the attempt of getting same." He continued in the remainder of his speech to address the urgency of this new militancy to his "brothers" and "fellowmen," reiterating that the "salvation of our race depends upon the action of the present generation of our young men."[14]

UNIA women endorsed this new paradigm of black manhood, but they believed in a new womanhood as well. Indeed, the UNIA's propaganda was directed to both sexes. A call to members of black churches and lodges to organize UNIA divisions and send delegates to the 1921 UNIA convention stated that the UNIA

> wants every black man and woman to become an active member of the organization. If you have pride, if you feel that by co-operation we can make conditions better, if you believe that the black boy or black girl is the equal of other boys and girls of other races, then prove it now by co-operating to demonstrate our manhood and womanhood, not by talking, but by doing things.[15]

Women had been "doing things" for some time. When Garvey first began building the organization in the United States in 1918–19, he was greatly aided in his fledgling speaking tours by Henrietta Vinton Davis. A veteran stage actress already well known to black audiences, Lady Davis had been introduced into a public career in the 1880s by Frederick Douglass, for whom she had worked as an assistant in the Office of the Recorder of Deeds in Washington, D.C. Davis was one of the founding directors of the Black Star Line, and she emerged as one of the two women who became most prominent in the promotion of the shipping enterprise in the United States and the Caribbean. While Garvey spoke about emerging manhood in 1919–20, Davis chaired huge UNIA meetings at Madison Square Garden and Carnegie Hall. While Garvey himself never actually set foot on the African continent, Davis was in the forefront of the UNIA's Back-to-Africa campaign as a member of the three-person UNIA delegation that went to Liberia in 1924 to negotiate with president C. D. B. King about UNIA colonization plans. Davis was in turn a mentor to the younger M. L. T. De Mena, who emerged in 1925, leading mass meetings in Richmond, Norfolk, and other Virginia divisions and working as an organizer for the UNIA shipping line. She soon eclipsed Davis as a leader on the national scene. The two women were the primary organizers aboard the UNIA's *Booker T. Washington* when it made its maiden voyage from New York in 1925, stopping in Norfolk on the way to Cuba, Jamaica, and Panama. De Mena returned to Virginia later in the same year on a speaking tour with Amy Jacques Garvey. De Mena acted as a trouble-shooter to divisions suffering from factionalism. The *Negro World* reported that on these occasions De Mena "electrified" her audiences and won over a "magnificent following."[16]

Davis and De Mena to a great extent displaced the male model of militancy dominant in the movement. Both were frequently described by the adoring UNIA press as women warriors or black Joans of Arc. Davis herself went so far as to explicitly regender the politics of militancy that Garvey had articulated in his October 1919 Newport News speech, one-upping him in her use of the imagery of self-sacrifice. In a 17 October 1925 *Negro World* article called "The Exigencies of Leadership," she wrote that if and when "our men hesitate," then the "women of the race must come forward, they must join the great army of Amazons and follow a Joan of Arc who is willing to be burned at the stake to save her country."[17]

Davis became the first woman to officially join the upper echelon of national UNIA officers when she was elected international organizer at the international UNIA convention in August 1920 in New York. Some of the major issues facing the UNIA in Virginia were voiced at that same convention by Newport News delegate Nellie G. Whiting. Whiting's comments from the floor of the convention addressed Jim Crow conditions in Newport News. She was particularly perturbed by the double standard in business, whereby white merchants profited by providing goods and services to black residents but African Americans were excluded from both wider business development and civil opportunities open to whites. Foreshadowing the "Don't Buy Where You Can't Work" campaigns and boycotts that women UNIA members joined in the 1930s, Whiting observed, "We are segregated in the Eastern section of the city. All of our people are huddled together over in the one section, yet white men are allowed to come over there in our section and set up their stores and sell to colored people." Whiting proceeded to describe the realities of the Newport News shipyards. Her description countered the idealistic vision of freedom conjured up in Garveyites' minds by the Black Star Line ships. The Black Star Line's appeal lay in several layers of liberating promise. One was that of blacks in the position of leadership, with the powerful image of African Americans at the helm.[18] Another was that of black business enterprise, with the promised development of trade and exchange of natural resources among people of African descent and between the United States, Africa, and the Caribbean. The freedom of movement manifested in black-owned ships was another basis for support. And the ultimate political message of liberation connected to the Black Star Line was the planned future use of the ships, not for trade, but for repatriation of oppressed African Americans to a more independent life in Africa. These hopes, which organizers like Davis and De Mena were so good at stirring within the breasts of their UNIA audiences, were in sad contrast to the reality of the shipping industry as Whiting described it. "Our men and boys work in the shipyard; they are segregated there. The white man goes to one window for his pay and the colored man goes to another. Our men there are building ships. When we ride on the ships we are put in one corner; the white people can walk anywhere they want to go." In her statements about daily life in Virginia, Whiting also put something on the record on behalf of women. She noted that economic inequities between black and white were matched by a sexual double standard with regard to black and white women. Whites supposedly enforced strict segregation in residences, workplaces, and public settings, but at the same time, Whiting observed, sexual harassment was the norm: "white people," she said succinctly, "won't leave our girls alone." Whiting also addressed the conservatism of black ministers who opposed the Garvey movement and tried to suppress it in Newport News, partly out of fear of losing scarce economic support and local political clout for themselves and their churches to the UNIA. In her simply put but far-reaching social analysis, Whiting also had something to say about the racialized nature of education in Virginia. The schools were designed to perpetuate white supremacy. Whiting described them to her fellow UNIA delegates as places where the "white man lets the white children study books in order to keep going upwards, and they deny us the use of the same books in order to keep us down, but give us books instead to study that will lead us to worship the white man and keep ourselves down." [19]

Liberty University

The purchase of Liberty University was one way of consciously "going upwards" and counteracting the kinds of conditions Nellie Whiting had described. The UNIA purchased the school in 1926. It had been in operation in Virginia since 1881, when it was founded by Hampton Institute graduate and former slave John J. Smallwood, a resident of Richmond. By the time the UNIA began negotiating for the property, Smallwood had passed away, and the name of the school had been changed from the Temperance Industrial Collegiate Institute to the Smallwood Memorial

Institute, and then, in 1922, to the Smallwood-Corey School when it merged with a black Baptist school formerly in Portsmouth. In 1926 it had a Richmond-based African American board of directors; and its president and vice-president, Caleb Robinson and Dr. J. G. St. Clair Drake, were both Garveyites. Its faculty included Minna Thorpe, Miss S. M. Gantt, and J. H. Blackwell, Ph.D., of Richmond, whose wife, Anna Jordan Blackwell, was a teacher at Maury Street High School in Richmond and a leading member of the First Baptist Church, the Binga Foreign Missionary Society, and the Council of Colored Women's Clubs of Richmond. She was described as "a speaker of unusual ability of her sex." The Blackwells' two sons were a doctor and a lawyer, and their daughter was the wife of a Petersburg merchant. Professor Blackwell was a leading member of the Richmond True Reformers, and when Garvey came to speak at the True Reformers Hall in July 1922, Blackwell spoke also. His wife was influential in bringing a summer camp for the Phillis Wheatley branch of the YWCA to the Smallwood-Corey School. Through the Blackwells the school was strongly connected to middle-class black society life in Richmond, and through Robinson and St. Clair Drake, both of whom lobbied hard for the transfer of the school to UNIA auspices, it was made part of a much more radical purpose.[20]

In March 1926, a few months before the successful transaction for the school was made by the UNIA, Robinson wrote a long, eloquent letter to white Richmond resident John Powell, asking for Powell's help in securing the school for the Garvey movement. Robinson explained that the school was located in the region where the first slaves had been brought from Africa to the United States, occupying the "spot where the second cargo of Negro slaves landed in 1622, and in sight of Jamestown . . . where the first cargo landed in 1619." The UNIA wanted to reclaim this land and use it to, in effect, reverse the process of the transatlantic slave trade by teaching Pan-African unity to those separated by the diaspora of slavery and preparing young Garveyites to meet the challenge of repatriation to a liberated Africa. "Because of the history of the place and its sacredness to our group," Robinson wrote, "we are deciding to make it the Southern Headquarters of the Garvey 'Back to Africa' movement, and have there a great school to teach and train boys and girls, men and women of African descent . . . to so train them there that when they depart to live in Africa they will on arriving be an asset and not a liability."[21]

Purchase of the school in July 1926 was part of an ongoing goal of the Garvey movement to establish schools that combined an Afrocentric curriculum with the teaching of technical skills that would be of use in a new society in Africa. When Garvey and Amy Ashwood founded the UNIA in Jamaica, Garvey planned to begin a school there based on the Tuskegee Institute model. As Amy Jacques Garvey explained, he wanted to

> open a trade school like Tuskegee. This would give practical help to the masses, who then had no such opportunity for training; at the same time he could inculcate in them race love, and strengthen his African program in the entire island. The trade school would in time furnish competent men and women as technical missionaries to be sent to the mother country—Africa.

With the death of Booker T. Washington and Garvey's move to the United States, the UNIA grew into a grassroots movement, but the interest in education remained, as evidenced by the oratory, editorials, and pageants of the UNIA, the classes taught through the UNIA auxiliaries and juvenile divisions, and later in a leadership correspondence course initiated by Garvey in the 1930s. With Garvey in prison in 1926, it fell to Amy Jacques Garvey and other UNIA leaders to negotiate for Liberty University. She described the institution simply as "a practical high school." UNIA Secretary General W. A. Wallace, in kicking off the Universal Liberty University Fund Drive, echoed Robinson's political view of the school when he proclaimed that "from this spot, our fore-parents were sold into slavery" and on 12 September 1926 "we return to dedicate it to the cause of African Redemption as FREE MEN." [22]

The UNIA encouraged every division to send at least two youngsters to the new school. The first to enroll were Genevieve Baker and Loretta Romer of New York, who, when they returned home for Christmas vacation, appeared at the UNIA's main Liberty Hall in Harlem. The *Negro World* described them as "highly intelligent young women" who "made brief but eloquent addresses in glorification of Marcus Garvey and Liberty University." The school, the *Negro World* reporter explained, was a

> distinct school for Negro young people, in which they may learn something about themselves and their race, and about Africa, their Motherland, which they could not learn in other race schools, nor in the white schools open to them. . . . To be taught that the Negro has as many rights as any other racial group and that he needs a country and flag of his own in order to make effective his rights, is something new in Negro education. [23]

The actual course of study advertised by the school included "Industrial, Scientific, Agricultural, Business, Domestic Science, Vocal and Instrumental Music, Normal, Bible Training, Physical Culture, Dressmaking, Plain Sewing, Typewriting, Stenography and Bookkeeping." School literature assured parents that their daughters would be protected by a "refined and cultured matron and the boys by a respectable warden" and that "they'll be safe from white psychology so in their older years they may praise and glorify your name." Although both boys and girls attended the school, girls made up the majority of the student body. Among them was Berniza De Mena, the daughter of Mme. M. L. T. De Mena. Berniza De Mena had been a standout in the juvenile division of the UNIA in New York before coming to Claremont at the age of fourteen. Her mother had come to the United States briefly from Nicaragua about the time Berniza was born in 1913, and then returned to Central America. She supported her daughter by working as a stenographer and teacher before beginning her career with the UNIA. She and Berniza immigrated from the Panama Canal Zone around 1923. Berniza was, like her mother, bilingual, and of mixed African, Latina, and white descent. She graduated with the final class of Liberty University in June 1929.[24]

The commencement ceremonies of Berniza De Mena's class make an interesting comment on the larger politics of Virginia at that time. In addition to helping shepherd Liberty University in the mid-1920s, Amy Jacques Garvey was emerging as a powerful political negotiator. The premier propagandist of the movement, she edited the woman's page of the *Negro World*, providing in the mid-1920s a forum for feminist and womanist thought and activity. She barnstormed the country as an orator and lobbied government officials to win the release of her husband from prison. She also produced the two volumes of the *Philosophy and Opinions of Marcus Garvey* (1923, 1925). Designed in part to win white support for Garvey's pardon, these volumes also offered the most concentrated argument regarding the UNIA's stand on race purity. In compiling statements from Garvey's speeches and editorials, Amy Jacques Garvey presented the UNIA position that miscegenation, in conjunction with the poverty induced by white denial of economic opportunities to black labor, was one form of race suicide, and that repatriation to Africa was the best hope for avoiding a future of genocide like that faced by Native American peoples. In accordance with these views, Amy Jacques Garvey had traveled to Virginia the year before Liberty University opened and orchestrated a coalition between Garveyites in Richmond and the members of the Anglo-Saxon Clubs of America, including president John Powell, who were working in favor of so-called racial integrity and repatriation legislation introduced in the Virginia General Assembly. She helped facilitate the appearance of white supremacists at local UNIA meetings in Richmond and personally introduced a speech by Powell at Liberty Hall in New York. In March 1926 she introduced the text of a repatriation resolution written for the Virginia General Assembly by one of the white supremacists who had been appearing at UNIA meetings in Virginia as a major plank at the UNIA convention held in Detroit. She urged UNIA delegates to take it to their own communities and start petition drives to win support for similar legislation in their home states.[25]

After the passage of the Racial Integrity Act of 1924, the Richmond white supremacists with whom Amy Jacques Garvey worked were primarily obsessed with the notion that Virginians of mixed Native American and African American descent were "passing" as Indian—and eventually as white—rather than being labeled black under the current law of the state. As one Anglo-Saxon Club supporter put it, individuals were slipping from "Indianoid negro to Negroid Indian, Negroid Indian to plain Indian, plain Indian to Indianoid White" and thus into marriage "to a white person" and passing as white.[26] The situation had come about in part because of a loophole in the law that allowed elite white Virginians the chance to continue to claim Pocahontas as one of their ancestors. In the midst of this controversy over the fine points of racial definition, Berniza De Mena's class at Liberty University staged a graduation pageant called "The Pioneer's Papoose."

Loretta Romer, who was finishing up her four years at the school, played the role of the "Indian Medicine man," and Raymond Kelly of Dayton, Ohio, played the lead, "Chief Tomahawk." The supporting cast included several Indian maidens: Berniza De Mena was one of them, as was Ila Purdy, the daughter of the president of the Alliance, Ohio, UNIA division; Miss Gregory Ann Dicks of Cincinnati; the "four Wooten sisters, of Savadge, Va., Miss Audrey Abrahams and Laurette Busby of N.Y., Miss Louise White and Eleanora Dicks of Cincinnati, Miss Velma Eddings of Cleveland, Miss Mercides Francis of Detroit and little Miss Alma Hunte, of N.Y., who was the Papoose." The leads featured class valedictorian Johnnie Mae Bryant of Cincinnati as the pioneer daughter; Mr. Solon Wooten of Savadge, Virginia, as the pioneer; Beaulah Tilghman of Philadelphia as the "Indian Princess"; and John Harrison of Cleveland as the "Messenger of Chief Arrowhead." During intermission Miss Gantt, one of the teachers, sang "When Ole Mammy Moon Swings Low."[27]

While white supremacists were worrying about African Americans passing as Indians, and the African American students at Liberty University were taking the stage in Indian garb, Amy Jacques Garvey was facing her own conflicts of identity as a UNIA leader. The purchase of Liberty University, her role in working with the Virginia white supremacists, and the national profile she had achieved during her husband's imprisonment caused deep factionalism in the Garvey movement. Some of it was over the movement's shift from its former radicalism to coalition with right-wing groups, but most of it was over Amy Jacques Garvey's role as a woman and her "first lady" power as the nonelected spouse of the president general. Two factions of the UNIA sued each other for control of Liberty University and UNIA operations. The male leadership headquartered in New York refused to take orders from a woman and challenged Amy Jacques Garvey's authority to form UNIA policy or direct UNIA affairs. While the *Negro World* responded to attacks on Amy Jacques Garvey by characterizing her as "helpless" and the perfect helpmeet, Garvey defended his wife from his prison cell as "loyal and loving" and urged "all of my friends to chivalrously protect the fair name of my wife from the vile and wicked tricks of my enemies." Mrs. A. S. Alexander wrote to the *New York Age* to lend a female spin on the allegations, stating that "these men are jealous of Mrs. Garvey because of her ability." "We Negro women," she wrote, want to say to those "weak-knees" men "who have not a third of Mrs. Garvey's intelligence, to stop trying to smother a woman of the race, because of their inability to compete with her." While the fur was flying, Amy Jacques Garvey continued to be anything but helpless. Defying her own husband's claim that she had "no connection with the school," she appeared on the lawn at Liberty University to welcome the Garveyites who had come to celebrate its opening day, and she did not stray from her discourse of support for women's rights within the organization.[28]

Berniza De Mena, meanwhile, represented the female hope of the future, the third generation of women's leadership and activism in the movement. After graduating from Liberty University she moved back to New York, where she became, like Amy Jacques Garvey before her, a writer and editor for the *Negro World* who specialized in women's issues. After editing a column for children in her first year on the paper, she began a column called "Womanly Ways" in 1930. In the paper's 14 June 1930 issue, while she was still a teenager fresh from her Liberty University education, she published an article calling for women's liberation within the movement. Decrying the defection of men from the UNIA, she took the rebellious position that women actually made better leaders than men: "The race, now, can only look to the women for help," she wrote.

> Men ARE capable of leading, but they generally lead the wrong way. Women, moreover, are more inspiring than men. They can stand the tests that man cannot stand . . . WOMEN! Wake up. Put your shoulder to the wheel, and show the men the real meaning of the word LOYALTY. If you begin now there should be no fear as to the further progress of this great organization.

Her status as heir to her mother's legacy was secure when a *Negro World* reporter described her, "a graduate of Liberty University," as a "little African Joan of Arc."[29]

NOTES

1. Excursion celebrations started on 12 September 1926, and classes commenced on 15 September. Preparations for the opening of Liberty University, or the former Smallwood-Corey School, received extensive coverage in the UNIA's *Negro World* newspaper, including articles, maps of the property, photographs of the buildings, lists of donors who had contributed to the purchase and maintenance of the school, and advertisements for the excursion (see 24 July, 31 July, 7 August, 21 August, 28 August, 4 September, 18 September, and 25 September 1926 issues).

2. See, for example, "50,000 Followers in Line of March as Convention Opens," *Pittsburgh Courier*, 6 August 1921; and "Garvey Followers Parading in New York," *East Tennessee News*, 10 August 1921, UNIA clipping file, Peabody Collection, Hampton University (HU). The *Courier* reported that the parade in New York on 1 August 1921 involved "from 5,000 to 10,000 Negroes from all parts of the United States and West Indies . . . some marching and others occupying seats in about 100 to 200 automobiles and auto buses." Women were very much a part of these parades. Cars holding UNIA dignitaries led bands and male regiments, followed by the Black Cross Nurses and a detachment of the Motor Corps, the woman's section of the African Legions, and finally delegations carrying banners from every state represented, including Virginia, North Carolina, and South Carolina. The *News* carried a photograph of the Black Cross Nurses marching and reported the text of various parade banners, including "The Negro woman is the greatest mother."

3. The Garvey movement was dedicated to the development of strong "race first" group consciousness and unity, including pride in black heritage, political identification with Africa, and knowledge of African cultures and history, among all peoples of the African Diaspora.

4. UNIA Collection, Western Reserve Historical Society, Cleveland (WRHS).

5. See Barbara Bair, "Ethiopia Shall Stretch Forth Her Hands unto God: Laura Kofey and the Gendered Vision of Redemption in the Garvey Movement," in *A Mighty Baptism: Race and Gender in the Creation of American Protestantism,* ed. Susan Juster and Lisa MacFarlane (Ithaca: Cornell University Press, 1996).

6. Among these was Benjamin F. Vaughan, whose correspondence to Edward Drummond about Harlem appears in the Drummond Papers, Valentine Museum Archives, Richmond, Va., and is the subject of a work in progress by Elsa Barkley Brown. See also Mrs. J. P. Giddings and Laura Johnson correspondence to Ethel Collins, 1940, WRHS. See also John Mitchell's *Richmond Planet* and P. B. Young's *Norfolk Journal and Guide.*

7. See "News and Views of the UNIA Divisions" sections of the *Negro World.*

8. The Black Star Line, along with its successor, the Black Cross Navigation and Trading Company, were UNIA maritime enterprises. The UNIA sold stock in the shipping lines to grassroots members of the movement and used the money raised to purchase and run a series of ships. One was an excursion boat used in New York. The others were used to make organizing tours down the eastern seaboard to the Caribbean and back. The goal, which went unrealized due to the UNIA's lack of capital, was to use the line to establish black-owned and -operated trade and passenger service between the United States, the Caribbean, and West Africa. Despite its failure as a business enterprise, the Black Star Line was an important symbol to Garveyites of the possibility of international black independence from white domination and control.

9. The photograph, along with one of Garvey's arch-rival W. E. B. Du Bois, is still there to see. Walker's home is open to public tours under the auspices of the National Park Service. On Walker's position on Garvey and Du Bois, see "The Garvey Movement and the Black Star Line," *St. Luke Herald,* 14 May 1921, HU. Walker was an officer in the local Richmond NAACP. *Richmond Planet,* 22 April 1922. On Walker's career in Richmond, see also Elsa Barkley Brown, "Constructing a Life and a Community: A Partial Story of Maggie Lena Walker," *Magazine of History* (Organization of American Historians) 7, no. 4 (summer 1993): 28–31.

10. Even though founded by white patronage and headed by a white administration, Hampton Institute (later University) represented the belief in the importance of higher education for black citizens and the creation of opportunities, through training, for African Americans to create careers in agriculture, the trades, and the professions, especially teaching and nursing. Hampton Institute was founded in 1868 by Samuel Chapman Armstrong, chief of the local Freedman's Bureau, to serve the freedpeople of the Hampton region. It was located on a farm purchased by the American Missionary Association and officially chartered as the Hampton Normal and Agricultural Institute in 1870. Booker T. Washington, founder of Tuskegee Institute in Alabama, was an 1875 graduate of Hampton and an early role model for the young Marcus Garvey.

11. The African Orthodox Church was formed out of Garveyism, and UNIA meetings followed the structure of church sessions, including the use of ritual, catechism, and the singing of hymns. A form of liberation theology was developed, which linked spiritual salvation to personal freedom from racist self-concepts regarding the relative worth of whiteness and blackness and the political independence of Africa from colonial rule. On the UNIA as a spiritual movement and UNIA theologians, see Randall Burkett, *Garveyism as a Religious Movement: The Institutionalization of a Black Civil Religion* (Metuchen, N.J.: Scarecrow Press, 1978); and idem, *Black Redemption: Churchmen Speak for the Garvey Movement* (Philadelphia: Temple University Press, 1978); on the Black Mammy monument, see *Richmond Planet*, 13 January, 27 January, 3 February 1923.

12. *Negro World*, 24 July, 28 August, 25 September 1926; *Richmond Planet*, 8 July 1922.

13. See, for example, "Black Cross Nurses Organize for Service," *Chicago Whip*, 13 November 1920: "When the next bugle call for war is sounded, when the next band of black boys march to fight the common enemy, they will . . . be accompanied by their own Black Cross Nurses." HU. Some black feminists prefer the use of the term *womanist* to describe their brand of feminism, partly to express separation from the historic racism of the white feminist movement, and partly in a desire to connote a sense of racial community and connectedness in conjunction with ideas of the personal liberation of women. The Black Cross Nurses, with their goal of empowering women in order to enable them to in turn better conditions for all African Americans, thereby ensuring both a better quality of life for individuals and group survival, fit in very well with this understanding of feminism. See Alice Walker, *In Search of Our Mothers' Gardens* (New York: Harcourt Brace Jovanovich, 1983), xi; and Patricia Hill Collins, *Black Feminist Thought: Knowledge, Consciousness, and the Politics of Empowerment* (New York: HarperCollins, 1990), 37–38.

14. Garvey reprinted this speech as one of his front-page editorial letters to the readers of the *Negro World*, 1 November 1919.

15. Undated *Negro World* clipping, HU.

16. *Negro World*, 5 September 1925; *Richmond Planet*, 31 October 1925. For Davis's and De Mena's careers, see Robert A. Hill et al., eds., *Marcus Garvey and UNIA Papers*, 7 vols. (Berkeley: University of California Press, 1983–90) (hereafter cited as *MGP*).

17. When Davis appeared in Los Angeles on an organizing tour, the Los Angeles *California Eagle* newspaper described her not just as a Joan of Arc but as "a broad, deep, very warm-hearted compassionate Amazon. . . . the Ethiopian Rachel of heroic mould." In a tribute to the movement's interest in nationalism and sovereignty, it also compared her to Betsy Ross. Reprinted in *Negro World*, 19 March 1921.

18. See, for example, "Shadyside on First Trip: Colored Captain at Helm," *New York Tribune*, ca. 8 August 1920, HU. The Black Star Line's *Shadyside* (an excursion

boat that went up the Hudson River, carrying in this instance delegates to the 1920 UNIA convention) was described as like an independent country: it flew under the UNIA's black, red, and green flag, and its "colored captain was monarch of all he surveyed."

19. Nellie Whiting's comments were recorded as part of the 1920 UNIA convention minutes, reprinted in Hill et al., *MGP*, 2:537. White theorists like Moses Drury Hoge were capable of recommending that literary work be abandoned completely in black schools in favor of concentrating on training a black agricultural and domestic labor force that would work in service of whites. *Negro Education in the City of Richmond, Va.* (Richmond, 1905). The "head" versus "hands" debate regarding black education was, of course, a long one. On the state of black education in the South, see also James D. Anderson, *The Education of Blacks in the South, 1860–1935* (Chapel Hill: University of North Carolina Press, 1988); and Howard N. Rabinowitz, *Race Relations in the Urban South* (New York: Oxford University Press, 1978), 152–81.

20. John J. Smallwood correspondence, Joseph Bryan Letterbook, 1895, 1897–98, Virginia Historical Society, Richmond; *Negro World*, 31 July, 18 December 1926; *Richmond Planet*, 17 June, 8 July 1922, 4 July 1925, 13 March 1926; Lester F. Russell, *Black Baptist and Secondary Schools in Virginia* (Metuchen, N.J.: Scarecrow Press, 1981), 101–3; Monroe Work, *Negro Year Book*, 6 vols. (Tuskegee, Ala.: Tuskegee Institute, 1912, 1914–15, 1916–17, 1918–19, 1921–22, 1925–26). As Russell demonstrates, the black Baptist church was enormously important in the founding of black secondary schools and colleges in Virginia. Among them was the Hartshorn Memorial Institute, founded in Richmond by the American Baptist Home Mission Society, which produced a corps of black women teachers and leaders. It became the Woman's College of Virginia Union University in 1923. See also Cynthia Neverdon-Morton, "The Colleges," in *Afro-American Women of the South and the Advancement of the Race, 1895–1925* (Knoxville: University of Tennessee Press, 1989), 10–67.

21. Caleb Robinson to John Powell, 26 March 1926, John Powell Collection, Special Collections, Alderman Library, University of Virginia, Charlottesville (UVA).

22. Amy Jacques Garvey, *Garvey and Garveyism* (1963; reprint, New York: Octagon Books, 1978), 13, 173; Hill et al., *MGP*, 6:338–39. The Tuskegee connection was also a link with Virginia because of Washington's training at Hampton Institute.

23. *Negro World*, 20 October 1926, 8 January 1927.

24. *Negro World*, 26 November, 25 June 1927.

25. *Negro World*, 27 March 1926.

26. Louise Burleigh to the editor, *Boston Evening Transcript*, 8 March 1926, typescript, box 3, UVA; Amy Jacques Garvey to Earnest Sevier Cox, 1925 correspondence, Cox Papers, Duke University; John Powell, *The Breach in the Dike: An Analysis of the Sorrels Case Showing the Danger to Racial Integrity from Intermarriage of*

Whites with So-Called Indians (Richmond, Va.: Liberty Press/Anglo-Saxon Clubs of America, ca. 1926).

27. The account of the graduation entertainment implies that few of the students at Liberty University were from Virginia. The five Wootens of Savadge are the only ones named from that state. The rest were from Ohio, New York, Pennsylvania, and North Carolina. If all the graduating students participated in the operetta, there were sixteen girls and five boys (not counting Miss Hunte, who it is implied was a small child). *Negro World,* 20 July 1929. Liberty University was bankrupt and forced to close in August 1929. Soon after, the buildings were vandalized. The institution never reopened.

28. Hill et al., *MGP,* 6:363–64, 365–66, 461, 462, 453; *Negro World,* 14 July, 21 July 1923, 20 March 1926; Alexander letter, *New York Age,* 6 March 1926, reprinted in Hill et al., *MGP,* 6:361.

29. *Negro World,* 14 June 1930, 25 April 1931.

Chapter Fifteen

A New Deal for Southern Women
Gender and Race in Women's Work Relief

Martha H. Swain

EDITOR'S NOTE: *Government spending during World War I produced boom times, and the economic expansion of the middle and late 1920s brought the "consumer durables revolution" of cars, radios, and refrigerators to many. The gross national product in 1929 had increased by 75 percent from 1909, and the income of the average American was a third higher in constant dollars than before the war. Yet there were flaws in the economy that would wreak havoc on an entire generation of Americans. Government tax policies favored the rich; the aggregate income of the twenty-four thousand richest families was three times larger than that of the six million poorest. High tariffs prevented Europeans from buying American goods to restore their economies. Government antiunion policies inhibited the growth of a counterbalancing force in manufacturing. A lack of federal controls permitted uncontrolled speculation in real estate, stocks, and bonds.*

Not all sectors of the economy shared in the prosperity of the twenties. Agriculture suffered from declining prices caused by overproduction and global competition, exacerbated in the South by a failure to diversify from dependence on antebellum staple crops and the expense of restoring fertility to exhausted fields, plus the devastation brought by floods, droughts, and the boll weevil. In addition, the textile and coal industries were plagued by high unemployment. Unfortunately, these were all major sectors of the southern economy. Most southerners were farmers, and they earned an average of $186 per year, compared to $528 for the rest of the nation. When Franklin D. Roosevelt called the South "the Nation's No. 1 economic problem" in 1938, he was describing a situation that had existed since the end of the Civil War.

With half of the nation's income going to only one-fifth of its families, the demand for durable goods was bound to decline, due to the average family's lack of purchasing power. High tariffs prevented Europeans from buying U.S. goods or selling in U.S. markets, so they were unable to pay their war debts to the United States or provide an alternative market for durable goods. Initially, prosperity had brought good returns on the stock market, which encouraged further investment; however, stocks could be purchased with as little as 10 percent down and the rest borrowed. The ease of purchase dramatically increased the number of sales. This enlarged demand for stocks drove prices up higher than their value; as a consequence, the wealth that resulted was largely on paper. When the inevitable slowdown in demand for durable goods occurred, stock prices fell. Buyers defaulted on their loans in such numbers that banks failed, depressing stock prices still further. Remaining banks tightened their loan policies by raising interest rates. Because the United States was the principal source of international credit, the Depression became worldwide. As inventories piled up, manufacturers, suppliers, and retailers cut back, firing employees. Families were forced to cut their budgets, reducing demand still further. By the winter of 1932 unemployment had reached 25 percent. Private charity could not cope with destitution on such a scale, nor could state and local governments, because their tax revenue had declined.

Roosevelt's New Deal brought hope and some relief, together with long-term change. The First Lady, Eleanor Roosevelt, highlighted the needs of women and minorities. The most important vehicle of relief was the WPA (Works Progress Administration), which prevented widespread starvation by providing material assistance and public work. Many young people were enabled to remain in school through the work programs of the NYA (National Youth Administration). Payments for taking crops out of production as a way to raise farm prices were less successful, for landowners often kept monies meant for tenant farmers or threw them off the land altogether. Long-term change resulted from the TVA (Tennessee Valley Authority), which built dams providing cheap electricity to attract industry in the seven-state valley, bringing eventual prosperity to one of the poorer regions of the South. The Rural Electrification Administration provided the possibility of electric lights, refrigerators, and electricity-driven machines to rural areas. The Social Security Act was of little value, however, for it excluded agricultural and domestic workers, categories that included most women workers, irrespective of race. The construction of low-cost housing projects in the larger towns and cities provided some of the poor with modern units and recreation facilities that they had never had. However, these projects were segregated, and racial ghettoization was reinforced.

The South was hard hit by the Great Depression, and black southerners were hit hardest of all. Desperation amplified racism. A group marched in Atlanta with banners proclaiming "Niggers, back to the cotton fields — city jobs are for white folks." Sexism was also reinforced. Married women were forced out of jobs to make way for men on the grounds that men were the family breadwinners. Nevertheless, major cultural changes were under way, propelled by the attacks on rural isolation represented by the radio, automobiles, a new network of paved roads, mail-order houses like Sears, Roebuck, and, perhaps most importantly, the movies. The New Deal relief agencies themselves spurred women's entry into social work, nursing, and other occupations. And the work that destitute women performed under government sponsorship was often the salvation of their families.

• • •

Long before the full impact of the Great Depression that began late in 1929 hit the South, the region's women ranked lower than men on economic indices of income and employment. By 1933 unemployment, poverty, and need for basic sustenance were facts in the lives of countless women, both urban and rural. But by the year's end in 1933 there was hope for improved circumstances through a new women's work program, under way with the Federal Emergency Relief Administration (FERA) and directed by Ellen Sullivan Woodward and virtually all-female national and state staffs. There were a number of administrative strictures common to all work relief projects that mitigated against women seeking work assignments. The prejudice of the lay public and local officials, particularly against minority women, presented additional difficulties. Nonetheless, Woodward's division made notable inroads against the obstacles it faced. From 1933 to 1943, women held "made work" jobs under three successive New Deal agencies on projects whose legacies remain until the present.[1]

During the so-called years of the locust, 1929–33, women's economic opportunities declined further than their previous lows. Urban workers lost jobs when the downturn reached their municipalities. Women workers in a range of mills and industries, most particularly textiles, suffered worse than even in previous years, as did sharecropper and tenant farm wives.[2] From Arkansas, where the extreme drought of 1930–31 wrought unbelievable hardship, one despairing widow wrote to the Red Cross, "I wish if you will please send me some clothes. Just enough to wear to the cotton patch," while a mother wrote, "I am near my row's end." Julia Kirk

Blackwelder has documented the "quiet suffering" among women in Atlanta, New Orleans, and San Antonio, where blacks bore the brunt of layoffs and harsh work.[3]

When local governments proved unable or unwilling to assist women, they wrote to Lou Henry Hoover, wife of President Herbert Hoover. Among the thousands of supplications mailed to the First Lady from 1929 to 1932, many were from the South. From Alabama came a request for used garments; similar pleas came from Louisiana and Kentucky.[4] A Sandersville, Georgia, woman begged for "some money to buy us some clothes and shoes"; some requests were for employment.[5] Many women found themselves in the plight of the South Carolina woman who wrote of a "nest egg" exhausted by her husband's illness that caused the couple to "really be up against it."[6] The letters were no different from those Lou Hoover's successor as First Lady received after March 1933.

Mrs. Hoover was correct in responding that only limited resources were available from the hard-strapped states or private charities. Even states that could have provided monetary aid had no governmental mechanism in place to do so. Documented cases point to the poverty of Alabama women whose direct assistance amounted to no more than $2.60 every two weeks.[7] In Mississippi, of the only thirty-four families that drew pensions in 1931, thirty were headed by widows.[8] No real help was forthcoming under two organizations set up by President Hoover, the President's Emergency Committee on Employment (PECE) and the President's Organization for Unemployment Relief (POUR).[9] Each had a women's division, but like the parent organization, it relied strictly on the voluntary cooperation of local municipalities, charities, churches, or women's clubs.[10]

What proved to be of some merit were the ideas generated by the women's divisions of PECE and POUR to create employment opportunities for women, albeit on a voluntary basis.[11] For Ellen S. Woodward, secretary of the Mississippi units of the two committees, it was instructive to study the work plans of other states and the periodic bulletins from the national women's program that came across her desk outlining "made work" endeavors.[12]

Harry Hopkins, the head of the FERA since its inauguration in May 1933, was greatly influenced by Eleanor Roosevelt and was determined to create a women's work program. In late August he appointed Woodward to direct the new Women's Division within the FERA. He accepted Woodward upon the recommendations of colleagues who knew of her work as executive secretary of the Mississippi State Board of Development, her involvement in the new State Board of Public Welfare, her direction of the PECE and POUR activities in Mississippi, and her related social welfare activities. He needed a woman administrator who was an effective organizer, able to manage diverse personalities and present his relief program in a favorable light to politicians. There is no evidence that he found her work wanting, for he retained her as an assistant administrator in the short-lived Civil Works Administration (CWA) from 1933 to 1934, and the Works Progress Administration (WPA), established in 1935.[13]

The challenge of putting to work a vast number of needy, unemployed women, especially those in the South, became evident to Woodward soon after she arrived in Washington in September 1933. At a White House Conference on the Emergency Needs of Women on November 20, the stark reality of the task ahead became apparent. Representatives of women's organizations in attendance reported on conditions existing in their locales. Alabama activist Patti Ruffner Jacobs had informed the Women's Bureau of the United States Department of Labor that there were six thousand unemployed clerical workers in Birmingham alone. Additionally, she reported that a new department store received five thousand applications for seventy-five advertised jobs. The need of Alabama women for income was no greater than that of women throughout the South.[14] Women's Bureau studies documented the low wages of workers in the hard-hit clothing and textiles industries, the depletion of what little savings women had accumulated, and the fact that resources of social service bureaus were inadequate to assist destitute women, circumstances common to the unemployed throughout the country, but exacerbated in the South.[15]

Woodward's first task was to create a Women's Division within each state, consisting of a state director, state supervisors for each approved statewide work project, and supervisors of designated districts in each state. State directors were women representing a range of experience that provided a sense of professionalism to the entire Women's Division. Some of the most effective programs in New Deal work relief had developed by the time the WPA began in 1935, because of the extent of need and the past experiences of the state directors.

Georgia's Jane Van De Vrede was a professional nurse of national stature and a former executive director of the Georgia State Nurses Association. Ella Graham Agnew was among the oldest of all state directors. A missionary in South Africa at the turn of the century, she returned to her native Virginia and, in 1914, became the first federal salaried home demonstration agent in the nation.[16] Ethel Payne was educated at Columbia University and the University of Chicago. She had worked with the national Young Women's Christian Association in New York and the Italian Relief Agency in Chicago before returning to Mississippi as a pioneer in social welfare.[17] Mary Weber, of Alabama, most recently had been a department superintendent of Woodward Iron Company, and Dot Kennan of Arkansas, an office manager of a finance corporation. Florida's Rolla Southworth was educated at the New York School of Social Work and had once worked at the Henry Street Settlement; Kentucky's director was Elizabeth Fullerton, a former rural case worker; Louisiana's was Edna Brenan and later Leo Spofford. Tennessee's was Elizabeth D. Coppedge. Mary K. Taylor, a former Fort Worth department store division head, directed the program in Texas, Margaret D. Davies in South Carolina, and May E. Campbell in North Carolina.[18] The regional supervisor for the South (Region 3) was Blanche Montgomery Ralston, a former state federated clubs president and journal editor in Mississippi, Coahoma County (Mississippi) Chamber of Commerce executive secretary, and state director of the Democratic women's division "Reporter Plan." Like most of the state directors, she had known Harry Hopkins when he had conducted Red Cross operations in the South after World War I.[19]

For many young women of the South, work relief social services offered an entrée into a new career. The task of administering means tests to relief applicants and certifying needy persons for work inundated state FERAs, necessitating the employment of trained social workers. Scholarships enabled a sizable number of young women to obtain graduate degrees in social work. The initial assignment given Marie L. Hoffman, the first person in the Mississippi FERA to hold a master's degree, was to supervise twelve graduate students entering Tulane University, where she had received her advanced degree in 1933. She became a pioneering FERA district supervisor and later an assistant director in the state WPA office. In South Carolina, thirty-one-year-old Alice Norwood Spearman, as director of the Social Service Department of the Marion County Relief Administration, was the first South Carolina woman to administer a county relief program. From Alabama, a child welfare worker, Loula Friend Dunn, became the FERA regional supervisor for eleven southern states and, after 1937, commissioner of public welfare for Alabama.[20]

While the FERA and CWA Women's Division heads competed with the men's construction work for project approval, it was at the county level that less-noticed foot dragging went on. "Women are not getting a fair share of the work," reported the Mississippi federated clubs president in January 1934. The CWA women's work leader in a southern Mississippi county met the kind of rebuff common to others. For three weeks her office was no more than a "big manilla envelope carried under her arm," for she was granted no office space. She concluded that it "was thought dangerous for a woman to be around the CWA headquarters."[21]

Under the FERA and the CWA, questions loomed, as they would in the WPA, about what constituted "woman's work." Woodward insisted that women "could and should work wherever work is," including manual labor, especially when it paid "men's wages," more remunerative than most of the women's service programs. A Leflore County (Mississippi) women's work official complained that the state CWA head had ruled that landscaping projects involving raking were "too hard for women," but he would approve projects "where the work is light, such as washing windows and scrubbing floors and walls." The disapproving office could have added that the pay for "light" women's work was lower.[22] Similarly, a North Carolina women's project leader was aghast to learn that CWA men directors ruled that furniture making was too strenuous for women. She knew many women who spent "weary days at such back-breaking work as plowing, chopping wood, scrubbing floors, dragging babies around, or bending over a wash tub for hours on end."[23] State officers appeared not to know what skills women possessed. Ethel Payne commented, "Every man has the idea that if a woman is trained, she is a stenographer, but if she isn't she can sew."[24]

In actuality, many women could not sew and had no skills at all. Although relief rules stated that applicants, men as well as women, were to be placed in areas of employment where they had a prior work history, numerous women had done no work except in common agricultural labor and in their own homes where conditions were substandard. Woodward and the state directors in the South, many of whom originated in small towns and had spent much time traversing the county seats and hamlets of their states, were well acquainted with the type of women in the largest category of needy clients.

Critics of the "traditional" women's work done on many of the FERA-CWA-WPA service (women's) projects would do well to recognize that it broke tradition and long-established patterns for masses of uneducated, often illiterate women with no prior work history other than in the fields to be employed at nonagricultural tasks away from home. The women's work program was supposed to enable women to maintain skills during the economic emergency or train them for employment when the Depression ended. The truth is that the majority of women certified for work relief were so bound to their families as household heads that they had virtually no mobility; thus movement into new lines of work was not promising. "The fact that a very large number of first priority women are unskilled creates many difficulties in trying to achieve a diversified program," Woodward informed Hopkins late in 1935, as the WPA got under way.[25]

Project designers in the Division of Women's and Professional Projects (WPP), as Woodward's section was reconstituted after 1936, were beleaguered by recurring problems inherent in administering effective projects for unskilled and semiskilled women, who accounted for 79.5 percent of all women on relief in 1935. The fact that in southern cities between 70 and 80 percent of women on relief jobs were unskilled weighted that figure.[26] Defenders of sewing activities rebutted detractors who scorned the projects as "female ditch-digging." Woodward feared that the "only alternative [for the unskilled] seems to be their return to direct relief," that is, the dole. She was determined that such women have the same opportunity as educated and professional women to earn work relief wages. Files on sewing projects offer glimpses into the lives of workers. After a small unit at Artesia, Mississippi, closed, its supervisor wrote President Franklin D. Roosevelt of one worker who with her five children subsisted on bread and water for two weeks while waiting for another assignment. Displaced women in North Carolina, a sympathetic congressman wrote to a constituent, "must have something to eat, some kind of roof over their head and some fuel to keep . . . warm."[27]

Most male WPA state chiefs frowned on sewing projects but offered no ideas about how to place small clusters of rural women in work accessible to their homes and under requisite supervision. As one North Carolina administrator put it, "Frankly our hearts don't palpitate over sewing rooms."[28] But even Lorena Hickok, Harry Hopkins's roving reporter who never minced words in pointing up shortcomings she saw in the WPA, saw merit in the projects. After visiting sewing rooms in Florida, she wrote, "I don't think you have any idea what they have done to women themselves. . . . Working in pleasant surroundings, having some money and food have done wonders to restore their health and morale." A sharecropper's boast that the $21 his wife drew at a WPA sewing room "just about takes care of everything" speaks volumes about the low standard of living of many clients.[29]

Sewing projects were enormously productive in their output of clothing and household items distributed to needy families. In Memphis, for example, between 1936 and 1938 sewers who annually added $200,000 to the city's payroll produced clothing worth $250,000. Atlanta women by the late 1930s had distributed over four million garments to individuals and public institutions.[30] When tornadoes devastated towns in Mississippi and Georgia in 1936, WPA output supplied welfare families who had lost everything. Ethel Payne reported from her state that the WPA clothing room at Tupelo "looks like Sears Roebuck." Of the eight million items produced in Kentucky by 1943, many had gone to children in rural and mining communities so that they could attend school.[31]

Still, as one of the most highly visible production-for-use WPA activities, sewing was a target for vociferous critics. Woodward could reasonably answer some, such as those from private manufacturers who charged unfair competition. After all, relief recipients of WPA-made articles hardly constituted a ready market for stores on Main Street. Woodward had more persistent difficulty in dealing with repeated assertions that minority women suffered discrimination. Even though sewing was developed for the unskilled or semiskilled, at a time when the WPA load in May 1940 in eleven southern states consisted of 22.9 percent blacks, only 7.4 percent of sewing wage earners were black women. They were given work assignments at more difficult tasks, for instance, stitching heavy fabrics instead of lighter textiles, or cleanup chores not expected of whites. They were the first to be released when congressional cutbacks closed projects, or else they were transferred to menial and demeaning work. In one of many such cases, Fayetteville, North Carolina, supplicants wrote of the "rampant discrimination" in the reassignment of sixteen black sewing project workers to yard cleanup. Honest efforts to investigate legitimate complaints led to dead ends. Local officials denied the charges, and victims of certain abuse feared reprisal if they were identified as complainants. Moreover, projects for black and Mexican American women were curtailed when congressmen received rebukes from employers, whether landowners or housewives, who resented the loss of their cheap labor to better-paying government relief jobs.[32]

Women's Division personnel developed two activities primarily to provide wages for black women, the Housekeeping Aide Project and Household Demonstration. Both were intended to ease the high unemployment among women who classified their occupation as "servant," a category claimed in 1934 in seventeen southern cities by fifty-two thousand blacks and only five thousand whites. Kentucky, for example, reported in 1933 that more than half its black women were out of work, three-fourths of them in domestic service.[33] As housekeeping aides, women who had minimal domestic skills gained training sufficient to send them into homes of needy families as "surrogate mothers" so that the caregiver there could work herself or children held home to nurse a sick family member could attend school. In the South most aides were black. Despite constant watchfulness from Washington, some local officials abused the system. San Antonio furnished one example where women, in this instance white, were sent to do "dirty and exhausting" work in homes of wealthy families.[34]

But where the program was properly run, it won praise as a genuinely humane social service that aided women household heads whose families were hard hit by illness or some other calamity that had halted income. At the same time it provided FERA or WPA wages to women who were unable to obtain assignments on other activities for which quotas were filled. Texas observers claimed that infant mortality had been reduced; Tennessee's final report emphasized the sheer relief to human suffering that housekeeping "Good Samaritans" rendered.[35]

In 1935 an Arkansas native, Alfred Edgar Smith, who was an investigator on black affairs for Harry Hopkins, began work for Woodward's office. In successive reports, he explored appropriate work opportunities for untrained black women "for which Federal, state, and local administrative officials admit having no solution."[36] The challenge led Woodward to conclude that training projects could be a function of her division that would make its program distinct from that for men. In 1935, with the express encouragement of Eleanor Roosevelt, the Women's Division launched the first of three Household Workers' Training Projects to set up centers to upgrade skills of domestic workers. In the South, where a preponderance of the projects existed, the centers were segregated and a vast majority of trainees were minorities. In Mississippi and Louisiana, all enrollees were black, but then the nationwide figure was 93 percent. The history of the program proves that Roosevelt, Woodward, and other reformers, including the liberal congressman from Texas, Maury Maverick, were wrong to believe that training household workers could actually increase wages and improve work conditions. It is a lamentable fact that

New Deal federal work relief was limited in what it could do to raise wages in the private sector. But the greatest failure of the Household Workers' Training Project is captured in Jane Van De Vrede's terse comment to Lorena Hickok, "The only trouble is that [blacks] won't go for it. They don't want to learn how to be servants."[37]

Both Congress and President Roosevelt made policy that worked against southern populations on relief. "Sponsors," either local organizations or state agencies, always underfunded in the best of years, had to meet most nonlabor costs. For the WPA women's projects, the sponsor was often a women's club or the local parent-teacher associations, organizations that either had limited resources or were too often dominated by provincial viewpoints about what segments of society should first be served. When Gay Shepperson, Georgia's WPA chief and the only woman to head a state program until Arizona appointed a woman head, tried to give blacks greater assistance, she alienated sponsors and was forced to back down or else cancel projects. Hence, blacks had no choice but to accept "half a loaf" or none at all. Similarly, when the Georgia Women's Democratic Club complained about integrated sewing centers, the practice was curtailed. Florida laws forbade whites from teaching blacks and vice versa, a stricture that hampered efforts toward mixed-race supervision in training in most other southern states as well.[38]

Finally, there were circumstances within black families that made it difficult for women to prove they were household heads, a firm requisite for certifying individuals for work relief. A husband was often absent so much he provided no assistance, yet he remained the legal household head. The seasonal nature of WPA programs for men inflicted hardships on a wife, who could not be accepted for WPA work even while none was available at the time for the husband.[39] Those and other concerns were explored at a special White House conference in April 1938 instigated by Mary McLeod Bethune and conducted by Eleanor Roosevelt and Ellen Woodward. Attended by a number of representatives of southern black women's organizations, the Conference on Participation of Negro Women and Children in Federal Programs adopted resolutions that were only perfunctory.[40] Had Congress ever appropriated sufficient funds for the WPA to operate independent of state or private sponsorship, work relief could have been conducted without deference to regional prejudices. It never happened, and in fact as the 1930s went on, Congress made deep cuts in federal relief that worsened problems with the states.

Difficulties and discriminations that beset work relief for southern women assigned to sewing or training should not cloud the success of other projects that employed almost half of women on relief. Probably the most popular of all Women's and Professional Projects activities was the School Lunch Project and its allied Gardening and Canning Projects. School lunches for undernourished and needy children came into their own under the WPA and were nowhere as welcome as in the South. Virginia's record was as impressive as that of any state: between January 1937 and April 1939, women on relief served nine million lunches. In Texas at the program's peak in 1941–42, 7,000 project workers were serving 250,000 lunches daily in 2,500 schools. Little wonder that local esteem for the WPA lunch ran as high in Texas as everywhere else in the South, and school officials touted the gains in student health, attendance, and demeanor.[41] Probably more than any other Goods Production project, WPA feeding programs left a true legacy and did much to augment passage in 1946 of the National School Lunch Act.

WPA nurses performed a myriad of duties: bedside care of mothers, promotion of oral hygiene, maintenance of clinics to treat specific diseases, and location of crippled children for therapy. Georgia's project bore the stamp of Jane Van De Vrede: by 1936 (in less than one year of WPA service), workers had immunized 184,000 persons against typhoid, 2,300 against smallpox, and 26,000 against diphtheria. WPA public health and nursing personnel replicated such work in all southern states.[42] Extensive library projects, popular in all southern states, were the cornerstones of eventual statewide library systems encompassing every county. It was in the South that librarians on relief delivered books by intrepid means: by packhorse in Kentucky, by flatboats in the Mississippi, Arkansas, and Louisiana Delta, and by houseboats that plied the streams in backwater counties.[43] There is no question that library service under the WPA was institutionalized and made permanent all over the South at the demise of work relief.

Women on relief performed other work that remains useful to the present. They worked at Historic Records Surveys and wrote local histories under the Historical Research Project. A Vital Statistics Survey, which operated under the nomenclature of Public Administration and under the Women's and Professional Projects division, employed women to check back records of births and deaths, work that was of considerable value to state departments of public health and for Social Security applicants after 1935. Independent of the WPA Divisions of Emergency Education and Recreation, Woodward's program included extensive nursery and recreation projects. Women mounted displays and performed research for public museums and schools and created traveling exhibits. All of this does not even touch upon the employment of women in the Four Arts Projects for Art, Music, Writers, and the Theatre. Historian Douglas L. Smith has concluded that "in terms of human impact," the women's service programs in the South "in some way touched almost everyone in every locality where they operated."[44]

Accurate figures for the total number of southern women employed by the WPA are difficult to obtain since final reports do not list numbers by region. Moreover, the WPA was chary of reporting employment on population groups by race or ethnicity. Until June 1940, women constituted between 12 and 18 percent of those on WPA rolls.[45] If an internal count for the Women's and Professional Projects made in mid-July 1937, showing an average of 27.6 percent women as WPA employees in twelve southern states compared to a national average of 18.2 percent, represented usual loads, then it seems likely that women consistently made a better showing in the South. (The matter of hourly wages is another thing.)[46] Because many workers were dropped from projects and others hired, or women were removed from relief rolls when they became eligible for assistance under Social Security, monthly WPA totals cannot tell how many *different* individuals drew relief wages.

Beyond work relief, southern women were beneficiaries of the New Deal in other ways that have not yet been explored to any extent. Women received homeowner loans and worker's and literacy education; they signed contracts as landowners under the Agricultural Adjustment Administration and benefited extensively, and gratefully, from rural electrification. They moved to new locales through rural resettlement and lived on subsistence homesteads. They won at least small gains under wage and hour clauses of the National Industrial Recovery Act and the Fair Labor Standards Act. Younger women enrolled in National Youth Administration work that replicated that of work relief in many ways.

Gender and race distinctions limited women to less assistance in the vast work programs of the FERA-CWA-WPA than that given men. Nevertheless, lasting gains resulted for many women from the multifaceted federal programs in the 1930s. Unlike the imprimaturs left on many of the construction projects, women's work relief has few monuments that testify to its consumer goods and services. Mississippi's Ethel Payne thoughtfully asked near the end of 1939 how to equate the lasting value of linear feet of paved sidewalks and airstrips with linear feet of books on a WPA library shelf. For a time, women's work relief was the salvation of workers and their families, and their communities benefited in incalculable ways.[47]

NOTES

1. For a summary essay on women's work relief in general, see Martha H. Swain, "'The Forgotten Woman': Ellen S. Woodward and Women's Relief in the New Deal," *Prologue* 15 (winter 1983): 201–13.

2. See Douglas L. Smith, *The New Deal in the Urban South* (Baton Rouge: Louisiana State University Press, 1988), chap. 1; Delores Janiewski, *Sisterhood Denied: Race, Gender, and Class in a New South Community* (Philadelphia: Temple University Press, 1985), esp. chap. 4; and Margaret Jarman Hagood, *Mothers of the South: Portraiture of the White Tenant Farm Woman* (New York: Norton, 1977), passim.

3. Nan Elizabeth Woodruff, *As Rare as Rain: Federal Relief in the Great Southern Drought of 1930–31* (Urbana: University of Illinois Press, 1985), 27; Julia Kirk Blackwelder, "Quiet Suffering: Atlanta Women in the 1930s," *Georgia Historical Quarterly* 61 (summer 1977): 112–24.

4. A. T. (Alabama) to Lou Henry Hoover (LHH), 10 September 1931; LHH to F.D.C. (Louisiana), 2 September 1931; M. D. (Kentucky) to LHH, 27 August 1930, all in Papers of Lou Henry Hoover, box 54, Herbert Hoover Library, West Branch, Iowa.

5. Mrs. R. B. (Georgia) to LHH, 5 October 1930; Secretary of LHH to Mrs. H. C. B. (Virginia), 10 November 1930, both in box 49, Papers of LHH.

6. Mrs. L. H. A. to LHH, 3 December 1930, box 49, Papers of LHH.

7. See Wayne Flynt, *Poor but Proud: Alabama's Poor Whites* (Tuscaloosa: University of Alabama Press, 1989), 286, 294.

8. Anthony J. Badger, *The New Deal: The Depression Years, 1933–1940* (New York: Noonday, 1989), 27.

9. On POUR ineffectiveness in the South, see Smith, *New Deal in the Urban South*, 40.

10. Report of the Women's Division, PECE, 12 December 1930, Record Group (RG) 73, series 12, box 1117, Hoover Library.

11. Undated release, Records of the Publicity Section, Women and Unemployment (PECE), RG 73, series 26, box 1143, Hoover Library.

12. Ellen S. Woodward (ESW) to Lillian Gilbreth, 11 February 1931, Women's Division (Miss.), RG 73, National Archives (NA); James Ford (Better Homes in America) to Gilbreth, 23 April 1931, RG 73, series 20, box 1132, Hoover Library.

13. A full treatment is in Martha H. Swain, *Ellen S. Woodward: New Deal Advocate for Women* (Jackson: University Press of Mississippi, 1995).

14. Patti R. Jacobs to Agnes L. Peterson, 20 November 1933, printed in *Proceed-

ings, White House Conference on Emergency Needs of Women, FERA Old Subject File, RG 69, NA.

15. Mary Elizabeth Pidgeon, "Employment Fluctuations and Unemployment of Women: Certain Indications from Various Sources, 1928–31," Women's Bureau Bulletin 113 (Washington, D.C.: Government Printing Office, 1933).

16. Register for Van De Vrede Papers, Georgia Department of Archives and History, Atlanta; Helen Wolfe Evans, "Ella Graham Agnew: New Occasions, New Choices" (graduate paper, Duke University, 1988), copy in possession of author.

17. More on Payne and her work is found in Martha H. Swain, "A New Deal for Mississippi Women," *Journal of Mississippi History* 46 (August 1984).

18. "They Know What They're About," *Democratic Digest* 13 (June 1936): 25.

19. Isabel Kinnear Griffin, "Five Regional Directors of WPA Projects," *Democratic Digest* 13 (June 1936): 22–23.

20. Register, Marie Hoffman Papers, McCain Library, University of Southern Mississippi, Hattiesburg; Marcia G. Synnott, "Alice Norwood Spearman Wright: Civil Rights Apostle to South Carolinians" (paper given at Third Southern Conference on Women's History, Rice University, 1994); Martha H. Swain, "Loula Dunn: Alabama Pioneer in Public Welfare Administration," in Mary Martha Thomas, ed., *Stepping Out of the Shadows: Alabama Women, 1819–1990* (Tuscaloosa: University of Alabama Press, 1995). In 1949 Dunn became the first woman executive director of the American Public Welfare Association.

21. Mrs. O. B. Taylor to ESW, 2 January 1934; Mayme O'Dow to George B. Power (Mississippi CWA head), 16 March 1934, both in FERA State series (Miss.) 453.2, RG 69, NA.

22. ESW, quoted in *Washington Post,* 3 March 1934; Mrs. H. E. Moorhead to ESW, 15 March 1934, FERA State series (Miss.) 453.2, RG 69, NA.

23. Quoted by Susan Wladaver-Morgan, "Young Women and the New Deal: Camps and Resident Centers, 1933–1935" (Ph.D. diss., Indiana University, 1982), 170.

24. Minutes of staff meeting, Jackson, dated 5 July 1935, WPA State series (Miss.) 660, RG 69, NA.

25. ESW memorandum to Hopkins, 10 December 1935, WPA General Subject File 230, RG 69, NA.

26. Lewis Merriam, *Relief and Social Security* (Washington, D.C.: Brookings Institution, 1946), 417; Smith, *New Deal in the Urban South*, 130.

27. ESW to Hopkins, 14 January 1937, WPA Division Records, WPP, RG 69, NA; Mrs. G. B. to FDR, 7 April 1936, WPA State series (Miss.) 651.4, RG 69, NA; Douglas Carl Abrams, *Conservative Constraints: North Carolina and the New Deal* (Jackson: University Press of Mississippi, 1992), 143 (North Carolina quotation).

28. Badger, *New Deal,* 206. The strongest contemporary indictment of sewing projects was Marie Dresden Lane and Francis Steegmuller, *America on Relief* (New York: Harcourt, Brace, 1938), 71–78.

29. Hickok is quoted in Richard Lowitt and Maurine Beasley, *One-Third of a Nation: The Reports of Lorena Hickok* (Urbana: University of Illinois Press, 1981), 173. The sharecropper quotation is from Badger, *New Deal,* 206.

30. Smith, *New Deal in the Urban South,* 131.

31. Ethel Payne to Wayne Alliston, 15 April 1936, WPA State series (Miss.) 661, RG 69, NA; George T. Blakey, *Hard Times and New Deal in Kentucky, 1929–1939* (Lexington: University Press of Kentucky, 1986), 59. All Final State Reports for the Women's and Professional Projects from the South attest to the outstanding productivity of the sewing projects.

32. Alfred E. Smith, "Race of WPA Workers," 31 July 1940, Smith Papers, Special Collections, University of Arkansas Libraries, Fayetteville; Abrams, *Conservative Constraints,* 175. Also see Raymond Wolters, *Negroes and the Great Depression: The Problem of Economic Recovery* (Westport, Conn.: Greenwood, 1970), 208; Richard Sterner, *The Negro's Share* (New York: Harpers, 1943), 251–52; Alberta Haynes, "WPA Practices Discrimination," *Woman's Voice,* February–March 1940, 5–6. Many complaints are in the Papers of the National Association for the Advancement of Colored People, Administrative Files C, box 418, Library of Congress. See also Jacqueline Jones, *Labor of Love, Labor of Sorrow: Black Women, Work, and the Family from Slavery to the Present* (New York: Basic Books, 1985), 216–20.

33. Jean Collier Brown, "The Negro Woman Worker," Women's Bureau Bulletin 165 (Washington, D.C.: Government Printing Office, 1938), 2–3; Philip S. Foner, *Women and the American Labor Movement from the First Trade Unions to the Present* (New York: Free Press, 1979), 301–2; Mary Anderson, "The Plight of Negro Domestic Labor," *Journal of Negro Education* 5 (January 1936): 66–72.

34. Phyllis Palmer, *Domesticity and Dirt: Housewives and Domestic Servants in the United States, 1920–1945* (Philadelphia: Temple University Press, 1989), 102–4; Julia Kirk Blackwelder, *Women of the Depression: Caste and Culture in San Antonio, 1929–1939* (College Station: Texas A&M University Press, 1984), 124.

35. WPA Service Division, Final State Reports, box 80, RG 69, NA.

36. Alfred E. Smith, "Report: Negro Clients of Federal Unemployment Relief," 31 December 1931, Smith Papers.

37. Roger Biles, *The South and the New Deal* (Lexington: University Press of Kentucky, 1994), 77; Blackwelder, *Women of the Depression,* 122; Lowitt and Beasley, *One-Third of a Nation,* 145.

38. Michael S. Holmes, *The New Deal in Georgia: An Administrative History* (Westport, Conn.: Greenwood, 1975), 80, 132. On Florida, see Margaret Batjer to Florence Kerr, 12 April 1939, WPA General Subject File 218.2, RG 69, NA; on Virginia, see Thomas C. Walker, *The Honey-Pod Tree: The Life Story of Thomas Calhoun Walker* (New York: John Day, 1958), 235–36. Walker was the state consultant on projects for blacks.

39. Margaret Leach to ESW, 15 May 1935, FERA State series (Miss.) 453.2, RG 69, NA; Smith, "Race of WPA Workers."

40. *Proceedings,* White House Conference on Participation of Negro Women and Children in Federal Programs, Papers of the National Council for Negro Women, Series 4, National Archives for Black Women's History, Washington, D.C.

41. Ronald Heinemann, *Depression and New Deal in Virginia: The Enduring Dominion* (Charlottesville: University Press of Virginia, 1983), 9; Ellen S. Woodward, "WPA School Lunch Program," *School and Society* 46 (17 July 1937): 91–94; Colleen I. Williams, "Work Relief as a Social Service Delivery System: The Experience of the WPA, 1935–1942" (D.S.W. diss., Tulane University, 1976), 227–31.

42. Van De Vrede's papers in the Georgia Archives reflect her influence. See her "How Georgia Nurses Are Employed and the Communities Served by the Georgia Emergency Relief Administration," box 1.

43. See Edward A. Chapman, *WPA Record of Program Operation and Accomplishment, 1935–1943,* vol. 6, *Library Services,* RG 69, NA.

44. Smith, *New Deal in the Urban South,* 144.

45. Federal Works Agency, *Final Report on the WPA Program, 1935–1943* (Washington, D.C.: Government Printing Office, 1946), 44.

46. This table is adapted from a report of the WPA Division of Research, Statistics and Records, dated 11 September 1937, found in WPA General Subject file 210.13, RG 69, NA.

Employment and Earnings of Women for Month Ending 31 July 1937

State	Women as % of Total Persons Employed	Average Hourly Wages
Alabama	20.8	.331
Arkansas	17.0	.437
Florida	28.6	.317
Georgia	33.1	.290
Kentucky	15.4	.306
Louisiana	18.4	.386
Mississippi	32.7	.316
North Carolina	37.3	.289
South Carolina	39.5	.277
Tennessee	19.3	.287
Texas	32.3	.290
Virginia	37.4	.292
Average—South	27.6	.318
Average—continental U.S.	18.2	.458

47. Ethel Payne, "Summary Report," 1939, WPA State series (Miss.) 651.3, RG 69, NA. Readers are directed to an important study by an economist, Nancy E. Rose, *Workfare or Fair Work: Women, Welfare, and Government Work Programs* (New Brunswick: Rutgers University Press, 1996). While she points to the shortcomings of work programs for women, and especially for blacks, she concludes that the job creation programs of the 1930s "provide models for alternative government policies during economic hard times" (31).

Chapter Sixteen

Searching for Southern Lesbian History

Pippa Holloway

EDITOR'S NOTE: *Only in the twentieth century have widespread explicit discussions of sexuality informed American life. Masculinity and femininity are today increasingly acknowledged to be socially constructed, changing from one era, region, and society to another. In examining the social constructedness of southern sexuality, three aspects of sexual identity should be differentiated. "Gender identity" refers to one's conception of oneself as either female or male. "Masculinity" and "femininity" refer to conformance to the traditional division of labor and customary heterosexual behavior patterns. "Sexual orientation" or "preference" refers to the gender identity of those with whom one desires physical intimacy. In the South these three aspects have always been complicated by the ubiquitous issue of race.*

Although only the most prosperous white farmers avoided having to use their women's labor in the field, the dominant culture's belief that women's work was domestic and farming (except for dairying) was man's work made Native American and African American women seem less than feminine. Native American men, who unlike male slaves, had some choice in the matter, generally refused to farm out of fear of emasculation, for in most Indian and West African traditional societies women were responsible for growing food to feed their families.

Euroamerican men came from patriarchal cultures where a belief in individualism and rights in property was strengthened with the rise of democracy. As owners of land, chattel, and other goods, they wanted to be able to identify the heirs of their body in order to pass on their estates. It was not always possible to ascertain who fathered a child, but who gave birth to the infant was not easy to hide, and female chastity was therefore an essential requirement of sexual ideologies of the middle and upper classes. The lower orders, not having to reckon with wealth, were more accepting of premarital sex. This was also true of traditional

Indian and West African societies, where land, although parceled out for individual use, belonged to the society and could not be alienated by its members.

The structure of the family also played an important role in sexual mores. In traditional African societies, marriage was not just a personal relationship but an alliance between lineages. Most, like the Yoruba, were patrilineages in which all of the sons lived together in one compound with their wives and children. The adult men lived in one building and each wife had her separate residence. In matrilineages like the Ashanti, the situation was similar except that the compound contained all of the sisters with their husbands and children. The cousins called themselves brother and sister, and all the adult members of the compound felt some responsibility toward their rearing. Unlike the nuclear Euroamerican family, such a structure could more easily absorb children conceived out of wedlock. Indeed, the purpose of marriage was to reproduce the lineage, so bachelors and spinsters were unknown. Barren women were stigmatized. Prebridal pregnancy assured a groom that his future wife would not disappoint him.

Lineages could not be replicated under slavery, so slaves developed "fictive kinship systems" in which all slaves on the plantation were referred to in kinship terms and in which those stripped of relatives through sales or death were taken in. Legitimacy had no saliency in African American life, and "outside children," those who were not the product of marriage, were treated the same as those who were. Becoming a parent marked entry into the adult world, and sex was seen as a normal and natural part of life. This contrasted with the European ambivalence toward sexuality, a response, perhaps, to the honor accorded celibacy in the medieval Catholic Church, its idealization of Mary as a passionless virgin, and its demonization of Eve as the temptress responsible for evil in the world. As long as southern ladies could be placed on pedestals of purity, white men could be assured of legitimate heirs whose unimpeachable white ancestry would maintain the color line of a biracial society. All of the progeny of mixed unions could then be classified as black, thereby ridding them of any threat to white hegemony.

Where did the reigning sexual ideologies leave those who chafed at their strictures? Both southern black and white communities have a strong history of homophobia, perhaps based in part on the importance of children in African American culture, the requirements of patriarchal white society for legitimate heirs, and commitment to Christian fundamentalism. Traditional African societies encouraged self-reliance through female networks, and these practices were carried throughout the African Diaspora. Might they have provided an alternative source of emotional identification for some women? The nineteenth-century white belief that masculine and feminine characteristics were polar opposites may have resulted in "romantic friendships" among white women, because they had *so little in common with men that they had difficulty relating to them. Whatever the case may be, it was not until the twentieth century that opportunities for female economic independence provided the means necessary for the development of lesbianism defined as a community of common cultural practices.*

• • •

> We have realized that there is no such thing as "the" southern woman, for she came in many varieties of class, race, and ability. The reality, we have discovered, is neither so simple nor so glamorous as the myth. People have the disconcerting ability not to fit into the historian's categories, much less to fit the legends their descendants like to relate. The reality, when it finally emerges, is no less interesting and far more helpful in understanding ourselves than all the myths and fiction ever were.
>
> —Anne Firor Scott,
> "Historians Construct the Southern Woman"

It is in this theoretical spirit that I propose to describe the contours of southern lesbian history since the Civil War. The study of southern lesbians should not involve simply scanning the past and trying to find evidence that various southern women "did it" together. This kind of approach is basically futile for most of the South's history, and it has also been rejected on theoretical grounds by many scholars. Historians have demonstrated how ideas and social formations are products of specific historical circumstances, and more recently queer theorists have explicitly critiqued this "looking under rocks" method of studying sexuality.[1] How can we study southern lesbian history with full recognition of sexuality's historical construction and without imposing a modern semantic category, "lesbian," that oversimplifies and obscures the past? Studies of sexuality have shown that sex is historically specific, taking different forms and meanings in different times and places. Historians should not in good conscience use contemporary terms such as "lesbian" to describe people who did not identify themselves as such, nor can they assume that women who have engaged in same-sex sexual behavior in various times and places had anything in common with each other, let alone lesbians of today.

"Lesbian" is not the only category that can be scrutinized in light of these theoretical considerations. What kind of conceptual unity does the category "southern women" have? Not much. Southerners have had widely differing experiences, depending on their race, class, and region within the South—upper and lower, rural and urban. Do a white upper-class plantation mistress in North Carolina, a free black woman in antebellum New Orleans, and a poor black woman in rural Jim Crow Mississippi share anything that gives their common label "southern women" any meaning? I believe the answer is no; there is very little evidence that historians should make assumptions about commonalities between individuals because they can be joined in a semantic category. Instead, in writing southern lesbian history we should take some of our first lessons from historians of southern women, like Anne Scott. That is, we should recognize that our categories are not only problematic but dangerous in their ability to elide difference and create myths about the past. However, keeping this in mind does not necessitate abandoning the subject and ceasing to write history. "Southern lesbian" is a troublesome category, but historians can still try to write their history, while being careful to embed it in the larger context of female sexuality, sexual deviance, and normality.

The study of southern lesbians has, thus far, been barely undertaken. Scholarship on lesbian and gay history has been dominated by community studies, almost none of which have been about the South, and national studies that mention the South only as part of a larger national narrative.[2] While there is much to be learned from scholarship on other parts of the country, there is also much that scholarship on the South can contribute to the history of sexuality. In addition to the history of sexuality, there are two other historical subfields from which southern lesbian history will rely heavily: women's history and southern history. Earlier generations of historians often ignored women's history, in part because women's experience is difficult to locate in traditional historical sources. More recent historians of women have had greater success documenting women's experiences by using different kinds of sources and by approaching traditional sources more creatively. Historians of southern lesbians will need to take a similarly imaginative approach toward historical evidence.[3] Southern history has emphasized the importance of rural people, cultures, and experiences. Most chronicles of lesbian and gay history, however, have a distinct urban bias. Furthermore, since for most of U.S. history the majority of African Americans have lived in the South, studying southern history offers a window into the experiences of a group of Americans who are often overlooked by historians of sexuality. How were African American women's constructions and experiences of sexuality different from those of white southerners? How did African American women's sexuality vary by class and region? How did African American churches interpret and delineate female sexuality?

Because of its roots in southern history, women's history, and the history of sexuality, southern lesbian history can illuminate how female sexual desire is constructed in a regionally specific way. Lesbians; women who engaged in sexual, emotional, and/or physically intimate relationships with other women; women who participated in interracial, premarital, or extramarital sex; and others constitute a population that has been defined in various times and places as "deviant." As scholarship of the last two decades has illustrated, the construction of sexual deviance is entwined with the construction of the sexually "normal" and "healthy." By asking who is marked as deviant and when, we can also learn about who is considered normal.[4] In this sense, the study of southern lesbians is the study of all southern women, because it explores the sexual possibilities open to women, how these options changed over time, and when, how, and why individuals challenged the limits of these possibilities. Rather than thinking that by contextualizing same-sex sexual activity in this broader realm of women's sexuality we might be marginalizing the history of lesbians, lesbian sexuality can be seen as central to an understanding of all kinds of female sexuality in the South.

This theoretical perspective can help guide research and writing in southern lesbian history. While there are many potentially fruitful areas of research, in the remainder of this essay I will discuss some key themes and periods that I see as having the potential to illuminate important issues in southern history and the history of sexuality. Studies based on non-southern sources have defined the historiographic questions of the history of sexuality. Southern history can bring new perspectives on these issues, and more important, contribute new ways of delineating and organizing this field.

Studies of women's intimacy and sexuality in the nineteenth century have focused on "romantic friendships"—the emotionally and sometimes physically intimate relationships in which many middle- and upper-class white women engaged during the eighteenth and nineteenth centuries. Close female friendships were quite common among women who had not yet married, and often endured long after marriage. Women who lived with their birth families established these relationships with neighbors or relatives who were of similar ages. The "female world" that fostered intimate attachments between middle- and upper-class white women thrived in the large, rapidly spreading women's boarding schools that were established in the nineteenth century. "Adolescent crushes" became part of the unique culture at northeastern women's boarding schools in the later part of the century, and much has been written about them by historians of sexuality.[5] Letters between these women have provided insight into the high degree of affection and passion between correspondents.[6] Women's friendships are relevant to the study of lesbian history for a variety of reasons. Whether or not any of these women had what we would label sexual relations is less important than the fact that these friendships delineated a female-centered sphere of emotional closeness and support outside the realm of marriage. These friendships were one kind of relationship that some women participated in exclusive of men, and thus they are relevant to our understanding of the options for same-sex relationships that women had in this historical period.

Did white southern women engage in the same kind of friendships that have been well documented among white northern women? Some historians have argued that southern women engaged in romantic friendships as did other nineteenth century women. Carroll Smith-Rosenberg's landmark article on women's intimate relationships, "The Female World of Love and Ritual: Relations between Women in Nineteenth-Century America," relied on evidence from women all over the country. In Smith-Rosenberg's eyes, this "literate middle class" transcended geographic and religious boundaries, and thus, women across the nation were involved in these close friendships. The work of Lillian Faderman drew similar conclusions about women's relationships without regard to geographic regions, but she went even further than Smith-Rosenberg by searching for romantic friendships between women in both England and the United States.[7]

While scholars have made little effort to identify any regionally specific variations among women's relationships, historians of men's sexuality in the nineteenth century have granted more influence to region. The nineteenth-century cultural ethos that not only made possible but encouraged these ties between women brought forth a comparable kind of friendship between young men, which has been documented by Anthony Rotundo and Martin Duberman. Rotundo has pointed out that some men engaged in similarly intense emotional and physical relationships, though unlike women, nineteenth-century men generally confined these relationships to the early years of their life.[8] Rotundo's work studied men in the "northern United States," and Duberman wrote about a physically and emotionally intimate relationship between two young men in antebellum

South Carolina. Duberman argued that these men's relationship was a product of the region's particular sexual system: "The American South of the later part of the eighteenth century and early part of the nineteenth century was (for privileged young, white males) one of those rare 'liberal interregnums' in our history when the body could be treated as a natural source of pleasure and 'wanton' sexuality viewed as the natural prerogative—the exemplification even—of Manliness."[9]

This is not the place to debate the veracity of Duberman's claims about southern sexual mores, but it is relevant to question why men's sexuality has been seen by historians as a product of regional differences, whereas women's has not. The implication is that women's lives were less tied to particular historical circumstances than the lives of men. Men were connected to the public world of politics and economics, which is easier to identify as regionally distinct, whereas women remained in the private sphere of the home and family.

If, in fact, romantic friendships in the South were indistinguishable from those in the North, this is a significant blow to arguments in favor of southern uniqueness. The postbellum South had a unique sex and gender system, marked by the ideal of white southern ladyhood and chivalric white masculinity.[10] The South's racial caste system, its primarily rural population, and its conservative and deeply held religious traditions have all been seen as combining to produce and uphold a different sex and gender system in the region. The peak years of women's romantic friendships also saw the South's isolation from the rest of the country, the ensconcement of ideas about the purity of white womanhood in the wake of supposed sexual threats from black men, and the reaction against "outside" cultural practices and traditions illustrated by the development of the myth of the "Lost Cause." If women's relationships were actually similar across regions, the importance of these factors is significantly diminished.

However, the South *was* different, particularly with regard to sexual and gender issues, as well as racial ones; it is more likely that historians such as Smith-Rosenberg and Faderman have simply been remiss in ignoring the uniqueness of southern women's relationships. Although Smith-Rosenberg asserted that women across the United States engaged in these relationships, most of the evidence she presented came from northeastern sources.[11] Regionally specific studies of women's relationships can point out the similarities and differences between the South and the rest of the country. Two historians have begun the task of examining southern women's romantic friendships and pointing out the distinctively southern elements of these ties. In a recent article, Joan Cashin explored the correspondence of two white southern sisters, demonstrating the importance of female friendship in their lives and the existence of a distinct, gendered culture among southern women. This work is important because it illuminates some of the uniquely southern elements of these women's lives, such as their advocacy of secession and their linking of their ideas on gender to their ideas on politics. Similarly, Christie Anne Farnham's book on women's higher education in the antebellum South documents romantic friendships between southern students, pointing out the different character of these relationships in the South. These works on the antebellum period hint that further studies of women's relationships after the Civil War will raise more questions about the nature of southern distinctiveness and challenges to national narratives of the history of sexuality.[12]

Studying southern women's boarding school friendships will involve more than simply asking whether southern women did the same thing as northeastern women. Higher education for white southern women developed differently than in the North, and educational facilities for African American women were scarce during these years. Historians can inquire whether friendships between young women at southern schools were different in that later period, and whether middle-class African American women had similar friendship ties.[13]

However, southern women's history also calls into question the usefulness of the romantic friendship/boarding school friendship model for understanding intimate attachments among southern women. These women were the minority among southern women, and our general understanding of southern women's sexuality should not be based on the experiences of that small group. Research on women in poor and rural communities might be more fruitful in illuminating emotional bonds between southern women, as well as their various sexual experiences.

The question of whether some of these relationships, either romantic friendships in general or boarding school friendships in particular, were seen as potentially sexual is debated by historians. Smith-Rosenberg argues that close female friendships were not seen as problematic or deviant, but were instead "socially acceptable." Despite the physical nature of the intimacy of many of these women, there was no suspicion that they engaged in sexual (and therefore deviant) behavior. Lillian Faderman has presented evidence that these relationships were considered innocent and asexual until a certain point in time—probably linked to the emergence of medical studies of homosexuality—when changing ideas about women's sexuality raised the possibility that some women could engage in "impure," and thus sexual, physical contact. Others have argued more recently that these kinds of intimate relationships were never viewed without some suspicion.[14]

The root of this discussion is a debate over how ideas about sexuality are transmitted and received. Theories about how medical models about sexuality filtered down into the minds of the general populace must consider that different regions had different levels of access to scientific knowledge and accorded different authority to that discourse. Lisa Duggan's work on the trial of Alice Mitchell, a young Memphis, Tennessee, woman who murdered her female lover in 1892 when their elopement was aborted, is a good beginning for explorations of the relationship between region and medical/scientific models of sexuality.[15] Racial tensions in Memphis around lynching and anti-lynching crusades set the stage for a particular set of concerns and interpretations of white womanhood, and racial issues were embedded in this trial. More studies of female sexuality in the nineteenth-century South can further explore how the southern racial system intersected with sex and gender in these years.

By the end of the nineteenth century, much of the nation was being transformed by industrialization and urbanization, and historians of sexuality have conceptualized the first two decades of the twentieth century as turning points in American sexual experience. Much of the country saw changing patterns of marriage, reproduction, sexual practices, and socialization in these years. There is also some of the earliest evidence in this country of gay men's communities and cultures.[16] In the South, however, these years were marked more by stagnation than change. World War I brought a tide of African American migration out of the region, most remained in the South during these years, and neither white nor black saw much of the urbanization and prosperity that enveloped the rest of the country.[17]

The focus on changes in northern urban areas leaves many questions about southern women unanswered. Did young, single "women adrift" in southern cities engage in sexual practices similar to those of women in New York and Chicago? Is there any evidence of "Boston marriages" among southern women? If there were, how can we account for them? John D'Emilio's landmark article "Capitalism and Gay Identity" tied the decline of the family as the unit of production and the rise of wage labor with the possibility of a "homosexual identity." While D'Emilio did point out that the wage-based economy emerged very slowly in different parts of the country, there is still much room for the exploration of these different paths of industrialization. Historians of southern industry have noted that life as a mill worker and life as a sharecropper were in many ways more similar than different. In mill towns, for example, most family members, including children, worked in the mills. Were these family-based economies or free labor economies? Future studies may show that the introduction of wage labor was less significant in changing sexual identities and experiences than the social and cultural context in which people lived.[18]

Another way to get some insight into the impact of urban life on southern lesbians and female sexuality could be to study some of the women of the Harlem Renaissance and black female blues singers of the 1920s and 1930s. Many were immigrants from the South who lived most of their adult lives in the North. Depending on how one defines "southern" and "lesbian," Mabel Hampton, Ma Rainey, Josephine Baker, Bessie Smith, Angelina Weld Grimké, and others fit into this category, and their experiences can be used to ask questions about southernness and migration.[19] While there have been historical studies of some of these women, no one has looked at them as a group of southerners.

The next key turning point in lesbian history was World War II. While cultural changes such as the spread of consumer culture were important for the development of lesbian identities and communities, the most important and more easily quantifiable changes stemmed from the further industrialization and growth of cities that occurred rapidly as a consequence of the war. These years saw the development of lesbian communities and cultures across the nation, and this was true of the South also. Two interrelated institutions facilitated the formation of lesbian communities and identities: the military and gay bars. Service in the military or work in defense industries brought more and more unmarried women to urban areas, where they met, formed friendship networks, and established intimate relationships. In their free time and with their usually small but significant disposable income, they provided the clientele for lesbian bars in some cities. In many more cities, they joined gay male patrons at bars that served a mixed gender population. There is evidence that southern cities developed gay and lesbian bars similar to those in the rest of the country. By the 1950s cities such as New Orleans, Atlanta, and Richmond had gay and/or lesbian bars, and by the end of the decade some southern cities had chapters of the Mattachine Society or other homophile groups.[20]

Again, this raises the question of southern distinctiveness, and again the experience of southerners who identified as lesbians can help us understand the region's history. Did the economic changes of the 1940s—industrialization and urbanization—bring about the development of southern lesbian communities that were indistinguishable from the rest of the country? Are cultural institutions—the region's sex and gender system—so malleable that they can be transformed in a decade's time by economic change? Or did distinctly southern elements persist?

The last three decades have provided rich sources for historians of lesbians, because growing numbers of women publicly identified as such, formed political and social groups, wrote books, and left records that historians can mine. In addition, many historical subjects from these years are still alive, making oral history interviews feasible. The South has followed the pattern of the rest of the country in this area, and southern lesbians have been quite visible in the last three decades.[21] Yet the South remains distinct from the rest of the country, and the experiences of southern lesbians reflect this. Sexuality becomes a particularly rich area of study in southern history in these years because the region had more than its share of anti-gay politicians and political movements. Anita Bryant's Florida campaign in the mid-1970s was followed in the 1980s by Senator Jesse Helms's spearheading of anti-gay legislation in Congress. The religious right became a factor in United States politics in the 1980s, receiving a great deal of its support from southerners; and anti-gay rhetoric has been a key component of both their agenda and their popularity. Further evidence of the South's continuing uniqueness is the number of southern states that have maintained legal bans on same-sex sexual activity, a majority being in this region.

Comparisons between the South and the rest of the country between 1970 and 1990 could illuminate some important questions about these years. Was the South more anti-gay than the rest of the nation? While the South had its share of anti-gay politicians, they were far from scarce across the United States. Similarly, historians can inquire about the impact of conservative political movements on lesbians. Did the efforts of the religious right make southern lesbians more or less likely to form political and social organizations, or is there no discernible regional difference? How does lesbian history intersect with gay history in the South and how does this relationship compare to the rest of the country?

Lesbian history and the history of sexuality more generally are relatively new areas of inquiry for historians, and consequently there are many gaps to be filled and much work to be done. Scholars have proposed an initial framework and periodization for this field, but these will continue to be modified as elements of regional distinctiveness are taken into account. This scholarship will fill gaps in knowledge about an important group of southern women, thereby enhancing women's history in general. Furthermore, this will enrich our understanding of southern history, especially the extent to which national cultural, social, and political movements take unique forms in the southern region.

NOTES

I would like to thank Susan Hartmann, Leila Rupp, Birgitte Soland, and Jennifer Terry for reading drafts of this essay.

1. My ideas about this have been influenced by the work of Lisa Duggan, especially her article "The Discipline Problem: Queer Theory Meets Lesbian and Gay History," in *Sex Wars: Sexual Dissent and Political Culture,* ed. Lisa Duggan and Nan. D. Hunter (New York: Routledge, 1995), 194–206, in which she argues that scholars of lesbian and gay history put forth some of the earliest arguments for the social construction of sexuality and its historical specificity. For other theoretical works on historical constructions of sexuality, see Donna Penn, "Queer: Theorizing Politics and History," *Radical History Review* 62 (1995): 24–43; Robert Padgug, "Sexual Matters: Rethinking Sexuality in History," in *Hidden from History: Reclaiming the Gay and Lesbian Past,* ed. Martin Duberman, Martha Vicinus, and George Chauncey, Jr. (New York: Meridian, 1989), 54–64; Joan W. Scott, "The Evidence of Experience," in *The Lesbian and Gay Studies Reader,* ed. Henry Abelove, Michele Aina Barale, and David Halperin (New York: Routledge, 1993), 397–415.

2. One of the few published works on gays in a southern city is John Howard, "The Library, the Park, and the Pervert: Public Space and Homosexual Encounter in Post–World War II Atlanta," *Radical History Review* 62 (1995): 166–87. An excellent study of a lesbian community is Elizabeth Kennedy and Madeline Davis, *Boots of Leather, Slippers of Gold: The History of a Lesbian Community* (New York: Routledge, 1993). Nationally oriented works include John D'Emilio, *Sexual Politics, Sexual Communities: The Making of a Homosexual Minority in the United States, 1940–1970* (Chicago: University of Chicago Press, 1983); Alan Berube, *Coming Out under Fire: A History of Gay Men and Women in World War Two* (New York: Free Press, 1990); Lillian Faderman, *Odd Girls and Twilight Lovers: A History of Lesbian Life in Twentieth-Century America* (New York: Columbia University Press, 1991).

3. The omission of women's history in the work of professional historians of

previous generations is, of course, due to more than just problems with sources, and is instead a product of the structure of social power and social relations. Examples of recent works that have approached historical sources in a new light to locate women include Lisa Duggan, "The Trials of Alice Mitchell: Sensationalism, Sexology, and the Lesbian Subject in Turn-of-the-Century America," *Signs* 18 (1993): 791–814; Victoria Bynum, *Unruly Women: The Politics of Social and Sexual Control in the Old South* (Chapel Hill: University of North Carolina Press, 1992); Suzanne Lebsock, *The Free Women of Petersburg: Status and Culture in a Southern Town, 1784–1860* (New York: Norton, 1984).

4. For a discussion of these theoretical questions, see Jennifer Terry, "Feminist Lineages of Deviant Historiography," in *Feminists Revision History*, ed. Ann-Louise Shapiro (New Brunswick: Rutgers University Press, 1994).

5. Martha Vicinus, "Distance and Desire: English Boarding School Friendships, 1870–1920," in *Hidden from History*, ed. Duberman et. al., 212–29; Carroll Smith-Rosenberg, "The New Woman as Androgyne: Social Disorder and Gender Crisis," in *Disorderly Conduct: Visions of Gender in Victorian America* (New York: Knopf, 1985), 245–96; and Nancy Sahli, "Smashing: Women's Relationships before the Fall," *Chrysalis* 8 (1979): 17–27.

6. The seminal work on these friendships is Carroll Smith-Rosenberg, "The Female World of Love and Ritual: Relations between Women in Nineteenth-Century America," *Signs* 1 (1975): 1–29. See also Lillian Faderman, *Surpassing the Love of Men: Romantic Friendship and Love between Women from the Renaissance to the Present* (New York: Morrow, 1981); idem, *Scotch Verdict* (New York: Morrow, 1983); Leila Rupp, "'Imagine My Surprise': Women's Relationships in Historical Perspective," in *Hidden from History*, ed. Duberman et. al., 395–410; Martha Vicinus, "'They Wonder to Which Sex I Belong': The Historical Roots of Modern Lesbian Identity," *Feminist Studies* 18 (1992): 467–97; Lisa Moore, "'Something More Tender Still Than Friendship': Romantic Friendships in Early-Nineteenth-Century England," *Feminist Studies* 18 (1992): 499–520; Marylynn Diggs, "Romantic Friends or a 'Different Race of Creatures'? The Representation of Lesbian Pathology in Nineteenth-Century America," *Feminist Studies* 21 (1994): 317–40.

7. Smith-Rosenberg, "Female World of Love and Ritual," 3; Faderman, *Surpassing the Love of Men*.

8. E. Anthony Rotundo, "Romantic Friendship: Male Intimacy and Middle-Class Youth in the Northern United States, 1800–1900," *Journal of Social History* 23 (1989): 1–25; Martin Duberman, *About Time: Exploring the Gay Past*, rev. ed. (New York: Meridian, 1991), 1–23.

9. Duberman, *About Time*, 12.

10. Many general works of southern history treat the issue of southern distinctiveness. A recent overview of this question can be found in Dewey Grantham, *The South in Modern America: A Region at Odds* (New York: HarperCollins, 1994).

11. It is not possible to ascertain from the footnotes which of the letters Smith-

Rosenberg cited are from southern women, though some of the women were identified as living in the South when the letter was written. Interestingly, only women in the Upper South—Virginia, North Carolina, and South Carolina—are cited. See Smith-Rosenberg, "Female World of Love and Ritual," nn. 12, 22, 41, 48, 56, 68.

12. Joan E. Cashin, "'Decidedly Opposed to *the* Union': Women's Culture, Marriage, and Politics in Antebellum South Carolina," *Georgia Historical Quarterly* 68 (1994): 735–60; Christie Anne Farnham, *The Education of the Southern Belle: Higher Education and Student Socialization in the Antebellum* South (New York: New York University Press, 1994). See also Steven M. Stowe, "'The *Thing* Not Its Vision': A Woman's Courtship and Her Sphere in the Southern Planter Class," *Feminist Studies* 9 (1983): 114–30. For some primary sources on southern women's friendships, see Joan E. Cashin, *Our Common Affairs: Texts from Women in the Old South* (Baltimore: Johns Hopkins University Press, 1996), especially the chapter on friendships, 81–122.

13. Lisa Duggan labels the friendship between Alice Mitchell and Freda Ward in Memphis "an ordinary, if excessive, schoolgirls' romantic friendship—in Memphis, such relations were called 'chumming.'" Duggan, "Trials of Alice Mitchell," 798.

14. Smith-Rosenberg, "Female World of Love and Ritual"; Faderman, *Surpassing the Love of Men*. Scholars who argue that some of these relationships were seen by some contemporaries as problematic include Vicinus, "Distance and Desire"; Diggs, "Romantic Friends or a 'Different Race of Creatures'?"; Moore, "Something More Tender Still Than Friendship"; Sahli, "Smashing"; and Smith-Rosenberg, "The New Woman as Androgyne." Smith-Rosenberg's position in this article somewhat qualifies her earlier work, in that she points out that the New Woman was seen on some level as a threat to the social order.

15. Duggan, "Trials of Alice Mitchell," 791–814.

16. George Chauncey, *Gay New York: Gender, Urban Culture, and the Making of the Gay Male World, 1890–1940* (New York: Basic Books, 1994).

17. Studies of the southern economy and industrialization include James C. Cobb, *Industrialization and Southern Society, 1877–1984* (Lexington: University Press of Kentucky, 1984); and Gavin Wright, *Old South, New South: Revolutions in the Southern Economy since the Civil War* (New York: Basic Books, 1986).

18. Studies of women's social and sexual lives in these cities include Joanne Meyerowitz, *Women Adrift: Independent Wage Earners in Chicago, 1880–1930* (Chicago: University of Chicago Press, 1988); and Kathy Peiss, *Cheap Amusements: Working Women and Leisure in Turn-of-the-Century New York* (Philadelphia: Temple University Press, 1986). Bertram Wyatt-Brown has searched for Boston marriages in the South in *Southern Honor: Ethics and Behavior in the Old South* (New York: Oxford University Press, 1982), 251. John D'Emilio, "Capitalism and Gay Identity," in *Powers of Desire: The Politics of Sexuality*, ed. Ann Snitow, Christine Stansell, and

Sharon Thompson (New York: Monthly Review Press, 1983), 100–116. Jacqueline Hall et al., *Like a Family: The Making of a Southern Cotton Mill World* (Chapel Hill: University of North Carolina Press, 1987).

19. Joan Nestle, "Excerpts from the Oral History of Mabel Hampton," *Signs* 18 (1993): 925–35; Gloria T. Hull, "'Lines She Did Not Dare': Angelina Weld Grimké, Harlem Renaissance Poet," in *The Lesbian and Gay Studies Reader*, ed. Abelove et al., 453–66; Eric Garber, "A Spectacle in Color: The Lesbian and Gay Subculture of Jazz Age Harlem," in *Hidden from History*, ed. Duberman et al., 318–41; Mab Segrest, "'Lines I Dare': Southern Women's Writing," in *My Mamma's Dead Squirrel: Lesbian Essays in Southern Culture* (Ithaca: Firebrand Books, 1985). For insight about cultural interactions of southern migrants to Chicago, see James R. Grossman, *Land of Hope: Black Southerners and the Great Migration* (Chicago: University of Chicago Press, 1989).

20. Mentions of gay bars, communities, and organizations in southern cities can be found in D'Emilio, *Sexual Politics, Sexual Communities*, 49, 50, 110, 152–57, 163–64, 199 n. 201; Berube, *Coming Out*, 105, 106, 111, 116, 124, 271; and Howard, "The Library, the Park and the Pervert." See also Elly Bulkin, "An Old Dyke's Tale: An Interview with Doris Lunden," *Conditions* 6 (1980): 28; and various books, poems, and essays by Dorothy Allison, Minnie Bruce Pratt, and Mab Segrest.

21. A good start for locating articles about southern lesbians in recent years is Clare Potter, ed., *The Lesbian Periodicals Index* (Tallahassee: Naiad, 1986). A variety of other sources can provide insight into female sexuality in this later period, and perhaps also for earlier years, including newspapers, and legislative, police, and medical records. In addition, demographic information from census records can indicate patterns of work, family size, education, and so on.

Chapter Seventeen

Second Wave Feminism(s) and the South
The Difference That Differences Make

Jane Sherron De Hart

EDITOR'S NOTE: *One might have expected that any major challenge to racism would arise outside the South, for African Americans who had migrated to the Northeast, Midwest, and West Coast, although still oppressed by racism, had greater opportunities than those who remained there, and liberal whites who resided in those regions increasingly expressed a growing commitment to equality after World War II. But surprisingly, the Civil Rights Movement originated — not just in the South — but in the Deep South, where activists faced the greatest threats.*

The bus boycott that black women set in motion in Montgomery, Alabama, in 1954 initiated a decade of protests aimed at ending second-class citizenship and integrating African Americans into the mainstream. The struggle was carried forward by students, primarily from college towns across the Upper South, who developed a potent weapon in sit-ins, which succeeded in desegregating much of this part of the region. Freedom rides on buses traveling into the Deep South exposed the use of violence by white racists and their governments, and in so doing built a cadre of committed activists out of black and white students, now from the North as well as the South, who had suffered together in the struggle. The movement was based in the black church, where female members composed the backbone of the protests. Student organizations, especially SNCC (Student Nonviolent Coordinating Committee), formed the cutting edge of the movement, organizing voter registration drives in rural areas. All these groups joined together in major demonstrations in cities like Birmingham, where police brutality and white violence, captured on national television, sickened Americans throughout the country.

The high point of the movement was the March on Washington, coming a century after the Emancipation Proclamation of 1863. The Reverend Martin Luther King, Jr., constructed a bridge between the races with rhetoric that resonated with Christian symbolism and democratic values. If the movement could elicit little change from southern power structures, its nonviolent strategy, which highlighted the lawlessness of its opponents, gained advocates outside the South. They were able to bring pressure on Congress and presidents Kennedy and Johnson to pass the Civil Rights Act of 1964, ending segregation, and the Voting Rights Act of 1965, ending disfranchisement.

The Civil Rights Movement brought attention to the ways society defined and restricted individuals and groups merely on the basis of looks — in this case, skin color, hair, and facial features. To arguments drawn in the past from democratic ideals and Christian morality were added a social science analysis of socialization and roles. Other groups (like Native Americans, the disabled, gays and lesbians) were quick to see the power of this approach and adopted it with many successes.

The largest of these groups were feminists. World War II had brought women into the workforce in increasing numbers, but demobilization returned men to most of these jobs. The media extolled the happy homemaker, idealizing domestic life in the fifties. But the postwar economic boom drew more women into educa-tion and jobs, and divorce rates rose. When Betty Friedan published The Femi-nine Mystique in 1963, she sparked a movement of women who could not find complete satisfaction in living through service to their husbands and children — women who aspired to an identity of their own. In 1966 NOW (National Organization for Women) was formed with Friedan as president to lobby for legal and policy changes that would promote women's equality.

The South — home of the traditional southern lady — was surprisingly also the place where a more radical branch of the women's movement evolved. Frustrated by how difficult it proved to gain leadership roles in the Civil Rights Movement and noticing that, whereas men were "spokespersons," women ended up fixing coffee and doing mailings, some black and white women in SNCC began to see an analogy between the way society treated blacks and the way it treated women: both were ascribed characteristics that people assumed to be natural and inherent but that were in actuality the product of socialization and assigned roles. When the student movement was increasingly influenced by black nationalism in the mid-sixties, whites who were expelled continued their activism in the New Left, especially in anti–Vietnam War protests. But women found the same situation re-created: their desire to be treated as equals was trivialized and ridiculed by men in the movement. Out of these experiences came the women's liberation wing of feminism, which spread rapidly across the nation through informal consciousness-raising groups patterned on the Civil Rights Movement's rap *sessions. These groups posed a more fundamental challenge to society than prior calls for eliminating obstacles to women's access to the world of men. By looking at socialization and societal roles as the source of gender inequality, they undermined the entire gender system.*

Yet, there were many southern women who felt they had much to lose with the altering of the gender contract; and, not surprisingly, the issue was further complicated by race. Now, however, the distinctiveness of the South was only evident in the depth of its reaction to feminism, for the same reaction was reflected in the national experience.

● ● ●

The feminist movement of the 1960s was, in reality, many movements. Referred to as feminism's second wave as distinct from an earlier surge that occurred around 1910, cresting with the passage of the Nineteenth Amendment giving women the vote, it was embraced by some southern women, rejected by others. That southerners of both sexes would resist the dismantling of gender hierarchy came as no surprise. States that in 1920 refused to ratify the Nineteenth Amendment included much of the old Confederacy: Delaware, Maryland, Virginia, North Carolina, South Carolina, Georgia, Alabama, Mississippi, Louisiana, and Florida. A half century later, many of those same states refused to ratify the Equal Rights Amendment (ERA), a simple statement that read, "Equality of rights under the law shall not be denied or abridged by the United States or by any State on account of sex."

Explanations for rejection are familiar. Southerners are religious, and Protestant fundamentalism takes seriously scriptural injunctions concerning the subjection of women. Southerners are traditionalists; suffrage and especially feminism challenged traditional relationships of gender, race, and class embedded deep in self and society. Southerners are suspicious of federal intervention, and both amendments evoked linkages to Washington and to racial equality that local elites believed threatened their power to govern.

This essay, however, focuses not on those who rejected equality but rather those who embraced feminism and the divisions that separated them from one another. Southern feminists confronted issues of gender, race, and class as well as questions about the definition of feminism that were dealt with in the ideology and scholarship of the national movement a full decade later. Thus, southerners were among the first feminists to learn the difference that differences make.

The Making of Southern Feminists

In a journey from civil rights to women's liberation, college-age women with a deep commitment to racial equality left the shelter of middle-class families, often against strenuous parental objections, for the dangerous work of the Civil Rights Movement. Joining picket lines, creating freedom schools, canvassing for voter registration, and enduring jailings, they acquired new organizing skills and new role models in the form of courageous African American women like Fannie Lou Hamer, a Mississippi sharecropper. Movement involvement also generated a heightened sense of self-worth and greater commitment to equality. But along with that commitment came the realization that men who embraced the principle on behalf of racial equality were not prepared to extend it to include sexual equality.[1]

White women were frequently relegated to domestic chores, treated as sex objects, and denied a voice in decision making. When Student Nonviolent Coordinating Committee (SNCC) leader Stokely Carmichael joked that the only "position for women in SNCC is prone," he encapsulated views that, if not his own, reflected all too accurately the feeling of many males in SNCC. By 1967, when black nationalism forced white women out of the movement, they began organizing on behalf of their own liberation. New understandings of the political resiliency of the white power structure and the deep structures of black poverty left them impatient with liberalism and critical of capitalism. Recognition that sexism, like racism, was institutional as well as personal sealed the commitment of these movement veterans to fundamental change.[2]

Older women who had reared their children during the resurgent domesticity of the Cold War years discovered, as did Lady Bird Johnson, that feminism was not just for their daughters. That discovery often began with the reading of *The Feminine Mystique,* Betty Friedan's indictment of domesticity, which gave voice to years of unarticulated dissatisfaction and yearning. One such reader, a white middle-aged housewife from a little town in North Carolina, had staunchly maintained that all she had ever wanted to be was a wife and mother. She had explained her community activism in terms of noblesse oblige. After reading *The Feminine Mystique,* she wrote to one of her daughters, "I absolutely agree with everything she said, with one exception—the bit about penis envy. I certainly never wanted a penis and I don't know any other woman who does." But if

Friedan's reader was unfamiliar with Freudian theory, she knew more than she had been prepared to admit about gender-based discrimination. Of all those years of activism in her church, the Parent Teacher Association, the Women's Club, the American Association of University Women, and finally the County School and Hospital Boards, she subsequently confessed, "I had to do something to keep my sanity." What she had really wanted to do was serve in the state legislature. "I always knew I could do a better job than most of those men in Raleigh."[3]

In letters to North Carolina's U.S. senator, Sam Ervin, written when Congress was debating the ERA, southern women of all ages and backgrounds poured out their resentment of patriarchy, paternalism, and gender bias. On engraved stationery and lined notepads, they wrote of personal experience with workplace discrimination: lost income, lost promotions, lost benefits, and sexual harassment. We women, wrote a librarian, "have never known anything except discrimination."[4]

Others wrote of their resentment at being handicapped by hundreds of discriminatory federal statutes as well as the many state laws denying them equal treatment. Outraged at being assigned the "legal status of a child," they protested that married women still lacked complete control over their own property: as late as 1970, North Carolina law required the written assent of the husband before a wife could convey her real property to someone else. Still others were adamant about what one woman referred to as the "protective custody" to which her sex was assigned. "We do not need any special protection, we do not need social concessions or social supervision, we do not need any law that treats us differently from other citizens." "We are not," wrote one woman, "the weak-minded, weak-bodied, weak-spirited individuals you take us for." Criticizing Ervin's insistence that equality would actually penalize women, especially with respect to military service, another wrote, "I could care less about the dower right, the alimony business, the child custody bit.... I have already done my military service and am an honorably discharged (1946) veteran.... Stop putting down North Carolina women."[5]

North Carolinians were not the only southern women who felt put down. A female Mississippi legislator wrote,

> As a State Senator, I succeeded in getting Mississippi women the right to sit on juries (1968); the opposition's arguments were appalling. When women began hiring me in order to get credit, I became upset at the discrimination I saw. After I was divorced in 1970, I was initially denied a home loan. The

effect was one of the worst traumas I have suffered. Denial of a home loan to one who was both a professional and a member of the legislature brought things to a head.[6]

Whatever the experiences that radicalized, action followed. Those identifying with women's liberation created consciousness-raising groups on university campuses and in urban areas in the early 1970s and organized alternative institutions. In the university town of Chapel Hill, North Carolina, a group of graduate students and young faculty members founded a nonsexist day care center called the "School for People under Six." They joined together in a collective called Lollipop Power to write and publish nonsexist children's books. In New Orleans, feminists founded battered women's shelters while those in other cities formed rape crisis centers.[7]

Women who felt more comfortable in women's rights organizations than in the less structured groups associated with women's liberation joined state and local branches of national feminist organizations such as the National Organization for Women (NOW) and the National Women's Political Caucus (NWPC). The latter focused on the small number of women in government, encouraging women to run for elective office and plying government officials with lists of women qualified for appointments on state and local boards and commissions. NOW members wrote letters in support of congressional legislation that would extend minimum wage coverage to domestic workers, provide equal access to credit for all women, and secure passage of the ERA. NOW chapters in university towns pushed for equal access to university scholarships, often joining with the few women on the faculty to secure equity in hiring, pay, and promotion for female faculty. Within universities themselves, feminist faculty initiated sex discrimination suits and women's studies programs, pushed for the hiring of more women on the faculty, more courses on women in the curriculum, and equitable resources for female athletes. Feminist lawyers litigated sex discrimination suits, utilizing new federal legislation forbidding discrimination in employment and educational facilities.[8]

While the impetus usually came from women, like-minded men also joined the struggle. Some were outsiders who had been enticed to the region by professional opportunities, others had roots deep in southern soil; virtually all were liberals. For example, the two state senators sponsoring a bill ratifying the ERA in the North Carolina legislature in 1973 were both native sons. One was the son of one of the few southern congressmen who had refused to sign the Southern Manifesto, a declaration pledging resistance by "all lawful means" to school integration mandated by the Supreme Court's *Brown* decision; the other was the great-grandson of a pro-suffrage state legislator.[9]

Family tradition was no doubt a factor as well in the decision of a Texas lieutenant governor to mentor an avid feminist and active Democrat who would eventually become governor of Texas herself. In the 1970s Ann Richards was working as campaign manager and administrative assistant for Texas legislator Sarah Wedding, the young Austin lawyer who argued the landmark abortion rights case, *Roe v. Wade*, in 1973. William Hobby, she recalled, was "the first man who talked to me about politics as an equal." But then Hobby had grown up in a family that took women seriously. His mother, Oveta Culp Hobby, had served in the Eisenhower cabinet in the 1950s and, as governor, William P. Hobby, Sr., had pushed the woman suffrage bill through the Texas legislature.[10]

But if feminism as an ideology presupposed a set of principles that men as well as women could embrace, not all women and certainly not all men chose to do so. The struggle to ratify the ERA provided dramatic evidence of their resistance.

Resistance to Feminism

The amendment, intended only to remove sexual bias from common, statutory, and constitutional law, had passed Congress by overwhelming majorities in both houses. Sent to states in 1972, many rushed to ratify, among them Texas, Tennessee, Kentucky, and Maryland. Soon, however, the ERA encountered unanticipated opposition. By 1975, with the approval of only three more states needed to secure the amendment, national attention focused on the South. Seven southern states could be virtually written off: Virginia, Georgia, South Carolina, Alabama, Arkansas, Louisiana, and Mississippi. But North Carolina and Florida were likely to ratify. Accordingly, women both for and against the amendment mobilized in unprecedented numbers until narrow defeats in 1982, the deadline for ratification, secured the ERA's demise. Finding out who opposed the amendment and why reveals much about the opposition not just to the ERA but to feminism in the South and the nation.[11]

Anti-ERA activists in North Carolina, where the amendment failed, and in Texas, where it passed, were remarkably similar to ERA supporters in socioeconomic background. A little older, somewhat less educated and

affluent, and more likely to be housewives than pro-ERA women, opponent activists were less likely to have grown up in politically active
families and less likely to hold professional and managerial jobs, if they
worked outside the home. The chief difference between the two groups,
however, was ideological. Anti-ERA activists were politically and religiously more conservative. At home ideologically with the New Right,
their leaders were identified with conservative organizations like the John
Birch Society, Eagle Forum, Women for Constitutional Government, and
Daughters of the American Revolution. Locally, activists were likely to
have been leaders in church groups or organizations traditionally concerned with children such as the Girl Scouts.[12]

What made these self-described "family-oriented" women so intensely
oppose the ERA? Americans who claim to believe in equality often become profoundly apprehensive when the principle is identified with specific governmental policies they consider to be intrusive and unreason-
able. When supporters of the ERA said that implementation of a
constitutional ban on sex discrimination would be left to the Supreme
Court, conservatives of both sexes were reminded that this was the same
court that had not only mandated integration but prohibited prayer in
public schools and struck down bans on birth control, abortion, and
pornography. Court-enforced sexual equality, like racial equality, many
Southerners believed, would further diminish the power of state and local
governments and the right of individuals to live as they chose. As one
woman wrote her U.S. senator: "*Forced* busing, *forced* mixing, *forced* housing. Now *forced* women! No thank you!" In what was also an obvious
reference to racial integration, another pleaded, "Please don't desexigrate
us."[13]

Such logic illuminates charges, mystifying to ratificationists, that the
ERA would destroy the family. Although amendment supporters correctly
pointed out that the amendment had nothing to do with private relationships, social conservatives were unconvinced; they had seen what a federal agenda in feminist hands looked like at the International Women's
Year Conference in Houston in 1977. A meeting subsidized by American
tax dollars and attended by the wives of three presidents had endorsed
not only the ERA but government-sponsored child care, federal funding
of abortions for poor women, contraception for minors without parental
consent, and gay rights. Such endorsements intensified conservatives'
fears of a post-ERA world invoked by anti-ERA spokeswoman Phyllis
Schlafly of Illinois in which mothers, no longer financially able to remain

at home, would be forced to surrender their children to government-sponsored day care, whose personnel would supplant parental authority with loyalty to the state.

Feminists believed that theirs was a struggle for justice and liberation— liberation from economic inequities, social roles, and cultural values that denied rights and limited autonomy. To require all women to endure constraints dictated not by biology (sex) but by culture (gender) was to deny freedom, autonomy, and self-determination to half the population simply because they were born female. To women who did not consider themselves oppressed, "liberation" appeared not as an attack on traditional gender categories but rather an assault on women's security and very identity. Fusing feminism and the ERA, an antiratificationist begged her senator not to vote for the amendment, insisting that she did not want to be liberated. "My husband," she wrote, "works for me and takes care of me and our three children, doesn't make me do things that are hard for me (drive in town), loves me and doesn't smoke, drink, gamble, run around or do anything that would upset me. I do what he tells me to do. I like this arrangement. *It's the only way I know how to live.*" Insisted another, "I am a widow, have three children, and work to make ends meet. I am still against ERA. I am a woman—and want to be treated as a woman." Still another pleaded, "A few women want to be men," but "don't force all of us to be one. Please."[14]

When ERA supporters responded that treating women as individuals for legal purposes rather than classifying them by sex had nothing to do with the household division of labor, social etiquette, or the masculinization of women, their reassurances fell on deaf ears. The free-floating anxiety aroused by the enormity of the social change demanded by feminism had acquired concrete focus in the ERA. Opponents' predictions of the terrible consequences that would result from ratification (decriminalization of rape, destruction of the family, etc.) were not as important as the function such statements served: to indict what Schlafly called the "unisex" society and affirm traditional gender categories. For women living in a world in which personal identity, social legitimacy, economic viability, and moral order were rooted in traditional gender categories, calling those categories into question in the name of gender-neutral law meant that feminists must want men and women to be "the same." Finding it difficult to separate gender from sex—to see gender as a social construction—ERA opponents could only conclude that this latest drive for equality was not only absurd ("you can't fool Mother Nature") but dangerous. By alerting women to this danger, Schlafly revealed that the issue was not whether women should stay at home minding the children and cooking dinner—Schlafly herself did not do that. The issue was the meaning of sexual differences between men and women.[15]

In the early years of the movement, most feminists minimized those differences, believing that reproductive control and work in the public sector had made women's lives more like men's. Antifeminists inflated those differences. Their response was a measure of their belief that women (and men) are eternal in their attributes and unchanged by events and their anger and distress at changes that had already occurred for which they held feminism responsible: rising divorce rates, increases in female-headed households, legalized abortion, gay and lesbian couples, permissive lifestyles, and so on. Such perceptions tell us much about why gender equality came to be seen as problematic by so many southerners. But it would be erroneous to conclude that the feminist movement in the South was therefore a much smaller, less robust version of the national movement.

Diversity within Southern Feminism

As a portrait of southern feminism, this sketch is inadequate because historians have written little about second wave feminism and even less about the movement in the South, and because the women portrayed are virtually all white. The portrayal of the national movement looks very similar. To be sure, important black women are included: Pauli Murray, the North Carolina–born civil rights activist, lawyer, poet, and Episcopal priest who was a founder of the movement; Aileen Hernandez, organizer for the International Ladies' Garment Workers' Union and a founding member of NOW and its second president; New York Congresswoman Shirley Chisholm, a founding member of NOW and the NWPC; writers and intellectuals like Alice Walker, Toni Morrison, and bell hooks; and Eleanor Holmes Norton and Mary Frances Berry, both lawyers, university professors, and government officials. There were also organizations like the short-lived National Alliance of Black Feminists, the Third World Women's Alliance, and the Combahee River Collective, a radical Boston-based group. Nonetheless, the portrait of feminism drawn from most national accounts remains predominantly white, even when Chicana and Asian American feminists are included.[16]

Might that portrait change if we expand our angle of vision to encom-

pass women of color who may have entertained a more expansive definition of feminism than what we associate with the mainstream movement?
To pose the question has an important advantage. It allows us to look at
feminism in the South not simply as a stunted offshoot of a more powerful
national movement, but as representative of the mainstream movement.
As is so often the case where race is concerned, what we initially presume
to be characteristic of the southern experience proves to be less a matter
of southern exceptionalism than of the national experience.

First, did the potential exist for a more inclusive movement that would
embrace women of different backgrounds and sexual orientations with
different visions of feminism? To answer that question we have to consider many factors, among them a long tradition of African American
feminism. In 1892, Anna Julia Cooper wrote in *A Voice from the South*, "The
colored woman of today occupies . . . a unique position in this country. . . .
She is confronted by a woman question and a race problem." black
women, she argued, should not be passive and subordinate in their relationships with black men; and black men should not criticize women's
efforts to obtain equal rights. Equality of the sexes, she insisted, would
mean that black women would be able to share the leadership burden in
the struggle against racism.[17]

Richmond's Maggie Lena Walker, who became arguably the first female bank president in the nation, was yet another black feminist, suffragist, and civil rights activist, but feminism was not confined to super-
achievers or to elite women of color. A black-owned Richmond
newspaper reported on the outcome of a 1916 women's basketball game
between African American public school teachers. The contest was billed
as the Feminists versus the Suffragists. When woman suffrage was finally
achieved, black women in southern cities from Mobile to Richmond,
many of them no doubt part of the black women's club movement, lined
up to register to vote. Their presence, which often elicited rejection and
even threats of violence, signaled their conviction that racial and sexual
oppression were indivisible.[18]

Although a self-conscious white feminist movement waned in the post-
suffrage decades, African American feminism did not. Emphasizing self-
definition and empowerment within a humanistic vision of community, it
was embedded in black women's activism, suffusing their struggles
against lynching and for community development and civil rights. Moreover, as progressive women of both races placed integration at the top of
their agenda in the years after World War II, the two groups infused new

energy into an equally important tradition, that of interracial cooperation, which had taken root in the South under white supremacy, as black and white clubwomen warily engaged in dialogue about social problems in their communities. Cooperation on a wide range of activities during World War I had generated interracial friendships and networks in a number of southern states, out of which an interracial movement developed in the 1920s. Small and seldom as aggressive in its challenge to segregation as black women wished, the movement, which had as one of its institutional bases the Council on Interracial Cooperation, continued to attract progressive women of both races in the 1930s and 1940s.[19]

Perhaps no organization was more effective in introducing new generations of southern women to interracial work than the Young Women's Christian Associations (YWCA) on college and university campuses. Regional Y conferences provided powerful interracial experiences, as one young white woman attested during the summer of 1944: "The only difference between us at Conference," she wrote, "was the color of our skins and no one noticed that—we were truly all God's children and it was a grand experience. There were three Dorothys at Conference—I was the only white one and the other two put me in the shade with their talents."[20]

With the Supreme Court's 1954 decision mandating integration, interracial cooperation gained new momentum. When local and state officials vowed to close public schools rather than allow desegregation, white women in Atlanta organized HOPE (Help Our Public Education), mobilizing thirty thousand white Georgians around a campaign for "open schools." More to the point, the fight led to even more direct cooperation as white HOPE women, a largely middle-class constituency, joined with middle-class black women to form Partners for Progress to urge compliance with the Civil Rights Act of 1964.[21]

If the Civil Rights Movement provided women of both races new opportunities for cooperation, it also produced a cadre of black movement veterans able to give voice to contemporary feminism. Their names have been overshadowed by those of men like Martin Luther King, Jr., but Ella Baker and Ruby Doris Smith were also immensely effective leaders. Baker, a southerner who had spent much of her adult life as a civil rights activist and organizer in both the North and South, was a key figure in the Southern Christian Leadership Conference (SCLC) in 1957. Dispatched by King to Shaw University in Raleigh, North Carolina, her alma mater, she organized SNCC in 1960 and functioned as a much respected adviser during its most effective years. Describing her involvement with SCLC, she recalled that "as a woman, an older woman, in a group of ministers who . . . [were] accustomed to having women largely as supporters, there was no place for me . . . in a leadership role." Hence her determination to see to it that SNCC embodied the principles of grassroots democracy and decentralized, group-centered leadership that would provide opportunities for women, among others, to initiate projects and influence strategy.[22]

While SNCC proved more militant than other civil rights organizations and its cadre of young male leaders less sexist than some SCLC ministers, being a woman in the organization did not always guarantee equal treatment, as Ruby Doris Smith and other young black activists learned. Joining at the age of seventeen during her freshman year at Spelman College in Atlanta, Smith became, in the words of veteran civil rights activist James Foreman, "one of the few genuine revolutionaries in the black liberation movement." Yet her extraordinary leadership, administrative skills, and legendary toughness did not protect her from virulent attacks by SNCC men when she assumed a major leadership position in 1965. Although Smith's years as an activist were brief—she died of a rare blood disease in 1966—there were other black women for whom the male chauvinism experienced in the movement generated a political consciousness that was self-consciously feminist. While most would continue to make racial equality their top priority, some enlisted in the women's movement, among them Septima Clark, a longtime civil rights worker of Baker's generation.[23]

A feminist consciousness was not restricted to an activist elite but was shared by thousands of African American women in the South. Poll surveys conducted nationally in 1972 revealed that 62 percent supported efforts to improve women's status in society, compared to only 45 percent of their white sisters. When asked how they responded to women's liberation groups, 67 percent were sympathetic, compared to only 35 percent of white women. By 1982, when pollster Louis Harris focused in on North Carolina in an effort to gauge support for passage of the ERA, he found that black women were the amendment's strongest supporters.[24]

What such figures suggest is that when second wave feminism emerged, substantial numbers of black women in the South were aware of what Cooper had articulated over a half century before: the double jeopardy involved in being both black and female. It was a political consciousness born of day-to-day experience, self-scrutiny, and self-understanding as well as a long tradition of community activism. Add to that a tradition of interracial activism that had taken shape during the worst years of racial repression and expanded in the years following World War II, and the building blocks for an interracial feminist movement would seem to have been in place. Why, then, were the possibilities unrealized?[25]

The Difference That Differences Make

Race, of course, was key, but in ways that are more complicated than we might assume. The development of contemporary feminism occurred in the mid- to late sixties—precisely the point at which the southern Civil Rights Movement, with its emphasis on integration through nonviolent civil disobedience, had been eclipsed by the Black Power Movement. Accompanying the new rhetoric of militance and separatism associated with black power was new debate about black manhood and women's "place." The "place" for the already "hyper-liberated" black woman, militants insisted, was not on the barricades but in the bedroom producing babies for the black nation. The impact of this resurgent machismo was reinforced by the Moynihan Report on the black family, an analysis that echoed concerns previously voiced by black sociologist E. Franklin Frazier.[26]

Written for the U.S. Department of Labor by then Harvard sociologist and now New York senator Daniel Patrick Moynihan, the report explored the "tangle of pathology" within the black community and its relationship to female-headed households. Moynihan blamed single mothers. They raised their children in a female culture that made it difficult for sons to develop into psychologically healthy men. Even in two-parent households, black women often held the jobs and therefore the power in their families.[27]

Moynihan's concern with female dominance struck a sympathetic chord with young black male militants. Some even insisted that black men had been "emasculated," not only by the white man, but by their own women. Even many moderates agreed on the need for a sexual division of labor in the black household that replicated the traditional white model then under attack from feminists for its rigidity and indifference to the individual talents and needs of both sexes.[28]

The timing, therefore, could hardly have been worse for incipient black feminists who were attempting to forge a political consciousness out of their unique racial and sexual interests. They had to demonstrate the "double jeopardy" of being female and black at the very moment they were being labeled castrating matriarchs by many black men. More difficult still, they had to demonstrate that they could be both pro-woman and pro-black at the moment when militant black male leaders (and some notable black women) demanded *black* solidarity—and white feminists insisted on *female* solidarity. It was a tall hurdle to jump, and white feminists, despite good intentions, did not make it easier.[29]

It is tempting to assume that, as white middle-class southerners, these women would naturally have been more racist than feminists elsewhere. But that assumption is not supported by the available evidence. While we have no survey data that provide a reliable profile of southern feminists or a satisfactory measure of their racial liberalism, we do have data on pro-ERA activists. Not all white southern feminists were ERA activists nor were all ERA activists self-identified feminists. Nevertheless, it is possible to draw a reasonably accurate profile of southern white feminists from these data. Predominantly middle-class, well educated, cosmopolitan in outlook, liberal in politics, and if religious, affiliated with churches and synagogues that were either liberal or "mainstream," most were married. If they were in the workforce, they were likely to hold professional or managerial jobs. Socialized in families where parents tended to be college-educated and politically active, these women had continued their own political education in professional associations, women's organizations, and liberal groups. They had frequently joined forces to fight racism and the Vietnam War, to free political prisoners, and to oppose capital punishment. Indeed, for those who came of age in the sixties, civil rights had been the cause of choice. Whatever their age, they were citizens who believed in equality and individual rights—not as familiar abstractions, but as promises to be fulfilled. Activism was part of their self-definition.[30]

This profile indicates that most white southern feminists were neither more nor less racist than those elsewhere. This is not to say that they were free of racism, but many would continue to fight it in themselves and others precisely because they felt a particular responsibility to do so as southerners. Like their counterparts nationally, many were also middle- and upper-middle-class. Class, as the writer Rita Mae Brown reminds us, is not simply an analytical concept associated with Karl Marx. "Class involves your behavior, your basic assumptions about life. Your experience (determined by your class) validates those assumptions, how you are taught to behave, what you expect from yourself and from others, your concept of the future, how you understand problems and solve them, how you think, feel, act." Indeed, growing up in the South often assured an awareness of class that sometimes eluded women elsewhere. A recent study of interracial activism in Durham, North Carolina, during the civil rights era suggests that race was an easier barrier than class for both black and white women to overcome.[31]

Consider the consciousness-raising group. Its purpose was to bring together in a caring, supportive, noncompetitive setting women accustomed to relating intimately not with other women but with the men in their lives. As these women shared experiences, a sense of common problems would emerge that led participants to understand how profoundly their lives had been shaped by a society in which being female dictated what they could be and do. This process could have provided an opportunity for women from different backgrounds to discover commonalities, probe differences, and develop a sense of solidarity but for problems of time and trust. Yet feminism—as Oscar Wilde said of socialism—took all one's evenings. Time was scarce for less affluent women who bore the multiple burdens of wage work, housework, and child care and who often were heads of households. Community work often was a higher priority. Trust was also in short supply. Nobel Prize–winning author Toni Morrison put the matter bluntly: black women "look at white women and see the enemy—for they know that racism is not confined to white men." They feel "no abiding admiration of white women as competent, complete people." Cushioned by privilege, white women seldom became "real adults." Her words rang true to countless southern blacks who, having spent their days in other women's kitchens, concluded that white women rested on pedestals polished by black women. Adding to the mistrust was the problem of sexual competition, as SNCC veterans had discovered. In the heady atmosphere of sexual freedom that was part of the cultural revolution of the 1960s, black men and white women had self-consciously broken the ultimate taboo. For black women struggling with negative images of black femininity and white standards of beauty, sexual competition from white women intensified old resentments. More to the point, these sexual liaisons endangered the black community in ways that many young white women were unable to appreciate.[32]

Such differences in day-to-day experiences bred not only distrust but differences in problems and priorities. Although many black feminists could agree on the need for less rigid social roles, equal education and employment opportunities, legal rights, adequate child care, access to family planning, and even abortion rights, some of their most pressing concerns—sterilization abuse, welfare and prison reform, public housing, and household workers' rights—were of little interest to white women.[33]

Work was perhaps the issue on which there was greatest divergence. College-educated white feminists, especially those with professional degrees, sought freedom from sex-based discrimination that denied them meaningful, well-paid work outside the home. Their demands were legitimate, but from the perspective of black women, who had always been in the labor market, where they were relegated to the least rewarding jobs, such demands lacked legitimacy. As they saw it, the problem came not from discrimination but from "boredom, gentle repression and dishpan hands." What white women wanted, they charged, was access to elite male jobs and black nannies in order to achieve fulfillment; black women sought better jobs simply to survive. They were well aware that white women's ability to work outside the home was dependent on black women's labor as housekeepers and child minders. Thus it was easy for black feminists to conclude that the priorities of elite white women were inconsistent with feminists' own ideology of universal sisterhood. Dorothy Bolden, a black maid in Atlanta for twenty-two years and one of the founders of an organization for domestic workers, put the matter clearly: "I was very proud to see them [white women] stand up and speak when it started. I'm glad to see any group do that when they're righteous and I know they have been denied something . . . [but] you can't talk about women's rights until we include all women. When you deny one woman of her rights, you deny all."[34]

Differences between black and white feminists were not only experiential and perceptual but ideological. At the heart of mainstream feminism was the notion that male domination was the most fundamental form of oppression—a notion that seemed ludicrous to women whose entire lives had been oppressed by racism. Troubling, too, was radical feminists' critique of the family as a source of oppression. Women of color concluded that feminism, as articulated and practiced by white feminists, was too narrowly defined, too indifferent to race and class, too antimale and antifamily. Dismissing the mainstream movement as an exercise in self-indulgence by spoiled white housewives yearning to carry briefcases was unfair, but there was much in black women's critique with which white feminist scholars would later agree. Mainstream feminism had privileged gender over race and class and treated the experience of white heterosexual women as universal. Although family often is a source of male domination, it can also be a base of emotional support as well as a source of resistance to other forms of oppression like racism.[35]

The problem lay in how each side handled differences. White feminists welcomed black feminists to the movement in principle, soliciting their token involvement in practice, but many never acknowledged their ignorance of these women's lives. Nor did they acknowledge the extent to which they were prevented from learning by their own personal discomfort in interacting with women they perceived to be unlike themselves. Even fewer appreciated the ways feminist theory and practice were exclusionist, and fewer still fully understood the extent to which dismantling gender hierarchy also required dismantling hierarchies of race and class. Put simply, they never fully understood why they might need to substantively change "their" movement to fit "others' " needs. Just being a feminist was tough enough, especially in the South. For black feminists, it was difficult to regard white women as sisters, especially when white sisters seemed to think that verbally acknowledging biases was the same as doing something about them.[36]

Differences, however, were not resolved by racial separatism. Those black women who formed the short-lived National Black Feminist Organization discovered that class mattered. The Atlanta chapter, for example, was never able to overcome barriers between middle-class and working-class black women. Even the New York members of the Third World Women's Alliance, a socialist-feminist offshoot of SNCC, discovered that familiarity with Marxism did not make it easier to recruit working-class sisters. White feminists also stumbled over class barriers. Feminist scholar Nancie Caraway describes in *Segregated Sisterhood* the discomfort and resentments she had experienced as a young white southerner from a blue-collar background and a "hick town."[37]

In allowing differences to separate them, feminists gave comfort to those whose dominance rests on the power to divide. Conservatives, capitalizing on a grassroots backlash against racial and sexual equality in the 1970s, sought to steer social policy rightward in the 1980s. As a result, feminists everywhere had to fight hard to maintain gains already won during the Reagan-Bush years.[38] But if the 1980s was a decade in which feminists in the political arena found new initiatives curtailed by a Republican administration and an increasingly conservative Supreme Court, it was also a decade in which feminists in the academy finally came into their own. Black feminist scholars, like their activist sisters who had distanced themselves from the racism of the women's movement and the sexism of the civil rights and black nationalist movements, refused to concede feminism to those who would marginalize the experiences of minority women. They insisted that differences—whether of race, class, ethnicity, or sexual preference—be taken seriously. Gender oppression, they maintained, is not the only form of oppression nor indeed always the primary form; more often than not, it interacts with and compounds other forms of oppression. They also insisted that feminism itself be redefined. Consider sociologist Deborah King's reformulation: "Any purposes, goals and activities which seek to enhance the potential of women, to ensure their liberty and afford them equal opportunity and to permit and encourage their self-determination represent a feminist conciousness, *even if it occurs within a racial community."* [39]

As these ideas were developed, expanded, and publicized at scholarly conferences and in professional journals and books, historians of women began to rethink the way women's history is written.[40] Increasingly, white scholars recognize that it is essential to take into account the different experiences of women of color, just as it is imperative to recognize that feminism has multiple voices—that feminism is, in fact, feminism*s*. As a result, historians are writing a very different history—one that is both more complex and more accurate. As a consequence, we can look forward to a portrait of the South that will look quite different from our original sketch. Recall, for example, the young women in SNCC in the 1960s. Our initial focus, like that of most historians, was on young white southerners whose discovery of sexism in the Civil Rights Movement led them to act on behalf of their own liberation. But we must also keep in view those young southern black women in SNCC who also took part in that discovery. It was principally to their African American sisters that white activists addressed their 1965 memo "Sex and Caste," which pointed out ways women as well as blacks are subordinated. If the exodus of white feminists from SNCC represented a protogenic event in the history of radical feminism, the decision of black women who understood the message but chose to remain was no less significant—and no less feminist—although it was not seen as such by white activists at the time or by white scholars subsequently. Indeed, the episode itself now emerges as paradigmatic, not just for the South but for the nation. White feminists and feminists of color from New York to California would repeat the process of separation over the next decade as they too discovered the difference that differences make.[41]

Shifting our focus to include African American women and an expanded definition of feminism alters our understanding in other ways as well. It suggests why older black women in the movement—the Ella Bakers and Fannie Lou Hamers—proved to be such compelling role models for a younger generation of female activists. Although these black women would not have described themselves as feminists, their actions exemplified the core themes of African American feminism with its emphasis on multiple forms of oppression and empowerment.

This more inclusive focus also challenges customary interpretations that ignore contemporary feminism's southern roots and the distinctive contribution of the South's black women. It raises such questions as, Do earlier forms of African American feminism call into question our periodization of second wave feminism? If the basic narrative of mainstream feminism should be braided from the outset to include multiple strands of feminist activism, do we still begin with the politicization of white women? Should the movement continue to be characterized as predominantly middle-class? The questions abound, but at the very least they alert us to the distinguishing features of a new historical portrait. Most certainly the faces will be numerous and darker. The paint will also be layered, conveying the richness of texture and a complexity that befits both the multiple ideologies and practice we term "feminism" and this diverse entity we call "the South."

NOTES

A much abbreviated version of this essay was presented at Mississippi State University in 1994 under the auspices of the Mississippi Humanities Council. I am indebted to Christina Greene, Darlene Clark Hine, and Kathryn Nasstrom for their careful comments on the penultimate draft and to Dennis Ventry for his research assistance.

1. Sara Evans, *Personal Politics: The Roots of Women's Liberation in the Civil Rights Movement and the New Left* (New York: Knopf, 1979); see also idem, "Tomorrow's Yesterday: Feminist Consciousness and the Future of Women," in *Women of America: A History*, ed. Carol Ruth Berkin and Mary Beth Norton (Boston: Houghton Mifflin, 1979), 390–415. This and the following paragraph rely heavily on *Personal Politics*, chaps. 2–4.

2. Mary King, one of the white women protesting the treatment of women in SNCC, insists that Carmichael was personally responsive to their concerns, if

others were not. I have chosen to use her version rather than Evans's, because King was a participant. See Mary King, *Freedom Song* (New York: Morrow, 1987), 450–52.

3. Johnson's observation is quoted in Caroline Bird and the Members and Staff of the National Commission on the Observance of International Woman's Year, *What Women Want: From the Official Report to the President, the Congress, and the People of the United States* (New York: Simon and Schuster, 1979), 68. Response to *The Feminine Mystique* is contained in an undated letter to the author from Ruby S. De Hart, 1964.

4. Letters to Senator Sam J. Ervin from Linda Votta-Sullivan, September 28, 1970; Elizabeth Lansing, December 17, 1970; Pamela Oliver, February 26, 1972; Eunice Storey Deerhake, February 28, 1972; Carol Barnes, March 7, 1972; Margaret W. Bennett, March 16, 1972, all in Samuel J. Ervin Papers, Southern Historical Collection, University of North Carolina, Chapel Hill. See also Ruth Easterling to Ervin, August 28, 1970; Barnes to Ervin, February 20, 1972, both Ervin Papers.

5. Letters to Ervin from Mollie Weaver, March 14, 1972; Gayle Bynum, October 19, 1971; Mrs. F. D. Le Brecht, October 14, 1971; Deerhake, March 22, 1972, Ervin Papers.

6. Quoted in Carolyn Hadley, "Feminist Women in the Southeast," *Bulletin of the Center for the Study of Southern Culture and Religion* 3 (March 1979): 10.

7. Information in this paragraph is based on participant observation beginning in 1968; conversations with Sara Evans, then a graduate student at the University of North Carolina at Chapel Hill and one of the founders of the School for People under Six; Paula Goldschmidt, a sociologist and feminist activist formerly of Chapel Hill; and Mary Capps, a New Orleans activist.

8. Participant observation and conversations with Martha McKay, founder of the North Carolina Women's Political Caucus; Florence Glasser, head of the NCWPC talent bank; Tennala Gross, NCWPC activist; Miriam Slifkin and Nancy Drum, North Carolina NOW activists; and Meyrissa Schoonmaker, feminist lawyer. See also Glasser, Gross, and Drum and Slifkin Papers, University of North Carolina at Greensboro Library; NOW Papers, Schlesinger Library, Radcliffe College, Cambridge, MA; Joan S. Carver, "Women in Florida," *Journal of Politics* 41 (August 1979): 941–55; Carolyn Hadley, "Collective and Individual Problems of Feminist Leaders: An Inquiry into Social Process Factors Affecting Women's Concerns in the Southeastern United States" (Ph.D. diss., Florida State University, 1979).

Southern feminists were also prominent in national efforts to eradicate sex-based discrimination in the professions. The historical profession provides a case in point. Willie Lee Rose and Jane Sherron De Hart chaired committees set up for that purpose by the American Historical Association; Anne Firor Scott was the first chair of the Organization of American Historian's Women's Committee.

9. Reference is to state senators Charles Deane, Jr., and Willis P. Whichard. Deane volunteered and Whichard agreed to sponsor because of his grandfather

and his concern for his daughters' future. See Deane to Elizabeth Petersen and Patricia Locke, September 22, 1972, Petersen Papers, University of North Carolina at Greensboro Library; interview with Willis P. Whichard, September 17, 1979.

10. Richards quoted in "The Titan of Texas," *Vogue*, August 1991, 247.

11. For a fuller account, see Donald G. Mathews and Jane Sherron De Hart, *Sex, Gender and the Politics of ERA: A State and the Nation* (New York: Oxford University Press, 1990). For the Florida struggle, see Joan S. Carver, "The Equal Rights Amendment and the Florida Legislature," *Florida Historical Quarterly* 60 (1982): 455–81.

12. Theodore S. Arrington and Patricia A. Kyle, "Equal Rights Activists in North Carolina," *Signs* 3 (1978): 660–80; David W. Brady and Kent L. Tedin, "Ladies in Pink: Religion and Political Ideology in the Anti-ERA Movement," *Social Science Quarterly* 36 (1976): 564–75; and Kent L. Tedin, "Religious Preferences and Pro/Anti Activism on the Equal Rights Amendment Issue," *Pacific Sociological Review* 21 (January 1978): 55–63.

13. Violet S. Devieux to Senator Sam J. Ervin, Jr., March 23, 1972, Ervin Papers. The plea not to "desexigrate" was made at hearings held on March 11, 1975, by the North Carolina General Assembly (author as participant observer). For a fuller discussion of the attitudes of conservative southern legislators, see Mathews and De Hart, *Sex, Gender, and the Politics of ERA*, esp. chap. 7.

14. See Phyllis Schlafly, *The Power of the Positive Woman* (New Rochelle, NY: Arlington House, 1977). The symbolic significance of both conferences for opponents was evident to participant observers at the Houston meeting and the pro-family conference in Washington called to counter the White House Conference on Families. See copies of notes of Roxie Nicolson and Donald Mathews (author's possession); Rebecca E. Klatch, *Women of the Right* (Philadelphia: Temple University Press, 1987), 122–27. For quotes, see Lois J. Watkins to Representative Margaret Kessee, February 24, 1973, author's files; Mrs. Carl A. Embler to Senator Cecil Hill, February 17, 1977, Hill Papers, ERA, North Carolina Department of Archives and History, Raleigh, NC.

15. For a fuller analysis of the concerns of antiratificationist women, see Jane Sherron De Hart, "Gender on the Right: Meanings behind the Existential Scream," *Gender and History* 3 (1991): 246–67; and Mathews and De Hart, *Sex, Gender, and the Politics of ERA*, esp. chap. 6.

16. Histories of the movement are relatively few. Evans's *Personal Politics* remains a classic study of the origins of the women's liberation movement. See also Judith Hole and Ellen Levine, *Rebirth of Feminism* (New York: Quadrangle, 1971). Jo Freeman, *The Politics of Women's Liberation: A Case Study of an Emerging Social Movement and Its Relation to the Social Policy Process* (New York: Longman, 1975) focuses more on the women's rights segment of the movement in the early years. Alice Echols, *Daring to Be Bad: Radical Feminism in America, 1967–1975* (Minneapolis: University of Minnesota Press, 1989) traces the shift from radical feminism to

cultural feminism. For the more recent history of radical feminism, see Nancy Whittier, *Feminist Generation: The Persistence of the Radical Women's Movement* (Philadelphia: Temple University Press, 1995).

Failure to include the perspective of feminists of color led to a series of books, including Toni Cade Bambara, ed., *The Black Woman: An Anthology* (New York: Signet, 1975); Michele Wallace *Black Macho and the Myth of Superwoman* (New York: Dial Press, 1978); bell hooks, *Ain't I a Woman: Black Women and Feminism* (Boston: South End Press, 1981); Angela Davis, *Woman, Race, and Class* (New York: Vintage, 1981); Gloria Hull et al., *All the Women Are White, All the Blacks Are Men, but Some of Us Are Brave* (Old Westbury, NY: Feminist Press, 1982); bell hooks, *Talking Back: Thinking Feminism, Thinking Black* (Boston: South End Press, 1989).

17. Anna Julia Cooper, *A Voice from the South by a Black Woman of the South* (Xenia, OH: Aldine, 1892), 120–45; quote, 135. Cooper, whose book has been called the first black feminist publication, was born into slavery in Raleigh, NC, in 1858, the daughter of a slave and a white master. A lifelong educator and leader, she received her Ph.D. from the Sorbonne in 1925. See Louise Daniel Hutchinson, "Anna Julia Haywood Cooper," in *Black Women in America: An Historical Encyclopedia*, ed. Darlene Clark Hine, Elsa Barkley Brown, and Rosalyn Terborg-Penn (Bloomington: Indiana University Press, 1993), 1:275–80. Cooper's feminism was of a distinctive African American feminist tradition that struggled for liberation from the dual oppression of racism and sexism. See Patricia Hill Collins, "The Social Construction of Black Feminist Thought," *Signs* 14 (summer 1989): 745–73; idem, *Black Feminist Thought: Knowledge, Consciousness, and the Politics of Empowerment* (New York: Routledge, 1990); and Beverly Guy-Sheftall, *Words on Fire: African-American Feminist Thought* (New York: New Press, 1995).

18. Another early feminist was Lotte Rollin, a member of an elite Charleston family. See Rosalyn Terborg-Penn, "The Rollin Sisters," in *Black Women in America*, ed. Hine et al., 2:990–91. On Walker, see Elsa Barkley Brown, "Womanist Consciousness: Maggie Lena Walker and the Independent Order of St. Luke," *Signs* 14 (spring 1989): 610–33. For Richmond teams, see Suzanne Lebsock, "Woman's Suffrage and White Supremacy: A Virginia Case Study," in *Visible Women: New Essays in American Activism*, ed. Nancy Hewitt and Suzanne Lebsock (Urbana: University of Illinois Press, 1993), 62–100. Lebsock also documents efforts of black women in Virginia to register and vote. For an account of North Carolina black women's voting efforts, see Glenda Gilmore, *Gender and Jim Crow: Women and the Politics of White Supremacy in North Carolina, 1896–1920* (Chapel Hill: University of North Carolina Press, 1996). Attempts of black women to vote in other southern states are documented in Rosalyn Terborg-Penn, "African American Women and the Woman Suffrage Movement," in *One Woman, One Vote: Rediscovering the Woman Suffrage Movement*, ed. Marjorie Spruill Wheeler (Troutdale, OR: New Sage Press, 1995), 151–54, and Elna C. Green, *Southern Strategies: Southern Women and the Woman Suffrage Question* (Chapel Hill: University of North Carolina Press, forth-

coming 1997), chap. 5. See also Ann Gordon, ed., *African-American Women and the Vote,* (Amherst: University of Massachusetts Press, forthcoming 1997).

19. On African American feminism, see Patricia Hill Collins, "Feminism in the Twentieth Century," in *Black Women in America,* ed. Hine et al., 1:421–25. The organization of Birmingham suffragists nearly split in two in 1913 over a resolution condemning segregation. That a minority of southern white women were prepared to embrace such a resolution suggested the potential for interracial cooperation during and after the war. See Green, *Southern Strategies,* chap. 5. For early efforts at interracial cooperation, see Gilmore, *Gender and Jim Crow,* chap. 7; Jacquelyn Dowd Hall, *Revolt against Chivalry: Jessie Daniel Ames and the Women's Campaign against Lynching* (New York: Columbia University Press, 1979), 77–128; and Evelyn Brooks-Higginbotham, *Righteous Discontent: The Women's Movement in the Black Baptist Church, 1880–1920* (Cambridge: Harvard University Press, 1993), 197–98. See also Cynthia Neverdon-Morton, *Afro-American Women in the South and the Advancement of the Race, 1895–1925* (Knoxville: University of Tennessee Press, 1989); Stephanie J. Shaw, *What a Woman Ought to Be and to Do: Black Professional Women Workers during the Jim Crow Era* (Chicago: University of Chicago Press, 1996).

20. Susan Lynn, *Progressive Women in Conservative Times: Racial Justice, Peace and Feminism, 1945 to the 1960s* (New Brunswick: Rutgers University Press, 1992), 40–67, quote on 57–58.

21. Kathryn L. Nasstrom, "Women, the Civil Rights Movement, and the Politics of Historical Memory in Atlanta, 1946–1973" (Ph.D. diss., University of North Carolina, Chapel Hill, 1993).

22. Quoted in Paula Giddings, *When and Where I Enter: The Impact of Black Women on Race and Sex in America* (New York: Bantam, 1984), 312. Among the SCLC leadership, Ralph Abernathy was apparently least inclined to work with women as equals. See also Aldon Morris, *Origins of the Civil Rights Movement* (New York: Macmillan, 1984), 102–4, 109–15. On the extraordinary organizational role of black women in the Civil Rights Movement, see Charles M. Payne, *I've Got the Light of Freedom: The Organizing Tradition and the Mississippi Freedom Struggle* (Berkeley: University of California Press, 1995), 265–83.

23. Cynthia Griggs Fleming, "Black Women Activists and the Student Nonviolent Coordinating Committee: The Case of Ruby Doris Smith Robinson," *Journal of Women's History* 4 (winter 1993): 64–81; James Foreman, *The Making of Black Revolutionaries* (New York: Macmillan, 1972), 475; Ann Standley, "The Role of Black Women in the Civil Rights Movement," in *Black Women in the Civil Rights Movement: Trailblazers and Torchbearers, 1941–1965,* ed. Vicki L. Crawford, Jacqueline Anne Rouse, and Barbara Woods (Brooklyn: Carlson, 1990), 183–245; and Grace Jordon McFadden, "Septima P. Clark and the Struggle for Human Rights," in *Black Women and the Civil Rights Movement,* ed. Crawford et al., 85–98.

24. Louis Harris and Associates, "1971 American Women's Opinion Survey, no. 2137" (New York: Louis Harris and Associates, 1971); and idem, "1982 ERA Survey

in North Carolina, no. 8221029" (New York: Louis Harris and Associates, 1982). Support for feminism on the part of non-elite southern black women who migrated to the North is also evident in M. Rivka Polatnic, "Poor Black Sisters Decide for Themselves: A Case Study of 1960s Women's Liberation Activism," in *Black Women in America*, ed. Kim Marie Vaz (Thousand Oaks, CA: Sage, 1995), 110–30.

25. On the relationship between black women's experience and consciousness, see Collins, *Black Feminist Thought*.

26. E. Franklin Frazier, *Black Bourgeoisie* (New York: Collier Books, 1962). On black machismo and black matriarchy, see hooks, *Ain't I a Woman*, 177–89. Larry Delano Coleman's characterization of black women as "hyper-liberated" is quoted in E. Frances White, "Africa on My Mind: Gender, Counter Discourse, and African-American Nationalism," *Journal of Women's History* 2 (spring 1990): 73–97. See White also for the relationship between black nationalism and feminism. Resentment at the way black nationalists defined the role of women is much in evidence in manuscripts of black feminist organizations, whether socialist feminist or liberal feminist. For example, in a four-paragraph history of the Third World Women's Alliance, one paragraph focuses on definitions of women by black men in the movement, while another paragraph is devoted to an attack on the concept of black matriarchy. See "Third World Women's Alliance: Our History, Our Ideology, Our Goals," TWWA, History and Goals, series 24, box 4, folder 19, Records of the National Council of Negro Women, Bethune Museum and Archives, Washington, DC.

27. [Daniel Patrick Moynihan], *The Negro Family: The Case for National Action* (Washington, DC: U.S. Department of Labor, 1965).

28. See, for example, Eldridge Cleaver, *Soul on Ice* (New York: Dell, 1968), 162; Amiri Baraka, *Raise Race Rays Raze: Essays since 1965* (New York: Random House, 1971), 248; Giddings, *When and Where I Enter*, 314–21; and hooks, *Ain't I a Woman*, 180–82.

29. "Double Jeopardy" is the title of an essay by Frances Beal in *Sisterhood Is Powerful*, ed. Robin Morgan (New York: Vintage, 1970), 340–53. Even so respected a figure as Dorothy Height argued that "the status of the Negro man and his position in the community" was the Negro woman's major concern. See Freeman, *Politics of Women's Liberation*, 41. Quite apart from the cult of virility associated with the black nationalist movement was the legitimate concern that feminism would divert energy from the struggle for black equality and liberation. Leaders of the National Black Feminist Organization would later argue that some women actually joined the organization in order to undermine it, because they saw it as diversionary. See Beverly Davis, "To Seize the Moment: A Retrospective on the National Black Feminist Organization," *Sage: A Scholarly Journal on Black Women* 5 (fall 1988): 43–47.

30. Arrington and Kyle, "Equal Rights Activists," 660–80. See also Mathews and De Hart, *Sex, Gender, and the Politics of ERA*, esp. chaps. 3–5. While the

Arrington and Kyle data apply only to North Carolina, survey data on ERA pro- and antiratification activists in other states are sufficiently consistent with these data to suggest that the North Carolina profile fits many other southern white ratificationists and feminists. The fit is not exact, however. While those ratifica- tionists who did not embrace the feminist label did identify with the women's movement, radical feminists did not initially and, in some cases, ever involve themselves in the ratification struggle, dismissing it as reformist and diversionary.

31. Rita Mae Brown, "The Last Straw," in *Class and Feminism*, ed. Charlotte Bunch and Nancy Myron (Baltimore: Diana Press, 1974), 14–23; quote 15. bell hooks, who grew up in the South, suggests that, on the basis of her experience with fellow students at Stanford University, southern women, black and white, are more aware of class and racial differences than white women in other areas of the United States—an observation that my own experience confirms. See hooks, *Feminist Theory: From Margin to Center* (Boston: South End Press, 1984), 11. On the greater difficulties of bridging class differences, see Christina Greene, "'Our Separate Ways': Women and the Black Freedom Movement in Durham, North Carolina, 1940s–1970s" (Ph.D. diss., Duke University, 1996).

32. The problem of time was succinctly articulated by one of the women interviewed by black feminist and psychologist Brenda Eichelberger in "Black Feminism: Is It Necessary? A Critique of Eight Black Feminist Interviews," Records of the National Alliance of Black Feminists, series 6, box 6, Bethune Museum and Archives. Eichelberger's interviews also contain useful material on perceptions of white women. See also Toni Morrison, "What the Black Woman Thinks about Women's Lib," *New Times Magazine*, August 22, 1971, 14–15, 63–64, 66; quotes 15, 64. Morrison also noted the anger black women felt toward white women engaged in interracial sex and toward their partners who were "talking black and sleeping white." The tensions generated by this behavior in SNCC, discussed by Evans in *Personal Politics*, have been most effectively captured in fictional form in Alice Walker, *Meridian* (New York: Harcourt Brace Jovanovich, 1976).

It should also be noted that consciousness-raising groups were often more homogeneous in terms of members' social background than were more bureau- cratic feminist organizations. The explanation lies in the fact that people with similar backgrounds were more likely to share values and norms, thereby making it easier to arrive at a consensus so critical for collectivist groups. Also friendship networks were the primary means of recruiting new members for c-r groups. See Myra Marx Ferree and Beth B. Hess, *Controversy and Coalition: The New Feminist Movement* (Boston: Twayne, 1985), 85.

33. Even topics for discussion in c-r groups differed. Black women in Chicago, for example, wanted to discuss relationships between black men and white women, media depictions of black women, employment opportunities, lack of housing mobility, racially coded credit policies, and so on. They had little interest in such problems as corporate sexism in upper management or sexist admission

policies to exclusive men's clubs. See Carol Kleiman, "When Black Women Rap, the Talk Sure Is Different," *Chicago Tribune*, June 1, 1975, sec. 5, 13. NOW's resistance to minority issues prompted its former president, Aileen Hernandez, to resign, charging that NOW's interest in minority women was prompted primarily by the desire to involve them in the ERA struggle. See Paula Kassell, "Race Issue Stumbling Block to Sisterhood," [Press] Clippings, 1974–79, series 1, box 1, Records of the National Alliance of Black Feminists, Bethune Museum and Archives; "Ex-President of NOW Calls Group 'Racist,' " *San Diego Union*, October 21, 1979.

34. Eichelberger, "Black Feminism: Eight Interviews"; "Dorothy Bolden," in *Nobody Speaks for Me: Self Portraits of Working Class Women*, ed. Nancy Seifer (New York: Simon and Schuster, 1976), 138–77; quote 170.

35. This critique of white feminism, voiced by black feminists like Frances Beal as early as 1970, received its classic statement by the Combahee River Collective in 1977 and has been elaborated in the writings of other black feminist intellectuals. See Beal, "Double Jeopardy," 351–52; Combahee Collective, "A Black Feminist Statement," in *All the Women Are White*, ed. Hull et al., 13–22; and, for example, hooks, *Feminist Theory*, chaps. 3–5.

36. A classic example of the naïveté that caused good intentions to fail is the organization of a community forum in Fayetteville, NC, by white feminists. Planners designated one of the six panels to address "minority women" and invited black women to be five of the twenty speakers. One of the three white women in charge of publicity later confessed that the publicity committee "had not *personally* contacted a single Black women's organization, much less considered trying to co-plan or co-sponsor with such a group: and . . . [we] had no notion of the doubts or risks that Black women in our town might have about our endeavor." When those attending the forum turned out to be overwhelmingly white, "we questioned our publicity, instead of our perspective on power." See Minnie Bruce Pratt, "Identity: Skin, Blood, Heart," in Elly Bulkin, Minnie Bruce Pratt, and Barbara Smith, *Yours in Struggle: Three Feminist Perspectives on Anti-Semitism and Racism* (Ithaca: Firebrand Books, 1988), 30. I am indebted to Christina Green for calling the Pratt essay to my attention.

37. New York's Third World Women's Alliance consisted primarily of "students, ex-students, teachers and . . . professionals." As "petit-bourgois" black women, they could be "revolutionary," but they could not seem to involve "workers." See MJ to Sisters, May 22, 1972, Third World Women's Alliance Correspondence, 1972–74, folder 12, box 4, series 24, Records of the National Congress of New Women, Bethune Museum and Archives, Washington, DC. For Caraway's background, see Nancie Caraway, *Segregated Sisterhood: Racism and the Politics of American Feminism* (Knoxville: University of Tennessee Press, 1991), 18–19.

38. Divisions among oppressed groups have always worked to the advantage of those in power. For example, in North Carolina in the early years of the twentieth century, conservatives became convinced that eite white suffragists

would countenance and, in some areas, even encourage the voting of black women, and that suffragists also intended to use the ballot to improve the pay and working conditions of female operatives in the state's mills and factories. For the ways these men responded to the prospect of gender solidarity, see Sarah Wilkerson-Freeman, "Women and the Transformation of American Politics: North Carolina, 1898–1940" (Ph.D. diss., University of North Carolina at Chapel Hill, 1995). For a fuller discussion of conservatives' efforts in the ERA struggle, see Mathews and De Hart, *Sex, Gender, and the Politics of ERA*. For a journalistic survey of the conservative backlash, see Susan Faludi, *Backlash: The Undeclared War against American Women* (New York: Crown, 1991).

39. This enterprise was shared by feminist intellectuals and scholars of color. Among the writings of the former, see Audre Lorde, *Sister Outsider* (Trumansburg, NY: Crossing Press, 1984); hooks, *Ain't I a Woman*; and idem, *Feminist Theory*. Early works of feminist scholars include Hull et al., *All the Women Are White*; and Gloria Josephs and Jill Lewis, *Common Differences* (Boston: South End Press, 1981). See also Bonnie Thornton Dill, "Race, Class and Gender: Prospects for an All-Inclusive Sisterhood," *Feminist Studies* 9 (spring 1983): 131–50; Collins, "Social Construction of Black Feminist Thought"; Angela Harris, "Race and Essentialism in Feminist Legal Theory," in *Feminist Legal Theory*, ed. Katherine Bartlett and Roseanne Kennedy (Boulder: Westview, 1991); Hazel Carby, "White Woman Listen! Black Feminism and the Boundaries of Sisterhood," in *The Empire Strikes Back: Race and Racism in '70's Britain* (London: Hutchinson, 1982); and Deborah K. King, "Multiple Jeopardy, Multiple Consciousness: The Context of Black Feminist Ideology," *Signs* 14 (autumn 1988): 42–72.

40. For the critique of existing scholarship on women in the social sciences and history by African Americans and other feminist scholars of color, see, for example, Maxine Baca Zinn, Lynn Weber Cannon, Elizabeth Higginbotham, and Bonnie Thornton Dill, "The Costs of Exclusionary Practices in Women's Studies," in *Making Face, Making Soul Haciendo Caras: Creative and Critical Perspectives by Women of Color*, ed. Gloria Anzaldúa (San Francisco: Aunt Lute Foundation Books, 1990); Evelyn Brooks-Higginbotham, "Beyond the Sound of Silence: Afro-American Women in History," *Gender and History* 1 (spring 1989): 51–67; idem, "African-American Women's History and the Metalanguage of Race," *Signs* 17 (winter 1992); Antonia Castaneda, "Women of Color and the Rewriting of Women's History: The Discourse, Politics, and Decolonization of History," *Pacific Historical Review* 61 (1992): 501–33; Aida Hurtado, "Relating to Privilege: Seduction and Rejection in the Subordination of White Women and Women of Color," *Signs* 14 (summer 1989): 833–55. Some of the criticism has also come from white scholars. See, for example, Margaret A. Simons, "Racism and Feminism: A Schism in Sisterhood," *Feminist Studies* 5 (summer 1979): 389–401.

41. For the experiences of Chicanas, see, for example, Velia G. Hancock, "La Chicana, Chicano Movement and Women's Lib," *Chicano Studies Newsletter*, Uni-

versity of California at Berkeley, February–March 1971; Alfredo Mirande and Evangelina Enriquez, "Chicana Feminism," in *La Chicana: The Mexican-American Woman* (Chicago: University of Chicago Press, 1979), 234–43; and Alma Garcia, "The Development of Chicana Feminist Discourse, 1970–1980," *Gender and Society* 3 (1989): 531–44. On Asian American feminism, see Esther Ngan-Ling, "The Feminist Movement: Where Are All the Asian Women?" in *Making Waves: An Anthology of Writings by and about Asian American Women*, ed. Asian Women United of California (Boston: Beacon Press, 1989); and William Wee, "Race vs. Gender: The Asian American Women's Movement," in *The Asian American Movement* (Philadelphia: Temple University Press, 1993), 72–100. See also Cherríe Moraga and Gloria Anzaldúa, *This Bridge Called My Back: Writings by Radical Women of Color* (Watertown, MA: Persephone Press, 1981).

Contributors

Adele Logan Alexander is an assistant professor of history at George Washington University. Author of *Ambiguous Lives: Free Women of Color in Rural Georgia, 1789–1879,* she has contributed essays to a number of collections, including "'She's No Lady, She's a Nigger': Abuses, Stereotypes, and Realities from the Middle Passage to Capitol (and Anita) Hill," in Anita Faye Hill and Emma Coleman Jordan, editors, *Race, Gender, and Power in America.*

Barbara Bair is associate editor of the Jane Addams Papers Project of Duke University. One of the editors of the *Marcus Garvey and UNIA Papers* for the University of California Press, she is a former fellow of the Virginia Center for the Humanities and the Virginia Historical Society. Her latest book is *Though Justice Sleeps: African Americans, 1880–1900.*

James Taylor Carson is an assistant professor of history at Queen's University, Kingston, Ontario. He has published articles on southern Indians in *Ethnohistory,* the *Journal of Mississippi History,* and *Agricultural History* and is currently preparing for publication a manuscript entitled "Searching for the Bright Path: The Mississippi Choctaws from Prehistory to Removal."

Joan E. Cashin is an associate professor of history at Ohio State University. She is the author of *A Family Venture: Men and Women on the Southern Frontier* and *Our Common Affairs: Texts from Women in the Old South,* as well as numerous articles on southern history.

Jane Sherron De Hart is a professor of history at the University of California, Santa Barbara, and former director of women's studies at the University of North Carolina, Chapel Hill. She is co-winner of the 1990 American Political Science Association's Victoria Schuck Prize for *Sex, Gender, and the Politics of the ERA: A State and the Nation,* and coeditor of *Women's America: Refocusing the Past.* In addition to publishing a book on arts policy and numerous articles, she is completing a book entitled *Defining America: Gender, Sexuality, and National Identity.*

Christie Anne Farnham is an associate professor of history at Iowa State University and former director of women's studies and member of the Afro-American Studies Department at Indiana University. She is founder of the *Journal of Women's History,* which she coedited from 1988 to 1996. Her publications include *The Education of the Southern Belle: Higher Education and Student Socialization in the Antebellum South.*

Jean E. Friedman is an associate professor of history at the University of Georgia. Author of *The Enclosed Garden: Women and Community in the Evangelical South, 1830–1900,* she is currently completing *Ways of Wisdom in the Early Republic: The Diary of Rachel Mordecai.*

Darlene Clark Hine is the John A. Hannah Professor of American History at Michigan State University. Her books include *The Rise and Fall of the White Primary in Texas, Black Women in White: Racial Conflict and Cooperation in the Nursing Profession, 1890–1950,* and *Hine Sight: Black Women and the Re-Construction of American History.* She is also editor of the award-winning *Black Women in America: An Historical Encyclopedia* and coeditor of *"We Specialize in the Wholly Impossible": A Reader in Black Women's History.*

Pippa Holloway holds an M.A. in history from the University of North Carolina, Greensboro, and is completing a Ph.D. in history at Ohio State University, where her research focuses on the history of sexuality in the South.

Johanna Miller Lewis is an associate professor of history at University of Arkansas, Little Rock; the codirector of the National Dunbar History Project; and a consultant for public history institutions. Her publications include articles on the North Carolina backcountry and *Artisans in the North Carolina Backcountry.*

Timothy J. Lockley is a lecturer in U.S. history at the University of Warwick. He is a doctoral candidate at the University of Cambridge; his dissertation explores biracial encounters between non-elite whites and African Americans in the Georgia lowcountry before 1830.

Audrey Thomas McCluskey is an assistant professor of Afro-American studies at Indiana University. Her recent publications include "We Specialize in the Wholly Impossible: Black Women Founders and Their Mission," in *Signs*; and "Teaching across the Barriers," in *Transformations*, which she coauthored. She is completing a book on Mary McLeod Bethune.

Anne Firor Scott is the W. K. Boyd Professor Emerita of History at Duke University and a past president of the Organization of American Historians and the Southern Historical Association. Her publications include *The Southern Lady* and *One Half of the People: The Fight for Women's Suffrage*, which she coauthored.

Nina Silber is an associate professor of history at Boston University. She wrote *The Romance of Reunion: Northerners and the South, 1865–1900* and coedited *Divided Houses: Gender and the Civil War* and *Yankee Correspondence: Civil War Letters between New England Soldiers and the Homefront*.

Martha H. Swain, Cornaro Professor of History Emerita at Texas Women's University, now teaches at Mississippi State University. She is the author of *Pat Harrison: The New Deal Years*, *Ellen S. Woodward: New Deal Advocate for Women*, and articles on southern women and prominent people from the Roosevelt and Truman eras. She is currently completing biographies of Lucy Somerville Howorth and Loula Friend Dunn.

Alice Taylor-Colbert is an associate professor of history, the chair of the Social Science Division, and the director of the Museum and Archives at Shorter College. She is also coeditor of the *Journal of the Georgia Association of Historians* and an editorial committee member of the *Journal of Cherokee Studies*. She has published several articles and is currently researching women in the family of Cherokee leader, Major Ridge.

LeeAnn Whites teaches in the department of history at the University of Missouri-Columbia. She is the author of *The Civil War as a Crisis in Gender: Augusta, Georgia, 1860–1890* and articles on nineteenth century gender relations.

Margaret Ripley Wolfe is a professor of history at East Tennessee State University and a past president of the Southern Association of Women Historians. Her most recent book is *Daughters of Canaan: A Saga of Southern Women*. She is general editor of the University of Kentucky Press's American Culture Series and is currently completing a biography of Eleanor Copenhaver Anderson.

Index